St Antony's Series

The St Antony's Series publishes studies of international affairs of contemporary interest to the scholarly community and a general yet informed readership. Contributors share a connection with St Antony's College, a world-renowned centre at the University of Oxford for research and teaching on global and regional issues. The series covers all parts of the world through both single-author monographs and edited volumes, and its titles come from a range of disciplines, including political science, history, and sociology. Over more than thirty years, this partnership between St Antony's College and Palgrave Macmillan has produced about 200 publications.

More information about this series at
http://www.palgrave.com/gp/series/15036

Jonathan Waterlow
Jacques Schuhmacher

War Crimes Trials and Investigations

A Multi-Disciplinary Introduction

palgrave
macmillan

Jonathan Waterlow
St Antony's College
University of Oxford
Oxford, UK

Jacques Schuhmacher
Somerville College
University of Oxford
Oxford, UK

St Antony's Series
ISBN 978-3-319-64071-6 ISBN 978-3-319-64072-3 (eBook)
https://doi.org/10.1007/978-3-319-64072-3

Library of Congress Control Number: 2017956722

Cover illustration: Forance / Alamy Stock Photo

Printed on acid-free paper

This Palgrave Macmillan imprint is published by Springer Nature
The registered company is Springer International Publishing AG
The registered company address is: Gewerbestrasse 11, 6330 Cham, Switzerland

For our families and friends
— JS & JW

The original version of this book was revised. An erratum to this chapter can be found at https://doi.org/10.1007/978-3-319-64072-3_11

Preface

In discussing our work on war crimes trials and investigations, we repeatedly found ourselves at the limits of our discipline's knowledge and expertise. Both the literature and our conversations with scholars from different fields working on the subject suggested we were certainly not alone in this perception, and so we decided to collaborate to draw together experts from numerous different fields to cross the disciplinary boundaries which both separate and limit us. Even within a given field, it is all too easy to get lost in the minutiae. In many ways, the danger of specialization can be that we come to know more and more about less and less. This is especially limiting when considering a subject area which requires extensive cooperation between, and knowledge of, other disciplines.

Seeking a resolution to this situation, we established an interdisciplinary research network on war crimes trials and investigations at the University of Oxford, which hosted two international, interdisciplinary workshops, and an eight-week seminar series featuring contributors from numerous disciplines involved in the study of this subject area. To ensure a broad range of perspectives, we invited contributors not only from the UK, but also Europe, Russia, North and South America, and Australia.

Although there are many scholars working on war crimes investigations and trials at different universities and policymaking institutions around the world, they tend to present their research at conferences dealing with specific countries, wars, or broader questions, such as gender or the mentalities of the perpetrators. In the context of such conferences, there is normally little room for the discussion of the fundamental questions surrounding the investigations and trials themselves. There is also an understandable reluctance at conferences and other formal academic settings to reveal areas of weakness or the limitations of one's disciplinary approach and to learn about other approaches from a foundational level.

Our network therefore aimed to provide a forum in which these fundamental issues could be addressed, and by directly promoting open and frank reflection on the limits of individual disciplines and how each can benefit from the input of others (in part by recognizing how they already unconsciously, and/or uncritically, build upon each other). By promoting this atmosphere of openness and discovery, there was often a palpable sense of relief as we broke the implicit taboo on admitting to areas of ignorance, confusion, and misunderstanding. All contributors were to some degree surprised and relieved to find that, while they were aware of the weaknesses of their own discipline, other disciplines had their own shortcomings and areas of weakness, too. Discoveries such as these set the tone for the present volume, which exposes false certainties and thereafter develops stronger foundations for a productive, mutually enriching dialogue and cooperation between all the disciplines involved.

We decided to hold two workshops with the same participants: our experience is that when scholars from different disciplinary backgrounds come together, they frequently speak at cross-purposes due to elementary differences of approach and terminology. The first workshop therefore provided the foundations for the second by clarifying the key issues and drawing together the different interpretational frameworks and approaches developed by the various academic disciplines. This allowed us to untangle those differences, establishing common ground and analytical clarity. At the second workshop, we were able to deeply engage with the perspectives and insights—as well as the critiques and weaknesses—of our respective disciplines. Following the success of these two workshops, we invited specialists from other fields to present at the two-month seminar series which followed. This further enriched the development of both the Network and the present volume.

The fruit of these intensive days of debate and discussion is the collection now before you. To date, students and scholars have had to piece together disparate elements from various (often intimidating, jargon-heavy) handbooks and disciplinary overviews; this book provides a clear solution to this issue of fragmentation. It aims to provide a concise overview of each field's key interests, points of debate, evolution over time, or rationale for studying war crimes at all. As such it provides crucial orientation for readers from any discipline concerned with the study of war crimes trials and investigations and, it is hoped, will foster further valuable interactions in scholarship. Our aim in creating this volume is to provide the accessible entry-point which we wish had been available when we began our own research.

We could not have created the War Crimes Research Network without the facilities and financial support of The Oxford Research Centre in the Humanities (TORCH), as well as the generous additional funding from Oxford University Press's John Fell Fund. We would like to thank TORCH's first director, Stephen Tuck, for his keen interest in the Network's activities, and we must also thank everyone in the hardworking administrative team at TORCH.

St Antony's College provided the venue for the two workshops, and we would like to extend our warm thanks to Han Kimmett and the rest of the conference team for providing such a welcoming setting.

In the early days of the Network, we received valuable advice and suggestions from (in alphabetical order): Dapo Akande; Paul Betts; Donald Bloxham; Patricia Clavin; Martin Conway; Robert Harris; Joanna Innes; Rana Mitter; David Priestland; David Rodin; Lyndal Roper; Connor Sebestyen; and Serena Sharma.

The engagement and support of several other research centres and networks was crucial and eye-opening. We would specifically like to thank: Leila Ullrich and the Oxford Transitional Justice Research (OTJR) network; Hew Strachan and The Changing Character of War Programme (CCW); and David Rodin and The Oxford Institute for Ethics, Law and Armed Conflict (ELAC).

We would also like to extend special thanks to our colleague and friend, Jan Lemnitzer, who not only contributed to the volume, seminar series, and the workshops, but at our request undertook significant original research and supported the project in numerous other ways.

We would like to specifically thank the speakers at the Network's Seminar Series for their excellent and thoughtful contributions: Andreas Hilger; Jan Lemnitzer; Kerstin von Lingen; Brian Orend; Nikita Petrov; Tim Thompson; Leila Ullrich; and Annette Weinke.

We also learnt a lot from those who attended the Seminar Series and participated in the discussions: Roderick Bailey; Anja Bihler; Thomas Brodie; Elena Butti; Andrea Domenichini; Jack Doyle; Vincent Druliolle; Elizabeth Dykstra-McCarthy; Katherine Erickson; Suwita Hani; Jose Harris; Ruth Harris; Dan Healey; Christopher Huff; Fredrik Hjorthen; Jonathan Leader Maynard; Matilde Gawronski; Brian McCormick; Daniel O'Neil; Judith Pallot; Tien-Nhan Phan; Lijian Phil; Will Pooley; Sophie Rosenberg; Joanna Rozpedowski; Malcolm Spencer; Nick Stargardt; Steve Smith; Simon Unger; Zachary Vermeer; Jonathan Ward; John Watkins; Calum White; and Jennifer Wunn.

Thanks are also due the editorial team at Palgrave, the anonymous readers who supported and encouraged our project, as well as Halbert Jones and Matthew Walton, the editors of the St Antony's Series.

It gives us great pleasure to thank and to acknowledge the years of hard work that the contributors have put into this volume. Through the multiple meetings and several chapter revisions based on the often-challenging feedback from readers of other disciplines, their enthusiasm and support for the project never wavered.

We would also like to thank the following participants of the workshops:

Katie Engelhart of *Vice News*; Ozren Jungic; Ruben Reike; Kevin Reynolds; and Harry Rhea.

Finally, we would like to express our warm thanks to the European Commission.

Brussels, Belgium
December 2016

Jacques Schuhmacher
Jonathan Waterlow

Contents

1

War Crimes Trials and Investigations: Major Trends and Disciplinary Challenges

Jacques Schuhmacher and Jonathan Waterlow

In a world of continuing conflict, mass violence and foreign interventions—and with the terminology of 'war crimes', 'genocide' or 'crimes against humanity' widespread yet little understood both in academic disciplines and in the media—the wide contemporary significance and need for greater understanding of the language and theoretical perspectives applied to the subject of war crimes trials and investigations could hardly be clearer.

War crimes and atrocities represent a series of powerful challenges that play out in the courtroom, but whose significance extends far beyond the legal sphere. They legitimize international action against perpetrators; they determine how a post-conflict society is structured and struggles to make sense of and respond to atrocities both historic and present; and they inform the development of the international laws of war concerning prevention and intervention. For these reasons, we must study

The original version of this book was revised. An erratum to this chapter can be found at https://doi.org/10.1007/978-3-319-64072-3_11

J. Schuhmacher (✉)
War Crimes Research Network, University of Oxford, Oxford, UK

J. Waterlow
St Antony's College, University of Oxford, Oxford, UK

J. Waterlow, J. Schuhmacher, *War Crimes Trials and Investigations*, St Antony's Series,
https://doi.org/10.1007/978-3-319-64072-3_1

the conduct of these trials and investigations, as well as their priorities, limitations and contextual exigencies. It is only through the process of prosecution that we develop and propagate a vocabulary and interpretational framework for dealing with atrocities and war crimes and, as such, the study of these trials continues fundamentally to shape how we understand and respond to conflicts and mass violence in the world today.

A thorough understanding of how the knowledge informing war crimes trials was generated is essential, but is as yet significantly underdeveloped. Although war crimes prosecutions have been studied from numerous disciplinary perspectives, each of these has its drawbacks and limitations, as well as its specific points of focus. We believe these approaches will benefit greatly from dialogue. The subject is so complex that it is impossible to study without constant confrontations with issues outside of one's professional 'comfort zone'. A historian is inevitably confronted with complex questions of international law with which even specialists in the latter field continue to struggle; likewise, political scientists interested in conceptualizing genocide at an abstract level rely on historians' accounts, which themselves are constructed from the prosecutorial evidence generated in a given trial and political context. Perhaps most problematically, almost all disciplines draw unquestioningly on the evidence and conclusions of the forensic scientists who exhume and analyse the human remains of mass violence, but with little understanding of the significant limitations and subjectivity of the conclusions generated within that field. In other words, numerous disciplines build upon each other's works, but with little dialogue and, hence, very limited understanding of their respective foundations.

This book represents a first collaborative effort to establish a more systematic, integrated and original introduction to the study of war crimes investigations and prosecutions, anchored in history, but with a sharp awareness of the present-day and future implications. Contributors are experts in their respective fields, who write here with in-depth knowledge but in an accessible style with non-specialist readers borne strongly in mind. This volume intends to orientate rather than overwhelm, so these chapters are deliberately non-encyclopaedic: they do not attempt to describe a discipline from every angle or to cover the entire field. Rather, they highlight the major trends, debates, methods and approaches, and the interactions with and relevance of these to other disciplines.

To do interdisciplinary work, we must begin with a strong understanding of the other disciplines. We need this firm ground beneath our feet before we can begin more complex projects, so this volume aims to provide a clear introduction to neighbouring disciplines' work on the shared subject area of war crimes trials and investigations, allowing readers to develop their own work and knowledge beyond the traditional, artificial boundaries of their field.

The sequence of chapters mirrors both the chronological and disciplinary succession of the investigation and analysis of war crimes, proceeding from the initial gathering and study of evidence; on to the attempts to institutionalize and professionalize the prosecution of individuals for war crimes; and then the writing of histories based upon these events. We then turn to the ways these histories are thereafter used to generate analyses of the mentalities and psychologies of perpetrators of mass violence; before moving on, on the basis of all this, to theories and efforts at preventing future occurrences of mass violence; and, completing the cycle, philosophical reflections on the ethics and morality of war and conflict. This structure thereby demonstrates how each discipline builds upon others, but also how this process is cyclical, with the philosophical reflections and the theories of International Relations scholars feeding directly back into how wars are conducted and perceived by states and their leaders. This volume thereby encapsulates both the breadth of approaches to the subject and, crucially, their interdependence.

However, before we embark on this journey, it is vital that we orientate ourselves. The chapter, by Devin Pendas, provides an eagle-eyed view of the broad currents of how people have thought about and punished international crimes through the ages, from their earliest inception to the landmark post-Second World War Trials. He shows how important it is for war crimes trials to be situated in the history of their intellectual, philosophical and practical development, all of which are deeply interconnected. The aim is to establish common ground and a broader framework in which the more specialized chapters then sit. He illuminates the crucial themes which play a principal role in the more in-depth chapters, but which we must first understand in the broader perspective.

Each chapter will then outline, discuss and demonstrate a particular disciplinary approach, followed by a bibliographical essay which will offer crucial orientation for approaching the specialist literature in each case. These essays do not aim to be comprehensive, but instead provide a targeted overview of the most relevant and stimulating works. The book will thereby equip readers with what they need to know in order to use effectively the specialist literatures of different fields, to understand the principal debates and foci of particular disciplines, as well as the terminology those disciplines employ.

Each chapter endeavours to answer several key questions: What does this discipline do? What questions drive it in the study of war crimes? What tools, techniques, theories and so on, does it employ? How have its priorities grown and developed over time? And how, in the author's view, can their discipline both strengthen and be strengthened by others? In considering this latter point in particular, we explicitly asked contributors to be critical of their own disciplines and to consider with an open mind the most common concerns raised about them by others.

However, by initiating these reflections, neither we nor the authors are promoting interdisciplinarity for the sake of it. The aim of this book is not to offer unconditional praise or support for interdisciplinary approaches, but rather to explore where they can be of benefit, and where they fall short, or even become detrimental to analysis. We consider it a strength to complicate an orthodoxy rather than to offer straightforward 'answers'; indeed, the intention of approaching war crimes and investigations from multiple disciplinary perspectives is precisely to disrupt prevailing, rather balkanized assumptions and practices. This strongly critical approach is not aimed at undermining either trial processes or the disciplines which study them; on the contrary, the approach of identifying weaknesses honestly and without self-deception enables us ultimately to strengthen them both.

While handbooks and encyclopaedias provide comprehensive overviews, they frequently leave things at an abstract and theoretical level, offering little to no coverage or discussion of the numerous disciplinary 'toolkits' employed to study war crimes, trials and investigations. We therefore chose to include a case study in each chapter that illustrates how the respective disciplines work in practice, using examples drawn from cutting-edge research. Some of the cases are well-known, but we also draw into focus less famous, but extremely influential and telling, examples for the first time.

Overarching Themes and Key Issues

Although, from the perspective of the twenty-first century, holding trials after a conflict now seems like an obvious and natural step, in reality, ideas about having international tribunals at all have waxed and waned over the years. In considering their uncertain and uneven development, several overarching themes emerge and formed the subject of intense discussion at the workshops which preceded this volume. Therefore, in addition to the more specialized debates charted in the individual chapters, we highlight some of these broader issues here.

Terminology

The first of these concerns the aforementioned tension around the terminology we use to describe acts of mass violence and their prosecution. Often, when attempts are made to overcome interdisciplinary misunderstandings and divisions, scholars focus on issues of terminology, hoping that this will provide clarity, as though this alone would enable perfect dialogue across disciplines. In practice, these attempts rapidly devolve into one discipline trying to enforce its conventions on the others, especially lawyers, who can, with confidence, point to strict legal definitions which have tangible real-world consequences. However, legal terms do not emerge in a vacuum; rather, laws are birthed by specific political, cultural and social environments: as this volume shows, especially in the pieces by Pendas and Lemnitzer, these terms mean different things at different times, even in the courtroom.

Today, these terms may have a firmer, stricter legal definition, but they are also so widely used in the general and academic population that they continue to be surprisingly flexible. Although criminal lawyers express frustration at the imprecise way that everyone outside their discipline uses terms like 'crime against humanity', it is deeply limiting to think that they can own such terminology. Codification is self-evidently important, but legal definitions aim at binary outcomes (guilty/not guilty), whereas other fields are interested in many, more complex and less clear-cut questions and connections.

With this in mind, it is perhaps less surprising than one might have expected that, at the workshops which preceded this volume, terminological debates were not a big issue. These debates consume a great deal of energy, but ultimately produce more heat than light. The overwhelming feeling at the workshops was that an excessive focus on the specific terms used was counterproductive; it is an illusion to believe that we can definitively name and, thereby, somehow contain what are always complex and unique events. Even the classical tripartite division of 'perpetrator', 'victim' and 'bystander' rapidly breaks down when we examine particular case studies, dealing a serious blow to any theorists who would prefer their subjects to remain in orderly and cleanly divided categories. Instead, interdisciplinary discourse is most fruitful when we remain open to the perspectives of others.

The Holocaust Problem

The Holocaust is ever-present in the background of any discussions about mass violence and trials. As the single worst example of state-sponsored mass violence against a particular community in modern history, the Holocaust continues to mesmerize us not only due to its sheer proportions, but because it is synonymous with the dark side of Western modernity, and illustrates how technology and science can be harnessed to register, categorize and ultimately exterminate millions, all under the premise of rational action.

Thanks to Nuremberg and the subsequent trials, an unprecedented volume of evidence was generated, allowing researchers to probe numerous questions in unparalleled depth. Psychologists continue to be fascinated by the minds of perpetrators; philosophers grapple with the challenge presented by a shift in norms on such a wide scale; and, more concretely, scholars of Transitional Justice and International Relations—who frequently play an advisory role to modern states emerging from or at risk of descending into violent conflict—also use the Holocaust as the principal example of failures to be avoided in future.

Moreover, many scholars working on other instances of mass violence frequently use the Holocaust to give their own topics relevance and context:

both academics and the general public are so much more aware of the Holocaust than other atrocities that it functions as the default comparator and helps to illustrate the seriousness of other examples. This can have its drawbacks, however, because events do not always unfold according to the same formula and so there are limits to the usefulness of a Holocaust-centred approach to the study of mass violence. There is a problematic but understandable temptation to place the word 'Holocaust' in one's book title in order to generate interest, even if the relationship to the Holocaust itself is minimal. The unintentional side effect of this is to simultaneously make the Holocaust ubiquitous, but also to drain it of real meaning.

We must be cautious, therefore, not to allow the long shadow of the Holocaust to conceal from us the particularities and backgrounds of other cases. However, we must be equally aware that, at the other end of the spectrum, one finds a strong resistance to all comparisons between the Holocaust and other instances of mass murder, wherein comparisons are interpreted as somehow downplaying one or judging another to be 'worse'. This desire to emphasize 'uniqueness' is misplaced: comparison is essential to sharpen and contextualize our understanding of mass violence. In any case, the assumption that something is unique is itself based on an implicit comparison which goes silently untested.

Therefore, although this volume is not centred upon, nor structured around, comparisons to the Holocaust, it will become evident in the following chapters that its influence has and continues to shape how we approach the topic of war crimes and atrocities.

Western Bias/Neo-Imperialism

One of the most persistent and uncomfortable questions which arises when discussing the prosecutions and even analyses of war crimes is how far their implementation is merely an exercise in power relations? It is uncontroversial to note that international law has strong roots in Western imperialism and keeping other peoples subjugated, but the question is to what extent this continues to play a role today.

A common accusation is that Western countries get away with violations of international law, while only poorer nations have to fear that they will be held responsible for their actions. It is often pointedly remarked, for instance, that while the United States refuses to participate in the International Criminal Court (ICC; effectively rendering itself immune to prosecution), much of the Court's time is spent on prosecuting individuals from African countries. The picture becomes more complicated, however, when we consider the fact that the majority of African cases before the ICC have resulted from *self*-referrals. Justified concerns about asymmetrical power relations thus run the risk of denying agency to the countries that they seek to protect and empower (politically and emotionally volatile issues, which are explored in depth in the chapters by Han and Bellamy). We must also not forget that it can hardly be a straightforward case of imposing 'Western values' if the countries in question have officially declared their commitment to the international laws of armed conflict, which almost all countries in the world have done.

Nevertheless, charges of moral hypocrisy have gained traction due to high-profile cases of Western war crimes and atrocities which have, despite attempts to sweep them under the rug, become known but have remained insufficiently punished. When cases like the serial abuse of inmates at Abu Ghraib in Iraq, or the torture of prisoners at CIA dark sites emerge, it is hard to escape the impression that states of exception continue to be made for 'our boys', using euphemisms like 'excessive violence' restricted to a few 'isolated cases'. It often falls to scholars and journalists to assume the role of activists to point out these discrepancies which undoubtedly undermine the project of a universal set of moral and legal standards to which all nations are equally committed and answerable.

Nevertheless, although we must freely acknowledge that, like the disciplines themselves, this volume is rooted in a Western perspective (albeit with contributors from around the world), we continuously and openly acknowledge the limitations of this perspective, but we also do not let the debate end there. The alternative would be, as Brian Orend explores in his chapter, a potential regression into purely relativistic positions wherein, purely because of their origins, we would deny the possibility of finding a set of basic 'ground rules' for armed conflict and the punishment of their transgression which, even if not perfect (and, sometimes, intensely problematic), reduce the suffering of combatants and civilians alike. Under the guise of respecting all cultures equally, this toxic brand of relativism can effectively endorse terrible violence against innocents and, as such, is ultimately an act of intellectual cowardice.

Travelling Models

Talking in terms of 'impositions' and 'imperialism' does not do justice to the complex dissemination and adulteration on the ground of knowledge and practices. Instead of talking in terms of a forcible imposition of Western values, in this volume we repeatedly encounter trends perhaps best understood as 'travelling models'. These models of investigation, analysis, prosecution and post-conflict reconstruction often do arrive from outside, but their expertise, values and practices are often rapidly and necessarily adapted to local circumstances. Chapter 3, on Forensic Anthropology, shows how this continues to play out at the very earliest stages of investigation, but the theme reverberates throughout this volume.

What Does Success Mean?

Debates around war crimes prosecutions inevitably raise the perhaps unanswerable question of what would constitute a truly successful trial process. Each trial has to strike a delicate and maybe even impossible balance between the need to conduct them in a timely manner and have the appearance of fairness; and, beyond the judicial aspects, to mark a clean break with the past and to point the way towards a more humane future, and away from the possibility of regression and repetition. There is clearly a tension between these two points of emphasis which cannot be easily resolved.

War crimes trials resist simplification and we must bear in mind that evaluations of them change repeatedly over time. Consider, for instance, that the German and Japanese post-war trials have frequently been criticized as insufficient at the judicial level; yet, despite the lack of a comprehensive prosecution of war criminals, the peaceful history of both countries post-1945 has been an unparalleled success that continues to serve as a model for future action—something which certainly did not seem obvious immediately after the trials, when the general feeling domestically was one of resentment.

Given the scope of what trials attempt to accomplish on a judicial and societal level, Orend's and Bellamy's chapters raise the pointed question of why we would expect this process to be either simple, or without considerable problems and moments of compromise. As Bellamy puts it in Chap. 9, 'A Court charged with holding heads of government to account for atrocity crimes *ought to be* controversial, contested and difficult. If it is not, then it is probably not doing its job'.

All the same, there is an increasing shift towards the goal of truth and reconciliation as the key ingredients in any successful transition from situations of violence into peace, signalling a pragmatic realization that a comprehensive prosecution for all perpetrators after the cessation of violence is perhaps neither achievable nor desirable for the sake of a stable post-conflict order. Truth and reconciliation commissions, such as took place in post-Apartheid South Africa, provide a model which is increasingly influential in how the post-conflict situation is addressed. Such commissions have related but markedly different aims and forms, although they are clearly more successful if the desired aim is to defuse tensions, allow space for grief, permit confrontations within controlled environments and ultimately foster a sense of closure in a way that judgements of guilt and punishment rarely, if ever, achieve. This is at least a tacit recognition that the kind of clean slate that trials aim at can never be achieved by judicial processes alone.

Narratives of Progress

Despite the many criticisms which may fairly (and productively) be levelled at war crimes trials, it would be hard to deny that genuine progress is being made. Not only are such trials being conducted by international bodies rather than the winners of a given conflict—which can never escape the smell of victor's justice—strategies have been developed to pre-empt the need for trials by defusing potential outbreaks of mass violence before it is too late. As Bellamy's chapter showcases, the doctrine of the Responsibility to Protect (R2P) has been successfully put to the test in several instances. To be sure, these are still not without problems; the experiences of Iraq and Libya show us that interventions are intensely complex affairs which seldom provide a clear picture of 'good' or 'bad' sides to support or remove. However, the R2P philosophy represents a significant shift in international commitments to the principles of preventing, rather than merely punishing, mass violence.

A lot has been achieved, but there are new challenges and little cause for complacency. One thinks immediately of the actions of the ISIS, which confront us with mass violence that simply does not follow the anticipated script around which the instruments of international justice have been developed. Rather than hiding or denying their responsibility for atrocities, they document and propagate them with the aim of prompting armed conflict. In other words, they do not fear intervention; they seek to provoke it. It is seductive to focus on their use of modern technology (their use of social media, encrypted channels of communication to reach their supporters and the cinematic aesthetics of their propaganda videos); however, we should focus on the content of their communications, for this reveals a rationale that, although markedly different to our own, still follows their own version of justice. The group's interpretation of the conflict becomes apparent in the executions performed at sites and in the same manner where their own fighters or civilians had been killed in a fashion that they consider criminal. Troubling as it may be to say, these are, in essence, their own form of war crimes trials, about which our traditional models have little to tell us.

At the same time as we grapple with new phenomena, recent events draw us back into more traditional questions about states' responsibility for war crimes and atrocities. The shooting down of a civilian plane—MH17—over Ukrainian airspace in 2014 prompted competing investigations that sought to determine whether Russia or its proxies were responsible. Similarly, international investigations sought to clarify whether the Assad regime in Syria used poison gas against its opponents. In their essence, these cases would seem entirely familiar to audiences from a hundred years ago.

Both in the modern and these more 'traditional' cases, the media and scholarly debates surrounding them often start from scratch, without an awareness of the long-standing influences—historical and philosophical—that quietly inform our immediate reactions to these issues. Even as debates concerning the use of drones and private military contractors (most notably by the USA) imply that these are entirely novel concerns, as Orend's chapter reminds us, these are debates which emerge every time a new technology or practice is introduced to the battlefield. Indeed, the very concepts that soldiers should be employees of the state, or that killing should happen face-to-face, are not timeless norms, but have their own contingent histories.

Perhaps the most complex or widely influential 'modern' element of contemporary instances of mass violence is the rapidity with which the general population is kept informed about them. This continues to inflect attitudes towards conflict; yet, due to the speed and availability of conflict zone reporting, the media forces two very different contexts to constantly encounter each other. We experience a clash of wildly different norms of conduct: on the one hand, in any warzone, extreme violence is directly permitted, but, on the other hand, when this is shown to the domestic audience, it cannot help but strongly clash with their everyday norms and expectations of acceptable conduct. Indeed, social media exacerbates this jarring confrontation by undermining the traditional media's attempts to conceal the true extent of violence in these settings. One of the many consequences of this exposure has been to increase activists' demands for interventions and prosecutions—an example of which was the #Kony2012 campaign, the many complexities and ramifications of which are explored in Han's chapter.

Chapter Overviews

These broader issues find reflection in the character of each chapter in the volume, each of which incorporates both a critical introductory overview of their respective discipline and a specific case study to demonstrate that discipline 'in action'.

Forensic Anthropology

Although the analysis of human remains is the ultimate foundation of all evidence on which other disciplines rest, outside the fields of forensic science there is very limited knowledge of how that evidence is produced and understood. Scholars from other disciplines accept the findings of forensic science as 'hard' and immutable facts, but in reality, as Chap. 3 reveals, this evidence is, to a significant extent, an exercise in subjective interpretation, not dissimilar to how historians may interpret the archival record. It is therefore crucial to have an understanding of how this evidence is generated and the standards employed to uncover and assess that evidence, for it gives legitimacy to particular versions of events, especially in the courtroom. Without a thorough understanding of what the human record can and cannot tell us, all further research and conclusions rest on very shaky foundations.

The authors—who have worked directly on a wide variety of sites of mass violence—introduce the interests of Forensic Anthropology and its relation to human rights investigations, a relationship which is still, surprisingly, in its infancy. The authors then explore the different (socio-) physical anthropological approaches and contexts of their discipline, outlining the often very different standards and practices which are applied in different countries.

By comparing several case studies, they highlight the many differences which exist in the methodologies, legal status and even the intentions of forensic anthropological teams around the world. Not only is a significant degree of adaptability to local conditions—cultural as well as practical—essential to their work, but when protocols developed elsewhere are imported to a new context, serious problems can arise. For instance, methods developed to determine age, sex or racial backgrounds among one population simply cannot be—but often have been—transferred, unadulterated, to another. Indeed, their concept of 'travelling models'—of imported and imposed interpretative lenses—is an important theme which emerges time and again in the following chapters.

Anthropometrics

Chapter 4 continues the focus on the generation of evidence by turning to the discipline of Anthropometrics, an emerging field which is itself interdisciplinary, and which draws on both medical and economic datasets to establish the effects of indirect violence against non-combatants. There are long-running debates about the morality and possible criminality of blockades and sanctions against an enemy, because these disproportionately affect the most vulnerable in society and, as such, arguably constitute war crimes.

Whereas the forensic anthropologists showed the significant limitations of the conclusions they can draw from their analyses, the Anthropometric approach provides definite empirical clarity ('was there an impact on population health or not?') in cases which are often sucked into painful and long-running memory wars.

In specific cases, we recognize that sanctions or blockades are unacceptable—for example, the Sieges of Leningrad or Sarajevo—yet in others, they are uncritically deployed, as against Germany or Iraq. These debates often lead nowhere, however, because there is usually no clear evidence to demonstrate the violence or damage done to the people affected. This is where the field of Anthropometric analysis comes into its own, by providing evidence that is not as immediately obvious as, for example, a mass grave.

Using, among others, the example of the so-called British Hunger Blockade of Germany in the First World War, Mary Cox uses data collected annually by German school doctors to assess the impact of the blockade on those most susceptible to the effects of nutritional deprivation. The chapter therefore highlights the significance of using 'indirect evidence' (i.e. evidence that was not collected or generated for the explicit purpose of trial) for establishing, for the historical if not for the immediate trial record, the human nature and full scope of certain war crimes. Indeed, counter-intuitively, this seemingly cold data actually brings to life the true suffering of those involved—including the survivors, rather than solely the dead.

International Legal History

Evidence is vital for the establishment of trial proceedings; however, before we enter the courtroom, we must examine the development of the legal norms which cause us to consider certain acts war crimes at all. Although all disciplines make use of terms such as 'war crime' and 'atrocity', and refer to various conventions or precedents that give legitimacy to trials, most have little or no awareness of the improvised, often instrumentalized, and extremely complicated development of these terms as they gradually transformed from evocative labels to legal categories.

Therefore, to understand the origins of the twentieth- and twenty-first century tribunals, we need to explore not only what values and ideas inspired the creation of the legal order for wartime that was established by The Hague and Geneva Conferences, but also the practical and ad hoc steps of this process. This development owes as much to unintended consequences as it does to the pursuit of high-minded ideals. Chapter 5 shows convincingly that we must not take the Second World War and Nuremberg as our starting point in this story, but as just one more step along a longer, more twisted path. Jan Lemnitzer disrupts the narrative propounded by legal scholars of a linear development from medieval tribunals to current international trials, and carefully reconstructs the uneven and sporadic changes in moral and legal norms. In doing so, he explores the influence of events ranging from the notorious Armenian Genocide to almost entirely forgotten, but no less influential, precedents such as the 1904 Dogger Bank incident, in which the Russian Navy opened fire on British fishing boats.

In discussing these developing legal norms, he reminds us that the perception of acts which we would today consider war crimes has changed significantly over time. The very concept that killing non-combatants in wartime should merit international concern is surprisingly novel, and continues to be problematic to this day, not least in conflicts involving ethnic violence that draw their destructive potential from the assumption that whole communities are culpable for individual actions.

This development owes a great deal to the rise of modern mass media over the past century. Although media coverage today is often intensely critical of war in general, this was rarely so in the past. To the contrary, the media's role was, as an arm of the state, to mobilize societies in support of war by highlighting only the atrocities of the enemy. In this context, Lemnitzer explores the role of atrocity reports in nurturing demands for war crimes prosecutions to be initiated—documents which play a major role in several other chapters, but which as a source sit uneasily on the boundary line of evidence-gathering and propaganda. Nowadays, a more independent media continues to compile testimonies and images of atrocities before investigators set foot on the scene, often thereby taking on the role of activists agitating for an international response.

History

Having explored the ways evidence is gathered, as well as the roots and rationales of the trial medium itself, Chapter 6 examines the role of historians, who are involved both in the trials themselves, and in the ways they are remembered.

History as a discipline is not only vital to the study of war crimes and trials because of the obvious fact that historical accounts are what most people turn to in order to learn about these events, but also (and just as importantly) because other disciplines, especially the Social Sciences, build their own theories and interpretations on the work of historians without sufficiently appreciating the nature and limitations of this field. Peter Romijn examines those limitations, as well as the more problematic ways in which historians come to act as expert witnesses within trial processes. By working for state institutions and when taking the stand, many historians effectively canonize certain documents and interpretations, the impact of which extends far beyond academia, shaping popular memory and influencing future politics.

In this context, he presents specific case studies charting the experience, interpretation and legacy of German war crimes in the occupied Netherlands, as well as Dutch war crimes in the subsequent Indonesian War of Independence. This pairing is particularly revealing, as a nation now synonymous with international justice, due to the ICC sitting in The Hague, had, amid much media and emotional controversy, to publicly come to terms with their own colonial crimes.

With the exception of historians who are still working to establish the basic facts of a given mass violence event, historiographical debates do not focus on whether specific crimes were committed, but what these crimes can tell us about the experiences of conflict—of issues concerning identity; obedience to authority; processes of radicalization; how malleable our moral compass may be; and more. As such, the historian's approach is inherently (and increasingly) interdisciplinary. However, when historians and others engage in reflections on the actions of the perpetrators of war crimes, they frequently do so with little understanding of the complex theories and concepts developed by the Social Sciences to study these very issues, and which form the centre of the following chapter.

Violence Studies

The rich empirical and theoretical work from the disciplines of Social Psychology, Sociology and Cultural Psychology are especially useful in explaining the occurrence of crimes within a context of deliberate, systematic destruction, killing and harming. Violence Studies, which draws upon all these disciplines, engages with the persistent and troubling questions of the reasons behind mass violence, often using the same resources that trials employ, but seeking to understand, rather than specifically to punish, these acts.

Violence Studies does justice to the fact that people are not born perpetrators—something which may seem obvious, yet is quickly obscured when the language of 'evil' and 'monsters' is deployed to describe the perpetrators of mass violence. This forms part of a pan-disciplinary shift in focus away from military leaders and political elites who were put on trial, to the role and experiences of 'ordinary men' who are no longer seen as blameless puppets, but as agents in their own right, which Romijn also explores in his case studies (Chap. 6).

Approaching this field from a Violence Studies perspective means focusing on the concrete actions in question and the conditions of their emergence. These studies and theories have shaped broader understandings of mentalities, motivations and ideas of peer pressure and obedience. Defence attorneys in trials always, implicitly or explicitly, draw on assumptions about social dynamics and individual agency, most emblematically the issue of soldiers being unable to refuse superior orders, or of being so under the sway of ideological propaganda that they carried out war crimes because they feared that, if they did not, they would themselves fall victim to the same logics of destruction.

Many of these perspectives are based on such famous psychological studies as the Milgram Experiment, which, as Christian Gudehus shows, are simply not such clear-cut examples of obedience to authority as they are often portrayed. In general, Gudehus warns against the fetishization of theories which are not developed in relation to or with the intent to analyse war crimes. They generate ways of seeing, yet they do not provide unbreakable chains of causality. Rather, they provide a series of lenses through which we can examine particular cases, but we must be aware of their nature to shape what we see as we look through them.

This chapter argues that individual behaviour can only fully be understood by examining the social world that surrounds each acting person. However, in contrast to historians and political scientists, who tend to overemphasize the role of ideology, Violence Studies presents a more fine-grained reading in which local norms and exigencies can themselves becoming determining, even radicalizing, factors on the ground.

Moving from theories to a historical case study, Gudehus also examines the German violence against Belgian civilians during the First World War, the propaganda side of which appears in Jan Lemnitzer's contribution (Chap. 5). While Lemnitzer outlines the simplistic propaganda version of events ('German soldiers intentionally murder innocent civilians') which prompted calls for trials, Gudehus brings into focus the fact that German troops were acting in the belief—untrue, but genuinely believed by most—that armed Belgian civilians had committed war crimes against them. This is not about assigning blame, but shows how Violence Studies can enable us to penetrate the minds of perpetrators, bringing to light the surprising insight that German soldiers believed they were the victims in this situation—a profoundly different motivational context.

International Relations

Having covered how numerous disciplines discover, assess, help to prosecute, and then to learn lessons from war crimes and atrocities, we turn to the final stage, which is the attempt to take these lessons and apply them to modern policy in the effort to prevent future acts of mass violence.

Moving from the individual to the structures and contexts in which they operate, we turn now to the theories and toolkits generated by International Relations. War crimes trials take place and are legally addressed within a fundamentally international context and, as such, we need to grapple with questions of state sovereignty, international politics and how 'justice' is to be understood and enforced, lacking as we do a single, coercive institution to enforce it. International Relations (IR) forms the point at which academic study feeds directly back into the process of norm-setting and governmental decision-making, as the theories developed by IR scholars—who often work as political advisors—frequently constitute the models on which politicians then act.

Yuna Han breaks down the complex and emerging theories applied to the prosecution of perpetrators of war crimes and atrocities, and the attempts of fragmented international bodies to mediate and adjudicate these contexts. Chapter 8 makes it clear that war crimes trials are not only about attempts to end conflict, to bring about a sense of closure or even of reconciliation, but are often inexorably drawn into the local political and social dynamics of the country in which the crimes took place. Challenging notions of Western imperialism, Han focuses on the in-depth case study of Uganda's decision to self-refer to the ICC regarding the alleged crimes committed by the Lord's Resistance Army, to examine how the apparatus of war crimes trials can be instrumentalized by particular state actors against their rivals in domestic conflicts. Indeed, Han, like Bellamy in the following chapter, highlights the ways in which the ICC may not act as a deterrent so much as a bargaining chip in domestic power plays.

Responsibility to Protect

While Han's chapter focuses on international criminal justice, Alex Bellamy describes the innovative new doctrine of the 'Responsibility to Protect' (R2P), which in a sense works to remove any need for an apparatus of international trials and recognizes that punishment alone is not a sufficient deterrent. War crimes trials are, after all, an implicit admission of failure to prevent those crimes.

R2P asserts that states have the responsibility to protect their own populations from four specific crimes (genocide, war crimes, ethnic cleansing and crimes against humanity) and that, if any state fails in this duty, or moves towards the implementation of these acts, that the world must not turn a blind eye—as happened with such terrible consequences in Rwanda—and instead must intervene, as was the case in Libya.

However, in order to achieve this goal, R2P leads us into interesting grey zones. As in Kenya, efforts to protect the civilian population may well undermine attempts to prosecute certain perpetrators. This emphasis on stability within local cultures can also give rise to paradoxical cases where individuals may violate local norms *by not committing atrocities.* We might also recall Chap. 4, for while R2P accepts the use of international sanctions as a non-violent tool, Mary Cox demonstrates how these tactics can inadvertently and disproportionately affect the most vulnerable members of society.

Despite these moral quagmires, R2P is an astonishing story of success. While many of the pieces in this volume are in some sense pessimistic, Bellamy shows that in spite of significant difficulties, there are genuine beacons of hope. R2P stands out not because it is a laudable theory, but because it is being actively developed on the ground. Bellamy calls for other disciplines to participate in the growth and development of R2P because, in an important sense, R2P finally offers other largely academic disciplines a pathway to effect real change. While so many debates about war crimes and mass violence revolve around trying to ever-more precisely theorize and categorize the problem(s), in the process they often defer the possibility of action beyond the horizon. R2P, by contrast, insists that action must be taken before it is too late. Just because something can be recognized as intensely problematic does not mean that positive action cannot be taken. Relative success is still preferable to paralysis.

Moral Philosophy

Underlying the very concept of war crimes and trials for their perpetration, as well as the Responsibility to Protect, is a moral sense that mass violence against civilians or violence of particular kinds against combatants is wrong. It is crucial to appreciate that this view is historically contingent and has developed over millennia; just because the morality seems self-evident to us now does not mean that we should lose sight of how this perception was achieved. The volume thus concludes with a chapter that provides a systematic, panoramic view of the ethical and moral understandings of the three crucial stages of conflict: pre-war (*Jus ad bellum*), wartime conduct (*Jus in bello*) and post-war reconstruction (*Jus post bellum*), for all three are intrinsically defined by the concept of war crimes, real and imagined.

Not only is an understanding of these theories relevant to other disciplines' studies of wars and war crimes, but philosophers build and develop their theories on the basis of other disciplines' investigations and hence each relies on the other in a symbiotic relationship which must itself be analysed. Furthermore, recognizing that this is a Western tradition is crucial when we are confronted with actors who openly disregard not only the laws of war, but also the value system which underpins them.

Brian Orend showcases the unexpectedly hands-on role which philosophers—himself included—play in training soldiers by teaching them moral awareness in their decision-making. The inclusion of this aspect of their training—in the US army, at least—owes much to the experience of the Vietnam War, in which many soldiers who have now ascended to the top ranks felt a deep absence of moral guidance. Just as generational shifts can lead to calls for historical re-evaluations of past conflicts (as Romijn describes in Chap. 6), they can thus also lead directly to a change in attitudes and practices within the military itself, as well as in the societies involved in a given conflict.

The chapter examines the long philosophical tradition that informs our moral judgements about the initiation and conduct of war; this tradition underpins, consciously or unconsciously, all our attitudes to war and mass violence and continues to develop in dialogue with modern conflicts. It provides a highly sophisticated instrument for assessing war and war crimes and is often present in the discourse of other disciplines, yet it is not widely understood in its complexity and nuance. Orend's chapter describes and interrogates these vital connections.

The chapter explores in depth the three key elements that make up Just War Theory: *Jus ad bellum*, *Jus in bello* and *Jus post bellum*. In the first, Orend discusses how enemy war crimes or the threat of them are perhaps the most frequently cited justification for military intervention, and how rules have been developed to attempt to prevent (justifiable) conflict unfolding at all. Regarding *Jus in bello*, the conduct of war has largely been codified in international and humanitarian law, but has fundamentally been defined and developed philosophically. While many these days emphasize the problems and shortcomings of Nuremberg, in the context of his discussion of *Jus post bellum*, Orend offers an unapologetically enthusiastic defence of these groundbreaking proceedings and their continuing legacy.

We present this volume as a first collaborative effort to open and begin to build an effective and productive dialogue between disciplines. We have aimed to establish a systematic, integrated and original introduction to the study of war crimes prosecutions and investigations, and hope that it will provide a starting point for future collaboration.

Jacques Schuhmacher is Co-Director of the War Crimes Research Network at the University of Oxford. He is Vanessa Brand scholar at Somerville College, Oxford, where he is completing an AHRC-funded DPhil project on the Nazi investigations of Allied war crimes and atrocities.

Jonathan Waterlow is Co-Director of the War Crimes Research Network at the University of Oxford, and a Research Associate at the University of Bristol. He previously held a British Academy Postdoctoral Research Fellowship at St Antony's College, Oxford. He writes and podcasts at www.voicesinthedark.world.

2

Orientation: War Crimes Trials in Theory and Practice from the Middle Ages to the Present

Devin O. Pendas

Introduction

Few international developments in the twentieth century are more striking than the increasing use of law to punish perpetrators of mass violence, whether war crimes, crimes against humanity, or genocide. There has been both an expansion of the forms of mass political violence considered justiciable and an intensification of efforts to institutionalize prosecution at both the international and domestic levels. The permanent International Criminal Court (ICC) in The Hague is only the most dramatic recent example of this, but there have also been various ad hoc international tribunals and so-called 'mixed' tribunals with shared international and domestic jurisdiction. There has also been a parallel effort to enhance claims for universal jurisdiction over core international crimes over the past 20 years or so, though with decidedly mixed results. The question is what do we make of this expansion and intensification of law? How novel is it? If it is new, what accounts for it? And what political effects might it have?

D.O. Pendas (✉)
Boston College, Boston, MA, USA

J. Waterlow, J. Schuhmacher, *War Crimes Trials and Investigations*, St Antony's Series,
https://doi.org/10.1007/978-3-319-64072-3_2

The Legality of War

The first key question to address is whether there actually has been a change in the use of law to punish the core international crimes—war crimes, crimes against humanity, and genocide? Obviously, the laws of war, as a distinct subset of international law, or the law of nations, are far older than the twentieth century.[1] There is a long tradition, dating at least to the Stoics and elaborated in Medieval just war theory, of viewing war as 'a handmaiden of justice…[whose] purpose was not conquest or revenge or glory, but rather the vindication of the rule of law.'[2] While the laws of war were for the most part a matter of customary law until the nineteenth century, royal ordinances were sometimes issued for specific campaigns in the Middle Ages, and it was not uncommon for opposing sides to negotiate terms for the treatment of prisoners at the start of hostilities.[3] Until roughly the publication of Hugo Grotius's *On the Laws of War and Peace* in 1625, much of the doctrine of the laws of war operated under the rubric of a broad 'just war' theory. This held, inter alia, that war could only rightly be waged by a sovereign, in pursuit of a precise objective, and that objective had to be legally valid—an *iusta causa* or just cause. As the leading Medieval theologian, Thomas Aquinas put it, 'a just cause is required, namely that those who are attacked, should be attacked because they deserve it on account of some fault.'[4] The justness of that cause was held to be objective, a matter of law, not of conflicting (political) interpretations. 'As a result, it was impossible in principle for a war to be just on both sides. Wars were seen as inevitably just on one side and unjust on the other, depending on which party had the law objectively on their side.'[5]

This doctrine authorized offensive as well as defensive wars, and contained no intrinsic norms for the actual conduct of hostilities (*jus in bello*). However, because just war theory held that war was waged for the vindication of some objective, legal right, it was supposed to be waged without hatred of the enemy, a war 'against wrongdoing as such, and not against the wrongdoers as individuals.'[6] This dispassionate pursuit of a just cause constituted the *animus* or motive force of war. Again, according to Aquinas, 'it is necessary that the belligerents should have a rightful intention, so that they intend the advancement of good, or the avoidance of evil.'[7] This view suggested a prohibition on 'gratuitous or unnecessary violence against the enemy side, since the enemy soldiers were not, per se, the real target.'[8] In other words, there was an implicit doctrine of proportional violence in the natural law tradition, which held that *unnecessary* violence was unjust. This, in turn, implied that there should be some legal recourse for violations, although this was mostly a matter of self-enforcement.

This medieval natural law theory started to decline in the seventeenth century, in the context of the wars of religion and their aftermath. The dominant legal mind of the era, Hugo Grotius, helped to divorce the laws of war from natural law, by arguing that only states, not individuals, were relevant actors for the law of nations, and by shifting the focus from mental attitudes (*animus*) to actions.[9] Crucially, Grotius separated the conduct of war from principles that would also cover private morality. Gone were discussions of just motives and *animus*. War was considered a formal condition.

Grotius thus asserted that a 'war is often called lawful not from the cause from which it arises, nor, as is done in other cases, from the importance of its exploits, but because of certain peculiar legal consequences.'[10] On this account, the conditions of legality for a war were reduced to two. First, war was—and could only be—an act of state. (Pirates, brigands, and other non-state actors were summarily excluded from the rights of war.) The reason, according to Grotius, was that although states might on occasion act unjustly, that was not their *raison d'être*, as was the case with criminal bands. Rather, states are created 'for the enjoyment of rights.' This, according to Grotius, inclines them to respect 'agreements entered into with each state or in accordance with custom.'[11] In other words, states are inclined to respect the rule of law, and should, therefore, be accorded legal rights.

The second requirement for a legal war was that a formal declaration of belligerence be issued. This was linked to the first condition. 'The purpose [of a declaration of war] was, rather, that the fact might be established with certainty that war was being waged not by private initiative but by the will of each of the two people or of their heads.'[12] The formal legal declaration guaranteed the status of war as a sovereign act. This in turn had important consequences. War permitted acts that would ordinarily be illegal, and remained, even in wartime, morally dubious—most notably killing, but also the destruction of property and other acts of harm. A formally recognized state of war was thus imperative, since it granted what was in effect a legal excuse for otherwise criminal behaviour. If only one side was justified in fighting, then only that side's soldiers could avail themselves of the legal excuse that a state of war existed, meaning, in effect, that everyone fighting for the 'unjust' side was a war criminal. It was, therefore, crucial to Grotius's argument (and the subsequent development of the laws of war) that he denied the possibility of distinguishing the 'just cause' of any given war. 'Even in a lawful war, from external indications it can hardly be adequately known what is the just limit of self-defence, of recovering what is one's own, or of inflicting punishments; in consequence it has seemed altogether preferable to leave decisions in regard to such matters to the scruples of the belligerents rather than to have recourse to the judgment of others.'[13]

War thus created a 'licence to injure' that could not be evaluated objectively from an external or neutral position. This had important implications for the conduct of hostilities. On Grotius's account, the license to harm and kill granted by war applied not only to 'those who actually bear arms, or are subjects of him that stirs up the war, but in addition to all persons who are in the enemy's territory' and included even women, children, prisoners of war, and hostages.[14] Although Grotius did, at least, believe poisoning and rape remained impermissible in wartime, the key point was that acts of state granted legal immunity for a vast range of harmful acts against a wide array of targets. Many of these acts would subsequently come to be considered war crimes. But because, according to Grotius, the justness of a war—and the limits on self-enforcement of rights—could not be determined externally and objectively, the restraints that could be imposed on violence were also strictly limited, and largely at the discretion of the combatant sovereigns.

As Stephen Neff has pointed out, this Grotian move, to treat war as a formal act of state, divorced from questions of just cause, did not lead immediately to the dissolution of the older natural law tradition.[15] Grotius himself remained indebted to that tradition, discussing at some length just and unjust causes of war, before admitting that, in many cases, the true justice of a given conflict may be difficult to adduce and subject to legitimate disagreement. Though—in medieval fashion—he does claim that 'with reference to the thing itself, a war cannot be just on both sides, just as a legal claim cannot,' he, nevertheless, also concludes that 'it may actually happen that neither of the warring parties does wrong.' This is because, 'no one acts unjustly without knowing that he is doing an unjust thing, but in this respect many are ignorant. Thus either party may justly, that is in good faith, plead his case.'[16] For Grotius, the secular law of nations was a necessary supplement to natural law, given the unavoidable potential for ambiguity in the interpretation of the latter. Thus, the law of nations and natural law enjoyed a kind of synergy. Yet, in Grotius's assertion, that the justness of a given cause is ultimately subject to legitimate dispute and thus cannot be treated as an external, objective fact in the world, pointed in the direction of an increasing scepticism towards natural law.

According to James Q. Whitman, in an important recent study, the impossibility of unambiguously determining the just cause of a war (and thus branding one side as criminal) meant that, from the Early Modern period until into the nineteenth century, the laws of war were not primarily concerned with constraining violence. Rather, the core concept was what he terms the *jus victoriae*, the law of victory. The rules for war 'were not, for the most part, humanitarian rules of the kind that dominate in the law of war today…[Rather] they were the rules of the law of victory, rules that aimed to determine who the winner was and what the winner won by virtue of victory.'[17] Wars—as the natural lawyers of the Middle Ages had argued—were still seen as lawful actions for the redress of legitimate grievances, but because there was no jurist capable of adjudicating those grievances, sovereigns were left to their own best judgement regarding when to wage wars to settle them. Wars were, in legal terms, 'self-help,' available only to sovereigns, not private persons.[18] Consequently, as the influential German jurist and philosopher Samuel Pufendorf put it, 'the evils inflicted by right of war have properly no relation to punishment, since they neither proceed from a superior as such, nor have as their direct object the reform of the guilty party or others, but the defence and assertion of my safety, my property, and my rights. To secure such ends it is permissible to use whatever means I think will best prevail against such a person, who, by the injury done me, has made it impossible for me to do him an injury, however I may treat him, until we have come to a new agreement to refrain from injuries for the future.'[19] In this context, according to Whitman, the laws of war were concerned with the determination of victory, and the stipulation of the 'rights' vindicated by victory. Constraining violence hardly entered the picture.

Law and the Constraint of Violence in the Middle Ages and Early Medieval Period

What did this way of thinking about war—either the pure natural law theory of the Middle Ages or the mixed-variety of the Early Modern period—imply for implementation on the ground? Throughout the Medieval and Early Modern period, there were sporadic trials for waging unjust wars and, on occasion, even for waging wars unjustly—that is, for violations of *jus ad bellum* and *jus in bello*. This has led Geoffrey Parker to argue that 'The rules of war followed by most European societies both at home and abroad have thus displayed a remarkable continuity since the sixteenth century.... [A]lmost every excess, from the sixteenth century onward, has been subject by contemporaries to detailed scrutiny.... And if no excuse were available, moral condemnation and then legal sanctions ensued. Most of the actions today outlawed by the Geneva Convention have been condemned in the West for at least four centuries; only the degree and the extent of enforcement has changed over time.'[20]

This overstates the case. To condemn an action is not the same thing as prosecuting it. If one wishes to understand the history of war crimes prosecutions, one needs to look not simply at what acts were decried or prohibited (themselves rather different matters), but also at who was prosecuted for these acts, in which courts, and according to what procedures.[21] Here one notices rather substantial variation over time. In particular, one must be sensitive to the ways in which war crimes trials are never simply trials. By their very nature, such trials are political. This means that one cannot understand them without understanding the political stakes in a given trial, and the way these interact with the law. Political trials come in many shapes and sizes and the same goes for war crimes trials.[22] Some may be egregious show trials with preordained outcomes; others may be scrupulously fair efforts to pursue justice. Simply noting that the defendants were charged with similar offences, therefore, reveals little about the trials themselves. To what extent were pre-modern 'war crimes trials' attempts to 'constrain' the violence of war and punish the violation of shared norms, and to what extent were they exercises in the political legitimation of victory through the judicial *de-legitimation* of the loser? The answer varies enormously from case to case.

At one extreme, one might take the example of one the of earliest known 'war crimes prosecutions'—that of Conradin von Hohenstaufen, King of Jerusalem, convicted in 1268 for waging an unjust war condemned by the Pope in his attempt to assert his claim to the throne of Sicily. Conradin was convicted of what we would today call crimes against peace, as a 'disturber of the public peace ... and the usurper of a kingdom, which the pope had granted to another,' as well as, on some accounts, of war crimes for the 'excesses of his German soldiers.'[23] Conradin was tried and convicted by a panel of legal experts convened ad hoc for that purpose. M. Cherif Bassiouni calls this the 'first international criminal prosecution.'[24]

Yet, it would be absurd to consider Conradin's trial as an early example of or precursor to contemporary war crimes prosecutions for several reasons. First, as is in fact typical of many early 'war crimes trials,' Conradin's real offence was not aggression or atrocity, but political treason. Conradin, as a Hohenstaufen, had a traditional claim on the throne of Sicily. His Uncle, Manfred, served as Regent in Sicily and, in that capacity, had continued the long-standing Hohenstaufen conflict with the papacy. In 1258, having defeated the papal armies, Manfred took advantage of false rumours of Conradin's death to declare himself King of Sicily, thus usurping his nephew. In 1263, Pope Urban IV recruited Charles, Duke of Anjou and brother to the French King, to the papal cause by offering him the Sicilian throne. Charles defeated Manfred in 1266 and made himself King of Sicily. Later that year, Conradin invaded Italy to vindicate his claim to the Sicilian throne, only to be narrowly defeated and subsequently captured by Charles in 1268.

After Conradin's capture, Charles wanted to legitimate his claim to the Sicilian throne, which to that point rested largely on his military victories over Manfred and Conradin, and on Papal support, but which was not widely acknowledged by other European powers (especially in Spain and Germany). To this end, he summoned a panel of legal experts and demanded that they declare Conradin guilty of 'high treason and *lèse-majesté*.'[25] A majority confirmed the king's interpretation, no doubt feeling more than a little intimidated at a trial held in Charles's court, given the king's reputation for ruthlessness. Whatever the legal merits of the case, Conradin was convicted not for his conduct of the war (war crimes), or even for what we would today recognize as aggression, that is launching an unprovoked offensive war, but for his refusal to acknowledge Charles's sovereignty, and he was thus held to be in effect a rebel.

Second, even this allegation was hotly contested, since the Hohenstaufens had a traditional claim on the throne of Sicily; whereas Charles's legal claim rested almost entirely on Papal support, the validity of which was open to dispute. (Indeed, the question of the Pope's secular authority had been at the root of the conflict between the Pope and the Hohenstaufen Emperors since the days of Conradin's grandfather, Frederick I.) One of the members of Charles's own legal commission, the Neapolitan law professor, Guido von Suzara, evincing considerable personal courage, vigorously protested Conradin's conviction. 'Conscience and duty impel me to affirm that the indictment just read is not only too severe, but unjust. Conradin of Hohenstaufen did not come as a robber or insurgent, but honourably; in full belief and confidence of his rights. No one can say that Naples and Sicily are not the inheritance of the young prince.'[26] Another version even has Suzara in effect accusing Charles himself of a war crime for his treatment of Conradin: 'He [Conradin] was not even captured while attacking, but rather as he fled; and treating prisoners gently [*schonend*] is a command of divine as well as human law.'[27]

Third, the *tu quoque* (you also) problem that plagues most war crimes prosecutions was particularly acute in this instance. By its very nature, war involves reciprocal violence, and it is often all too easy to point to 'excesses' by both sides. Yet it is almost unheard of for victors to be prosecuted alongside the vanquished. (This is a problem which afflicts even supposedly neutral international tribunals, like the ICC, of which more is discussed later). Certainly, in Conradin's case, there is good reason to think that Charles's army was guilty of more egregious misconduct than the Hohenstaufen forces. Villari notes that, after Conradin's defeat, his captured soldiers 'were treated with unparalleled cruelty, being mutilated, beheaded, or even burnt alive.'[28] For their alliance with Conradin, Charles 'avenged' himself on the local nobility, 'martyring them to death with refined cruelty.'[29] Writing in the eighteenth century, Archibald Bower declared that Conradin's execution 'to this day must raise horror and indignation.'[30] Much more recently, Bassiouni has declared Conradin's trial a 'perversion of international criminal justice [that] demonstrated how justice could be used for political ends.'[31]

But what of later trials, those in the Early Modern period, which Parker points to as direct ancestors of the Geneva Convention? Here the record is more mixed, but one would be hard pressed, on the available evidence, to declare straightforwardly that 'war crimes trials' were commonplace. Records from the sixteenth and seventeenth centuries are spotty, but there are two collections of court martial records from the parliamentary army in the English Civil War that offer a useful snapshot of legal practice in the era. Taken together, these two collections convey the impression of an army overwhelmingly concerned with maintaining internal discipline and that addressed harm to non-combatants (mainly against property) only to the extent it impinged upon that discipline. Above all, what these courts martial policed was *unauthorized* violence, not violence against civilians per se.

The first collection—the court martial papers of the parliamentary army commanded by Sir William Waller in the period prior to the formation of Oliver Cromwell's New Model Army—cover a period from April to December 1644.[32] These included charges for five cases of insubordination or mutiny, three cases of insubordination and desertion, three cases of desertion alone, one case of drunkenness, one case of theft from a fellow soldier, one case of assault on a fellow soldier, two cases of killing a subordinate (for which both officers were acquitted, since they were putting down a mutiny), and one case of heresy. There was one case of murder, though the victim was not identified, so it is impossible to say whether it was a civilian or a fellow soldier. Only five cases concerned anything that could reasonably be called a war crime from our current perspective, all involving theft or the unauthorized seizure of civilian property. In one case, for instance, two soldiers took a doublet and a pattern for breeches from a local tailor and, in another, a soldier, Henry Stone, stole a shirt, apron, 'and some other triviall things' from an unspecified victim.[33] All three were subject to humiliation and discharge from the army. In another case, one William Quincy, quartermaster to Captain Guilliams's troops, together with several of his subordinates, was convicted of robbing a man on the highway, taking his horse, his money, and his sword, for which Quincy was hanged and one of his subordinates discharged. Of these cases, only Quincy's might potentially be viewed as a war crime, since the others appear to involve common theft. Quincy, on the other hand, may have intended the stolen horse and monies for his unit, since he was quartermaster, though the records are unclear on this point.

In any event, General Waller appears to have been concerned about the risk of unauthorized requisitions and plunder, since he issued guidelines on the requisition of civilian horses on two occasions. On October 11, 1644, he declared 'that no souldier upon what pretence soever shall from hence forth presume to plunder take away or change any horse or horses from any Countryman or other Traveller upon the Road, man or woman without order from the Generall, or other superior officer who hath power thereunto upon payne of Death without mercy.'[34] On December 7, this order was extended to cover 'Goods, sheepe, Cattle, horse or horses whether by exchaining or otherwise,' and to protect not only travellers, but also 'any man or woman comeing to or from the Markett.' Again, though, this prohibition only applied to acts done '*without* expresse order from the Generall or other superior officer having power thereunto.'[35] The clear implication is that the General and other superior officers could very well authorize such requisitions, if they so chose.

The Waller records thus reveal a limited willingness to protect the property of civilians, but only from unauthorized seizure. This seems to have been intended mainly to preserve discipline among the troops. Further, since this was a civil war, and Waller's army was operating in southern England at the time, there may have been a degree of solicitousness towards the local population in the hopes of securing their loyalty against the king. This possibility is hinted at in a further proclamation issued by Waller in June 1644, demanding that the local 'persons of

Quality' in Worster County 'shall speedily repaire to my head Quarters and according to the Ordinace of Pareliament enter in to the Nationall Covenant taken by both kindoms, as a sincere expression of their Right affection to Gods cause.' Waller promised that, for those who declared their loyalty in this manner, he would 'protect theire persons and estates from all insolencyes and prejudice by my army.'[36] Clearly, civilian loyalty was at a premium in the context of civil war, and Waller was not shy about securing it by extortion if necessary. Again, the implication is clear. He would seize property from any local notables who did not swear fealty to parliament.

In any event, even more revealing of the state of the laws of war at the time is the Articles of War that Waller required all of his soldiers swear to uphold. (According to John Adair, these likely predated the Civil War, and were probably a restatement of a previous, royal ordinance, which was appended to the courts martial records for reference purposes.)[37] These demanded, first and foremost, that a soldier be obedient to his 'lord and Soverayne' and his superior officers. Secondly, they prohibited blasphemy. Third, they required soldiers to 'content themselves with their places appointed,' meaning they had to accept service in whatever units the army required, and work willingly with other units in the army without resistance. This was intended to prevent an excess of localism or personal loyalty to commanders from fracturing the army, as was the requirement that soldiers serve under replacement officers when necessary. Finally, the articles did prohibit certain acts that resemble modern war crimes, requiring that 'every Souldier shall for his Honor sake, gladly favor and mercifully forebeare unto ye utmost of his powers, all women lying in childbed, or being with child or lately delivered to defend and suckour them from ye Rage of the Cruell and rude soudiers or others which follow the Camps and spoyls, also to defend all ministers aged men and women.'[38] In other words, the articles protected pregnant women and those with newborns, clergy, and the elderly. This was obviously a very restricted class of protected persons and left open the possibility of lawfully killing many other kinds of non-combatants.

The second set of records comes from a slightly different context. As Cromwell pursued Charles II's army into England, he left behind George Monck to finish up the campaign against Royalist forces in Scotland.

Monck's army set about reducing Royalist strongholds, most importantly at Dundee, which the Parliamentary troops assaulted on September 1, 1651, after a brief siege. Because the city governor, Robert Lumsden, had refused to surrender the city, Monck, in keeping with established military practice, gave his troops permission to sack the city for a 24-hour period. Anywhere from several hundred to over 1000 civilians were killed during the sack.[39] Monck himself estimated civilian casualties at 500. Further, one contemporary observer, John Nicoll, estimated that 'seven score women and young children were also killed.'[40] In addition, substantial material wealth was plundered, over 200,000 pounds sterling, plus diverse merchandise, according to Nicoll.[41] Another contemporary observer noted that 'the spoil is like to prove very great; were you here, you would not know a private soldier from an officer, divers of them having got gallant apparel.'[42]

The challenge for Monck after the sack of Dundee was to secure the peace of Scotland and reconcile the population to foreign occupation, all the while continuing to reduce Royalist strongholds. To that end, he deployed military justice. As Godfrey Davies puts it, the civil war had taught commanders that 'indiscriminate plundering both rendered permanent the hostility of enemies and irreparably damaged the morale of any army allowed such licence.'[43] Monck thus 'sought to obtain the acquiescence of the Scots by the impartial administration of justice and to secure their own supremacy by the maintenance of strict discipline in the forces under their command. The two objects were interdependent—both concerned the relations of an alien soldiery with a subject population.'[44] The hearts-and-minds strategy pursued by Waller in England loomed larger for Monck's forces in Scotland, since the loyalty of the population was even more doubtful, given the national as well as political and religious cast of the conflict. Courts martial were used to preserve discipline, and the hope was this would lead to peace between occupiers and occupied. Records are preserved of such courts martial from September 1651 to January 1652.

In this context, what is striking is that, as with Waller's courts martial records, a great many of the cases in the Dundee records concern matters of internal discipline, pertaining to the conduct of soldiers in relation to their superiors and one another. There are cases of fighting,[45] insubordination,[46] drunkenness, and swearing.[47] Unlike in Waller's court, there were also several charges of frequenting prostitutes, in which both the soldier and the woman were punished.[48] Desertion appears not to have been as much of a problem, perhaps because the troops were quartered in foreign territory and were, therefore, farther from home.[49]

Given the dual mandate of the courts martial—to preserve discipline and to reconcile the local population to Parliamentary occupation—it is perhaps not surprising that crimes against civilian property loom large in these proceedings, substantially more so than in the Waller records. Many of these concerned the perennial problem of Early Modern armies: the quartering of troops. As with most armies of the era, troops were frequently housed with local residents. This created potential problems, since soldiers could be tempted to claim quarters without authorization, disturbing local residents and undermining the authority of their superior officers. For instance, on December 9, 1651, four soldiers, two of them in custody, came to the house of one David Thompson, claiming they had orders to quarter there. They 'beate the deponent's servants for shutting the doore against them.'[50] When Thompson's wife demanded to see their orders, 'one of them, who had a pistol, said, there was his order.' The defendants also drank heavily and broke into Thompson's larder to get at his liquor, striking his wife when she attempted to stop them. One of the two defendants was convicted and sentenced to be lashed; the fate of the other is unclear.

Many cases, however, were more ambiguous. One of the more bizarre cases to be found in the Dundee court martial records concerns a dispute between Isabel Hamilton, Lady Arley, a local noblewoman, and one Lt. Greene, along with several of his subordinates.[51] Lady Arley asserted that Greene and his troops had come to her manor, claiming they had an order to quarter troops there, but would not show her the order. They kept threatening her and came over her wall when she refused to have the gates opened. They further set fire to the gates to force them open. Lt. Greene protested that he in fact did have an order from General Monck to quarter troops on Lady Arley's estate, that she refused his offer to show her said order, and that she was in general completely uncooperative with his troops. He added that his troops were at considerable risk while trying to enter the house grounds, 'being in the edge of the Highlands, where were many armed men. The Lord of the house being one of their head men as alsoe the time of the day (which was then almost spent).'[52] This, he explained, was why he had tried to force entry into the house.

Only when another local nobleman, James Mauley, Laird of Melgun, arrived, was a compromise reached. Lady Arley agreed to open her gates, and the soldiers agreed to spare her life and those of her servants. Once the gates were open, the soldiers seized various moveable goods. Lady Arley and her servants alleged this included personal property. One of the soldiers said they seized only war materials, including 'fower barrels of powder, 2 little ones and 2 greate, some musquetts and other guns and bulletts and stones in the windows, and 9 foote collours.'[53] The records are unclear, but it appears that after Lady Arley agreed to open her gates, soldiers quartered on her estate for some time.

In the end, the court tried its best to issue a Solomonic verdict. It declared that, on the one hand, Lady Arley's house was not a prize of war, but that, on the other hand, Lt. Greene had done nothing wrong in forcing entry. It did order that Lady Arley's property be restored to her 'except materials of warre' and that she receive the proceeds from the sale of any goods that had already been disposed of. It further granted her 50 'boules of oates' as compensation for food consumed by quartered soldiers. Given that Greene had legitimate orders for the quartering of troops and that military goods were found on the property, indicating likely support for Scottish Royalists, this might seem a surprisingly mild verdict. Yet, if one keeps in mind that the ultimate purpose of these courts martial was to secure a more quiescent occupation, this verdict makes more sense.

In another case, a landlord, one William Fergisson, alleged that the four soldiers quartered with him had 'bin disorderly' and that one of them had assaulted his elderly mother sick in bed by flinging coals from the fire on her.[54] The soldiers, on the other hand, countered that it was the landlord who had been drunk on the night in question, cursing and abusing the soldiers. One of the soldiers testified—in a manner sure to evoke the sympathy of the court—that Fergisson, 'coming in druke … came and pull'd the deponent by the arme, and ask't what rogue was that that had abused his Mother, and said, wee were all rogues and beggerly rogues, and if there were noe more souldiers then ther were townsmen they would soon have done with them.'[55] The other soldiers testified similarly, though with less political acumen, omitting any reference to the seditious claim about the town's ability to dispose of the occupation. In the end, the soldiers were acquitted and the landlord, William Fergisson, was convicted.

This mix of cases of clear-cut abuse by soldiers, orderly confiscations gone awry, and ambiguous circumstances of conflict between soldiers and civilians led the court to try to minimize the military footprint in the area. The court issued a proclamation: 'Whereas divers disorders are committeed by the souldiers stragling, and lying out of their quarters by abusing the country, and extorting victuals to the dishonor of the army and great prejudice of the country. These are to require all souldiers whatsoever belonging to this garrision, that they doe nott goe half a mile from the garrison without leave from their officers upon paine of severe punishment.'[56] The instrumental quality of military justice in this context could hardly be made plainer. What was at stake was the 'honor' of the army, and with it, the willingness of the local population to peaceably accept its authority. Any sense that civilian life and property was to be respected on grounds of general principle is almost entirely absent. It should hardly surprise us then that one soldier was able to successfully defend himself from allegations of illicit property seizure by asserting 'that hee knew nott that the plunder of the towne was done.'[57]

Given these examples of Medieval and Early Modern 'war crimes trials,' it would seem best not to overstate the degree of continuity with subsequent developments. Certainly, none of the courts martial from the English Civil War look very much like what one would expect from trials held under the Geneva Conventions of 1949, especially given that both sets of records make it clear that the killing of non-combatants and the destruction of civilian property could be authorized under an array of circumstances. To the extent that the Dundee example might be interpreted as demonstrating an implicit doctrine of military necessity, this is a far cry from the modern understanding. The sack of the city *may* have been done, in part, to intimidate other cities and encourage them to surrender. This is rather different from the contemporary understanding of necessity, which holds that violence against non-combatants is permissible only when '"concrete and direct" military advantages [can be] anticipated' and when these advantages are proportional to the harm done.[58] The indirect and potential advantage of intimidating other cities into surrender through the sack of Dundee follows an entirely different logic. As for the other crimes prosecuted, insofar as these pertain not to the internal discipline of the army, but to the protection of civilian life and (mainly) property, these only apply to *unauthorized* harm. These records make abundantly clear that commanders could, when they saw fit, *authorize* harm to civilians and that doing so would be perfectly within their legal rights.

Transformations in the Modern Era

Starting gradually in the nineteenth century, the situation began—haltingly and in limited contexts—to change. The United States took the lead in formally codifying the laws of war, with the so-called Lieber Code of 1863, promulgated shortly before the First Geneva Convention of 1864. The Lieber Code is often viewed as the origin of modern, 'positive' (i.e. written) laws of war, but it should be remembered that it also contained very strong exceptions for 'military necessity.'[59] Of course, at about that same time, the United States was also prosecuting Native Americans for killing women and children while defending their lands in Minnesota, 33 eventually being hanged out of an initial list of almost 300.[60] One scholar has observed of this incident: 'This early attempt to apply law to war (even though the U.S. government did not consider the ongoing battles with the Indians a war) produced a primitive from of political justice.'[61] Whether the formalizing initiative of the Lieber Code compensated for the barely disguised lynchings in Minnesota is debatable. Although the trend towards codification continued with The Hague Conventions of 1899 and 1907, it is clear that before the mid-twentieth century, the laws of war, though developing, remained underspecified and enforcement was arbitrary and inconsistent at best. Adam Roberts has argued that the history of efforts to codify and strengthen the laws of war in the late nineteenth and early twentieth centuries is an 'account of failure.'[62] Roberts emphasizes, in particular, the 'revival of barbarism' in the two World Wars as evidence of the limited impact of the nineteenth-century laws of war on the actual conduct of hostilities. Equally important is the fact that, even at their best, the laws of war, whether customary or codified, were seen in this era of imperialism as pertaining only to conflicts between 'civilized' nations.[63] Being civilized meant, among other things, having an identifiable and internationally recognized state, having a standing, uniformed military, and fighting in a manner consistent with European norms (e.g. in open battle, rather than raids).[64] That this understanding of 'civilization' was deeply racialized and more or less overtly intended to exclude colonized peoples should be clear. In this context, it is perhaps better to think of the World Wars as involving, not a revival of barbarism, but the re-importation of barbarism from the small wars of colonial conquest to the big wars of intra-European geopolitics.

In the second part of the twentieth century, the sporadic and largely ad hoc application of the laws of war began to change, starting of course with the International Military Tribunal and the American-led Successor Tribunals at Nuremberg.[65] Thereafter, starting as early as the 1970s and clearly picking up steam in the 1990s, it became increasingly common to prosecute perpetrators of wartime atrocities and other forms of mass political violence, in a process that Kathryn Sikkink has termed 'the justice cascade.'[66] These prosecutions have proceeded in both domestic and international courts. Famously, the UN created a permanent International Criminal Court in 1998 in Rome (with the court coming into existence in 2002) and, just as famously, the United States has declined to join the court, with President George W. Bush even going so far as to 'unsign' the Rome Treaty.[67] Despite US opposition (as well as that of China and Russia), the ICC has established itself as a functioning element of international governance. Enshrined in the Rome Statute is the jurisdictional doctrine of 'complementarity,' which gives domestic courts first crack at the mass crimes under the ICC's jurisdiction, thus formalizing joint domestic and international jurisdiction for war crimes, crimes against humanity, genocide, and (eventually) aggression.

As the christening of this trend as a 'justice cascade' implies, these twentieth-century developments have often been treated as unambiguously positive, serving the general goal of seeing justice done in the world and aiding in political transitions from authoritarian to more democratic and liberal regimes. Consequently, such prosecutions are often lumped together with other judicial-political processes, such as lustration and truth commissions, under the rubric of 'transitional justice.'[68] This historical trajectory has often been framed as a move from impunity, where political actors in wartime could literally get away with murder, to justice where at least major perpetrators will be held accountable and punished for their crimes.[69] Although acknowledging the limitations and ongoing challenges for justice, on this view, the trend towards criminal prosecutions for human rights violations broadly construed is seen as a clear improvement. According to Sikkink, 'The possibility of individual criminal accountability has provided useful but imperfect tools to activists, victims, and states to help diminish future violations. These human rights prosecutions will continue to fall far short of our ideals of justice, but they represent an improvement over the past.... The new world of greater accountability that we are entering now, for all its problems, offers hope of reducing violence in the world.'[70]

The underlying logic of this cautiously optimistic interpretation of the history of war crimes trials is twofold. First, there is the empirical claim that criminal prosecutions for political atrocities have beneficial effects, in the form of deterrence and democratization. This is the crux of Sikkink's argument, for instance. Her evidence comes mainly from Latin America and she argues that 'countries in Latin America that used human rights prosecutions have better human rights records than countries in the region that did not use such prosecutions, or used them less frequently.'[71] This may well be true, statistically speaking, but it does raise an important 'chicken or egg' question. Perhaps, the countries more inclined to protect human rights are those more likely to stage prosecutions for human rights abuses, and not the other way around? Be that as it may, the second underlying claim of the optimists' position seems more consequential. This second assertion is that normalizing prosecutions for human rights violations and war crimes may help to diminish levels of mass violence and atrocity generally by spreading human rights norms and helping to (re)constitute the rule of law.[72] This is less an argument about deterrence than about the spread of cultural norms.

Realism and Culture

Many scholars are sceptical of this optimistic account.[73] Typically, the sceptics of trials for mass atrocities argue from a position of international relations 'realism.'[74] At its most basic, according to this perspective, the international arena is characterized by an 'absence of an arbitrator or laws', which means that 'war [is] a possibility.'[75] Accordingly, international law is seen as nearly an oxymoron. Certainly, the notion that international legalism will have a significant impact on state actors is called fundamentally into question. To the extent that states obey international law, they do so because such compliance is seen as cheap and as consonant with the state's preconceived interests anyway. As Jack Goldsmith and Eric Posner put it, 'International law emerges from states' pursuit of self-interested policies on the international stage. International law is, in this sense, *endogenous* to state interest. It is not a check on state self-interest; it is a product of state self-interest.'[76]

This realist scepticism has its own limitations, however. For one thing, the development of criminal prosecutions for past atrocities has taken place as much in domestic courts as it has before international tribunals, so the realists' account of self-interested states acting in an anomic international arena is rather beside the point for major dimensions of the history of war crimes trials.[77] Moreover, the vision of an anarchic international sphere where states pursue self-evident geostrategic interests greatly underplays the role of ideology—an odd choice especially when talking about the twentieth century, where the significance of ideology would seem to be self-evident. In particular, it tends to treat the notion of 'national interest' as an a priori given, rather than a historically emergent category, with variable content. 'Realists' see state interest as invariant—the pursuit of maximum power in a competitive zero-sum game.[78]

This is overly simplistic. States view their interests differently over time and ideology is the framework which constitutes those interests. Adolf Hitler, for instance, was convinced that the Third Reich lacked sufficient 'living space' and needed to expand geographically in order to ensure the prosperity of Germans.[79] This was an ideological construct that completely missed the modern determinants of prosperity (like industry and trade) that were no longer dependent on geographical scale. To this, one must add the Nazis' pathological perception of the Jews as an existential threat, where no such threat was present. These ideological constructs were clearly wrong, yet they were very 'real' determinants of Nazi foreign policy. If pathological ideologies can forge 'national interests,' why not other, more 'positive' ideological constructs? There is no reason to think that obedience to, and enforcement of, international norms cannot sometimes come to be viewed as a compelling state interest, even if that too could be seen from a certain vantage point as an ideological (humanitarian) distraction from supposedly 'real' state interests. Of course, this implies that the reverse can be true as well and that states may lose interest in international law over time. For instance, under its former conservative government led by Steven Harper, Canada abandoned its previous leadership role as a member of the 'coalition of the willing' that led the push for creating the ICC, and adopted a more US-style scepticism of international legal institutions.[80] Yet, it is hard to see that anything fundamental had changed about Canada's actual strategic interests; the shift was an ideological one.

So, rather than naturalizing some notion of state interest, I would suggest an alternative grounds for scepticism regarding the potential of war crimes trials to effect social and political change. The optimists overstate their case for what war crimes trials can achieve because they tend to misapprehend the relationship between law and politics. (Politics is here being conceived broadly as the social organization of power relations.) The optimists see criminal prosecution as a means for taming mass violence through the application of law. The analogy is to the process whereby states came to, first, claim and, then, to actually operationalize a monopoly of legitimate force in the domestic sphere, the notion being that something analogous could be replicated on the international stage.[81] As A.H. Feller, General Legal Counsel of the United Nations put it in 1949,

> The trouble with international law is not that it isn't law, but that there isn't enough of it. The rules cover only a small part of the relations between states; many of the rules are only vaguely defined or their meaning is disputed; there are too many loopholes, too many opportunities for quibbling and evasion. If the system is to furnish a secure foundation for the world community it must be developed until its content approximates that of national legal systems.[82]

Legitimation Crisis and Legalism

Even the most diligent promoters of international legalism are forced to concede that (at least currently) there is no international executive akin to the domestic state, hence the frequent turn to culturalist arguments. War crimes trials succeed—the argument goes—because they effect a normative cultural transformation, leading to a rejection of the ideology or logic that led to violence in the first place. The goal and effect of such trials is, as Ruti Teitel puts it, 'the grounding within society of a normative shift in the principles underlying and legitimating the exercise of state power.'[83] War crimes trials do not need a global executive to be effective, on this argument; they just need to change people's values.

The question, then, is how such a normative shift might occur. Two issues are crucial here. The first is legitimacy; the second, legalism. One way for war crimes trials to induce normative shifts would be for people to view them as legitimate acts of law, and to accept their verdicts as 'just' and their lessons as meaningful, in effect because they respect the institution teaching those lessons and accept them, more or less, 'on authority.' The second path—legalism—focuses more on procedure than it does on either authority or specific didactic lessons. If people accept the legalism enacted in war crimes trials, they come to view such proceedings as the right *way* to address historic wrongs, and law as the proper mechanism because it embodies procedural fairness. This might effect a normative transformation—an embrace of liberal rule of law—without people needed to embrace either the specific authority of the tribunal as such or its particular lessons.

There are considerable problems with the notion of trials as didactic exercises, as Peter Romijn explores in-depth in his contribution to the present volume. They are subject to considerable confirmation bias in which people learn lessons they already 'knew' to be correct in advance. There is a marked tendency for people to learn the 'wrong' lessons (i.e. lessons different from those intended by the trial's architects), which may even reinforce the authoritarian tendencies the trial is supposedly intended to undermine. There is never one audience for a given trial, so there can never be one lesson learned. Trials are circumscribed by rules of evidence and procedure that may exclude numerous crucial historical questions relevant to political pedagogy. And all of this is true, even if the audience(s) accept the legitimate authority of the tribunal.

Setting aside these difficulties, however, establishing the legitimacy of war crimes trials (in the broadest sense) is itself quite challenging. Legal legitimacy is typically linked to the state, conceived not just as an institution exercising force, but one seen as *authorized* to use force. As Max Weber noted, a state is only a state if 'its administrative staff successfully upholds the claim of the *monopoly* of the *legitimate* use of physical force in the enforcement of its order.'[84] A state exists when people (its citizens) *accept* its use of force. The state's monopoly on force works, when it does, because it is widely accepted. Where it is not, we see failed states and civil wars.

So the question becomes, can war crimes tribunals come to be viewed as placing *legitimate* constraints on action, and their sanctions accepted as legitimate acts of force? In other words, can prosecutions for mass atrocity foster political legitimacy? Under what conditions? What kind of legitimacy? Moreover, are such trials *necessarily* democratizing? Or can they foster authoritarian legitimacy as well?

For 'war crimes trials'—domestic or international—to be accepted as legitimate, two conditions are necessary: such trials must be considered 'just' *and* they must be considered politically effective. The history of war crimes trials, from Conradin to the ICC, shows how difficult it is for them to meet these twin goals. For war crimes trials to be viewed as just, they must meet several criteria. They must be viewed as procedurally fair, not as show trials with foreordained outcomes. They have to be seen as (relatively) neutral and objective, not as 'victor's justice.' And they must be accepted as addressing the legitimate grievances of the victims, for retributive and—perhaps—for restorative justice, while not abusing the rights of the accused or punishing them disproportionately.[85] Justice, then, entails both fairness to the defendants and satisfying the needs of the victims. Each of these can be challenging in its own right, and it is not unusual for the two to stand in mutual tension.

In order to be politically efficacious, there is the very real possibility that one or the other of these requirements will have to be deliberately violated. The Nuremberg trials brushed aside concerns about ex post facto legislating and the inequality of arms between prosecution and defence, in order to bring charges against the full range of Nazi criminality. The subsequent Tokyo trial, even more than Nuremberg, was unavoidably viewed as biased victor's justice, given the ways in which the Asia-Pacific war intersected with the history of European and American colonial dominance in the region. And all too often, the burden of proof and the presumption of innocence mean that defendants who are 'obviously' guilty in the eyes of victims will have to be acquitted in the name of justice. These challenges are structural, not merely contingent. No war crimes trial system can fully evade them.

It may be that it is easier to legitimate war crimes trials in the eyes of survivor communities than among perpetrators and their supporters. After all, survivors frequently call for justice to be done hoping the dead will not have died in vain, that just retribution will vindicate some measure of their loss. Such trials can also satisfy the need many survivors feel to tell their story, so that the dead are remembered. For example, the Eichmann trial in Jerusalem served, in the words of Tom Segev, as 'therapy for the nation, starting a process of identification with the tragedy of the victims and survivors….'[86] In this case, however, the trial was widely viewed positively within Israel—by survivors and others—at least in part because it was linked not just to the suffering of victims, but to the Israeli state. 'The witnesses related, in agonizing detail, heartrending stories that revealed the helplessness of the European Jews, the betrayal of the nations, the heroism of the resistance fighters, the depth of the trauma, the cruelty of the Germans, and the pride of the Zionists. The overt message was the Jewish nation. The hidden message was the Jewish state.'[87] The legitimacy of the Eichmann trial was quite deliberately linked to the legitimacy of the Israeli state. In this case, the legitimacy of the trial was closely linked to the perceived legitimacy of the state of Israel itself. Where such an association with a state is missing, as with international tribunals, or where the legitimacy of the sponsoring state is itself in question, as with some post-transition regimes, it can be far more difficult to establish the independent authority of the tribunal.

The association with state legitimacy can be extended beyond domestic borders, at least under some circumstances. This may help to explain the otherwise paradoxical response to the Eichmann trial in West Germany. In 1962, fully 95% of Germans claimed to have followed the Eichmann trial at least somewhat closely and, of these, only 15% thought it would be better to not prosecute Nazi crimes at all.[88] This stands in marked contrast to German attitudes towards Nazi trials conducted under their own domestic jurisdiction, where, in 1964, fully 57% of Germans opposed conducting any further trials for Nazi crimes.[89] More generally, Germans had been deeply sceptical of efforts to prosecute Nazi crimes since shortly after the end of the war. The percentage of Germans who viewed the Nuremberg Trial as 'fair' fell from 78% in 1946 to 38% in 1950.[90] There was widespread hostility to both the Allied war crimes trails programmes and to trials for Nazi crimes in domestic German courts, and substantial organized efforts, both by unofficial civil society groups and the German government, to provide legal aid to the accused and to pressure the Allies for early release.[91]

German support for the Eichmann trial thus stands in contrast to their opposition to both Allied and West German Nazi trials. The reasons for this dichotomy are complex, but I would suggest that they related to Konrad Adenauer's strategy of, in effect, 'offshoring' the response to the Holocaust. Adenauer pursued a dual strategy. First, he put enormous pressure on the Allies to release German 'war condemned' (*Kriegsverurteilte*) in the context of German rearmament and NATO membership—an effort that was enormously successful, such that by the mid-1950s hardly any Nazi criminals were still imprisoned by the Western Allies. This coincided with a precipitous decline in the prosecution of Nazi perpetrators in domestic West German courts, where the number of prosecutions fell from a high of 1819 in 1948, to 809 in 1950, and a mere 21 in 1955.[92] At the same time, however, against substantial opposition from within his own Christian Democratic Party, Adenauer was able to push through a programme of reparations to be paid to the state of Israel, as the successor to the Jewish diaspora exterminated by the Nazis.[93] This transformed the legacy of the Holocaust from a question of domestic German politics into an issue of foreign policy. This could be readily embedded in a Cold War framework, especially after Israel emerged as an anti-Soviet force once various Arab states moved into the Soviet orbit after the Suez crisis in 1956. The point ultimately was to substitute reparations for trials—a strategy that, if Adenauer's electoral success in the 1950s is any indication, found considerable favour with West German voters. It seems, then, that while many Germans were willing to concede to the Israelis the right to hold one trial for the Holocaust, they were generally opposed to any broader or more systematic efforts at accountability for Nazi crimes.

This points to a structural dilemma intrinsic to trials for mass atrocity. Such crimes are, by definition, political in nature, which makes it all but impossible for their prosecution to be seen as 'above politics,' as may be the case with ordinary domestic criminal trials. It is exceedingly difficult for such trials to be viewed as neutral and non-partisan. Thus, it is likewise exceedingly difficult for them to be viewed as legitimate by both victim and perpetrator communities simultaneously. Yet if they are to effect a substantive change in political culture, such legitimacy is indispensable. (Indeed, it is presumably more important that perpetrator communities embrace a normative transformation, since they were the ones who abused power in the first place.)

This problem may be particularly acute in instances where the courts are run by parties to the given conflict, like the Nuremberg or Tokyo trials after World War II, which were widely criticized as victor's justice, and not just by the defendants. Justice Radhabinod Pal's dissenting judgement in the Tokyo trial, which dismissed the whole proceedings as biased and unjust on these grounds, continues to resonate—especially, but not exclusively, among Japanese nationalists—to this day.[94] But even more purportedly neutral tribunals, like the ICC, suffer from this problem. The fact that, to date, 10 of the 11 open investigations at the ICC involve African nations has created a serious risk that the court will be perceived as a neocolonial court 'for Africans only'.[95] (*On this complex issue, see Yuna Han's contribution to this volume—Eds.*) Even domestic courts have a hard time escaping perceptions of partisanship in dealing with mass atrocities, since perpetrators rarely admit guilt or acknowledge the legitimacy of the proceedings.

If it can therefore be difficult for war crimes tribunals to establish the broad legitimacy required to promote normative transformations in political culture when it comes to their substantive 'lesson,' it may be easier (though far from easy) for them to demonstrate the value of legalism. Legalism itself is a term that is often deployed pejoratively. Judith Shklar certainly meant it this way when she popularized the term in 1964, when she described it as confusing morality with mere rule-following.[96] Yet I would suggest that legalism has its virtues, for all that it may risk a stultifying formalism and pedantic rule-following. The essence of legalism is the view that the procedure for reaching an outcome matters more than the outcome itself. In other words, a fair trial is more important than a just trial.

If the goal of war crimes trials is to effect a normative transformation in political culture, in attitudes towards state power, then it makes sense to focus on valorizing procedural limitations to state violence. Due process of law is among the most venerable such constraints. The state's monopoly on legitimate force is at its most legitimate when it operates through pre-established rules that protect the due process rights of those to be coerced. To be sure, perfectly fair trials can and do lead to unjust outcomes, especially if justice is conceived as encompassing political as well as metaphysical considerations. Many criminal trials under authoritarian regimes follow the letter of the law punctiliously, whether we are talking about ordinary courts (though not the *Volksgerichthof*) during the Third Reich, or the criminal courts of South Africa under apartheid.[97]

Nevertheless, trials are probably better at teaching legalism than they are at history lessons. For instance, for all that the West German public tended to reject the pedagogy of Nazi trials, whether in the immediate post-war years or the later decades of the post-war period, it would be wrong to conclude from this that 'war crimes trials' in the broad sense failed to make any contribution to (West) Germany's 'liberalization learning process.'[98] In occupied Germany, conservative and right-wing jurists organized a campaign to aid Germans accused of crimes against humanity in both Allied and German courts.[99] What was most significant about this effort was that, while it explicitly sought to exculpate perpetrators of Nazi crimes, it did so in the language of liberal legalism and due process rights. In particular, Germans argued that prosecuting crimes against humanity, whether in Allied or especially German courts, violated the principle *nullum crimen sine lege* (no crime without prior law)—the prohibition on ex post facto law. They argued, in the words of one German judge, such ex post facto prosecutions damaged 'a fundamental principle ... the violation of which during the Nazi period was justifiably subject to severe attacks.'[100] This judge, Hodo von Hodenberg, was a member of the right-wing Heidelberg Circle dedicated to aiding accused Nazi war criminals. Yet, he did not defend them on substantive or nationalist grounds, but rather on procedural ones. This kind of argumentation helped, I would argue, to deradicalize the right-wing German judiciary after World War II, pushing them to embrace a procedural legalism they had rejected during the Weimar Republic with disastrous consequences for German democracy. Whether this kind of unintended liberalization can be found in other contexts is a matter for empirical investigation, but I would suggest that this might offer the best hope for using war crimes trials for liberalizing purposes. The mere fact of holding fair trials may be what matters the most.

Trials for mass atrocities—whether war crimes, crimes against humanity, or genocide—have come to occupy a central role in both international and domestic politics at the start of the twenty-first century. If their history gives cause for caution regarding the prospects of them radically taming mass violence or transforming authoritarian political cultures, there are at least some reasons for guarded optimism as well, so long as one realizes the limitations intrinsic to the legal form.

The present volume offers reflections on the methods, procedures, substance, and possible future of war crimes trials in this broad sense. These reflections come from scholars and practitioners. They are necessarily interdisciplinary in nature, since war crimes trials draw on expertise from across the human sciences. Jurists, anthropologists, forensic scientists, political scientists, and historians all have contributions to make to understanding how this complex phenomenon has operated and continues to operate. In part, this is because post-war trials have used both eyewitnesses and experts from a wide variety of fields—forensic pathologists, historians, psychologists, and even handwriting experts. They have drawn on—and provoked debates within—social psychology, political science, and jurisprudence, among others. In other words, war crimes trials are both susceptible to analysis from a variety of perspectives and themselves rely on the insights of a wide range of disciplines. They can thus only be approached interdisciplinarily. While it might be too much to ask to expect that even a broadly interdisciplinary study can resolve all the open questions and the many ongoing challenges confronting war crimes prosecutions, we can nevertheless hope to at least pose some of the most pressing questions and point in the direction of potential answers.

Bibliographical Essay The historiography of 'war crimes trials' in the broad sense is quite substantial and growing rapidly. In part, this is because the term 'war crimes trials' itself is rather capacious—covering war crimes trials in the proper sense of trials for the violation of the laws and customs of war, but also trials for a myriad of other mass atrocities, including crimes against humanity and genocide. These include crimes committed both during wartime and outside the context of formal or even asymmetrical military conflict (e.g. the ICC investigation of Uhuru Kenyatta for violence associated with the 2007 Kenyans elections, though the case was eventually dropped). One might even add to the category consideration of various para-judicial procedures for dealing with mass political violence, such as truth commissions and, perhaps, even reparations and restitution procedures.

Given the scope of this literature, I will focus here on the historiography of criminal trials, international and domestic, leaving aside the para-judicial procedures. This literature can be divided into three general categories: (1) histories of international criminal and humanitarian law; (2) synthetic analyses of war crimes trials, often with a theoretical inflection; and (3) countless case studies of individual trials, both well-known and obscure. Each of these categories has much to offer students of war crimes trials, but only by reading through all three categories can one gain a sense of the full scope of the phenomenon.

At the broadest level, there are general histories of international law, which includes but is not limited to, international criminal law. One can still profit from older works, like Hirsh Lauterpacht's *The Function of Law in the International Community* (Oxford: Oxford University Press, 1933) or Arthur Nussbaum, *A Concise History of International Law* (New York: Macmillan, 1947). Crucial but troubling is Wilhelm Grewe's *The Epochs of International Law* (Berlin: DeGruyter, 2000). Originally published in German in 1984, the book is based heavily on Grewe's 1944 *Habilitationsschrift*, written in Berlin during World War II but never published. Strongly influenced by Carl Schmitt, Grewe sees international law as merely an expression of the strength of various hegemonic states from the late Middle Ages through the post-war period.

The best general modern history is Stephen C. Neff, *Justice Among Nations: A History of International Law* (Cambridge: Harvard University Press, 2014). *The Oxford Handbook of the History of International Law*, ed. by Bardo Fassbender and Anne Peters (Oxford: Oxford University Press, 2012) offers a particularly broad overview, covering most of the globe from antiquity to the present. Narrower in focus but indispensable is Martti Koskenniemi, *The Gentle Civilizer of Nations: The Rise and Fall of International Law, 1870–1960* (Cambridge: Cambridge University Press, 2004).

More focused than these general histories of international law as such are works that concentrate on the history of international criminal law and/or the laws of war. The best single-volume work is Stephen C. Neff, *War and the Law of Nations: A General History* (Cambridge: Cambridge University Press, 2008). Equally valuable are Geoffrey Best's two volumes: *Humanity in Warfare* (New York: Columbia University Press, 1980) and *War and Law since 1945* (Oxford: Clarendon Press, 1994).

Most of the preceding books deal only in passing with the actual administration of justice. They deal with international law generally, or international humanitarian law more narrowly, as *systems*, but only rarely investigate the operation of these systems on the ground. Obviously, individual case studies can help fill in this gap, as well as addressing the uses of domestic law for prosecuting mass violence, but there are precious few efforts to offer what might be termed an operational history of international humanitarian law or the administration of justice. To the extent such volumes do exist, they come from political scientists or legal academics seeking to build a general theory of how international law does and/or should work. See, e.g. Charles Anthony Smith, *The Rise and Fall of War Crimes Trials: From Charles I to Bush II* (Cambridge: Cambridge University Press, 2012) or Kathryn Sikkink, *The Justice Cascade: How Human Rights Prosecutions are Changing World Politics* (New York: Norton, 2011). Highly influential but excessively Whiggish is Garry J. Bass, *Stay the Hand of Vengeance: The Politics of War Crimes Tribunals* (Princeton: Princeton University Press, 2002). Despite its brevity, the best single volume of this sort is Gerry J. Simpson, *Law, War and Crime: War Crimes, Trials, and the Reinvention of International Law* (Cambridge: Polity Press, 2007).

There are also institutional histories of international tribunals. For a general overview, see Yves Beigbeder, *International Criminal Tribunals: Justice and Politics* (Basingstoke: Palgrave Macmillan, 2011) and William A. Schabas, *The U.N. International Criminal Tribunals: The Former Yugoslavia, Rwanda, and Sierra Leon* (Cambridge: Cambridge University Press, 2006).

The history of the International Criminal Court is for obvious reasons still in its infancy, as is the tribunal itself. See Benjamin N. Schiff, *Building the International Criminal Court* (Cambridge: Cambridge University Press, 2008); William A. Schabas, *An Introduction to the International Criminal Court*, 4th ed. (Cambridge: Cambridge University Press, 2011); Bruce Broomhall, *International Justice and the International Criminal Court: Between Sovereignty and the Rule of Law* (Cambridge: Cambridge University Press, 2004); and David Bosco, *Rough Justice: The International Criminal Court in a World of Power Politics* (Oxford: Oxford University Press, 2014).

Finally, there is by now a cottage industry in case studies of individual trials. Many of these focus on trials for Axis crimes after World War II, starting with Nuremberg and expanding to include the vast number of further trials in Europe and Asia. An overview of the vast literature for Europe can be found in my essay: Devin O. Pendas, 'Seeking Justice, Finding Law: Nazi Trials in the Postwar Era, 1945–1989' in *The Journal of Modern History* 81 (2009) and in Kim Christian Priemel, 'Consigning Justice to History. Transitional Trials after World War II,' *Historical Journal* 56 (2013). It remains more difficult to get an overview of the literature on Asia, but some key works include: Yuma Totani, *The Tokyo War Crimes Trial: The Pursuit of Justice after World War II* (Cambridge: Harvard University Press, 2009), Philip Piccigallo, *The Japanese on Trial: Allied War Crimes Operations in the East, 1945–1951* (Austin: University of Texas Press, 1979), and Allan A. Ryan, *Yamashita's Ghost: War Crimes, MacArthur's Justice and Command Accountability* (Lawrence: University Press of Kansas, 2014).

Notes

1. Stephen C. Neff, *Justice among Nations: A History of International Law* (Cambridge: Harvard University Press, 2014).
2. Stephen C. Neff, *War and the Law of Nations: A General History* (Cambridge: Cambridge University Press, 2005), 10.

3. For Royal Ordinances, see Theodore Meron, *War Crimes Law Comes of Age: Essays* (Oxford: Clarendon Press, 1998), 1–2; for bilateral agreements on prisoners, see Gunther Rothenberg, "The Age of Napoleon," in *The Laws of War: Constraints on Warfare in the Western World*, ed. Michael Howard, George J. Andreopoulos, and Mark R. Schulman (New Haven: Yale University Press, 1994), 89, 90.
4. Thomas Aquinas, *Summa Theologica*, vol. 2 (New York: Benziger Brothers, 1947), 1360.
5. Neff, *Justice among Nations*, 69.
6. Ibid.
7. Aquinas, *Summa Theologica*, 1360.
8. Neff, 70.
9. Neff, *War and the Law of Nations*, 85.
10. Hugo Grotius, *The Law of War and Peace*, trans. Francis W. Kelsey (New York: Bobbs-Merrill, 1925), 630.
11. Ibid., 631.
12. Ibid., 639.
13. Ibid., 644.
14. Ibid., 646, 648–649.
15. Neff, *War and the Law of Nations*, 86.
16. Grotius, *Law of War and Peace*, 565.
17. James Q. Whitman, *The Verdict of Battle: The Law of Victory and the Making of Modern War* (Cambridge: Harvard University Press, 2012), 189.
18. Ibid., 201.
19. Samuel Pufendorf, *De Jure Naturae et Gentium Libri Octo*, trans. C.H. and W.A. Oldfather (Oxford: Clarendon Press, 1934), 1298.
20. Geoffrey Parker, *Empire, War and Faith in Early Modern Europe* (London: Penguin Press, 2002), 167–168.
21. For an important effort to undertake precisely such an investigation, which emphasizes the long-term persistence of an 'outlawry doctrine' that undergirds international criminal law throughout the post-Roman west, see Ziv Bohrer, "International Criminal Law's Millennium of Forgotten History," *Law and History Review* 34, no. 2 (May 2016): 393–485. Bohrer, like Parker, emphasizes the long-term continuity in international criminal law, going even further and tracing that continuity back to late antiquity. Obviously, the argument presented here stresses instead elements of discontinuity and rupture.

22. For a broader examination of these issues, see Jens Meierhenrich and Devin O. Pendas, "Political Trials in Theory and History," in *Political Trials*, ed. Jens Meierhenrich and Devin Pendas (Cambridge: Cambridge University Press, 2016), 1–64.
23. Archibald Bower, *History of the Popes*, vol. 3 (Philadelphia: Griffith and Simon, 1845), 14; Pasquale Villari, *The Two First Centuries of Florentine History*, vol. 1 (London: Fisher Unwin, 1894), 248.
24. M. Cherif Bassiouni, *Introduction to International Criminal Law* (Dodrecht: Martinus-Nijhoff, 2012), 1047.
25. Karl Hampe, *Geschichte Konradins von Hohenstaufen* (Insbruck: Wagner, 1894), 312.
26. Richard Roth, *Kaiser, King, and Pope*, trans. Mary E. Ireland (Minneapolis: Augsburg Publishing, 1917), 189.
27. Friedrich von Raumer, *Geschichte der Hohenstaufen und ihrer Zeit*, vol. 4 (Leipzig: Brockhaus, 1878), 378.
28. Villari, *Two First Centuries*, 247.
29. Hampe, *Geschichte Konradins*, 311.
30. Bower, *History of the Popes*, 14.
31. Bassiouni, *Introduction to International Criminal Law*, 1047.
32. John Adair, "The Court Martial Papers of Sir William Waller's Army, 1644," *Journal of the Society for Army Historical Research* 44 (1966): 205–223.
33. Ibid., 218.
34. Ibid., 219.
35. Ibid., 220. Emphasis added.
36. Ibid., 215.
37. Ibid., 221.
38. Ibid., 221–222.
39. Trevor Royle, *The British Civil War: The Wars of the Three Kingdoms, 1638–1660* (New York: Palgrave Macmillan, 2004), 609.
40. John Nicoll, *A Diary of Public Transactions and Other Occurrences, Chiefly in Scotland, from January 1650 to June 1667* (Edinburgh: The Bannatyne Club, 1836), 58
41. Ibid.
42. Cited in Godfrey Davies, "Introduction," *Dundee Court-Martial Records, 1651* in *Miscellany of the Scottish History Society (Second Series)*, vol. 19 (Edinburgh: University of Edinburgh Press, 1919), 5.
43. Davies, "Introduction," 5.
44. Ibid., 5–6.

45. See, e.g. Ibid., 33.
46. See, e.g. Ibid., 21, 35.
47. See, e.g. Ibid., 12.
48. See, e.g. Ibid., 14, 17.
49. There is one example of a soldier absent without leave, but he was also charged with theft. Ibid., 20.
50. Ibid., 42.
51. Ibid., 21–30.
52. Ibid., 23.
53. Ibid., 26.
54. Ibid., 43.
55. Ibid., 44.
56. Ibid., 45.
57. Ibid., 13.
58. Geoffrey Best, *War and Law since 1945* (Oxford: Oxford University Press, 1994), 326.
59. John Fabian Witt, *Lincoln's Code: The Laws of War in American History* (New York: Free Press, 2012).
60. Larry McMurtry, *Custer* (New York: Simon & Schuster, 2012), 43
61. Peter Maguire, *Law and War: An American Story* (New York: Columbia University Press, 2001), 35.
62. Adam Roberts, "Land Warfare: From Hague to Nuremberg," in *Laws of War*, 116.
63. Devin O. Pendas, ""The Magical Scent of the Savage": Colonial Violence, the Crisis of Civilization and the Origins of the Legalist Paradigm of War," *The Boston College International and Comparative Law Review* 30 (Winter 2007): 29–53.
64. Gerrit W. Gong, *The Standard of 'Civilization' in International Society* (Oxford: Clarendon Press, 1984).
65. Geoffrey Best, *War and Law since 1945* (Oxford: Oxford University Press, 1994).
66. Kathryn Sikkink, *The Justice Cascade: How Human Rights Prosecutions are Changing World Politics* (New York: W.W. Norton, 2011).
67. Benjamin N. Schiff, *Building the International Criminal Court* (Cambridge: Cambridge University Press, 2008), 167–181.
68. Ruti G. Teitel, *Transitional Justice* (Oxford: Oxford University Press, 2000).
69. Yves Beigbeder, *International Justice against Impunity: Progress and New Challenges* (Leiden: Martinus Nijhoff, 2005).

70. Sikkink, *Justice Cascade*, 262.
71. Ibid., 167.
72. Ibid., 169–174.
73. For my own scepticism about the general prospects for criminal prosecutions for mass violence, see Donald Bloxham and Devin O. Pendas, "Punishment as Prevention? The Politics of Prosecuting Génocidaires," in *The Oxford Handbook of Genocide Studies*, ed. Donald Bloxham and A. Dirk Moses (Oxford: Oxford University Press, 2010), 617–637.
74. Paradigmatically, see Jack L. Goldsmith and Eric Posner, *The Limits of International Law* (New York: Oxford University Press, 2006). For a critique of this 'realist' position, see Jens David Ohlin, *The Assault on International Law* (Oxford: Oxford University Press, 2015).
75. Raymond Aron, *Peace and War: A Theory of International Relations* (New Brunswick, NJ: Transaction Publishers, 2003), 51.
76. Goldsmith and Posner, *Limits of International Law*, 13.
77. Beth A. Simmons, *Mobilizing for Human Rights: International Law in Domestic Politics* (Cambridge: Cambridge University Press, 2009).
78. John J. Mearsheimer, *The Tragedy of Great Power Politics*, updated ed. (New York: W.W. Norton, 2014).
79. For a recent overview, see Timothy Snyder, *Black Earth: The Holocaust as History and Warning* (New York: Tim Duggan, 2015).
80. Ryan Liss and Joanna Langille, "It's Not Just the Drought Treaty: In International Law, Canada Has Withered," *Globe and Mail*, 29 March 2013. Accessed 5 September 2013, http://www.theglobeandmail.com/commentary/its-not-just-the-drought-treaty-in-international-law-canada-has-withered/article10549743/. It is as yet unclear whether the new Prime Minister, Justin Trudeau, will reverse course.
81. Robert H. Bates, *Prosperity and Violence: The Political Economy of Development* (New York: W.W. Norton, 2001).
82. A.H. Feller, "We Move, Slowly, Toward World Law," *The New York Times*, June 5, 1949, SM 10.
83. Teitel, *Transitional Justice*, 213.
84. Max Weber, *Economy and Society*, ed. Guenther Roth and Claus Wittich (Berkeley: University of California Press, 1978), 54.
85. Martha Minow, *Between Vengeance and Forgiveness: Facing History after Genocide and Mass Violence* (Boston: Beacon Press, 1998).
86. Tom Segev, *The Seventh Million: The Israelis and the Holocaust* (New York: Hill and Wang, 1993), 11.

87. Hannah Yablonka, *The State of Israel vs. Adolf Eichmann* (New York: Schocken, 2004), 120.
88. Regina Schmidt and Egon Becker, *Reaktionen auf politische Vorgäge: Drei Meinungsstudien aus der Bundesrepublik*, Frankfurter Beiträge zur Soziologie, vol. 19, with a preface by T. W. Adorno and L. V. Friedenburg (Frankfurt: Europäische Verlagsanstalt, 1967), 108.
89. Institut für Demoskopie, *Verjährung von NS-Verbrechen. Ergebnisse einer Schnellumfrage* (Allensbach am Bodensee: Institut für Demoskopie, 1965).
90. Anna J. and Richard L. Merritt eds., *Public Opinion in Occupied Germany: The HICOG Surveys, 1949–1955* (Urbana: University of Illinois Press, 1980), 11, 101.
91. The literature here is by now quite substantial. For a good starting place, see Norbert Frei, *Vergangenheitspolitik: Die Anfänge der Bundesrepublik und die NS-Vergangenheit* (Munich: C.H. Beck, 1996).
92. Adalbert Rückerl, *NS-Verbrechen vor Gericht: Versuch einer Vergangenheitsbewältigung* (Heidelberg: C.F. Müller Juristischer Verlag, 1984), 329.
93. Nicholas Balabkins, *West German Reparations to Israel* (New Brunswick: Rutgers University Press, 1971).
94. Pal published his dissent first in Calcutta in 1948. It remains in print in Japan today. See R.B. Pal, *Dissenting Opinion of Justice R.B. Pal, Tokyo Tribunal* (Tokyo: Kokusho-Kankokai, 1999). For Pal's lingering influence, see e.g. Norimitsu Onishi, "Decades after War Trials, Japan Still Honors a Dissenting Judge," *New York Times*, 31 August 2007.
95. See e.g. the debate, "Is the ICC targeting Africa inappropriately?" available at: http://iccforum.com/africa and John Mukum Mbaku, "International Justice: The International Criminal Court and Africa' Brookings Institute," Africa Growth Initiative (Working Paper). https://www.brookings.edu/wp-content/uploads/2016/07/03-foresight-international-criminal-court-africa-mbaku-1.pdf/
96. Judith N. Shklar, *Legalism: Law, Morality, and Political Trials* (Cambridge: Harvard University Press, 1986[1964]), 1.
97. On German courts, see Ingo Müller, *Furchtbare Juristen: Die unbewältigte Vergangenheit der deutschen Justiz* (Munich: Kindler, 1987). For South Africa, see Jens Meierhenrich, *Legacies of Law: Long-Run Consequences of Legal Development in South Africa, 1652–2000* (Cambridge: Cambridge University Press, 2000).

98. Ulrich Herbert, "Liberalisierung als Lernprozeß. Die Bundesrepublik in der deutschen Geschichte—eine Skizze," in *Wandlungsprozesse in Westdeutschland: Belastung, Integration, Liberalisierung 1945–1980*, ed. Ulrich Herbert (Göttingen: Wallstein, 2002), 7–51.
99. I tell the full story of this effort and its consequences in Devin O. Pendas, "Retroactive Law and Proactive Justice: Debating Crimes against Humanity in Germany, 1945–1950," *Central European History* 43 (September 2010): 428–463.
100. Oberlandesgerichtspräsident Celle Dr. Frhr. von Hodenberg to Herrn Oberlandesgerichtspräsident der britischen Zone, 3 October 1946, BAK, Z 21, Bd. 784, Bl. 23–24.

Devin O. Pendas is Associate Professor of History at Boston College. His publications include *The Frankfurt Auschwitz Trial, 1963–1965* (2006) and, as co-editor, *Political Trials in History and Theory* (2016), as well as numerous articles on the history of Holocaust trials, international law, and war crimes trials in a global perspective.

3

Forensic Anthropology: Whose Rules Are We Playing by?—Contextualizing the Role of Forensic Protocols in Human Rights Investigations

Tim Thompson, Daniel Jiménez Gaytan, Shakira Bedoya Sánchez, and Ariana Ninel Pleitez Quiñónez

Forensic Anthropology and Human Rights Investigations

Forensic science is a discipline which takes validated scientific methods and protocols and applies them to legal questions and contexts. The 'forensic' part merely refers to the context of application, by which we

---

T. Thompson (✉)
Teesside University, Middlesbrough, UK

D. Jiménez Gaytan
Forensic Anthropology Section, National Institute of Forensic Science of Guatemala (INACIF), San Carlos University, Guatemala City, Guatemala

S. Bedoya Sánchez
Max Planck Institute for Social Anthropology, Halle, Germany

A.N. Pleitez Quiñónez
European Association of Social Anthropology and the Interdisciplinary Network of Studies on Latin American Memory, San Salvador, El Salvador

J. Waterlow, J. Schuhmacher, *War Crimes Trials and Investigations*, St Antony's Series,
https://doi.org/10.1007/978-3-319-64072-3_3

mean a legal setting. As such, the word 'forensic' does not imply a special type of method *per se*. In this way, many scientific practices can be assimilated into forensic science, depending on the specifics of the case, and anthropology is one such example. Forensic anthropology itself is a sub-discipline of physical or biological anthropology and uses the same methods and approaches. There is, therefore, the possibility for an anthropologist to work on forensic and archaeological material, since the skillset is largely (although not entirely) the same.

It was only in the mid-1980s that forensic science was applied in a substantive and organized way in investigate human rights violations with a view to taking these cases through the courts. In this respect, the first human rights forensic team was formed by a group of Argentine students in the summer of 1984, initiated by the renowned American anthropologist and osteologist Clyde Snow, who had come there in February that year with a delegation of forensic scientists from the American Academy for the Advancement of Science.[1]

The Argentine Forensic Anthropology Team (EAAF) excavated the graves of the individuals who disappeared and were murdered during the military dictatorship in Argentina, which ruled from 1976 to 1983. In a significant contrast to the application of forensic science in Europe and the United States, the team's approach emphasized the development of relationships with families and survivors of political violence, as well as the importance of historical inquiry (including both documentary and oral sources) to accompany and precede the work of exhumation.[2] Across the following decades, EAAF positioned itself as a key player in developing forensic anthropological 'expertise' elsewhere in Latin America, facilitating the expansion of forensic knowledge and the establishment of other agencies, such as the Guatemalan Forensic Anthropology team (later known as the Guatemalan Forensic Anthropological Foundation, FAFG); the Uruguayan Forensic Archaeological Group (GIAF); and the Colombian and Peruvian Forensic Anthropology teams (EPAF).[3] Since then, they have also worked outside of Latin America—for example, in parts of Europe and Africa.

Following their lead, several NGOs (such as Physicians for Human Rights, the Centre for International Forensic Assistance, and Inforce) have worked in the area of forensic investigations of atrocity crimes, albeit with rationales and mandates that differ profoundly from the Latin American regional teams. As a result, there has been a substantial expansion of various guidance and best practice documents concerning forensic methods and knowledge.[4]

In all cases, the formation of Human Rights forensic teams is accompanied by the adaptation of interpretative protocols, the creation of selection processes, funding models, and internal forms of assessment for the data collected. In their sum, these choices become the frameworks within which forensic expertise and knowledge is carried out, transported, transposed, and de-territorialized from its original settings.[5]

As an analytical concept, these 'traveling models' are defined as 'an analytical representation of particular aspects of reality created as an apparatus or protocol for interventions in order to shape this reality for certain purposes'.[6] They are the inevitable result of the relationship between how we know and order our world and the diverse social and material technologies that mediate this.[7]

Forensic Anthropology in Practice

Forensic anthropology, which is a sub-discipline of biological anthropology, developed as a discipline in the twentieth century, although its modern origins lie in the 1870s with the work of Thomas Dwight (Stewart, 1979), and there is an argument to be made that we could extend this back to the earlier work of the likes of Alphonse Bertillon. In essence, forensic anthropology is the application of human osteological knowledge to forensic settings; however, as the discipline has developed, so has this definition, with some practitioners now arguing for a broader meaning which includes the examination of the soft tissues, the ways in which the body decomposes and so on. Still, the classic definition comes from Stewart, who notes that it '...is that branch of physical anthropology which deals with the identification of more or less skeletonized remains known to be, or suspected of being, human ... the identification process undertakes to provide *opinion* regarding sex, age, race, stature, and such other characteristics of each individual involved as may lead to his or her recognition'.[8]

We highlight the word 'opinion' because the level of interpretation within forensic anthropological practice is often overlooked by those outside the discipline. The forensic expert offers *opinions* based on what he or she examines—not the kind of black-and-white statements which those outside the discipline frequently expect. Historically, the forensic expert was defined as such based on his or her technical knowledge and practical experience in the field. More recently, in the United States (although other countries are adopting the philosophy if not the specifics), the demand for standardization within the forensic sciences has led to the development of the Daubert criteria. The Daubert criteria define the requirements for a discipline if it is to be accepted within the courts. Of particular interest to forensic anthropologists are the new requirements to state error rates for the techniques used and the need for accepted standards. This has led to a 'quantification of forensic anthropology' which has resulted in some practitioners becoming uncomfortable with the experiential and interpretive aspects of forensic anthropology.[9]

At its core, then, forensic anthropology examines the human body. This examination tends to focus on the skeletal hard tissues of the body (and hence differs from forensic pathology, which focuses more on the soft tissues), and in the forensic setting these tend to derive from contexts where there has been a period of significant decomposition, burning, commingling, and other disruptions to the body. In these settings, other forensic techniques such as DNA profiling and fingerprint identification may well fall short.

Contexts of mass violence are a key example of this. In order to identify human skeletal remains, the forensic anthropologist must establish the biological identity of the remains. This is referred to as the osteo-biological profile and includes estimation of sex, age-at-death, stature, ancestry or race, and, sometimes, the genetic profile. The word 'estimating' is crucial in forensic anthropology because the age and stature are never given as exact numbers. Even the estimations of sex have a percentage of reliability. This all reflects the fact that human variation exists within and between population groups with regard to skeletal size and shape.[10] The comparison of the osteo-biological profile with other elements can be enough to situate the remains within a network of social and legal identities.

Despite being an 'identification science', the osteological profile created often lacks the specificity needed to positively identify someone, and so must be used in conjunction with other forensic disciplines, such as odontology or radiography.

The reconstruction of the facts surrounding the death of the victim therefore becomes very important for identification purposes; this is the contextual reconstruction. Although many authors believe that this kind of identification is only ever tentative and, thus, cannot be relied upon, others (e.g. the Guatemalan team) have adopted this model of identification. In many cases, the contextual reconstruction provides very useful information regarding the identity of the deceased—for example, interviewing the relatives or those close to the victims, not least if they were eyewitnesses to the killing and burial of the bodies (and, indeed, if they were the ones who buried the bodies).

Another benefit of practising forensic anthropology in human rights contexts is that it can be performed successfully with limited resources. This point is reiterated by Baraybar (2008) and then by Fowler and Thompson (2015) in their discussions on the use of technological methodologies in human rights investigations.[11] As an example, it currently costs the Guatemalan Forensic Anthropological Foundation (FAFG) approximately 300 US dollars to run a DNA sample; because of this high cost, only skeletons from open-context cases (those where the victims are unknown, as opposed to closed-context cases where the victims are in fact known and the forensic scientists focus on verification rather than identification of the dead) are sampled for DNA analysis. As well as being expensive, identification through DNA profiling is slow, taking time and resources to produce analysis for every single case. DNA analysis also relies on the presence of suitable ante-mortem comparison samples and databases—which again may not be present.[12] Interestingly, in Spain it has been noted that there has been some hostility towards the use of DNA analysis because it is felt that it has not delivered the kind of firm results that geneticists argued it would.[13] By comparison, osteological identification requires less time and, so, provides faster results for the next of kin as well as the legal system. For organizations such as the FAFG, which depend on donations for funding, these very practical considerations are key.

International Guidance on the Practice of Forensic Anthropology in Human Rights Investigations

There are international guidelines for the practice of forensic anthropology in human rights investigations, but they are certainly not without their drawbacks and limitations. *The Manual on the Effective Prevention and Investigation of Extra-Legal, Arbitrary and Summary Executions* (or the Minnesota Protocol) of 1991 provides a general framework as well as the steps for conducting what is labelled a 'proper forensic investigation'.[14] Medical examiners and forensic anthropologists use the protocol as a reference point when a violation of human rights is under investigation. The Manual on Effective Investigation and Documentation of Torture and Other Cruel, Inhuman or Degrading Treatment or Punishment from 1999, better known as the Istanbul protocol, was initiated by the Human Rights Foundation of Turkey (HRFT) and supported by several members of Physicians for Human Rights USA (PHR USA). It is considered to be a guideline for the evaluation and treatment of possible torture victims as well as an aid to the investigation of facts surrounding the torture and how to report any findings to the relevant institutions—be they local or international (like the International Criminal Court).

Both protocols represent worldwide parameters for forensic investigations, but it is the Minnesota protocol that addresses procedures for the treatment and analysis of skeletal human remains buried in mass graves. Although the Minnesota protocol does not mention the chain of custody (i.e. the documented and recorded transfer of forensic evidence from one person or investigative department to another), it does highlight the importance of marking every skeletal remain with unique and unmistakable code numbers. This not only helps with the subsequent technical procedures, but also incidentally ensures the chain of custody because the code can prove that the skeleton recovered in the field is the same that will later be analysed in the laboratory, and thus ensures that the final identification will correspond to the remains that were recovered and are to be buried.

However, international protocols like the Minnesota Protocol do not specify the best way to construct an osteo-biological profile. They only describe what elements should be in a complete profile. The technical procedures are the responsibility of every team and, in many cases, are influenced by the scientific tradition of which they form a part. Thus, the international protocols provide the general guidelines for investigations (what elements or information should be sought by the investigators), while the internal protocols used by the individual forensic teams are adapted from these general guidelines and add new specific procedures appropriate to the needs of the local context. This will include the need to address the issue of 'population specificity' whereby osteological methods developed using one population group are applied to another. Without this validation, the protocol can be considered not only inaccurate but also ineffective (this has resonance with the Daubert criteria discussed previously).

For example, the international protocols strongly suggest that the determinations of race is a basic procedure in the physical analysis. Yet, in Guatemalan forensic analysis, this is not viewed as important. Race or ancestry determination has been discarded through the years since the estimation of race in the Guatemalan population helps very little to differentiate the indigenous from the mestizo population. In contrast, within the US and European traditions, the estimations of race or ancestry are viewed as a significant part of the identification process. It is also relevant for evidentiary issues and in legal settings for establishing the type of crime that was being committed (e.g. genocide, crimes against humanity, etc.). This is a particularly interesting example of how protocols can be slow to develop and then become steadfast when finalized, to the detriment of forensic practice. There is a growing body of work that now argues that race does not exist as a biological category, pointing to the osteological and genetic evidence to argue that such categorization is entirely socially constructed with regard to the body.[15]

A similar issue concerns the application of methods of age estimation, where again there is little in the way of international guidance. In Guatemala, almost every method for age estimation has not been validated for the local population, which is problematic when you consider that these methods are conceived for Caucasian populations with different lifestyles and environmental stresses. A similar experience has been seen in the Former Yugoslavia where population-specific standards from the United States were used. This resulted in some inaccuracies in the osteo-biological profiles created, although these have since been resolved following systematic collection and analysis of this new population data. This issue is discussed further by Kimmerle, while Schaefer and Schaefer and Black provide appropriate examples of this in practice with regard to age-at-death calculations.[16] Note that while methods developed from new population data are tested and then published in the academic literature, this seems to have been more common with data from the Former Yugoslavia than for countries in South and Central America, as we have seen above.[17]

The final example of the problems that international guidance can create in the application of forensic science to human rights investigations relates to identifying the cause of death. For example, in the FAFG protocols, the recognized causes of death are those injuries that affect the skull, cervical vertebrae and thorax. If the injury affects a vital centre like the brain (evident in complete fractures or massive loss of bony tissue), the heart or the major veins in the neck, it can be classed as the cause of death. Yet in the United States and in Europe, the determination of cause of death is the pathologist's responsibility, not the anthropologist's. Here we find issues surrounding cultural relativism, whereby international protocols like the Minnesota Protocol are created with European and US expertise and, yet, inevitably applied insensitively to other parts of the world. It is difficult to comprehend then how experts in forensic anthropology cannot determine the cause of death in their own countries, but can do so in other countries at the recommendation of international protocols for the treatment of human remains in human right violations.

Case Study Examples: Knowledge-Transfer in Forensic Anthropological Practice

The practice of forensic anthropology cannot appear out of nowhere. Despite a desire to investigate human rights abuses, specific technical and scientific knowledge is required. But where does this come from? This has been handled differently in different contexts, but all struggle with a degree of inherent paternalism from one country to another. We provide three different case examples to illustrate these issues—(1) where experts from one country are invited into another, (2) where experts developed through the process of (1) then travel to a neighbouring country to assist and (3) where experts from multiple countries descend on another country in a collaborative and collective response.

1. Argentina

This team has come to work on several cases in collaboration with different organizations, including Tutela Legal and the Comisión Provincial de Derechos Humanos de La Rioja (CPDH). The team has also worked with Pro-Búsqueda and the National Search Commission for Disappeared Children. These NGOs work to gather and present exhumation requests to the appropriate authorities, while the EAAF itself performs the technical procedures—which include preliminary research, excavation, laboratory work and DNA testing.

As described by Salado and Fondebrider, the work of the Argentine Team was divided into three phases: preliminary research, archaeological recovery of the bodies and associated evidence and laboratory analysis.[18] The latter phase had two objectives: to identify the victim and also the cause of death. We will now explain the method used in the excavations performed by EAAF from fieldwork observations. The first research stage is conducted prior to the excavation and, in general, the NGOs with which the team is working provide support to conduct this initial research, serving as a link between the family members and the EAAF.

In the excavation stage, the remains are totally uncovered in order to identify the position in which they were found in the excavation pit. Photographs are taken, as well as drawings, diagrams and field notes to document the state of the remains and the excavation pit. To ensure accuracy, it is important for this contextual evidence to include measurements establishing the location of the pit on a grid with 3D measurements.

Once these elements have been documented, the team can proceed to collect the remains. At this time, a representative from the prosecutor's office and a medical examiner must be present. Even if the team is officially conducting the excavation, others must also be present to document the findings. At that time, it is important to pass the soil through a sieve in order to see if projectile shells are found. The bodies are then usually numbered and extracted, with the remains closest to the surface taken first, although as mentioned by Salado and Fondebrider, each case may require a different strategy.[19]

The laboratory work is conducted at the medical examiner's office. The remains are arranged anatomically and the pre-mortem and post-mortem injuries are analysed to determine the cause of death. Photographs are taken and a laboratory report sheet is filled out. Depending on the state of conservation of the remains, DNA samples may be taken for laboratory analysis.

Clearly, the exhumation processes may vary depending on the institution conducting the procedure. The majority of exhumations have been performed by the Medical Examiner's Office, but, in some instances, these exhumations were done without any investigation request. In these cases, the grave sites were excavated and the remains were transferred directly to the families for burial. Other cases have included laboratory work to inventory everything found in the pit. Over time, and as a result of the influence of the Argentine team, the EAAF methodology has been incorporated into the exhumation processes of other teams. Little care was taken in extracting the remains during the first exhumations; now, depending on who performs the procedure, there is generally greater documentation in the field and in the laboratory.

2. Guatemala

The first exhumation related to the decades-long violence in Guatemala (1962–1996) took place in 1991 and the Guatemalan team was created between 1991 and 1992. The Truth Commission (CEH) estimates that the number of disappeared or killed in the Internal Armed Conflict in Guatemala is approximately 200,000 people, of which at least 42,000 are victims of enforced disappearance. Of the known human rights violations, 93% are attributed to the National Army and other paramilitary groups. The Truth Commission registers 662 massacres in 17 of the 23 departments of the country (CEH 2006, II). Since the start of the Internal Conflict in 1962, there were moments when the violence increased. From 1978 to 1983, the violence was expressed in government policies called

'*Tierra Arrasada*' ('razed land') and '*Fusiles y Frijoles*' ('rifles and beans').[20] These policies were designed to undermine the social base of the guerrilla movements by attacking the civilian population. In the second half of the 1980s, organizations comprised of widows and other family members of people who were missing, killed or buried in clandestine graves during the conflict began to put pressure on Guatemalan society for answers regarding the death or disappearance of loved ones. This context of social pressure created the conditions which lead to the first exhumation in Guatemala in 1991.

By the end of 1992, the Guatemalan Forensic Anthropology Team (EAFG) was born with the aid of anthropologist Clyde Snow, the Argentine Forensic Anthropology Team (EAAF) and young students from Guatemala and other countries. The first exhumations of the newly created Guatemalan team took place in 1992, in which experts from the EAAF, United States and Chile (from the Chilean Forensic Team), as well as pathologists from the judicial system participated together.[21] In 1997, the EAFG changed in juridical status and was transformed into the Guatemalan Foundation of Forensic Anthropology (FAFG).

During this period, the FAFG and other institutions working in Guatemala have created new protocols and modified pre-existing ones. Although the FAFG has written its own protocol for the search of forced-disappearance victims, called the Research Proposal, it is clearly influenced by the International Committee of the Red Cross' protocols. Nonetheless, modification allowed for the incorporation of new epistemological knowledge and clauses to better suit application in the context of the Guatemalan internal conflict. Therefore, it can be seen here that forensic practice brought into the country by teams from neighbouring states still required alteration to best fit the nature of the conflict and subsequent human rights investigations here.

3. Europe

One of the most interesting features of the forensic reaction to the mass violence in the Former Yugoslavia and in Spain is the nature of the international response. In both contexts, forensic practitioners from many different countries have come together under the auspices of a range of interested bodies, agencies and institutions to contribute to the investigation and analysis of the victims of these events.

The fighting in the Balkan region of Europe represents one of the deadliest periods of conflict on European soil in modern times. For example, in the fighting in Croatia between 1991 and 1995, more than 14,000 war-related deaths have been recorded, while the Balkans region more widely is thought to have seen over 40,000 people go missing.[22] The extent of the violence (including deaths, disappearances and related migrations) has been referred to as a humanitarian crisis.[23]

The internationalization of the response is perhaps not surprising. For example, much of the forensic work in this region has been driven by the international tribunals and the developing international judicial system and, as such, it is likely that the international significance of these investigations provided the political will from interested States to support the forensic work being undertaken.[24] This international interest is also a function of the fact that, for some of those later prosecuted, the charge of genocide has been raised.[25] The complex nature of this legal charge—and the strength of evidence required to convict a person for genocide—also necessitated the need for leading forensic experts to be involved. Further, the sheer range of grave sites, deposition locales, taphonomic (decomposition) factors at work and so on required the contribution of a correspondingly wider range of expertise and experience from practitioners who were familiar with the specialist techniques and approaches required.[26] The scale and number of these investigations also had cost and resource implications, and these could not be met by the Balkan countries alone.

The other well-studied and well-discussed context of mass violence in Europe is in Spain. The Spanish Civil War (1936–1939), followed by the brutal dictatorship of Francisco Franco (which ended with his death in 1975), is thought to have resulted in over 110,000 missing and over 150,000 people killed away from the battlefields.[27] This more prolonged length of time, combined with the vast majority of the killing being the result of extrajudicial and reprisal executions, means that the nature of this context differs significantly from that in the Former Yugoslavia.[28] Another key difference between the two contexts is in the importance of archival records and documentation in Spain.[29] This is not to say that there are no similarities between the two contexts. The victims of the Spanish violence are also recovered from a wide range of depositional environments and display a variety of taphonomic changes, which also demands a high degree of forensic expertise which is only likely to be found in the international, rather than national, scientific community.[30]

Nonetheless, although international forensic experts were also involved in the investigation of these crimes, they tended to be coordinated through local Spanish interest groups or NGOs, rather than international institutions as they were in the Former Yugoslavia. Language skills were also a significant issue when it came to the use of foreign practitioners, as an understanding of Spanish was critical, whereas foreign practitioners speaking local languages was actively discouraged in the Former Yugoslavia for security and safety reasons. Time is also a key factor here in the differing nature of the international forensic teams used in these two regions. The investigations in Spain occurred long after the actual acts of violence, and as such the technical infrastructure and expertise is in place within the State to coordinate these cases. By contrast, the Former Yugoslavia was still in the process of active recovery and rebuilding following very recent fighting during the forensic investigations—thus, differing levels of international support were required. Indeed, the prosecutions in Spain were also a matter internal to the State, whereas in the Former Yugoslavia, as has been noted above, these prosecutions were subject to fledgling international law.

International Forensic Protocols in the Field—Whose Rules Are We Playing By?

Clearly, forensic anthropology has developed into a significant contributor to human rights investigations. The development of teams and expertise around the world and the transportation of these teams and expertise to other nations and contexts is a challenge, especially with regard to maintaining appropriate standards of practice. Attempts have been made to develop and establish common modes of practice—although these have been critiqued for failing to take cultural differences into account.[31]

The human rights work in Guatemala is a useful example of this last point. Forensic anthropological practice in Guatemala works within four disciplines: social anthropology, forensic archaeology, forensic anthropology (physical analysis of the remains) and, more recently, forensic genetics. We refer to this as the 'Guatemalan Model' and, as such, it can be seen to differ from the basic requirements laid out above and is illustrative of the developments that can occur in different contexts of work as a result of the specific social, political, financial and other conditions at play. Due to these deep contextual sensitivities, it is an example of the potential limitations of the far more generalized international protocols.

A particular difference in this model is the social-anthropological phase. This is the stage in which social anthropologists are reconstructing the social and historical context of every case selected for investigation. This includes the reconstruction of all events around the disappearance or death of the victims, the most important tool of which is the pre-mortem interview. This allows investigators to gather testimonial information from relatives and witness alike; the information gathered is used to build up the personal story of the victims—the ante-mortem profile—which includes, sex, age, stature, medical history (previous illness, dental records and pre-mortem trauma). In some cases, the relatives buried the bodies and were eyewitnesses of the assassination of their loved ones. Often, however, the ones who witnessed the disappearance or the killings are not the same people who witnessed the burial. In other cases, they only know that the national army, the guerrilla or other paramilitary groups took their relatives prisoner, after which they never saw them again. The 'Guatemalan Model' therefore provides extra information for the forensic investigators than the international protocols require since the latter are more focussed solely on the examination of the body.

The internationalization of forensic work in Europe prompts similar discussions to those above which have tended to focus on South and Latin America. The issue of appropriate standards for use in the Former Yugoslavia was actually raised within the courts when the defence asked specific questions about the appropriateness of the standards used on Bosnian populations.[32] This issue was so serious that the ICTY Office of the Prosecutor investigated it internally.[33] This may partly explain the reason why more population-specific data has been published for this region in comparison to other parts of the world.

In Spain, the situation has been slightly different, since the questions have not been raised in a court setting and thus, as Ferllini argues, there has been no formal investigation of whether appropriate standards have been used.[34] As discussed above, it is then the responsibility of the anthropologist to interpret the general international protocols within this specific situation.[35] It seems, then, that protocols have been applied in the Spanish case that have been devised in other countries. Of interest, though, is the fact that in 2013 the Spanish Association of Forensic Anthropology and Odontology published their 'Recommendations in Forensic Anthropology' aimed at guiding practitioners working in this setting.[36]

The final point to raise with regard to the work undertaken in the Former Yugoslavia and Spain is that, at times, the actual prosecutions have occurred in different countries from the crimes—in the Netherlands (The Hague) in the former case, and Argentina in the latter example. This raises further questions about how protocols refined in one country may then be interpreted in another—and suggests that some form of global consistency will be required if this is a trend moving forward.

What the different case studies in this chapter show is the need for a clear and conscious awareness of where the protocols being used come from and how they are then developed to suit local contexts. In other words, we always need to know whose rules we are playing by and why.

While there is no doubt that forensic anthropologists working in human rights contexts demand a certain level of professionalism and competence, there is still much debate about the need for international standards. As forensic work from around the world becomes more visible and open for discussion, this debate remains key to the continued success of forensic anthropology as practised in the challenging contexts of mass violence and human rights violations.

Bibliographical Essay The development of the concept of mass atrocities and the need to document and address human rights violations can clearly be seen to derive from the conclusion of the Second World War, although there are threads that stretch back further. A collective shock at what occurred and a sense of bearing witness to a failure of humanity led to intense work to ensure that such mass murder and degradation could not happen again. From this effort, we can see not just the creation of the

International Criminal Court, but also an acceptance of the concept that such crimes should be investigated on the international stage, using international expertise. Yet, as we know, any process that involves the courts requires the collection of evidence. One component of this is the use of forensic science. Forensic science refers to any scientific method or technique that is applied to a legal context. In routine police investigations, most forensic work tends to be of a lab-based, biological nature—such as the identification and examination of body fluids or the amplification of DNA.

This is slightly different in human rights investigations; yet, despite the fact that criminality of this nature still requires evidence to be presented in the courts, the literature surrounding the application of forensic science to the investigation of human rights violations is comparatively modern. Proving guilt in these contexts is challenging, but requires the use of the forensic sciences to examine and analyse the human remains and associated artefacts that are recovered during an investigation. Evidence of violence, murder and destruction of the physical body and social identity is only really attainable from the body itself.

Of the forensic sciences, forensic archaeology and anthropology are particularly useful in these contexts. Forensic archaeology focuses on the detection, location and recovery of human remains. In human rights work, the deceased are often buried and so investigations require careful use of archaeological techniques to excavate the remains, while maintaining bodily integrity and without losing any forensic intelligence and evidence that might be present. In the United Kingdom, the volume edited by John Hunter (*Studies in Crime: An Introduction to Forensic Archaeology*, London: Batsford, 1996) was crucial in giving such an approach a spotlight. Archaeology has a long history, and the fundamental methods have not changed significantly over the years, and so this work still retains some relevance. More recently, academic work in this area has tended to explore the differences in philosophy and traditions from one county to another, and how this then impacts on the application of these archaeological methods to forensic (burial) situations. W.J. Mike Groen et al.'s *Forensic Archaeology: A Global Perspective* (Chichester: Wiley-Blackwell, 2015) is a timely and thorough example of this. In contrast, forensic anthropology tends to focus on the body itself, and what this can tell us. Forensic anthropology is useful in these mass violence contexts because the body is often decomposing or fragmented in some way, but this does not necessarily impede the creation of an osteo-profile (demographic information) from the remains by the anthropologist.

In some ways, the separation of forensic archaeology and anthropology is artificial, and it is entirely possible for a given practitioner to undertake both the forensic archaeological and anthropological investigations; the positioning of the line between the two disciplines (if, indeed, present) shifts from country to country. These differences, and the significance of this separation, are explored in a number of volumes. Back in 2003, Thompson drew together a special edition of the journal *Science and Justice* ('Forensic anthropology in the United Kingdom—Current trends, problems and concerns', *Science and Justice* 43.4) which teased apart some of these issues and the implications of this separation. Following this, volumes by Megan B. Brickley and Roxana Ferllini, eds., *Forensic Anthropology: Case Studies from Europe* (Springfield: Charles C. Thomas, 2007) and Dennis Dirkmaat's impressive edited volume, *A Companion to Forensic Anthropology* (Chichester: Wiley-Blackwell, 2012) gave clearer illustrations of these national differences by providing a range of examples of practice from a number of different countries.

Other forensic sciences, such as DNA profiling, have their uses, but in human rights investigations are often compromised by the environmental context and taphonomic pathways that the bodies have been exposed to. Forensic taphonomy is particularly influential, but the myriad of postmortem influences on the body and the impact of these on human identification were not considered in a holistic and comprehensive manner until the publication of the classic volume *Forensic Taphonomy: The Postmortem Fate of Human Remains*, edited by Marcella H. Sorg and William D. Haglund (Boca Raton: CRC Press, 1997). Subsequently, a second volume has been produced, and other recent edited volumes on the subject have brought together state-of-the-art methods and interesting new case study examples; however, none have had the impact on the field of that first publication.

Forensic archaeology and anthropology have attracted a lot of attention in the academic literature in recent years. This collective work can largely be separated into two categories—work that examines technical aspects and methodologies, and work that examines the application of those methods. The publications in the former category are numerous, and tend to focus on individual methods being published and validated in academic journals. Some volumes have attempted to bring these together, with the most significant of these the volume by Jane Buikstra and Douglas Ubelaker (*Standards for Data Collection from Human Skeletal Remains* (Fayetteville: Arkansas Archaeological Report Research Series, 1994). Despite its age, this is still a key text in the investigation of human rights violations, but it is now supplemented with the likes of Margaret Cox's edited volume, *The Scientific Investigation of Mass Graves* (Cambridge: Cambridge University Press, 2013) and Bradley Adams and John Byrd's work, *Commingled Human Remains: Methods of Recovery, Analysis, and Identification* (Amsterdam & Boston: Elsevier, 2014), which specifically explores the challenging nature of commingled mass graves. Here, one of the key tasks is the individualization of the bodies, to ensure that subsequent identification techniques are effective and accurate. In the latter category, the effectiveness of forensic archaeology and anthropology has been explored and probed by Roxana Fellini (*Forensic Archaeology and Human Rights Violations* (Springfield: Charles C. Thomas, 2007)) and Elisabeth Anstett and Jean-Marc Dreyfus (*Human Remains and Identification: Mass Violence, Genocide, and the 'Forensic Turn'* (Manchester: Manchester University Press, 2015)) who noted, amongst other issues, the cultural clashes and tensions that are evident when practitioners from one country go to ply their trade in another. These tensions, and the globalization of the forensic investigation of human rights violations, are also deconstructed in the volume by Zoë Crossland and Rosemary Joyce (*Disturbing Bodies: Perspectives on Forensic Anthropology* (Santa Fe: SAR Press, 2016))—a book which arose from an exciting residential week of discussions at the School for Advanced Research in Santa Fe, and is a tangible illustration of the need for those working in the investigation and analysis of the human remains from human rights violations to come together to discuss and dissect their philosophies, practice and practitioners.

Notes

1. Thomas Keenan, "Getting the Dead to Tell me What Happened: Justice, Prosopopoeia, and Forensic Afterlives," in *Forensics. The Architecture of Public Truth*, ed. Forensic Architecture (Berlin/New York: Sternberg Press, 2014), 35–55.
2. Ibid.
3. Mehmet Yaşar İşcan and Horacio Elbio Solla Olivera, "Forensic Anthropology in Latin America," *Forensic Science International* 109 (2000): 15–30.
4. Margaret Cox, "A Multidisciplinary Approach to the Investigation of Crimes against Humanity, War Crimes and Genocide: The Inforce Foundation," *Science & Justice* 43 (2003): 225–227. Margaret Cox, Ambika Flavel, Ian Hanson, Joanna Laver and Roland Wessling, *The Scientific Investigations of Mass Graves. Towards Protocols and Standard Operative Procedures* (Cambridge: Cambridge University Press, 2008).
5. Andrea Behrends, Sung-Joon Park and Richard Rottenburg, "Travelling Models. Introducing an Analytical Concept to Globalisation Studies," in *Travelling Models in African Conflict Management. Translating Technologies of Social Ordering*, ed. Andrea Behrends, Sung-Joon Park, and Richard Rottenburg (Leiden and Boston: Brill, 2014), 1–40.
6. Ibid.
7. Sheila Jasanoff, *States of Knowledge. The Co-Production of Science and Social Order* (London: Routledge, 2004).
8. Thomas Dale Stewart, *Essentials of Forensic Anthropology* (Springfield: Charles C. Thomas, 1979), ix.
9. Tim Thompson, "Deconstructing the Ideal of Standardization in Forensic Anthropology," in *Disturbing Bodies: Perspectives on Forensic Anthropology*, ed. Zoë Crossland and Rosemary A. Joyce (Santa Fe: School of Advanced Research Press, 2015), 63–84.
10. Rebecca Gowland and Tim Thompson, *Human Identity and Identification* (Cambridge: Cambridge University Press, 2013).
11. Jose Pablo Baraybar, "When DNA is Not Available, Can We Still Identify People? Recommendations for Best Practice," *Journal of Forensic Sciences* 53 (2008): 533–540. Gillian Fowler and Tim Thompson, "A Mere Technical Exercise? Challenges and Technological Solutions to the Identification of Individuals in Mass Grave Scenarios in the Modern Context," in *Human Remains and Violence*, ed. Élisabeth Gessat-Anstett and Jean-Marc Dreyfus (Manchester: Manchester University Press, 2015), 117–141.

12. Baraybar, "When DNA is Not Available".
13. Francisco Ferrandiz, "Exhuming the Defeated: Civil War Mass Graves in Twenty-First-Century Spain," *American Ethnologist* 40 (2013): 38–54.
14. *The Manual on the Effective Prevention and Investigation of Extra-Legal, Arbitrary and Summary Executions* (or the Minnesota Protocol) of 1991.
15. Gowland and Thompson, *Human Identity and Identification.*
16. Erin H. Kimmerle, Richard L. Jantz, Lyle W. Konigsberg and Jose Pablo Baraybard, "Skeletal Estimation and Identification in American and East European Populations," *Journal of Forensic Sciences* 53 (2008): 524–532. Maureen Schaefer, "A Summary of Epiphyseal Union Timings in Bosnian Males," *International Journal of Osteoarchaeology* 18 (2008): 536–545. Maureen Schaefer and Sue M. Black "Comparison of Ages of Epiphyseal Union in North American and Bosnian Skeletal Material," *Journal of Forensic Sciences* 50 (2005): 777–784.
17. Douglas H. Ubelaker, "Issues in the Global Applications of Methodology in Forensic Anthropology," *Journal of Forensic Sciences* 53 (2008): 606–607.
18. Mercedes Salado and Luis Fondebrider, *El desarrollo de la antropología forense en la Argentina* (Buenos Aires: Asociación Andaluza de Médicos Forenses, 2009).
19. Ibid.
20. Gabriel Aguilera et al., *Dialéctica del terror en Guatemala* (Costa Rica: Ciudad Universitaria Rodrigo Facio, 1981). Historical Clarification Commission, *Guatemala: Memory of Silence* (Guatemala City: Historical Clarification Commission, 1999).
21. Jiménez Gaytan and Daniel Alonzo, *Contexto Histórico y Desarrollo de la Antropología Forense en Guatemala (1954–2011)* (Guatemala: Escuela de Historia, Área de Antropología, Universidad de San Carlos de Guatemala, 2011).
22. Mario Slaus, Davor Strinovic, Vedrana Petrovecki, Davor Mayer et al., "Identification and Analyses of Female Civilian Victims of the 1991 War in Croatia from the Glina and Petrinja Areas," *Forensic Science International Supplement Series* 1 (2009): 69–71. Fowler and Thompson, "A Mere Technical Exercise?".
23. Slaus, Strinovic, Petrovecki, Mayer et al., "Identification and Analyses".
24. Kimmerle, Jantz, Konigsberg and Baraybard, "Skeletal Estimation".
25. Melanie Klinker, "Proving Genocide? Forensic Expertise and the ICTY," *Journal of International Criminal Justice* 6 (2008): 447–466. Melanie

Klinker, "Karadžić's Guilty Verdict and Forensic Evidence from Bosnia's Mass Graves," *Science & Justice* 56 (2016): 498–504.
26. Fowler and Thompson, "A Mere Technical Exercise?". Melanie Klinker, "Proving Genocide?". Slaus, Strinovic, Petrovecki, Mayer et al., "Identification and Analyses".
27. Roxana Ferllini, "Human Rights Investigations in Spain," *Annals of Anthropological Practice* 38 (2014): 65–80. Ríos, Luis, José Ignacio Casado and Jorge Puente Prieto, "Identification Process in Mass Graves from the Spanish Civil War I," *Forensic Science International* 199 (2010): e27–e36.
28. Roxana Ferllini, "Human Rights Investigations in Spain".
29. Ríos, Casado and Prieto, "Identification Process".
30. Roxana Ferllini, "Tissue Preservation and Projectile Context in Spanish Civil War Victims," *Journal of Forensic and Legal Medicine* 17 (2010): 285–288. Roxana Ferllini, "Human Rights Investigations in Spain," *Annals of Anthropological Practice* 38 (2014): 65–80.
31. Hugh Tuller, "Identification versus Prosecution: Is it that Simple, and Where Should the Archaeologist Stand?" in *Disturbing Bodies: Perspectives on Forensic Anthropology*, ed. Zoë Crossland and Rosemary A. Joyce (Santa Fe: School of Advanced Research Press, 2015), 85–101; Tim Thompson, "Deconstructing the Ideal of Standardisation".
32. Baraybar, "When DNA is Not Available".
33. Ibid.
34. Roxana Ferllini, "Human Rights Investigations in Spain".
35. Ibid.
36. Ibid.

Tim Thompson is Professor of Applied Biological Anthropology in the School of Science & Engineering, Teesside University, UK. He has published extensively in peer-reviewed journals and books, mainly on the topics of bone diagenesis and taphonomy and the application of forensic anthropology in the field. He was co-author of *Human Identity and Identification* with Dr Rebecca Gowland (Durham University) and senior editor for the book *Forensic Human Identification*. In addition, Tim is on the editorial boards for the *Journal of Forensic Sciences*, *Journal of Forensic and Legal Medicine* and *Human Remains and Violence*. He is Editor-in-Chief of the journal *Science & Justice*, and is a practising forensic anthropologist who has worked at home and abroad in a variety of forensic contexts.

Daniel Jiménez Gaytan is Coordinator of the Forensic Anthropology Section at the National Institute of Forensic Science of Guatemala (INACIF) and Interim Professor of Anthropology at San Carlos University, Guatemala. He has worked as a forensic anthropologist on more than one hundred cases related to the political violence during the Guatemalan Civil War (1960–1996). He has provided expert testimony in the genocide trial against former president Efrain Rios Mott and the trial of Sepur Zarco, in which two former military personnel were convicted of committing war crimes against the indigenous population.

Shakira Bedoya Sánchez is affiliated to The Latin American Observatorium for Crime Policy and Criminal Law Reform (OLAP) and the Max Planck Institute for Social Anthropology. She holds a doctoral degree in Law from the Albert Ludwigs University of Freiburg, Germany. She was previously a doctoral researcher at the Max Planck Institute for Foreign and International Criminal Law. In 2012 and 2013, she was a visiting scholar at the University of Cambridge, UK. In Berlin, she was a postdoctoral fellow at the Rechtskulturen programme and a visiting scientist at the Free University. In 2015, she was a researcher at the University of Oslo.

Ariana Ninel Pleitez Quiñónez is a sociocultural anthropologist working on issues of heritage and historical memory. She is a member of the European Association of Social Anthropology and the Interdisciplinary Network of Studies on Latin American Memory. She has worked in various exhumation processes with the National Search Commission. At present, she is a curator of exhibitions at the Dr. David J. Guzman National Museum of Anthropology, San Salvador. She is currently developing research to renovate the permanent room of 'Native and Afro-Descendant Peoples', and is a curator of the exhibition of human rights violations during the war in El Salvador.

4

Anthropometrics: The Application of Anthropometrics to Identify and Assess War Crimes

Mary Elisabeth Cox

The nutritional status of an individual—and how that person's health may have been affected due to changes in his or her environment—is a biological condition independent of moral decisions, political opinion, or belief. If a child receives insufficient calories or nutritional content for a prolonged period, is forced to survive without sufficient shelter or warmth, or is subjected to a dangerous disease environment, extreme labour, or abuse, the child's physical health and growth is negatively impacted. A competent medical professional can easily assess nutritional deprivation in a child through examination. Hallmarks of deprivation are nutrient-related diseases such as pellagra or rickets. Other indicators include reduced stature and delayed puberty. But when assessing whether or not an entire population or group has suffered nutritional deprivation, an interdisciplinary subset of economists, anthropologists, human biologists, and historians increasingly rely on anthropometrics.

Anthropometric history is the practice of using physical measurements of past peoples to understand their nutritional status. Anthropometrics

M.E. Cox (✉)
Faculty of History, University of Oxford, Oxford, UK

J. Waterlow, J. Schuhmacher, *War Crimes Trials and Investigations*, St Antony's Series,
https://doi.org/10.1007/978-3-319-64072-3_4

comes from the Greek words 'anthro' (ανθρώ), meaning human, and 'metric' (μετρι), meaning measure. The word itself was first coined by Johann Sigismund Elsholtz, in his thesis *Anthropometria*, in 1654,[1] yet the use of anthropometric measurements goes back even earlier, particularly in the visual arts, to better understand the proportionality of the human body.[2]

Today when economists, historians, and anthropologists talk about anthropometrics, and anthropometric history in particular, they usually mean the process of using physical measurements of a group of peoples in order to assess that group's overall nutritional status. When there are changes in the overall physical measurements of a population, those changes could reflect shifts in diet, living conditions, and the disease environment. If an entire population or subpopulation increases or decreases in height, for example, then some exogenous factor may be responsible. Anthropometric historians look at groups rather than at single individuals or families, so that variation due to genetics or personal circumstances can be reduced.

Although scientists have been applying basic statistical methods to try to understand human growth and heredity for centuries, the widespread statistical use of heights to inform living conditions is much more recent. Sir Francis Galton discovered that the heights of children 'regress to the mean' from their parents' heights.[3] He found that adult offspring of very small parents tend to be smaller than average but larger than their parents, and that adult offspring of very tall parents tend to be taller than average but smaller than their parents. Regression to the mean is a statistical phenomenon that extends well beyond human height.

Anthropometric and statistical surveys were made in the nineteenth century as part of social movements to measure living conditions in factories.[4] And conscription data, which often included minimum stature requirements for service, have been recorded for centuries. Yet it was not until the late 1960s and early 1970s that historical anthropometric data were used to assess living standards in the past.[5] The term 'living standard' has different meanings and includes different indicators. The terms 'living standards' and 'well-being', as used throughout this chapter, are synonyms for 'nutritional status,' which is:

> a net measure; it represents the net energy that has been used for growth once the demands of body maintenance, resistance to disease, play, and work have been satisfied. If nutritional status is inadequate, a child or young person will not grow, either not at all or less than he or she would do under more favourable circumstances ... Inadequate growth will result in children and adults who are stunted—short compared to some recognized standard—or wasted, light by comparison to some such standard ... The primary evidence of nutritional status lies in our bodies and particularly in our height and weight.[6]

French historian E. Le Roy Ladurie is credited as the first to apply modern methods to historical anthropometric data in order to assess changes in living standards and, especially, differences between social classes.[7] Since that time, the use of anthropometric history has grown widely and become deeply rooted in the social sciences. Anthropometric methodology has been used to elucidate changing nutritional status of African American slaves,[8] changes in living standards of civilians in Russia during the eighteenth and nineteenth centuries,[9] living standards of workers during the Industrial Revolution, health disparities between urban and rural peoples, the effects of colonization on the nutritional status of both the colonizers and the colonized, differences in health due to regimes, gender and age biases in societies, and more.[10] The common thread in these studies is the use of anthropometric data to discern the well-being of large groups of people. Other types of data used to infer well-being, such as wages, and imports and exports, are oftentimes unavailable, unreliable, or deemed insufficient as a measure of well-being when used in isolation. This is in part because vulnerable groups such as women and children have traditionally been left out of the equation of wage labour since much of the labour they performed was not monetized. Often, data on their marketplace consumption are missing as these data were viewed as having little importance to economic momentum. Similarly, variability in wages—particularly for labourers—may not yield a clear index of standards of living, since such economic fluctuations may not directly translate into changes in household diet. Economists and others increasingly view biological welfare and human growth as an essential component in understanding well-being.

Interdisciplinary Issues

Analyses detailed in this chapter suggest the utility of anthropometrics for the field of war crimes studies in general. Even with its inherent limitations, anthropometrics can shed important light on the nutritional and physical consequences of alleged war crimes independent of the highly fraught political and moral dilemmas of deciding whether a certain case should, or should not, be considered a war crime. As discussed, the nutritional status of a human being is a biological fact and is not determined by recourse to political or judicial opinions. Although few human endeavours will ever be perfectly unbiased, anthropometric analyses can be seen as a step towards empiricism in the consideration of populations subjected to alleged war crimes. While it is ultimately the responsibility of lawmakers, jurists, and courts to decide on the occurrence of war crimes, the use of anthropometric history can help inform those decisions.

Anthropometric analysis is an interdisciplinary tool—economists, historians, anthropologists, and medical fields all use it—and skills inherent in each of these disciplines are vital to properly interpret its implications. Basic human growth and nutrition should be understood, and statistical competency and a knowledge of econometrics are necessary to generate hypotheses on what may have affected changes in measured heights and weights over time. Most important, all of these findings must be rooted in historical and social contexts to have meaning, which often requires analysis by historians and anthropologists. In the application of anthropometric history to war crimes, this interdisciplinary nature of anthropometric history becomes even more pronounced. Without reference to the other disciplines described in this book—such as forensic anthropology and archaeology, legal history, violence studies, and the ethics of war—anthropometric analysis can add little value to our understanding of war crimes or genocide. Some of the problems related to other disciplines considered in this volume are also obstacles faced by anthropometric historians. For example, issues surrounding data assessment for forensic anthropologists find echoes in anthropometric history, such as when skeletal remains are used to assess heights of deceased peoples.

Beyond the primary aim of showing how anthropometrics might be used in examining war crimes, this chapter can be used as a starting point for students who would like to learn more about anthropometrics generally, although many other excellent sources exist that do this. More than anything, this chapter has been written for colleagues in other disciplines with interests in war crimes.

Anthropometric history, though previously not admitted as evidence in courts of law, is a potential analytical tool for alleged war crimes when used alongside other sources of evidence. Clearly, anthropometric evidence will not be useful in assessing all kinds of war crimes. Atrocities committed during armed conflict are diverse, and one methodology will never be sufficient to assess all types of crimes. Torture can be more easily corroborated by scars, testimony, and discarded weapons and instruments used to inflict pain. Mass murders can be assessed by locating graves, taking evidence from survivors, and studying forensic evidence.

Anthropometrics is best suited as a tool for understanding war crimes committed against entire populations, such as mass starvation, food blockades, forced migrations, and expulsions. This is because, as mentioned, anthropometrics measures the living standards of an entire population. These indicators can reveal not only how severe changes in living conditions may have been, but also, with sufficient data, how wide their scope may have been. They tell us little about spontaneous or short-lived acts of terror. Rather than measuring a brief moment or singular act of violence, anthropometric data can show slow-moving aggression and violence that may have lasted months or even years.

Anthropometrics can be used to measure the biological standard of living of populations in any situation where data of sufficient quality and quantity can be found. Thus, they can be used to clarify situations in which living standards are not fully understood, including testing accusations of certain kinds of war crimes in which a population is under siege.

The issue of time lag remains significant. Anthropometric history cannot inform criminal proceedings concerning recent war crimes where the interference with normal human growth patterns has not been of sufficient duration to produce measurable effects. Instead, anthropometric history will prove more useful in establishing crimes contested in 'memory wars', such as the Ukrainian Holodomor, or in supporting claims for compensation by a victimized generation, such as those individuals afflicted by the Dutch famine of 1944.

The following are general situations where anthropometric history could be utilized with regard to war crimes:

1. The use of anthropometric evidence can expand our understanding of the scope of past atrocities, when other types of evidence already strongly suggest that war crimes occurred. This is useful, because it not only adds (either positive or negative) evidence for past atrocities, but it might also be helpful in understanding how widespread atrocities may have been, corroborating evidence presented by survivors.
2. The use of anthropometrics can provide evidence for situations in which the scope of disruption and deprivation is disputed, and which might then be used by others to determine whether or not war crimes were committed.
3. The use of anthropometrics can provide evidence in recent political situations where accusations of atrocities have been made, but the level of harm is unknown.

An underlying thread uniting these three uses—and indeed the *raison d'être* for the use of anthropometrics to gain a snapshot of a people's nutritional status—is that specificity and accuracy humanizes an entire population. To be able to state, with confidence, that a group was not only deprived, but how deep the level of deprivation actually was, and that various social classes suffered more or less than others, that particular ages or genders were more vulnerable, and to accurately determine when deprivation or well-being was at its apogee or nadir, gives a reality and veracity to the human condition that simple generalities cannot. Humans have understood this intrinsically for thousands of years. As Homer wrote, with exquisite detail, in the violent battles scenes of the Iliad:

> But Maris charged Antilochus,
> Sweeping in with his lance,
> Enraged for his brother,
> Planted himself before his corpse but Thrasymedes,
> Quick as a god, beat him to it—he stabbed
> before Maris stabbed—no miss! right in the shoulder,

> the Argive's spearpoint cracked through the bony socket,
> shearing away the tendons, wrenched the whole arm out
> and down he thundered, darkness blanked his eyes.[11]

Here, the poet explicates violence not only for shock value—although in his account explicit violence is described throughout—nor is it only to demonstrate the strength of the victor. These recurring, detailed descriptions of how individuals lost their lives actualize and humanize individuals who suffered and died. Anthropometrics can help to humanize an entire population. As shown elsewhere in this volume, oral testimonies and forensic anthropologists also humanize deceased individuals or very small communities who have been the victims of war crimes. With anthropometric history, it is possible to estimate the nutritional status of entire populations or subpopulations, while assessing the more particular questions of which groups experienced the most deprivation, how sharp that deprivation may been, and its duration. Such details humanize large groups in a unique way. Evidence for mass war crimes ultimately is more than a matter of statistics, and often requires specificity of suffering, including questions of who, what, and where.

Thus, the expansion of anthropometric history to legal proceedings is both natural and fitting. In its precision, even for groups and subgroups, it humanizes. And, as mentioned, anthropometric history has exposed controversial issues from the past—such as the finding that the biological living standard of many African Slaves in North America was better than the living standards of many contemporary, but poor, Europeans.[12] Surely, exploring and commenting on difficult situations is not something anthropometric historians have shied away from in the past, nor should it be avoided now. It is not known, after all, what will be found.

The rest of the chapter is organized as follows: first, I discuss the types of data that are used in anthropometric analysis, including the strengths and weaknesses of different types of data anthropometricians normally have access to. This is done both to further explain how anthropometric history works, and also to inform those in other fields about some of the limitations anthropometric historians need to contend with. Next, I give practical examples, using anthropometric studies that have been or could be completed, of three kinds of situation when serious anthropometric analysis might be useful to those deliberating on whether or not war crimes have been committed. Finally, I offer a brief conclusion.

Data Sources Commonly Used in Anthropometrics

One area anthropometric historians must constantly wrestle with, beyond discovering or excavating available data, is assessing the quality and applicability of the data they use for analysis. Understanding and acknowledging the strengths and weaknesses of data being used for analysis are extremely important. Anyone trying to understand an anthropometric article or book should become familiar with the type of data being used, as well as the various strengths and weaknesses they may contain.

Conscription Data

One of the most common sources of anthropometric data from the past comes from conscription records. This is unsurprising—conscription was and still is one of the most conspicuous instances where a person could have their height and weight officially recorded. Men were measured when joining the army. Further, this kind of data often reflects men drawn from many different regions in a kingdom or region. This diversity allows for differences in location to be accounted for. There are biases with this sort of data, of course—often there were minimum height requirements for a man to join the army, thereby excluding the shortest men from the sample. Minimum requirements often changed over time depending on how large the supply of potential soldiers was, and on how desperate the recruiters were. Likewise, men may have tried to exaggerate or minimize their height depending on how eager they were to join the army. Another issue with conscription data is that, very often, only certain kinds of men joined the army. Missing may be large proportions of the well-to-do, for example, or the entrepreneurs who would rather not fight.

The problem of self-selection is minimized somewhat in periods of universal conscription. Yet here too, conscription data may not fully reflect heights and weights of men in the broader population. For example, in some cultures, people could buy out another person to take their place.[13] For these reasons, conscription data, even taken in times of universal conscription for specific ages, are never perfect. Perhaps the most serious issue of using conscription data is that they seldom are representative of more than 50% of the population. Women in the past were not soldiers, and do not figure in these sources. So, assumptions of total living standards for a given population taken from soldier's heights may only be inferred. Very often, in times of serious deprivation, inequality in distribution, even within households, existed between males and females. There are plenty of examples where the division of resources between males and females, including nutritional quality and calories, was anything but equal.[14,15,16]

Hospitals and Prison Records

Another source of data commonly used in anthropometric history comes from prison records and other institutions. Inmates and criminals were often measured both at the time of incarceration, and again when they were released.

This kind of data is often limited to the types of people who entered prisons—typically, those with few economic means. However, when questions on the living standards of the poor are an issue, as well as the changing effects that incarceration may have had on people over time, these data can offer significant insights. Did repeat offenders have higher living standards in jails than they did in their own—free—communities?

A great boon of using prison data as a source of anthropometric data over conscription data is that, frequently, such data include women. Both men and women were incarcerated, so this allows for an estimate of interhousehold nutritional allocation—before individuals were even incarcerated. Some of the great work on prison records includes the study of English, Scottish, Irish, and Australian inmates.[17]

Many hospitals also record anthropometric measurements. While patients may be measured when they come in for check-ups, we might in general expect patients measured in a hospital to be lighter than those not visiting, as people go to hospital when they are unwell. This may on its own be interesting, depending on the questions being asked, but the data most commonly extracted by anthropometricians from hospital records are the weights and heights of newborns.[18] An entire literature within anthropometric history relates to the validity of basing health on birth weight.[19]

Measurements of Children

Less readily available in earlier periods, but still assessable, are measurements from children. These were most often taken at schools, hospitals, orphanages, and other institutions such as prisons or armies (for older children), or other venues described above.

Starting in the late nineteenth century, many children across Europe and the United States were measured in schools. This occurred for a multitude of reasons. First, schooling for children became much more common in the nineteenth and twentieth centuries and, in many countries, universal. These increased educational opportunities facilitated large-scale measurements. At the same time, anthropology was popular at the turn of the twentieth century, and interests in human growth were increasing. People were also concerned about poverty and interested in eugenics. Most often, measurements of school children were collated at the grade-school level of the school where the measurements were taken. A single table would be produced containing the mean height for a given age and sex, rather than list the specific measurements taken of each individual. One may still make powerful inferences from these averaged data, but, in general, data given for individual people are the most valuable. When data are averaged, interesting variability is obscured.

The benefit of much of the childhood anthropometric data is its broad coverage: both genders are often included, and socio-economic background can often be determined by the school the child attended. As schooling became more and more universal, an expansive coverage of the population was included, and thus, more detailed pictures of nutritional status can be derived. Children who were measured were still growing. Their continual growth allows for a more detailed analysis, such as the prediction of the pubescent growth spurt and tracing of the human growth curve. We can more precisely pinpoint when living standards changed because we see it immediately through alterations to childhood growth curves, rather than having to infer changes later on from adult measurements.

Constraints inherent with childhood data taken from schools are that the data are most often found in collated tables. This has, as noted, the effect of dampening individual variation. Also, not all of childhood can be captured in school records: measurements for two- to five-year-olds are less common, which is an important phase of childhood growth. School records also cease at ages as young as 14, far too young to capture the adolescent growth spurt, especially in males, who often left school as labourers or military conscripts. Further, the pubescent growth spurt itself can complicate observed differences because it is not synchronized between the genders. This results in differences in delayed growth trajectories between males and females.

Anthropometrics and Bioarchaeology

An emerging field in anthropometrics comes from the expertise of archaeologists. Here, bones are dug up out of the earth, and measured. An entire skeleton is not needed to estimate the height of the individual, and there are various rules governing the estimation for overall height.[20] Estimated heights based on the archaeological evidence are then used and analysed in a similar way to other sources of anthropometric data. Furthermore, measurements of bone density and make-up can also give clues to the nutritional status of the individual being measured.

A benefit of this kind of anthropometric source is that it allows us to go back much further in time, long before height and weight measurements were recorded. Because it is the actual archaeologist measuring the human bones, they can make decisions on needed measurements, rather than relying solely on historical data recorded by others. This can sometimes yield increased confidence in archaeological findings beyond those solely reliant on historical records,[21] although, just like forensic anthropologists, there are trade-offs for decisions made.

There are a few obvious weaknesses in this kind of research. The first is the sheer cost, both in monetary terms and in time, of digging up and measuring bones of deceased people. Anthropometrics assumes a reasonably large sample size to weed out genetic bias and other individual discrepancies. The bones of many diseased individuals must be dug up and measured before the anthropometric analysis can begin. Second, not all kinds of peoples in the past were buried, or at least not in ways that are easily ascertainable. Burial was sometimes restricted to the elite. And, finally, even in societies where people were buried, and centuries have passed in the interim, it may not be appropriate for cultural or religious reasons to dig up graves and measure bones in this way.[22] However, in the case of mass graves associated with wartime atrocities, it should be possible to get some sense of the nutritional status of the population prior to death, if the remains of enough individuals are measured.

Individual Studies

Health reports issued by governments and international agencies,[23] individual studies by doctors or scientists,[24] and records from refugee or, potentially, concentration camps, tend to be less common, but they do exist. When located and discovered, these can be greatly beneficial.

Other Sources of Anthropometric Data

Very recently, in a creative burst of energy, one economic historian spent a great deal of time in the archives of old tailor shops in London, acquiring measurements made to fit clothes. These included chest and waist circumference and much more, giving her a guide as it were, almost to the entire body, and certainly to the waist/hip ratio, which can be a good indicator of diseases like diabetes and heart disease.[25] While not many others have taken this up yet, the scope for expansion is definitely there. In a similar vein, a few academics have used costumes of ancient people, such as metal armour, to estimate height.[26]

Current Anthropometric Studies for Contemporary History

Today, development economists might use a person's height, weight, body mass index (BMI), arm circumference, and skin flaps to assess nutritional status. These will be sampled from a large group of people, and then used to make statements on the overall health of the population. Many of these measurements are also taken by government agencies in developed countries. Children are often still measured at schools. Soldiers are still measured when they enlist. Babies are still weighed at birth. In survey studies, many anthropometric studies have been done as part of larger studies. For example, the World Health Organization and the Food and Agriculture Organization (FAO) set standards and categories of BMI to define predetermined standards into various levels of 'chronic energy deficiency' and 'obesity'. The decisions for cut-off lines for these standards are made by groups of medical professionals and, as a result, are somewhat arbitrary. A woman aged 20–40 with a BMI lower than 20 would be categorized as suffering from chronic energy deficiency (CED) by the WHO, while a woman of the same age with an equal BMI would be considered normal by the FAO.[27]

These scores are then collected for an entire population, and the per cent of individuals suffering from CED are then assessed, assisting aid organizations in directing further aid. While these debates can be frustrating for those of us who then have to decide which definition to use in our research (I tend to cite both), they represent a great deal of progress in our understanding of health. A person with a low BMI would be deemed to have suffered nutritional loss whether they lived in the 1980s or in the 1880s.

Similarly, auxologists—scholars who study physical growth—have created 'modern standards'. Several different studies and sets of modern standards have been made. Modern standards show not the ideal of a healthy population, but the anthropometric measurements of heights and weights for males and females that can be expected to be found in a society with adequate nutrition.[28] Differences in ethnicities are accounted for. It has been found that the height potential for peoples across the globe is roughly the same, except for parts of Asia. Thus, comparisons from the past, as well as to current situations where there might be reason to believe that nutrition is inadequate, are made to these sets of modern standards as a means of assessing how severe the nutritional status may have been. Modern standards serve as both a way of assessing the heights a population could have been expected to reach in a society with sufficient nutrition and adequate disease environment, and they also make the various studies of anthropometric history comparable with each other.

How Anthropometric Data Are Used

Once data are obtained, their source and nature should be clearly articulated, including how many people were measured, where the data came from, and how living standards differed within the population, as indicated by an individual's or population's height, weight, BMI, or other anthropometric measurements, from a healthy population.

After data have been collected and transcribed, we can then begin to make comparisons. The most basic comparison is to use times-series calculations to compare the population with itself—perhaps to the very same individuals, or to others from a very similar timeframe or background. An example of this is the comparison of a person's weight when they enter an institution, such as a jail, to their weight when they leave. Similar comparisons could be made to the entrance and exit of individuals to the poorhouse, the military, school, or orphanage. One might also compare a group of adult men measured in London in 1870 to adult men measured 10, 20, or 50 years earlier to try to see short-term changes in living standards. Similar work can be done to look at differences between war and post-war, for example.[29] Comparisons can be made between two places with a shared history and similar natural resources, but that differ radically in political control—for example, between people in North and South Korea.[30]

Usually, comparisons are further made by comparing the historical population in question to 'modern standards' in height, weight, or BMI. Again, a modern standard is simply a standard taken from a modern population that shows the average heights and weights people can be expected to reach in a given population with adequate inputs (adequate nutrition, positive disease environment, etc.). These standards are not the ideal height and weight, but rather represent the actual anthropometric measurements of large groups of peoples, and are derived from large studies of peoples. Because human population gene frequencies are relatively static at most alleles[31] (in the absence of immigration, emigration, or small founder-type events, population gene frequencies take thousands of years to change), it is unlikely that the differences in nutritional status as measured by weight and height between one or two generations, or even five or seven generations, are due to genetic changes. Thus, modern standards are used as a benchmark of what peoples could have reached in a given time if they had been provided with sufficient inputs for their needs. By using modern standards as a benchmark of comparison, this then makes different historical groups more comparable to one another.

Those who make these assessments on nutritional status—typically, economists, economic historians, anthropologists, archaeologists, and medical professionals—do so as empirically as possible, publishing their results in peer-reviewed journals. This then allows others—an international court or tribunal, ethicists, the press, and others involved with determining criminality—to make their own judgement. There are three key reasons for this: First, every situation will be different. One can imagine a case where a tiny percentage of a given population are grotesquely starved, criminals or prisoners of war, for example, and another where millions of people experience deprivation severe enough to alter human growth, such as in the Democratic People's Republic of Korea (DPRK).[32] (I am giving these only as possible examples, but both have been chosen because there have indeed been small-scale studies in both instances—without the charge of war crimes.) A small percentage of people were severely starved in the first example, whereas a much higher number of people and percentage of the population suffered in the second, but perhaps not as intensely as those in the prisoner of war camp. These examples highlight the need for other scholars or jurists to determine what is more important in different situations: severity, duration, or the number affected. Those of us who practise the use of anthropometrics to assess living standards are best qualified to state what those living standards were or are, but not to make complex decisions impacting law. This is only complicated when working with population data, rather than with individual data, because, as mentioned, population data dampens population variability due to the individual differences. If an entire population shows deprivation, then very likely even though the numbers are averaged, deprivation itself is not averaged among the population itself. The privileged will be better off, while the most destitute could be suffering quite severely. The averages will not show this.

Applicability

Because anthropometrics as a field of study is still unknown to many, much of this chapter has by necessity focused on explaining what anthropometrics is, the types of sources available, how it has been used to understand the nutritional status of various populations, and how it might be applied to the study of war crimes. This has left little space for application, but there are several concrete examples where the use of anthropometric methodology could easily be put into practice and utilized by decision makers dealing with war crimes and crimes against humanity.

- *Anthropometrics can be used as evidence in current political situations where accusations of atrocities have been made, but the level of harm is unknown.*

As briefly mentioned, some work has already been completed on assessing living standards in North Korea under the rule of the DPRK, yet no one has yet used these empirical studies to analyse alleged war crimes. In particular, the work of Daniel Schwekendiek and his colleagues in Germany and in Korea is noteworthy. Through a variety of means, he and his collaborators have gathered anthropometric measurements of one kind or another from North Korea.[33] They have used these in order to compare differences in the nutritional status of North and South Koreans. Their findings suggest acute and widespread nutritional deprivation of the people in North Korea. The discovery, for example, that children from North Korea compared to children in South Korea were 3–4 cm shorter and weighed 1 kg less suggests intense nutritional deprivation.

Data they collected in 2002 show the differences in height between children in North and South Korea to be on average 8 cm, an extraordinary discrepancy.[34] While their sample sizes are large enough to be statistically valid, due to the extreme difficulty in acquiring data in a closed society, more research in this area would be useful. In this instance, jurors and others could use these anthropometric studies, alongside other kinds of sources, to make decisions on criminality of the DPRK in regards to its own people as is being currently investigated by the United Nations Human Rights Council. The findings of Schwekendiek are severe. Because the population he is studying is still living, perhaps the results themselves could be used to call for more studies, and more measurements. While data are limited, on their own these records still give an estimate of the level of deprivation experienced by the population as a whole of the survivors.

- *Anthropometrics can be used to expand our understanding of the scope of past atrocities, when other kinds of evidence already strongly suggest violence.*

Two examples immediately come to mind. First is the Armenian Genocide, for which the world recently marked the hundredth anniversary. Still disputed by some, but nearly universally accepted by academics, this atrocity rests mainly on disagreement over the number of people murdered. While anthropometrics itself might have little to say on this, if the anthropometric data were available, a study of the survivors, could be another way of tackling the problem. And even for those who are already convinced of the genocide, understanding the scope of deprivation experienced by those who were able to live through it, deepens and broadens the amount of suffering understood.

One anthropometric study that has been done on a known past atrocity relates to an incident which occurred in North America in the 1830s, namely the Indian Removal Act. In 1830, the Indian Removal Act was passed by the United States Congress. This Act removed the right of indigenous Americans to continue living on their native lands in the southeast United States unless they agreed to become part of and assimilated into Western culture. Members of the Cherokee Nation were particularly affected by this legislation. Those who would not take US citizenship and reject their culture and heritage were forced to walk hundreds of miles and resettle on the other side of the Mississippi. Some 15,000 people, including women and children, were forced to march. Of these, 4,000 individuals died en route, on what became known as the 'Trail of Tears', but even for the survivors, great suffering ensued. These people were removed from their native lands which had provided food, medicine and housing.

The Trail of Tears is universally considered to be one of the more tragic episodes in US history, not only for Native Americans, but for all Americans and for all indigenous peoples. The forced expulsion of some 15,000 people by order of the US government is an uncontested blight on the character of the nation. How might anthropometrics further inform our understanding of this already dire situation?

If anthropometric data were found on the survivors, then we would have a more precise means of measuring how widespread the physical impact of the expulsion may have been. This would include deprivation that occurred during the march, but also during resettlement. We could actually give some kind of meaning—beyond stating the number of people who died—estimating the percentage of people who suffered various levels of deprivation. Even if the numbers are not what we expect—perhaps everyone suffered a little, and a few suffered a great deal; or perhaps everyone was severely nutritionally deprived—the results would be illuminating.

Some might argue that such analysis and information at this point is meaningless. We already know and have evidence that people died, and it is obvious that some level of nutritional deprivation took place. Yet empirical articulation of how much deprivation occurred, and for whom, not only aids in a better understanding of the crime in its own right, but also serves as a form of respect. In regard to Armenia, very little is actually known about how people died, when they died, and precisely where. Understanding the details of the severity of nutritional deprivation for Armenians brings a sense of reality to a period and people that may otherwise seem distant. The motivation to understand and document suffering can guide practitioners as we work to avoid future instances of genocide or war crimes. The additional use of anthropometric sources adds to this understanding.

In the case of the North American indigenous people of the Cherokee nation, we do not know what the results will show. Although other evidence exists which suggests that great physical suffering existed for these people, not to mention the emotional shock and economic hardship of their experiences, the biological standard of living of the survivors has not yet been assessed.

Fortunately, at least two publications by anthropometricians relate to the biological standard of living of Native Americans during the nineteenth century. One used anthropometric data that was taken on Native American scouts who assisted Americans.[35] Another study of the anthropometrics of Native Americans goes back much further, to the work of Franz Boas. Before he became famous as the father of modern anthropology, Boas took expeditions across the United States in which he conducted anthropometric surveys of the indigenous peoples he met there. This included the Cherokee in 1891, which may include the measurements of individuals who experienced the Trail of Tears. These records were saved and collected at the Smithsonian Natural History Museum in Washington DC, the American Philosophical Society, and at other archives and libraries across the United States, probably because of Boas's later prominence.[36] His massive and thoughtful studies of Native American anthropometrics were forgotten for decades as his later and more prominent work on growth and anthropology took dominance.[37] Recently, however, others have assessed and explored the data Boas collected.[38] Perhaps there are other existing collections of Native American measurements recorded by those who were not to become as famous as Boas that could also be utilized.

While these studies on indigenous peoples have not been specifically applied to the question of the effect of expulsion on Native Americans, or exclusively on the Cherokee peoples alone, they show the possibility of locating and exploring anthropometric data for Native American peoples—those who might otherwise be considered outside the kinds of records that were kept by the US government. They also demonstrate how the data might be handled, including the various biases and issues related to it. Although the specific question on the effects that the Trail of Tears may have had on the nutritional status of survivors has not yet been specifically explored, it seems very possible to do so.

- *Anthropometrics can be used as evidence to test situations in the past where the scope of disruption and deprivation is disputed.*

For the past hundred years, the nutritional status of German civilians during the First World War has been debated. Some suggest that deprivation for civilians was severe, while others argue that such claims were exaggerated. What might have remained an issue confined to the discourses of public health became a political issue following the First World War when the British naval blockade was continued throughout the Armistice until after the Treaty of Versailles had been signed. The debate was particularly linked with the question of whether or not the British blockade of Germany, which included food and fertilizer among many other goods, had been legal. Some Germans were anxious to evoke sympathy after losing a long and painful war. Blaming former enemies for harming women and children was one way to do this. Certainly, the blockade reduced the number of calories available for German civilians to consume, yet so too did poor internal German policy for managing distribution.

I have written a monograph on the nutritional status of women and children in Germany during and immediately following the First World War.[39] While the book does not make claims about war crimes, it does show through a variety of sources—including measurements of heights and weights for approximately 600,000 school children—that deprivation was severe for some civilians in Germany, but that it varied greatly depending on status. Age, gender, social class, and even stratum within families impacted how much people suffered during the War. It also varied in its timing. Thus, the particular is made visible amongst a mass of statistics, while claims of hunger and deprivation are made for the country as a whole.

The famous historian of the First World War, Jay Winter, has claimed that the British blockade against Germany during the First World War 'did not fall short of being a war crime'.[40] The charge remains political, and the legality of the British blockade is still debated. One piece of evidence that might be considered when addressing the question of war crimes should be my anthropometric findings. If I had found no continuing nutritional deprivation for German civilians beyond the cessation of wartime hostilities, any intent to harm German civilian populations could be disputed. However, the continuation of what the Germans termed the 'hunger blockade' beyond the period when the Germans gave up arms, combined with documents of the Allied discussions after the Armistice, could be considered as evidence for vengeance and intentionality in prolonging the suffering of women, children, and other non-combatants. Still, on its own, deprivation as expressed in changing heights, weights, and body mass, does not prove intent, or illegality.

Conclusion

In this chapter I have tried to introduce the field of anthropometric history—what it is, what it can tell us, and how it has been used to answer various questions about the past. I have suggested how it can be used alongside other disciplines as an additional source of evidence in questions about war crimes, and have emphasized that this sort of empirical analysis is most suited for augmenting or addressing situations outside of more traditional sources such as witnesses, diary entries, and photographs, because it gives a snapshot of the nutritional status of populations. Yet even alongside other quantitative sources, such as mortality statistics, anthropometrics is important because it gives a measure of deprivation of those who survived. With anthropometric data, an entire life nutritional profile can be created, whereas mortality data is final; only those who die are counted.

Casting the methodological net of war crime jurisdiction wide enough to include serious anthropometric assessments, both of living and dead populations, delineates long-term serial deprivation. This specificity is unique, and cuts through broad-stroke claims of calamity or normality. Were circumstances so severe that they affected many people's growth patterns, or were they not? Those tasked with the final judgement can use the empirical work of anthropometric historians to understand how a possible war crime affected human growth of many people—a nuance not possible with other methods—and then, ultimately, to make verdicts of guilt or innocence. The limits are bounded by our ability to find reliable data, and by communication between the empirical assessors themselves and the legal and moral judges. It is hoped that this chapter might aid in spurring future conversations.

Bibliographical Essay Over the last decade, there have been a number of excellent introductions to anthropometric history which cover some of the major themes and debates in the past 30 years. These include the thorough introduction and summary by Timothy Cuff on EH.Net. See Timothy Cuff, "Historical Anthropometrics" in Robert Whaples, ed., *EH.Net Encyclopaedia* (August 29, 2004). The reader is also referred to Richard Steckel's article "Heights and Human Welfare: Recent Developments and New Directions", in *Explorations in Economic History* 46 (2009); and Roderick Floud et al., eds., *The Changing Body: Health, Nutrition, and Human Development in the Western World since 1700* (Cambridge: Cambridge University Press, 2011).

Below are a few of many anthropometric publications that are either introductions to the field, or are critical discussions of methodology. Readers should refer to the bibliographies of the books and articles included here for further specific areas of application. The uses of anthropometric methods to address different themes of study are varied. As previously mentioned, anthropometric history has been used to study standards of living and changes in living standards for people at the time of the industrial revolution, slaves and slave-holders, subjects of the Roman Empire, the colonized and colonizer. Anthropometric history has also been used to measure the long-term effects of famine, gender inequalities within families and society, differences between urban and rural populations, as well as socio-economic differences within single populations. Criticisms relate most closely to sample bias in datasets used. Again, each source below can be used by readers as a jumping-off point for further explorations. There are many other sources that could be included, but due to space constraints I have only chosen to highlight a very few. Bodenhorn, H., T. W. Guinnane, and T. A. Mroz, 'Sample-Selection Biases and the Industrialization Puzzle', Journal of Economic History 77/1 (2017), 171–207.

This is perhaps one of the most serious recent criticisms of anthropometric history, and one that other anthropometric historians are beginning to respond to. In it, the authors challenge the data used in the famous 'Antebellum Puzzle', which asks why height (a proxy for nutritional status) was declining in the United States during a period of economic growth. It is now believed that this occurred because of growing inequality and increases in the price of food. Bodenhorn, Guinnane, and Mroz turn the puzzle, and its supposed solution, on its head. They argue that there was no 'Antebellum Puzzle' because there were no decreases in heights during this period. Most of the evidence rests on height data taken from volunteer armies, which means the data suffers from self-selection bias. Furthermore, most anthropometric datasets are not based on random samples. The authors use the example of the Antebellum Puzzle—something that has been much written about and debated—to argue more broadly that the field of anthropometric history does not take sample selection bias seriously enough.

Timothy Cuff, "Historical Anthropometrics", in Robert Whaples, ed., *EH.Net Encyclopaedia* (August 29, 2004).

This is a free and open-access article which introduces the field of anthropometric history and discusses some of the main debates within the discipline. This source is particularly useful for students because it cites the main scholars involved in each debate and includes a brief bibliography of key publications.

Roderick Floud et al., eds., *The Changing Body: Health, Nutrition, and Human Development in the Western World since 1700* (Cambridge: Cambridge University Press, 2011).

A recent introduction by some of the most prominent scholars in the field. This book introduces important concepts such as the nutritional status of living, the basal metabolic rate (BMR), physical activity level (PAL), human health, mortality, and economic growth since 1700. Changes of body size and composition over the centuries are considered. This superb and thorough discussion lays a strong foundation for anthropometric history.

John Komlos and Brian A'Hearn, "The Decline in The Nutritional Status of The U.S.

Antebellum Population at the Onset of Modern Economic Growth," National Bureau of Economic Research, Working Paper no. 21845 (2016).

This article is one of several serious responses to the criticisms of anthropometric history made by Bodenhorn, Guinnane, and Mroz on sample selection bias related to the Antebellum Puzzle. Komlos and A'Hearn show that compensation of soldiers during the Antebellum Puzzle was increasing, compared to that of civilians. Hence, the supposed bias seen by Bodenhorn, Guinnane, and Mroz should go in the other direction (i.e. increased rather than decreased heights). They also show that Bodenhorn et al. failed to exclude migrants from their study. When Komlos and A'Hearn account for this, the Antebellum Puzzle reappears. This is a convincing response to the specific criticisms of the Bodenhorn et al. paper on the Antebellum Puzzle, although it touches only lightly on broader criticisms of anthropometric data collection.

Richard H. Steckel, "Heights and Human Welfare: Recent Developments and New Directions", *Explorations in Economic History* 46 (2009).

Richard Steckel, one of the early pioneers of using anthropometric history to understand shifts in living standards, wrote this summary of the state of the field of anthropometric history, pointing to a vibrant and continued future. This article traces the rise of modern economic history and its acceptance as an interdisciplinary area of study evidenced by the increased numbers of anthropometric history articles and books published each year. Steckel's article also summarizes some of the many diverse academic controversies within anthropometric history.

Notes

1. Stanley J. Ulijaszek, Francis E. Johnston and Michael A. Preece, eds., *Cambridge Encyclopedia of Human Growth and Development* (Cambridge: Cambridge University Press, 1998), 446.
2. Ibid., 448.
3. Francis Galton, "Regression towards Mediocrity in Hereditary Stature," *The Journal of the Anthropological Institute of Great Britain and Ireland* 15 (1886): 246–263.
4. For example, Edwin Chadwick led anthropometric surveys of British child factory workers in the 1833, as did Edwin Horner in 1837. In 1872, the Parliamentary Commission did another anthropometric study

of children, in part, to be able to enforce the law on the age of child-workers. Anthropometric studies of children were completed on the other side of the Atlantic as well, though in part to understand human growth rather than to enforce age-limit requirements. See for example Henry Bowditch, "The Growth of Children, Studied by Galton's Method of Percentile Grades," Reprinted from *The Twenty-Second Annual Report of the State Board of Massachusetts* (Boston, 1891).

5. For a wonderful and more thorough overview of the field, see Richard H. Steckel, "Heights and Human Welfare: Recent Developments and New Directions," *Explorations in Economic History* 46, no. 1 (2009): 1–2; Beyond anthropometric publications being published in top mainstream economic, development, and human biology journals, its own journal has even been established, *Economics and Human Biology*. Major academic publishers such as Cambridge University Press, Oxford University Press, Princeton University Press, and Routledge have all published major monographs in anthropometric history, and continue to do so. For an excellent recent example, see Roderick Floud, Robert W. Fogel, Bernard Harris and Sok Chul Hong, eds., *The Changing Body: Health, Nutrition, and Human Development in the Western World since 1700* (Cambridge: Cambridge University Press, 2011).
6. Floud et al., *The Changing Body*, 11.
7. Emmanuel Le Roy Ladurie, Nicole Bernageau and Yvonne Pasquet, "Le Conscrit et l'ordinateur: Perspectives de recherches sur les Archives Militaries du XIX siecle Français," *Studi Storici* 10, no. 2 (1969): 260–308. For brief English discussions on the importance of Le Roy Ladurie's work, and excellent introductions to anthropometric history in general, see John Komlos, *Nutrition and Economic Development in the Eighteenth Century Habsburg Monarchy: An Anthropometric History* (Princeton: Princeton University Press, 1989), 24–25; Roderick Floud, Kenneth Wachter and Annabel Gregory, *Height, Health and History: Nutritional Status in the United Kingdom, 1750–1980* (Cambridge: Cambridge University Press, 1990); Timothy Cuff, "Historical Anthropometrics," *EH.Net Encyclopedia*, ed. Robert Whaples (29 August 2004); Boris Mironov, *The Standard of Living and Revolutions in Russia, 1700–1917*, ed. Gregory Freeze (New York: Routledge, 2012), chapter 2.
8. Robert Margo and Richard Steckel, "The Height of American Slaves: New Evidence on Slave Nutrition and Health," *Social Science History* 6, no. 4 (1982): 516–538.

9. Please see the recent top seller in Russian anthropometric history: Mironov, *The Standard of Living*.
10. Steckel, "Heights and Human Welfare".
11. Homer, *The Iliad*, trans. Robert Fogels (New York: Penguin, 1998), 380.
12. Stanley L. Engerman, "The Height of US Slaves," *Local Population Studies* 16 (1976): 45–49; Robert W. Fogel and Stanley L. Engerman, *Time on the Cross: The Economics of American Negro Slavery*, 2 vols. (Boston: Little, Brown & Co., 1974).
13. A man in a certain region of Russia in the nineteenth century, for example, could select another man in his stead. Often, a community was told they must give a certain number of military-age men for the army and, here too, there was some leniency.
14. See for example, Sara Horrell and Deborah Oxley, "Crust or Crumb? Intrahousehold Resource Allocation and Male Breadwinning in late Victorian Britain," *The Economic History Review* 52, no. 3 (1991); Sara Horrell, David Meredith and Deborah Oxley, "Measuring Misery: Body Mass, Ageing and Gender Inequality in Victorian London," *Explorations in Economic History* 46, no. 1 (2009).
15. Siddiq Osmani and Amartya Sen, "The Hidden Penalties of Gender Inequality: Fetal Origins of Ill- Health," *Economics and Human Biology* 1, no. 1 (2003): 105–121.
16. Sally Macintyre, "Inequalities in Health: Is Research Gender Blind?" in *Poverty Inequality and Health. An International Perspective*, ed. David A. Leon and Gill Walt (Oxford: Oxford University Press, 2004), 283–293.
17. Deborah Oxley, *Convict Maids: The Forced Migration of Women to Australia*. (Cambridge: Cambridge University Press, 1996); Cormac Ó. Grada, "Anthropometric History: What's in it for Ireland?" *Histoire & Mesure* 11, no. 1–2, no. 3 (1996): 139–166.
18. Joël Floris, Kaspar Staub and Ulric Woitek, "The Benefits of Intervention: Birth Weights in Basle 1912–1920," University of Zurich, Department of Economics, Working Paper No. 236 (27 October 2016).
19. Janet Currie and Enrico Moretti, "Biology as Destiny? Short- and Long-Run Determinants of Intergenerational Transmission of Birth Weight," *Journal of Labor Economics* 25, no. 2 (2007): 231–263; A. J. Drake and B. R. Walker, "The Intergenerational Effects of Fetal Programming: Non-genomic Mechanisms for the Inheritance of Low Birth Weight and Cardiovascular Risk," *Journal of Endocrinology* 180, no. 1 (2004): 1–16.

20. Nikola Koepke and Jörg Baten discuss some of these in their article "Agricultural Specialization and Height in Ancient and Medieval Europe," *Explorations in Economic History* 45 (2008): 127–146.
21. Richard H. Steckel, Paul W. Sciulli and Jerome C. Rose, "A Health Index from Skeletal Remains," in *The Backbone of History: Health and Nutrition in the Western Hemisphere*, ed. Richard H. Steckel and Jerome C. Rose (New York: Cambridge University Press, 2002), 61–93; Clark Spencer Larsen, *Bioarchaeology: Interpreting Behavior from the Human Skeleton* (New York: Cambridge University Press, 1997); Jane E. Buikstra and Lane A. Beck, eds., *Bioarchaeologya: The Contextual Analysis of Human Remains* (Amsterdam: Elsevier, 2006).
22. Ayao Edward Halealoha, "Native Burials: Human Rights and Sacred Bones," *Cultural Survival* 24, no. 1 (2000).
23. José Villar, Leila Cheikh Ismail, Cesar G. Victora, "International Standards for Newborn Weight, Length, and Head Circumference by Gestational Age and Sex: The Newborn Cross- Sectional Study of the INTERGROWTH-21 Project," *Lancet* 384, no. 9946 (2014): 857–868.
24. Walter Kruse and Kurt Hintze, *Sparsame Ernährung Nach Erhebung im Krieg und Frieden* (Dresden: Verlag des Deutsches Hygiene-Museums, 1922).
25. Sarah B. Campbell, "Waists, Health and History: Obesity in Nineteenth Century Britain," D.Phil. thesis, University of Oxford, 2014. Unpublished.
26. Koepke and Baten "Agricultural Specialization," 136.
27. See for example World Health Organization, *Comparative Quantification of Health Risks, Global and Regional Burden of Disease Attributable to Selected Major Risk Factors*, vol. 1 (2004), 63, compared to P.S. Shetty and W.P.T. James, "BMI as an Indicator of CED," in *Body Mass Index—A Measure of Chronic Energy Deficiency in Adults*, ed. P. S. Shetty and W.P.T. James (Rome: Food and Agriculture Organization of the United Nations, 1994). Both of these publications have slightly different cut-offs: A BMI of 18.5 for the FAO, and 20 for the WHO.
28. Richard H. Steckel, "Percentiles of Modern Height Standards for Use in Historical Research," NBR Working Paper Series on Historical Factors in Long Run Growth (October 1995), Historical Paper 75; J. M. Tanner, R.H. Whitehouse and M. Takaishi, "Standards from Birth to Maturity for Height, Weight, Height Velocity, and Weight Velocity: British Children, 1965. Part I," *Archives of Disease in Childhood* 41 (1966):

454–471; J.M. Tanner, R.H. Whitehouse and M. Takaishi, "Standards from Birth to Maturity for Height, Weight, Height Velocity, and Weight Velocity: British Children, 1965. Part II," *Archives of Disease in Childhood* 41 (1966): 613–635; Centers for Disease Control and Prevention, *Growth Charts* (2010).

29. Mary E. Cox, "Hunger Games or How the Allied Blockade in the First World War Deprived German Children of Nutrition, and Allied Food Aid Subsequently Saved them," *The Economic History Review* 68, no. 2 (2015): 600–663.
30. Daniel Schwekendiek "Height and Weight Differences between North and South Korea," *Journal of Biosocial Science* 41, no. 1 (2009): 51–55.
31. An allele is an alternative form of a gene, sometimes resulting in a different phenotype.
32. Daniel Schwekendiek and S. Pak. "Recent Growth of Children in the Two Koreas: A Meta-Analysis," *Economics & Human Biology* 7, no. 1 (2009): 109–112.
33. Schwekendiek managed to use anthropometric measurements taken by aid workers in children in North Korea. These are limited—because aid workers have not been allowed in for some time, and because the North Korean government does not wish their children to be measured by aid workers. Schwekendiek and his colleagues also used measurements taken from escaped North Korean refugees, and compared these to South Koreans of the same age cohort.
34. Schwekendiek and Pak, "Recent Growth," 109–112.
35. John Comlos and Leonard Carlson, "The Anthropometric History of Native Americans, C.1820–1890," *Research in Economic History* 30 (2014): 135–161.
36. Boas was not only interested in anthropometric measurements, but in culture and language. Much of his collection, a treasure-trove, is located in the archive of the American Philosophical Society, and referenced as 'Franz Boas field notebooks and anthropometric data, American Philosophical Society.'
37. Richard Jantz, David Hunt, Anthony Falsetti and P.J. Key, "Variation among North Amerindians: Analysis of Boas's Anthropometric Data," *Human Biology* 67, no. 3 (1995): 337–344; Richard Jantz, "The Anthropometric Legacy of Franz Boas," *Economics and Human Biology* 1, no. 2 (2003): 277–284.

38. E. J. Szathmáry, "Overview of the Boas Anthropometric Collection and its Utility in Understanding the Biology of Native North Americans," *Human Biology* 67, no. 3 (1995): 345–353.
39. Mary E. Cox, *Hunger and the Allied Blockade of Germany: Malnutrition and Humanitarian Aid, 1914–1924.* (Oxford: Oxford University Press, 2018).
40. As cited by Holger Holwig, "Total Rhetoric, Limited War: Germany's U-Boat Campaign, 1917–1918," in *Great War, Total War. Combat and Mobilization on the Western Front. 1914–1917*, ed. Roger Chickering and Stig Förster (Cambridge: Cambridge University Press, 2006), 189.

Mary Elisabeth Cox is a Departmental Lecturer in Economic and Social History at the University of Oxford, a William Golding Junior Research Fellow in the Arts, Humanities, and Social History at Brasenose College, Oxford, and a Visiting Fellow at the Hoover Institution, Stanford University. Her research focuses on the effects of war on the living standards of non-combatants at all levels of society.

5

International Legal History: From Atrocity Reports to War Crimes Tribunals—The Roots of Modern War Crimes Investigations in Nineteenth-Century Legal Activism and First World War Propaganda

Jan Martin Lemnitzer

Legal history is an ambitious undertaking, attempting not only to establish the origins of our current legal terms and norms, but also to track how our ideas of what justice is and how it should be achieved have developed and changed over time. This chapter discusses the way the history of war crimes trials has been written, and how the field moved away from a simple desire to find precedents for Nuremberg. In the second section, it charts the origins of the idea to hold war crimes trials from the mid-nineteenth century onwards, showing the influence key events had on these developments, from the Armenian Genocide to forgotten precedents such as the 1904 Dogger Bank incident. This section also invites the reader to explore the surprisingly murky and recent origins of key terminology such as 'crime against humanity' and, indeed, 'war crime' itself. Finally, the chapter explores the origins and interdisciplinary nature

J.M. Lemnitzer (✉)
University of Southern Denmark, Odense, Denmark

J. Waterlow, J. Schuhmacher, *War Crimes Trials and Investigations*, St Antony's Series,
https://doi.org/10.1007/978-3-319-64072-3_5

of the atrocity report—a very special public relations exercise designed to initiate war crimes prosecutions that is still used today.

Fruitful cooperation between lawyers, historians and other social scientists is a worthy cause, but the cultural and methodological differences run deep: as Alexandra Kemmerer recently wrote, 'lawyers tend to insist on precise terminology and pure doctrine. Historians (along with anthropologists, sociologists and political scientists) don't like the technicalities, the complex institutional architectures, the intricate cases and convoluted judgements'.[1]

Writing good legal history demands deep knowledge of the political and intellectual history of the time period in question as well as highly specialized legal knowledge. Therefore, scholars working in legal history tend to choose a further specialization, for example, in the history of criminal law, in Civil Law and its Roman origins, or in the different concepts of public law that developed in Europe or elsewhere. Among them is a small but growing field exploring the history of international law, attracting scholars with expertise in international law and the history and politics of international relations. Even more so than historians of criminal law, who often tend to focus on one state or empire, these scholars are well equipped to tackle the origins of international criminal law. Historians of international law have always had a strong research interest in the development of the laws of war, and it was the codification of these rules that proved to be the vital first step towards international war crime tribunals.

The problem they face is that the history of international criminal law was originally written by lawyers, and with a clear agenda in mind: finding historical precedents that could be used to counter allegations that the Nuremberg and Tokyo tribunals were prime examples of victor's justice. This has led to a disjointed parade of historical precedents, presented entirely out of context, and with the intention of showing that there was something natural and inevitable about the community of states beginning to hold war crimes tribunals in the twentieth century. The first part of this chapter explains why historians and lawyers view this narrative and the precedents used to support it with increasing unease. The second part briefly sketches the emerging picture of a more complex route to war crimes tribunals, with crucial developments in the late nineteenth century laying the foundations for a process that has developed in fits and starts, and was often interrupted by decades of inactivity. The third part provides a case study of the interdisciplinary origins of the atrocity report, a special kind of political document that is still used to promote the establishment of a war crimes tribunal. Yet, it is little known that the origins of the genre date back more than a hundred years, and were shaped not only by an increasing desire for global justice, but also by the needs of wartime propaganda.

Part I: Writing the History of International Criminal Law and the Problem of Precedents

Scholarly interest in the history of war crimes tribunals only began in 1945, as lawyers strove to legitimize the rather extraordinary tribunals established in Nuremberg and Tokyo. The abandoned attempt to try the German Kaiser after the First World War made a poor precedent, and both the farcical Leipzig War crime trials of the 1920s and the abandoned Istanbul trials of the same period had created the impression that war crime tribunals were simply a place where the vindictiveness of victor's justice met the obstructionist zeal of revisionism.[2] In this situation, there was a clear interest to establish that war crime tribunals rested upon much sounder historical foundations. Georg Schwarzenberger, a German lawyer who had fled from the Nazis to Britain, was the first to point towards an obscure episode in German late medieval history as the starting point of the legal development towards modern war crime tribunals.

Until this point, the trial of Peter von Hagenbach in 1474 would only have been known to medievalists, but now Schwarzenberger cautiously suggested that 'it may be held that this trial offers a much needed precedent (in a non-technical sense) of a case in which war crimes in the wider sense of the term—as used in the Charter of the Nuremberg Tribunal—have come before an international bench'.[3] Arthur Nussbaum, another German refugee lawyer, chose to embrace the Hagenbach case as the origin of a tradition that culminated in modern war crime tribunals in his highly influential 'Concise History of the Law of Nations', probably simply because such a precedent was 'much needed'.[4] Following Nussbaum and stripped of Schwarzenberger's many caveats, the case became ubiquitous in textbooks of international law and international criminal law, with leading international criminal lawyer Cherif Bassiouni claiming in 2010 that 'for all practical purposes and in accordance with contemporary standards, this established the first international criminal tribunal'.[5]

This is problematic for a number of reasons: first, the Hagenbach trial was not 'international' in the modern sense, but conducted by an assembly of towns that belonged to the dissolving Holy Roman Empire, and were united in their wish to reject the territorial pretensions of Hagenbach's overlord Charles the Bold. It has been argued that the various entities of the Holy Roman Empire were so independent that their interactions can be compared to modern international relations, but examples like this one based on the agency of a spontaneous league of disgruntled cities highlight the very different world of European politics before the Thirty Years War. Second, it was not a war crime tribunal, since the allegations concerned Hagenbach's behaviour as bailiff in a part of Alsace, and no legal doctrine of criminal responsibility was applied here that did not emerge from mediaeval vassal-overlord thinking, with its sometimes rigid rights and duties of knights. After intensive torture, he was convicted of crimes 'which he as a knight was deemed to have a duty to prevent', and ritually stripped of his knighthood before execution. Next to alleged violations of his feudal duties, Hagenbach was also formally charged for the introduction of a hugely unpopular consumption tax—a sentiment that is still understandable to human beings living in the twenty-first century, but not commonly dealt with before war crimes tribunals.

Moreover, by any standard, modern or contemporary, a trial that results in numerous villages being burned down in revenge by the brother of the defendant is not a triumph of justice, which is why it did not enter German history as an example of the power of the law.[6] Its 'discovery' in 1946 rather serves as an example of why historians warn about the need to look at such early cases on their own terms, and not present them out of context to make them fit into an agenda half a millennium later.[7] Curiously, when the case was first cited at Nuremberg, it was as precedent for extending the tribunal's remit beyond war crimes: US prosecutor Telford Taylor argued in the *Ministries* trial (prosecuting leading bureaucrats from the Foreign Office and other ministries) that Hagenbach should inspire the judges to indict high-ranking German officials for a variety of offences committed before September 1939. Unimpressed, the judges chose to entirely ignore the 'precedent'—a fact that the history sections of international criminal law textbooks usually omit.[8]

The second case commonly cited as a precursor to modern war crime tribunals is many centuries younger, but equally unpersuasive. Henry Wirz, a Swiss immigrant who had fought for the Confederacy in the American Civil War and been in charge of a prisoner of war camp in Georgia, was tried in Washington DC in August 1865 by a military tribunal composed of his former enemies. They found him guilty of war crimes, in particular the criminal neglect of his starving and ill prisoners, but also the direct murder of 13 prisoners. This was undoubtedly a war crime tribunal, and the precedent of a special tribunal set up by the victors of a recent conflict was useful for the 'pre-history' of Nuremberg. Yet, it was conducted in the frenzied atmosphere just after the assassination of Abraham Lincoln, and there are persisting allegations of it being little more than a show trial that was always bound to end in a public execution.[9] Former Southern general Robert E. Lee testified that the dire conditions at the camp were primarily the result of the Union's refusal to exchange prisoners and the general lack of food and medical supplies caused by the blockade of the South and the brutal 'scorched earth' campaigns conducted by the North, in particular that of General Sherman in Georgia. Similar arguments persuaded another military tribunal shortly afterwards to acquit the commander of a prisoner of war camp accused of war crimes—therefore, this case did not enter the 'pre-history' of Nuremberg as a widely known precedent.[10] Moreover, a key witness describing the murders committed by Wirz may have done so under a false name. Nevertheless, the attraction of this case for early twentieth-century lawyers was that the judges explicitly rejected Wirz's attempt to employ the 'superior orders' defence, so often claimed by German defendants before the Leipzig war crime tribunal.[11] Together, the trials of Hagenbach and Wirz are presented as somehow forming a coherent tradition leading towards international war crime tribunals and, thereby, make up for the problem that all calls for an International Criminal Court (ICC) had been consistently rejected since they were first raised by Gustave Moynier in 1872.

After the Precedents: Writing the History of International Justice Today

Nevertheless, the attempts by Moynier and others to achieve progress in international law through a mixture of professional practice and activism have fascinated a second wave of lawyers interested in the origins of their discipline. The end of all formal development of international criminal law caused by the Cold War all but ended the scholarly interest in its history, but those who persevered were now freed from the need to find precedents. Instead, they became increasingly interested in the biographies of leading international lawyers to find out how their predecessors had achieved progress in a nineteenth-century world that was often hostile to international courts. The best-known work of this type is Martti Koskenniemi's *Gentle Civiliser of Nations* that employed sociological approaches to track the successes and failures of leading lawyers and the establishment of the modern academic discipline of international law. Other authors have celebrated the pioneers of the movement for international arbitration or, indeed, Gustave Moynier's fight for an ICC.[12]

The most recent scholarship takes a more critical perspective: shaped by the ongoing disputes over the political nature of the ICC, scholars are now interested in the biases, mindsets and political purposes of these activist lawyers: for example, James Brown Scott's fight for a single international court, conducted through the *American Society for Judicial Settlement of International Disputes* he had founded in 1910, is now understood as inspired by a highly flawed reading of US history which assumed that the Supreme Court had united the various states in common purpose.[13] According to this logic, any alternative international court, such as one specifically for war crimes, had to be prevented to allow international law to succeed in its unifying mission. An even more critical school of lawyers highlights the imperial roots of international law, arguing that one of its main functions was always the suppression of non-European peoples.[14] This school of thought has obvious repercussions for the current debate as to why the ICC began as a project of European powers but now seems to focus its efforts on prosecuting Africans. The latest research in this field, sometimes labelled as the 'turn to practice', explicitly acknowledges the intimate relationship between the legal and political spheres and tries to explore the political circumstances that shaped the creation of new legal norms while trying to move away from Eurocentrism.[15]

A major branch of research looking specifically at war crimes developed as a response to the genocidal violence in Rwanda and Bosnia in the 1990s: historians and political scientists wondered how such horrible war crimes could occur amid ethnic conflict that did not seem markedly more severe than in many other places on the planet. The obvious questions raised were whether the veneer of civilization was much thinner than everybody had thought, and if there was a way to predict or even prevent large-scale atrocities. Moreover, were our notions of human rights and civilian immunity the manifestation of a genuinely human and universal desire to protect those members of our species who cannot defend themselves against wanton abuse and murder? Or were the emerging critics of the human rights agenda correct to argue that this entire concept of individual human rights was a recent Western invention that was now imposed on other cultures with imperialist zeal, whether labelled 'humanitarian intervention' or not? In other words, can we write *one* global history of war crimes?[16]

This new scholarly interest in war crimes and the creation of the ICC inevitably led to a fresh look at courts and tribunals. But while the triumphalist accounts of the Nuremberg and Tokyo tribunals were quickly replaced with more balanced histories of these trials, historians found it much more difficult to establish the roots of war crime tribunals before the twentieth century and, indeed, the First World War. For example, when Gary Bass designed his case-studies-based volume *Stay the Hand of Vengeance: The Politics of War Crime Tribunals*, his only case before the First World War was the plan of holding a tribunal to punish Napoleon in 1815—an idea soon dismissed as impractical and much more dangerous for the Bourbon restoration in France than simply banishing Napoleon to somewhere very remote.[17] So did the idea of war crime tribunals emerge spontaneously out of a desire to blame the German Kaiser for the horrors of the First World War, or did it have deeper roots? And if so, what is the real history of what we call human rights? And why are so many of the key terms, such as civilian immunity, war crimes, genocide or crimes against humanity, such recent additions to our vocabulary? The following section attempts a brief outline of how efforts to ban atrocities against civilians and codify the laws of war in the second half of the nineteenth century established the idea that such crimes should be tried before international tribunals in the early twentieth century.

Part II: From Atrocity to 'War Crime': The Early History of War Crimes Tribunals

Historians have rejected the notion of a direct path towards modern war crimes tribunals through the centuries, with a small number of key precedents like Hagenbach or Wirz as the key stepping stones. Recent work has shown that the limitation of violence against civilians was more than just an ambition of philosophers, but, for example, the early modern evidence that has been found is perhaps best described as emerging trade standards among the various bands of mercenaries that did much of the fighting at that time.[18] The main development that would ultimately lead to war crimes tribunals is the beginning of the codification of the laws of war in the second half of the nineteenth century. The Declaration of Paris had marked an important breakthrough in establishing the technique: having emerged as a by-product of the Paris peace conference that ended the Crimean War in 1856, it was the first time that the great powers made real efforts to encourage all nations to sign up to a treaty and make its provisions universally accepted law.[19] This approach of first having a conference to draft and vote on new treaties and then asking every state to join was repeated numerous times, leading to a network of international rules and obligations on a wide variety of issues such as postal and telegraph communications, transport, illegal drugs or sanitation.

The earliest conventions of this type tended to focus on the laws of war, establishing it as a clear contemporary priority: shocked by the vast bloodshed he saw at the battle of Solferino in 1859, Henry Dunant organized the conference that would pass the Geneva Convention for the Amelioration of the Condition of the Wounded in Armies in the Field in 1864, after having established the Red Cross organization one year earlier. The second major document of that time period was also primarily about preventing unnecessary suffering of soldiers: most major powers signed the 1868 St. Petersburg Declaration, which banned the use of particularly cruel types of ammunition. But there was more to this development than simply a desire to protect the soldiers, and the instructions to naval officers fighting in the Crimean War broke new ground with their explicit order to spare the life and property of civilians as far as possible. When the Admiralty in London demanded more comprehensive bombardments unhampered by such restrictions, the local commanders refused and cited the negative impact of bombarding civilians on global public opinion as the prime reason.

This new restraint was partly caused by the simple fact that news travelled much quicker via telegraph and reached a much wider audience in a new era of cheap newspapers and mass literacy. But there was a crucial second element that we are still struggling to fully understand: for whatever reason, public opinion in Europe and the United States began to place a much increased value on the protection of civilians in wartime. Slowly, older concepts of town communities that choose sides in a conflict and suffer the possible consequences as a community (e.g. the sacking of a town after its military defences had been overcome) were replaced by liberal concepts of individual rights: even if a town had picked the weaker side in a vicious civil war, its residents were still individuals and could expect their rights to life and property to be respected even by a successful invader. This applied particularly to women, children and the elderly, but the most active proponents of this new view were the communities of foreign merchants that, after 1850, could be found in almost any sizable settlement in the world—the widespread use of the formula 'civilian life *and property*' in this time period highlights the desire to see warehouses protected as well as civilian life.

The 1863 Lieber code, commissioned as a manual for the Union troops fighting against the Confederacy in the American Civil War, summarized the existing customary laws of warfare and was fully aware of the recent shift from community to individual rights. As German-American scholar Francis Lieber wrote:

> The almost universal rule in remote times was, and continues to be with barbarous armies, that the private individual of the hostile country is destined to suffer every privation of liberty and protection, and every disruption

> of family ties. Protection was, and still is with uncivilized people, the exception. In modern regular wars of the Europeans, and their descendants in other portions of the globe, protection of the inoffensive citizen of the hostile country is the rule; privation and disturbance of private relations are the exceptions.[20]

The aim of the manual was to provide a guide for the difficult task of balancing the protection of the innocent and defenceless with the sometimes grim requirements of military necessity. While some argue today that the German-American scholar Francis Lieber erred by granting officers too much leeway in the name of 'necessity', it was his written manual that exposed this tension in a way that was hard to overlook.[21] In other words, it raised the question of where precisely the line between a justifiable invocation of military necessity and an unjustifiable atrocity lay—exactly the kind of task fulfilled today by a court of law conducting a war crimes investigation.

Do We Need International War Crimes Tribunals?

The brutal fighting of the Franco-German War, which involved the bombardment of Paris and Strasbourg and the use of insurgent fighters in civilian clothes (the infamous *franc-tireurs*), led to both sides repeatedly accusing each other of overstepping that very line. This was the precise moment when Gustave Moynier made his famous call for an *international* tribunal to decide such questions and punish those who had overstepped the mark. The title of his brief pamphlet, calling for the 'creation of an appropriate international judicial institution to prevent and punish infractions of the Geneva conventions' is further evidence of the link between codification and an emerging desire to have an international court that could enforce these new rules. Moreover, the war had highlighted the need to clarify the rules for insurgency, counter-insurgency and military occupation, which led to a conference attended by 15 European powers in Brussels in 1874. The resulting Brussels Declaration established new limitations on the rights associated with military occupation and introduced a clear distinction between combatants and non-combatants. It also limited the concept of military necessity by stating that the belligerent's right to adopt whatever means they wished to injure the enemy was not unlimited, and that certain practices such as the use of poison or denying quarter to captured enemy soldiers were simply illegal. However, the treaty was never formally ratified, and a French call to establish a duty to punish war crimes in national courts was ignored by the other delegates.

Yet, the Brussels Declaration was no failure, since together with the *Oxford Manual of the Laws of War on Land* published six years later by leading academics, it proved the main inspiration for the rules adopted at the 1899 First Hague Peace Conference.[22] The Hague Peace Conference was initiated by the Russian Tsar, and while its main aim of European disarmament was a resounding failure, it marked two important breakthroughs: the 1899 Hague Convention on the Laws and Customs with Respect to War on Land was a comprehensive summary of the existing rules; signed by almost two dozen states, it was the first document with a credible claim for universal legitimacy. Crucially, the 26 states represented at the conference included extra-European powers like Mexico, Iran, Japan, China and Thailand. The second breakthrough was the establishment of formal legal procedures to resolve serious disputes between states: the Hague Convention on the Pacific Settlement of Disputes established a Permanent Court of Arbitration in The Hague, but also included a lesser-known forum called an 'international commission of inquiry'. In an unexpected twist, it was this more informal route to an international tribunal that almost paved the way for a universal system of international tribunals to deal with war crimes.

It all began in October 1904 with Russia's decision to send its Baltic Fleet around the world to turn the tide in its war with Japan. The fleet's gunners were put on high alert because of persistent rumours of a planned attack by Japanese torpedo boats in European waters, and when they encountered the Hull fishing fleet on the night of 21 October 1904, several vessels opened fire at the trawlers. The British public was incredulous that the Russian Navy might have accidently sunk a British trawler and killed and injured harmless fishermen plying their trade in the popular fishing grounds of the Dogger Bank, halfway between Denmark and the English East Coast. The Russian Ambassador Benckendorff was mobbed at Victoria train station amid speculation that the attack might have been deliberate.[23] Russia promised compensation and an immediate investigation to allay the calls for war, but soon the British government began to doubt whether this inquiry would amount to more than a whitewash for the fleet's commander, Admiral Rozhestvensky.

Britain's Foreign Secretary Lansdowne now demanded an *international* investigation, and spontaneously drafted a hybrid of a commission of inquiry as outlined in the 1899 Hague Convention on the Pacific Settlement of Disputes, and an internationalized court martial. Therefore, the judges representing the two powers concerned and three neutral ones would not be lawyers, but high-ranking naval officers.[24] When Prime Minister Balfour announced the tribunal, he emphasized that 'the persons found guilty by that tribunal will be tried and adequately punished'.[25] The press recognized that an international body trying individual officers of a great power was unprecedented, with *The Economist* commenting that Russia deserved great respect for agreeing to this extraordinary tribunal since 'it is never pleasant to throw your own officers over'.[26] In fairness, Russia's agreement to the tribunal's precise terms was partly brought about by the fact that the Royal Navy blockaded the Russian fleet in the Spanish port of Vigo and only allowed them to leave after four officers deemed to have been involved in the shooting had left their vessels and proceeded to face the tribunal in Paris.[27]

The idea was for the form of punishment to be determined by the Russian side, but the question of guilt to be decided by the international inquiry alone.[28] The tribunal explored the event of that tragic night in great detail and rejected the Russian claim that an attack by Japanese torpedo boats had actually occurred. It concluded that Russian officers had misidentified one of their own vessels as an attacker, and had fired hundreds of shells at the fishing fleet in the ensuing chaos without being compelled to do so by any military necessity. When the full report was published in the *London Times*, it carried the headline 'Russian admiral held responsible—the firing not justified'.[29] Other newspapers also used the language of criminal law, with *The Economist* noting that Rozhestvensky had been found 'guilty, with extenuating circumstances' and the *Chicago Tribune* claiming that 'whatever the extenuating circumstances, Rozhestvensky is condemned'.[30]

It was indeed the first time an international body had accused a leading officer of a great power of committing a war crime, even if in this case caused by negligence rather than criminal intent. Rozhestvensky was never punished for the events of the Dogger Bank, but was court-martialled after his defeat to the Japanese in the battle of Tsushima and died a recluse in 1909. Although forgotten today, the inquiry into the 'North Sea Incident' made headlines across the world, and was recognized as the first time that an international body applied criminal law. Andre Mandelstam, one of the lawyers representing Russia at the tribunal, wrote an article in the leading international law journal of the time suggesting that the precedent should be used to establish a mechanism for the punishment of violations of international law, based on the idea that an international body should act like a jury in a criminal trial and determine guilt and responsibility. In a second step, the state to which the convicted individual belonged would then determine the punishment.[31]

Naturally, the idea of extending the mandate of commissions of inquiry into criminal law was raised at the Second Hague Peace Conference in 1907, but the other delegates rejected this Russian proposal. They argued that this might lead to a situation where the use of such commissions in similar cases might be seen as compulsory, rather than remaining the sovereign decision of states.[32] In other words, it might lead to something looking very much like an ICC with compulsory jurisdiction. The drafters of the second Hague Conference are often accused of creating and codifying a vast body of law binding the military forces of the world, but forgetting to establish any international mechanism that might punish transgressions. As we have seen, this is incorrect: the drafters did not *forget* to establish a formal route for prosecuting war crimes, but explicitly rejected the idea. Yet, the response to the Dogger Bank tribunal had also shown that the general public was rather more open to the idea of putting individual officers before international tribunals than their governments.

What Is a 'War Crime'? Propaganda and the Law

Therefore, when Europe descended into the First World War, the laws of war lacked a specific tribunal but had just been codified to a remarkable extent, with the Second Hague Peace Conference passing 14 different conventions and declarations. Codification of the laws of war had now reached a scale, complexity and universal acceptance that made it possible to define 'war crimes' with great precision. Violence or abuse of civilians or captured enemy soldiers was not just morally unacceptable, but a clear violation of duties explicitly laid out in treaties and signed by all belligerents.[33] For that reason, it was also possible to describe some or all of the enemy's soldiers as 'criminals' in First World War propaganda. This began with propaganda posters showing facsimiles of the 1839 treaty on Belgian neutrality that Germany had violated with its invasion, but this line never excited working-class audiences and was soon replaced by a much more engaging propaganda focus on German violence against civilians in Belgium. Allegations of sexual violence proved particularly effective, and both the original invasion and the atrocities against Belgian civilians were collectively referred to as the 'Rape of Belgium'.[34]

It was this new form of 'atrocity propaganda' that led to the definition of the term 'war crime' in its modern meaning. In an article published in 1916 and arguing for the punishment of war criminals, Hugh Bellot still felt the need to explain the terminology in his second sentence: 'By war crimes I mean those acts of the armed forces of a belligerent against the person or property of the enemy, combatant or non-combatant, which are deemed contrary to the established usages of war'.[35] This explicit definition of the modern meaning of war crimes was necessary, since the term existed before but commonly referred to the kind of crimes that can only be committed in war, such as spying for the enemy. A particularly good example to show the shift in meaning is a 1917 debate in the House of Commons where a speaker raised the fate of Edith Cavell, whose execution was a famous symbol of anti-German war crime propaganda, but admitted straight at the beginning that 'it is not disputed that Miss Cavell was, according to the strict law of the War, guilty of a war crime' (in her case helping prisoners escape), before condemning her summary execution as the violation of a 'higher law'.[36]

The new propaganda focus on 'war crimes' had two distinct advantages: first, it allowed for propaganda that whipped up public hatred of the enemy and described events like the Belgian atrocities committed by the German army (and others that were fictional) as crimes, persuading even the doubters that this was a war between law and civilization on the one side, and lawlessness and savagery on the other. Second, the prospect of war crime trials after the end of the war allowed the government to calm the public when it demanded immediate and brutal reprisals, for example, against captured submariners or Zeppelin crews who were blamed for attacks that led to high civilian casualties. But the debates about the correct treatment of such suspected war criminals exposed a lack of certainty on core principles of the new war crime trial regime: when Churchill decided to put captured submariners into a harsher form of detention, Germany put 39 officers into a much less privileged form of captivity in reprisal.[37] Therefore, the government was criticized for putting the life and health of captured British soldiers at risk, and even came under attack for the principle behind the special treatment of submarine crews: Charles Cripps, First Baron Parmoor, questioned whether it was at all possible under international law to try a soldier for an offence committed under direct orders.[38] The Marquess of Crewe defended the government stance, while admitting it was 'a matter of opinion'. He argued that

> it is possible to overstate the extent to which the existence of orders, or of permission to perform a certain act, ought to be treated as entirely whitewashing those who perform the particular act. If you carry that argument to an extreme, the indiscriminate murders of civilians, the handing over of a town to rape and robbery, might be taken to be, if not actually commanded, at any rate authorized by the superior command.[39]

When Arthur Balfour replaced Churchill as First Lord of the Admiralty in late May 1915, one of his first acts was to inform Parliament that there was no longer any special treatment for captured submariners. He insisted that their behaviour had been criminal, but declared that 'the general question of personal responsibility should be reserved until the end of the War'.[40] This episode highlights the elegance of post-war trials as a political solution: it showed to the public that the outrageous acts would not go unpunished, while avoiding for now the need to engage in debates of vexed problems such as whether a submarine crew following orders to torpedo civilian vessels was excused by the principle of command responsibility or not. MPs even suspected that the government might be less than sincere in its commitment to put suspected war criminals on trial, and repeatedly asked whether it kept systematic records of war crimes that would allow it to pursue guilty individuals after the war.[41]

What Is a 'Crime Against Humanity' and Should It Be Prosecuted?

This promise to prosecute war crimes was not restricted to Germany, and when it was applied to Turkey's persecution of Armenians, it led to the legal re-definition of another crucial new term—'crimes against humanity'. The phrase had originally been used to describe universally condemned practices such as slavery or piracy,[42] but became popular as a colourful oratory device to condemn a wide variety of evils in the 1870s, and was notably used by anti-imperialist radicals to denounce British expansionism in the Zulu wars,[43] the Egyptian Invasion[44] and the Boer War in 1899.[45] Just before the First World War, 'crime against humanity' still carried no clear legal meaning and was used for issues such as the failure to promote a perfect union of English speaking peoples,[46] the failure to prevent a war between Britain and Germany,[47] or the failure to implement modern security measures in coal mines.[48] However, the phrase acquired its present status in one of the most remarkable documents of the First World War. After listing a number of places where massacres against the Armenian population had been committed since the middle of April 1915, 'with the connivance and often assistance of Ottoman authorities', the joint statement of Britain, France and Russia of 24 May 1915 continued:

> In view of these new crimes of Turkey against humanity and civilization, the Allied Governments announce publicly to the Sublime Porte that they will hold personally responsible for these crimes all members of the Ottoman Government, as well as those of their agents who are implicated in such massacres.[49]

Viscount Bryce was the first to raise the issue in Parliament in late July, claiming that according to information at his disposal the old intention of Abdul Hamid II 'to do what he could to exterminate the Christian population is now being carried out with frightful effectiveness'.[50] The government confirmed that information collected by the Foreign Office coincided with Bryce's, and that a warning had been issued to Ottoman authorities but had not had any effect in limiting the slaughter. All that could be done now was to 'repeat with emphasis' that the guilty should and would be punished.[51] Bryce later described the persecution, murder and deportations of Armenians as widespread, 'premeditated' and 'systematic'. In other words, it happened because orders had been given from above, and it happened throughout the Ottoman Empire. Bryce's speech precisely anticipated the modern definition of crimes against humanity as used in the ICC's Rome Statute, which criminalizes atrocities 'when committed as part of a widespread or systematic attack directed against any civilian population, with knowledge of the attack'.[52]

The First War Crimes Trials After the First World War

Once the Allies had won the war, it seemed a natural step to establish war crimes tribunals. Responding to public enthusiasm for the idea, Lloyd George even made a war crime tribunal for Kaiser Wilhelm II a central part of his December 1918 election campaign.[53] Lloyd George had French support for the idea, but encountered strong opposition from the United States. The American public was largely in favour of a trial, but the US delegation in Paris strongly argued that the multinational tribunal suggested by their European allies had no precedent in international law. The only precedent they accepted was that of Henry Wirz, whose war crime tribunal was being popularized by leading US lawyers at this time to justify the calls for further such prosecutions. Helpfully, Henry Wirz was now consistently remembered to have been of German, instead of Swiss, origin.[54] Once agreement for a trial of the Kaiser was secured, a further problem emerged: the Hague conventions banned many forms of war crimes, but they did not explicitly ban the aggression of one state against another, or the failure to respect general treaties such as that securing Belgian neutrality. For want of a better-fitting crime, Wilhelm II was charged with 'a supreme offence against international morality and the sanctity of treaties'.[55]

The Dutch decision to refuse the extradition of the Kaiser spared the Allies a potentially embarrassing trial.[56] Yet, the Versailles treaty had not only demanded the right to try the Kaiser but obliged Germany to deliver anyone accused of violations of the laws of war to be brought before a military tribunal (Art. 228), while guaranteeing only the defendant's right to name his own counsel (Art. 229). However, the Allies soon realized that securing the extradition of hundreds of high-ranking soldiers, many of whom were considered war heroes by the German population, would make any form of compliance with the treaty as a whole much more difficult for any German government. Moreover, it might invite unwelcome debates over whether war crimes were committed by the winners as well as the losers of the conflict. Therefore, it was decided to risk going along with the German demand of trying those accused of war crimes before national courts. Out of the number of the accused, the Allies selected a 'test list' of 45 cases where it was thought that the evidence was so compelling as to ensure a conviction in any court. Unfortunately, the German authorities found it a real struggle to locate all defendants, or find sufficient evidence to prosecute them; therefore, the Leipzig War Crime Trials at Germany's highest court only ever involved 12 cases. For the first time, a German court now considered novel concepts such as whether an illegal order exculpates the soldier following it, or at what point military action against civilians can never be justified by military necessity. When the court felt unable to see the second condition fulfilled in any of the cases, and dealt with the first problem by adjudicating that torpedoing a hospital ship was fine if covered by a direct order (*Dover Castle* case), but criminal behaviour if the submarine crew also machine-gunned any survivors drifting in the sea (*Llandovery Castle* case), it had sealed its reputation abroad. The sentence handed out in the latter case (four years in prison) was by far the highest—most defendants walked free or faced not more than a couple of months in prison. Despite the outcry abroad, many Germans felt the trials had been a national humiliation, not least because some soldiers were actually sent to civilian prisons—a severe violation of their military honour. With no clear will on the Allied side to enforce the continuation of such trials outside of Germany, the experiment ended in dismal failure.[57]

That lack of willingness to prosecute further was not only caused by the political situation in Europe, but also by the waning Allied will to continue the prosecution of Ottoman war criminals. The Treaty of Sevres included very similar rules regarding war crime trials and extraditions as the Versailles Treaty (Art. 226–228), with the addition of special rules designed to include those responsible for the Armenian genocide even if they were currently outside of the country (Art. 229–230).[58] However, the Allies agreed to a similar experiment as in the German case and permitted the Turkish side to conduct its own court martials. These proceedings never had a chance to rise above the major political conflict of the day over the future of the House of Osman and the Ottoman Empire, which would ultimately and amid much bloodshed lead to the creation of the modern state of Turkey. The tribunals quickly convicted a group of eight former high officials who had fled the country before the armistice, but during its year of investigations it became increasingly clear that the court was unwilling to convict anybody who was actually within reach of the authorities.

Frustrated, the British government ended the experiment by bringing dozens of suspects to its naval base in Malta and attempted to set up an international tribunal to try them for crimes against British soldiers and Armenian civilians. However, without the cooperation of the Turkish authorities, it proved impossible to compile evidence that did not only prove state-sponsored mass violence but also individual guilt. When the power struggle between the two competing governments in Constantinople and Ankara clearly shifted in favour of Kemal Ataturk, there was no longer any prospect of the necessary cooperation, and the suspects were returned in exchange for British prisoners of war.[59]

Do We Need an International Criminal Court?

After the attempts to try First World War criminals had ended in disaster, the old idea of an ICC was revived in the interwar period. An early proposal was rejected by the League of Nations Assembly since it was felt that there was no such thing as international criminal law; however, under the leadership of British lawyer Hugh Bellot, the International Law Association (ILA) embraced the cause and presented a draft statute at the 34th meeting of the organization in Vienna in 1926. The draft was accepted by the conference participants, but when Hugh Bellot died in the midst of the 35th ILA conference in Warsaw in 1928, the cause lost its most committed agitator. International criminal lawyers are perfectly entitled to point towards these efforts as the intellectual roots of their discipline, but it would be wrong to claim that this initiative or even the thinking behind it was embraced by the profession as a whole. The arguments of the critics were best summarized by James L. Brierly, holder of the prestigious Chichele Chair of International Law and Diplomacy at Oxford University, in his 1927 article 'Do we need an international criminal court':

> The notion that war crimes can be banished from war or even appreciably reduced by the institution of a criminal court is probably a delusion, akin to that more general delusion which believes that war can be more or less humanized by law; and even if this were not so, an international court to deal with war crimes after a war is over would still be undesirable, because the supreme need then is to calm the passions which the war has raised and to work for the prevention of another, and no conflicting aim is comparable in importance with that.[60]

It was the experience of the Second World War that changed the mainstream view within the legal profession, and convinced the Allies that putting major German and Japanese war criminals on trial was a better pathway to a safer post-war future than simply 'calming the passions'. As this brief historical outline has shown, this is not a story of slow but steady progress towards the ultimate goal of an ICC. Once the laws of war had been codified and universally accepted by all states, the criminalization of war crimes inevitably led to the idea of war crimes tribunals. These were tried and tested both before and after the First World War, and found to be fraught with political difficulties and fears about state sovereignty. When the idea was revived in Nuremberg and Tokyo, it was not because previous experience with such tribunals had been positive, but because of a clear determination not to let the German and Japanese crimes go unpunished, however difficult, expensive and unpopular the trials were going to be.

War crimes tribunals are about the human desire for justice, but whenever they were tried, it became clear just how difficult it can be to distinguish between justice and revenge. Moreover, the tribunals will always be expected to both conduct their business in the sober and detached way of an exemplary court of law, *and* to fulfil an important role in international politics. Once war crimes tribunals were revived in the 1990s, it soon emerged that it had not become any easier to meet the expectations of victims while rising above politicized justice.

Part III: The Intricate Genre of the Atrocity Report

The third part of this chapter looks at a type of document that is a very common interim step between a war crime being committed and a tribunal being implemented: the atrocity report. In particular, the two reports published under Bryce's name in 1915 and 1916 on German atrocities in Belgium and the Armenian massacres are perfect examples to study the transition from atrocity reports written by activists to a more professional setup that was deliberately interdisciplinary. Moreover, the contrasting fate of both reports—with one widely dismissed as peddling unfounded propaganda claims, and the other still seen as key evidence in a historical debate—encourages a closer look at the decisions the drafters took to ensure their report would survive the purgatory of world public opinion, both at the time of its publication and beyond.

The mission of every atrocity report is not just to alert the global public and world leaders to the fact that war crimes are being committed. Crucially, its task is to break through the cycle of accusations and denials by establishing a neutral and unassailable account of the events that places the occurrence of war crimes and the identities of the perpetrators beyond reasonable doubt. Yet, the challenge is enormous: often, with limited or no access to the territory where the crimes happened, authors of atrocity reports must work fast and write with journalistic flair to capture the attention of global media and persuade world leaders to take action and either intervene or establish a war crime tribunal. At the same time, their reports must be sober and factual to avoid allegations of sensationalism, and their contents must satisfy the sceptical mind of a lawyer. Thus, finding the right balance between the ambition to thoroughly vet evidence to ensure it would stand up in any future court, and the need to complete the report as quickly as possible to maximize its political impact, is at the very heart of human rights fact-finding.[61]

The obvious answer to the variety of different skills needed is to establish an interdisciplinary team, and this was the route taken in one of the earliest and most influential atrocity reports—the Bryce report on German atrocities in Belgium in 1915. Together with his report on the Armenian genocide published one year later, Bryce not only established the standards for atrocity reports, but also contributed significantly to the very development of our legal concepts of war crimes and crimes against humanity. Yet, the legacy of both reports is tarnished by the fact that they were products of British government propaganda intended to expose the misdeeds of the enemy, and a closer look at the circumstances of their creation offers fascinating insights into the mechanisms that shape the writing, the impact and the legacy of atrocity reports.

The First Atrocity Reports

Pamphlets describing the horrible deeds of enemy armed forces have been a part of wartime propaganda since the invention of print, but the origins of our modern genre of atrocity reports can be found in the late nineteenth century. Among the first ones was the Sassoun report of 1896, which investigated massacres against Armenian Christians in the Anatolian provinces of the Ottoman Empire. Amid warnings that disgust at the atrocities in Europe could lead to 'active interference' if the crimes remained unpunished persuaded the Ottoman authorities to set up a commission of inquiry, and further British pressure assured the active involvement of delegates from Britain, France and Russia.[62] While their instructions only asked them to 'superintend' the Ottoman inquiry,[63] the three foreign delegates immediately ensured the dismissal of the local governor.[64] When the Turkish commissioners refused to visit the site of an alleged atrocity, the foreign delegates simply rode out on their own and forced the other members to scramble after them. Upon arrival, they discovered numerous mass graves.[65]

In many aspects, the report jointly produced by the three foreign delegates reads very much like a modern investigation into mass atrocities: it clearly established why the account of the events given by the local military commander was implausible, emphasized the strategic use of sexual violence against minorities and included pages of tables linking specific victims, alleged perpetrators and the witnesses implicating them.[66] This is very similar to the attempts by current commissions of inquiry set up by international organizations to compile lists of suspects for future prosecution.[67] They also applied a rather modern concept to establish the personal responsibility of the commander due to his failure to prevent the crimes: in their judgement, his inaction when he must have known what Kurdish militias were doing nearby 'is as weighty a condemnation of his conduct as if the troops had directly participated in the engagement'.[68] The proximity of their instincts to modern feeling on human rights is further highlighted by their attempt to set up a rudimentary witness protection programme and to organize a relief effort for destitute refugees.[69] The criminal prosecution that the authors so clearly desired never happened, but their report shaped the perception of these events and Ottoman responsibility in European capitals.[70] The report explains why European governments were so quick to recognize the next wave of Armenian prosecutions in 1915 as organized by the Ottoman state, but it did not make a major public impact at the time it was written. Written jointly by the three diplomats, its intended audience was government bureaucrats and it was not designed for public impact, even though the Armenian atrocities were covered extensively in the press at the time. The outrage was particularly pronounced in the United States, where it dominated the foreign policies agendas of both candidates for the presidential election of 1896, and in September 1895, *The New York Times* labelled the atrocities the 'Armenian Holocaust'.[71]

Had the contents of the report become public knowledge, it might have tipped the scales in favour of intervention or stronger pressure on the Ottoman government, but the first report to single-handedly end atrocities through its public impact only came a few years later, during the Boer War (1899–1902). Alerted by rumours that as part of the counter-insurgency effort to contain Boer guerrilla units, women and children were held in internment camps where many died from malnutrition and disease, a group of peace activists sent welfare and women's rights campaigner Emily Hobhouse to South Africa. The Hobhouse report, published in 1901, caused an outrage and led to the establishment of the Fawcett Commission.[72] This government-endorsed group was perhaps meant to rebuke Hobhouse's claims, but after returning from South Africa it corroborated all of them, and, if anything, went further in its calls for immediate action. There was now no other political option but to take the camps out of the hands of the British Army and put them under civilian control.

Atrocity Reports and First World War Propaganda

From the beginning of the First World War, governments realized the potential for creating unusually effective propaganda by merging the activists' language and methods for creating public impact with the resources of government bureaucracy to investigate facts—this combination set the standard for modern atrocity reports. Significantly for the purposes of this volume, the government assembled a team of authors to ensure that their specialist skills in journalism, history and law would be combined to create a report that would easily translate into newspaper headlines around the world but withstand scholarly criticism. The committee responsible for the Bryce report on German atrocities in Belgium was handpicked and shows what professional skills and personal attributes were seen as necessary: it included four eminent lawyers, each of them knighted, and one of them (Sir Frederick Pollock) also being a distinguished legal historian; a further historian (H.A.L. Fisher) who was also a Liberal politician; and a journalist, the editor of the *Edinburgh Review*, Harold Cox, who had also briefly served as a Liberal MP. In other words, what was deemed necessary was a combination of legal, historical and journalistic skills and a close involvement with the governing political party.

All that was then needed was a distinguished personality who combined all these skills and attributes in one person, and enjoyed a particularly good reputation both in the land of the perpetrators (Germany) and that of the key target audience (the United States). Viscount Bryce ticked all these boxes and was an obvious choice to head the committee and lend his name to the final report. James Bryce had studied in Heidelberg,

Germany, and the book he published on the Holy Roman Empire in 1864 established his reputation as a historian both in Germany and the United Kingdom.[73] However, he was actually a lawyer, having been Regius Professor for Civil Law in Oxford for more than 20 years. He also had considerable journalistic skill, and had been one of the most outspoken critics of the treatment of Boer civilians during the recent war in South Africa, to the detriment of his career as a Liberal politician and MP. Crucially, he had served a highly successful spell as British ambassador to the United States between 1907 and 1913 and had many influential personal friends in US politics.

When the committee began its work, it had, of course, no access to the scenes of the alleged crimes, but could rely on a large number of witness statements taken from Belgian refugees in Britain. However, they never actually heard any witnesses themselves, despite public invitations to submit further evidence when the committee was set up.[74] The government had already asked barristers to examine the materials, and the Attorney General strongly hinted that further efforts by Bryce's committee to acquire fresh evidence were deemed unnecessary.[75] After all, next to the numerous witness statements there were 37 diaries from captured or killed German soldiers freely describing looting or summary executions in cases of suspected support of the enemy. Yet, the diaries contained no evidence of the sexual-sadistic outrages that had featured so prominently in propaganda stories. The accusations of rape, breasts cut off or babies murdered had had a particular impact in the United States, but whenever the committee tried to follow up on UK addresses where Belgian children with their hands cut off, or Belgian girls rendered pregnant by rape, were said to live, they never found any victims.[76]

Requests by individual committee members to hear witnesses again or probe deeper were rejected, and Bryce decided that the report should be organized around the 'big picture', presenting the atrocities by region to rely on the cumulative impression made by the large number of statements rather than some particularly atrocious ones. Harold Cox challenged key claims made in the draft report, including assertions that only evidence that would have been good enough to be put before an English court had been used, or that the barristers had taken the witness statements following clear instructions from the committee itself. Although all of Cox's criticisms were factually correct, the committee sided with Bryce. Only by threatening not to sign off the final report did Cox achieve some changes to the final version, in particular the removal of some doubtful cases of sexual violence.[77]

When the report was published, none of this mattered, since the propaganda claims of German depravity were now seen as confirmed facts. Wellington House, the British propaganda institution that distributed the report worldwide, was delighted: 'Even in papers hostile to the Allies there is not the slightest attempt to impugn the correctness of the facts alleged. Lord Bryce's prestige in America put scepticism out of the question, and many leading articles begin on this note'.[78] Moreover, the decision not to embark upon any ambitious investigation of the evidence allowed the committee to produce its report by early May 1915. Therefore, it was published just five days after the sinking of the *Lusitania* and permanently combined the Belgian atrocities and the sinking of the passenger steamer in American public opinion to form one coherent picture of German barbarism.[79] Bryce understood what was expected of him and delivered, and proved that with a professional, sober structure and the legitimacy of a highly qualified committee, even a report containing highly dubious and uncorroborated claims can be extremely effective propaganda.

However, its methodological flaws exposed the report to revisionist criticism in the interwar years, and they were ruthlessly attacked by pacifists who had never agreed with entering the war in the first place, pro-Germans who felt that Germany was being treated unfairly, and American isolationists who thought the United States had been lured into the war by British propaganda. Together, they exposed the close links between the Bryce committee and British propaganda units, the fact that it created a false impression of how its investigation was conducted, and that the British state seriously struggled to remember where it had deposited the original witness testimony.[80] Soon, the reputation of Bryce's report was in tatters. Yet, most modern historians who have examined the Belgian atrocities agree that, if anything, it underplayed the number of victims. The picture emerging from their research exposes a consistent pattern of male civilians being shot in what either was a remarkably aggressive response to real or imagined offences by civilians against the invading German army, or a deliberate use of force against civilians to crush all forms of resistance, legitimate or not, to push through Belgium as quickly as possible.[81] But during the interwar years, the flaws of the report made it possible to deny not just the allegations of sexual violence, but to dismiss the entire claim of German atrocities against Belgian civilians as Allied propaganda.

The 1916 'Blue Book': Documenting the Armenian Genocide

The atrocities documented in the second report published during the war by Viscount Bryce are on an even grander scale. As mentioned before, the massacres and deportations of Armenians in the Ottoman Empire led directly to the permanent re-definition of the term 'crimes against humanity'. Moreover, the Ottoman Empire was at war with Britain, and the Armenian genocide began on the very day that British and French troops landed at Gallipoli to gain control of the Bosporus. Yet, the motivation behind the commissioning of an atrocity report was subtly different from the German report, with important consequences. The intention behind the report was openly described in Parliament, and rather surprisingly, it was all about separating the violence committed by the Ottoman authorities from the Islamic religion. The debate of 6 October 1915 that directly led to the commissioning of the report by Parliament and its presentation as an official document one year later openly acknowledged that the famous warning of 14 May 1915 had been completely ignored by the Ottoman authorities and that, after the disaster of the Gallipoli campaign, a war crime tribunal was now a very remote prospect.[82] Yet, the Earl of Cromer, the former Consul-General of Egypt, argued there were important reasons why a report on the atrocities should be published as soon as possible:

> There are many special reasons why the facts should be made public. In the first place, it is very desirable to lose no opportunity to let the people of this country know for what we are fighting. We are fighting for a great many things, and one of the objects which I hope we may attain by the end of

> this war is that Armenia shall no longer, as it has done in the past and as I fear it does in the present, constitute a sort of Turkish shambles. In the second place, we have to remember that we have some 70,000,000 Mahomedan fellow-subjects, who naturally have a certain amount of sympathy with their co-religionists and would be unwilling to believe ill of them unless they have positive proof. My belief is that all the educated Mahomedans of India would look with as great a horror as we do ourselves upon the proceedings of the Turkish Government.[83]

Thus, the task was to explain why the dissolution of the Ottoman Empire was a good thing, and to ensure that the atrocities were recognized as state-sponsored rather than sectarian violence and motivated by political rather than religious aims. Once more, Viscount Bryce was entrusted with the task, and once more the report was shaped by the interdisciplinary combination of his training as a lawyer and the historical expertise of the main author—the young Oxford academic Arnold Toynbee.[84] Like Bryce, Toynbee cared deeply about the Armenian cause and had just published a book called 'Armenian Atrocities. The Murder of a Nation', with a foreword by Bryce. Yet, their report was not simply the product of their empathy, but also government propaganda. Toynbee had left his academic position to work for the Wellington House propaganda unit as 'Assistant Director USA propaganda' and 'pamphlet compiler'.[85] Wellington House also ensured the global mass distribution of the report and its quick translation into many languages—this is unlikely to have happened had the narrative of the Armenian catastrophe not suited the general line of propaganda against the Ottoman Empire so exceedingly well.

So should we dismiss the report as a further example of government-led wartime propaganda? Curiously, the initially lower political profile of this report compared to the one on the Belgian atrocities allowed Toynbee to assert a more stringent insistence on academic standards—instead of being outvoted by a committee like Harold Cox had been, he was able to resist Bryce's suggestion to organize the material in a way that focused on what he called the 'important and the striking', that is, those allegations that would most excite public opinion. He also tried to corroborate any evidence as much as he could with other sources, and dismissed material because, for example, the date seemed implausible.[86] There was less pressure to confirm specific claims that had been used in propaganda than there had been on the Bryce commission, and Toynbee and Bryce were free not to follow the frequent propaganda suggestions that Germany might be inciting Turkey to commit these atrocities. Like the Belgian report, the testimony is organized by region, but given the much more complex story told by this report, it includes a section on Armenian history and the context of the 1915 genocide. Toynbee resisted Bryce's suggestion to edit and shorten the many documents reproduced in full to create a more readable pamphlet: as he wrote to Bryce, 'cutting down of documents might give the wrong impression; it might suggest that we had omitted or suppressed material in other places, not merely to save space but to modify the effect of the evidence'.[87] Despite not having access to Anatolia, Toynbee could use a wealth of evidence: there were many witness reports from American missionaries or their Armenian correspondents, and one missionary even had access to consular reports from inside the Ottoman Empire written by US diplomats. Apparently, the State Department was happy to see them included in the report as long as their true origin was hidden and they were also described as witness statements from missionaries.[88] Next to the eyewitness reports, it also re-printed material published in Orientalist journals in Germany to show that even enemy publications acknowledged the reality of the Armenian massacres.

But while being far superior to the Bryce report on Germany, the report published as a parliamentary 'Blue Book' in 1916 did not entirely escape the demands of wartime propaganda. After all, as a memorandum jointly written by Prime Ministers Asquith and Stanley Baldwin in 1924 acknowledges, the Blue Book was 'widely used for Allied propaganda in 1916–1917 and had an important influence upon American opinion and upon the ultimate decision of President Wilson to enter the war'.[89] Yet, since some of the best evidence (the consular reports) was published under a 'false flag' and the names of the witnesses were kept secret to protect them and their families, there was no way to corroborate the authenticity of specific statements. To buttress the credibility of the testimony at the time of its publication in October 1916, Bryce persuaded well-respected scholars in Britain and the United States to 'verify' the report. This was rather disingenuous, since US civil rights campaigner and prominent anti-imperialist Moorfield Storey was a personal friend, and historian H.A.L. Fisher had been Bryce's most committed ally on the Belgian atrocities committee when it came to suppressing Harold Cox's concerns about the quality of the evidence. The third personality 'verifying' the report was Oxford don and Liberal politician Gilbert Murray, who since the 1913 wedding of his daughter Rosalind was Arnold Toynbee's father-in-law. All these individuals were highly respected but were, of course, in no position to vouch for individual statements made by missionaries in Anatolia.

Moreover, the authority of Viscount Bryce was soon once more employed to support a publicity campaign relying on images of gruesome sexual violence to make its point: a US movie based on the account of a female teenage Armenian refugee and called *Ravishing Armenia* included a slide at the beginning that stated 'Each scene and incident has been carefully verified by Lord Bryce'. Bryce's papers reveal that he had no involvement with the creators of the movie.[90] Published in Britain under the less sexually charged title 'Auction of Souls', British censors were shocked by a scene showing the crucifixion of naked Armenian girls and demanded its removal, as well as any reference to the Christian or Muslim religion in the subtitles. Again, concerns over inciting religious violence in British India weighed heavily on the minds of British officials, especially after the 1919 Amritsar massacre committed by British forces. The censors were so eager to avoid the false impression that the violence against the Armenians was linked to the Muslim faith that the film in its altered version appeared to portray senseless slaughter devoid of any political, ethnic or religious context.[91]

Given these close links with propaganda efforts in the Blue Book's creation, distribution and use in film, and the problem that those who explicitly vouched for its veracity were in no position to do so, it should not be presented to students as the equivalent of a modern primary source collection. Michelle Tusan is right to conclude that 'its problematic use as evidence at the time reveals why it remains so difficult to identify, prosecute, and obtain justice for victims of genocide, past and present'.[92] We simply cannot know whether these events happened exactly as described in the report. What we do know is that the testimony sounds perfectly plausible when compared to the many other pieces of evidence suggesting a systematic campaign to exterminate Armenians and other Christians, for which various German and Turkish sources not included in the Blue Book are particularly important.

Such distinctions matter since the question of the Armenian genocide is still a matter of political controversy today, and the unconditional respect Bryce's Blue Book still commands among many genocide scholars has inadvertently created an opening for deniers of the Armenian genocide to claim that the authors and methodology of the Bryce report on German atrocities are identical. By arguing that the one on Germany is discredited while the one on Turkey is still being hailed as a landmark document, it is possible to 'expose' the bias behind the allegations against Turkey. All that is necessary is to suppress two crucial facts: that the Bryce report on Germany makes some false claims but is overall correct, and that the Blue Book is not the only or even fundamental source material in existence to prove the historical reality of the Armenian genocide. In this distorted form, the argument is made not only by denialist websites,[93] but also by scholars holding academic positions at US universities like Justin McCarthy.[94] And he has an eager audience—in a presentation at a conference in Turkey in 2001 that is still available on the Turkish Foreign Ministry's website, McCarthy made the precise argument outlined above:

> The main falsification of history by the Armenian apologists lies not in what they say, but in what they do not say. They do not admit that much of the evidence they rely on is tainted because it was produced by the British propaganda office in World War I. For example, the 'Bryce Report' (…) has recently been reproduced by an Armenian organization, with a long introduction that praises its supposed veracity. Nowhere does the reprint state that the report was produced and paid for by British Propaganda as a way to attack its wartime enemies, the Ottomans. Nor does the reprint state that the other 'Bryce Report,' this one on alleged German atrocities, has long been known by historians to be a collection of lies.[95]

On the occasion of the 90th anniversary of the Armenian Genocide, the Turkish parliament invited McCarthy to give a lecture on 24 March 2005, where he once more referred to the 'false documents produced by the British Propaganda Office'.[96] Shortly afterwards, on 28 April, 550 delegates of the Turkish parliament signed a letter to the UK parliament, demanding an apology for the 1916 Blue Book. Parliament passed the matter on to the Foreign Office, which asked retired diplomat David Miller to look at the circumstances of the report's creation. The article cited earlier was published in August of that year in the *Journal of the Royal United Service Institute* to highlight that while the report's authors worked for British propaganda, they enjoyed considerable freedom during its creation. An official reply was sent in January 2006, offering to discuss the report, its history and its sources, but was met with no reply. Today, the Blue Book is still promoted by Armenian activists, who gave a copy of the first Turkish translation to every member of the Turkish parliament in 2009 and re-published the English edition one year later.[97]

The changing fates of the 1915 Bryce report into German atrocities in Belgium and the 1916 Blue Book describing the Armenian genocide are prime examples that war crimes investigations are never separated from the politics of their time, and indeed the politics of following generations. Despite its serious flaws, the Bryce report on Belgium contributed to the very idea that war crimes should not go unpunished, and that their perpetrators should not be able to hide behind commands given by their superiors. The Bryce report on Armenia did not only persuade global public opinion that the persecution of Armenians was widespread, state-sponsored and systematic. The fact that these three characteristics form the modern definition of a crime against humanity is a direct legacy of this document. Together, both reports set the standard for the emerging genre of the atrocity report as a document specifically written to establish the veracity of war crime allegations beyond reasonable doubt and thus reinforce the urge to prosecute the offenders. The Bryce reports merged the desire to achieve direct public impact of earlier pamphlets like the Hobhouse report with the resources of government bureaucracy: written by interdisciplinary teams with strong legal and historical skills, these prime examples of First World War propaganda stand at the beginning of what we now call 'human rights fact-finding'. Today, such reports are usually commissioned by international organizations, particularly the UN Human Rights Council,[98] and like the Blue Book they have explicit mandates to assemble evidence to facilitate the later conviction of perpetrators.[99]

Between Politics and Law: The Value of Interdisciplinary Approaches

Like the authors of the Bryce reports, these teams must find a solution to the fundamental contradiction at the heart of the process: the main purpose is political, to influence public opinion in as many countries as possible and to ensure that a debate over punishment of the guilty or even intervention is kept alive. Therefore, the report needs to be completed as quickly and distributed as widely as possible. On the other hand, it should also silence the doubters, remain detached from any partisan political agenda and compile evidence that would be overwhelming even in a court of law. To persuade sceptics at home or abroad, the report must be painstakingly researched and err on the conservative side in its claims to ensure that no single falsehood is used to discredit the entire report. The lesson of the Bryce reports is that half-truths and shortcuts can prove very costly indeed, and may potentially enable polemicists to deny that the crimes ever happened for generations to come. For the same reason, it is important that records of the investigation itself are kept and permanently archived, even in the digital age.

For a century, the answer to the demands of this thankless task has been the assembly of interdisciplinary teams to speed up the work and improve the quality of the decision-making. The composition of the team that wrote the best-known human rights report in recent years is a case in point: the international commission of inquiry on Darfur established in 2004 was led by individuals who brought both serious legal expertise and experience of politics or human rights campaigning. The report emphasized that they enjoyed the support of 'a legal research team and an investigative team composed of investigators, forensic experts, military analysts, and investigators specializing in gender violence'.[100] The team was helpless to prevent the atrocities, but their work was not in vain: when the ICC's Pre-Trial Chamber decided to extend the charges against Sudanese president Bashir and indict him with genocide, it cited the team's report as vital evidence supporting their decision to prosecute.[101]

This example shows that atrocity reports remain relevant and can even result in prosecutions at the ICC. The mix of interdisciplinary skills that is necessary for a successful outcome is only going to increase in complexity:

while film has been used from Nuremberg onwards as evidence in war crime trials, new investigation teams will need the expertise to validate footage filmed with smartphones, or establish the authenticity of social media posts.[102] At the same time, the inclusion of more scientists and forensic experts should not bring about the illusion that this type of work is apolitical: from their very origins in First World War propaganda to their current incarnation as UN human rights fact-finding, atrocity reports have always been political texts. Their authors must embrace their dual mandate of political impact and factual accuracy, as when they do their difficult work well and political circumstances align favourably, they can single-handedly bring about a war crimes prosecution and secure justice from afar.

Conclusion

As this chapter has shown, the nexus of politics and law is at the very heart of every inquiry into the past, present and future of war crimes trials and investigations. Just as atrocity reports are best compiled by interdisciplinary teams, the task of understanding the political contexts of key legal events requires a combination of historical and legal skills. Some lawyers are still prone to see historians challenging the established narrative of how international criminal justice came about as an attack on their discipline, while historians need to learn that simply providing historical context is not enough: they must master the intricate details of legal principles and doctrines and adopt the language of contemporary legal discourse to ensure their message is heard.

On a positive note, the field is rapidly moving away from a simplistic narrative based on dubious precedents and establishing a more nuanced account of how previous generations tried to balance the yearning for justice and the thirst for revenge in the aftermath of violent conflict. This involves the acceptance that the very idea of an ICC not only encountered strong scepticism from states, whether democratic or not, but also from within the legal profession. Moreover, many key concepts of the discipline that are often heralded as timeless expressions of universal values are relative newcomers to the discourse of international society.

Common terms such as 'war crimes', 'crimes against humanity' or even the very idea that victorious alliances in protracted military conflicts should run international tribunals prosecuting war criminals have all emerged during the downfall of international cooperation marked by the First World War. They were formed by a combination of practices and sensibilities that marked developments in international society immediately preceding the conflict, such as the detailed codification of the laws of war at the Second Hague Peace conference or the high public profile of the investigations of the North Sea Incident Commission, and the demands of wartime propaganda and politics. In war and in peace, the political nature of war crimes tribunals necessitates the establishment of a specific narrative that shows that the prosecutions of certain individuals is a good thing for international society as a whole—be it as a campaign promise in a wartime election or as an international commission of inquiry releasing a press statement. Likewise, it is the responsibility of historians, lawyers and other scientists working in this highly complex field to show that putting these narratives and the ways in which they have been formed under close scrutiny does not mean undermining but ultimately strengthening the idea that international criminal justice can be a force for good in international society.

Bibliographical Essay Serious academic study of the history of war crimes trials is a small and relatively recent field. While the Nuremberg trials have always attracted scholarly interest, it was only the adoption of the Rome Statute in 1998 and the subsequent establishment of the ICC that inspired works aiming to provide an overview of how the prosecution of war crimes has developed over time. The earliest example is Gary Bass's case-studies-based volume, *Stay the Hand of Vengeance: The Politics of War Crime Tribunals* (Princeton: Princeton University Press, 2002), which reflected the state of the field at the time with its heavy focus on the twentieth century. Covering the same time period but taking an even more critical approach towards exploring the tensions between politics and law was Gerry J. Simpson's *Law, War and Crime: War Crimes, Trials and the Reinvention of International Law* (Oxford: Polity, 2007). Simpson later teamed up with Kevin Jon Heller to edit what is currently the most important collection of essays in the field, *The Hidden Histories of War*

Crimes Trials (Oxford: Oxford University Press, 2013). This volume makes a serious attempt to investigate the pre-twentieth-century origins of war crimes prosecutions and includes an excellent discussion of the value of the trial of Peter von Hagenbach in 1474 as a precedent (although I disagree with the conclusion, as set out in my contribution to this volume), the legacy of French colonial law or the impact of the prosecution of the Armenians on the establishment of modern categories of international criminal law.

In a volume published one year later, David Crowe adopted a very different approach and combined the history of war crimes trials with a general history of war crimes and genocide (*War Crimes, Genocide, and Justice: A Global History*, New York/Basingstoke: Palgrave, 2014). He begins his overview in antiquity and makes a deliberate effort to cover developments outside Europe, especially regarding China, in an attempt to respond to current debates whether the quest for justice for victims of war crimes is a Western project or a more universal undertaking that can rightfully claim to speak for humanity as a whole. Michael Bryant's more recent volume, *A World History of War Crimes: From Antiquity to the Present* (London: Bloomsbury, 2015), shares this ambition of providing a global history of the evolution of the laws of war from the beginnings of human civilization, but deliberately puts the criminalization of war crimes into the wider context of placing restraints on war. From this perspective, war crimes trials are only the most recent manifestation of a much longer and broader struggle. What the struggle for war crimes trials and investigations was actually about is also the question at the core of a volume published still more recently: Mark Lewis, *The Birth of the New Justice: The Internationalization of Crime and Punishment, 1919–1950* (Oxford: Oxford University Press, 2016), which analyses the diverse reasons why legal and non-governmental organizations either supported or opposed ICCs, and explores the ideas and activism of leading lawyers such as Nicholas Politis, Raphael Lemkin and Hersch Lauterpacht. His work is a further challenge to the notion that the development of international criminal law was driven by one coherent liberal-progressive agenda, currently still the version presented to law students in the history sections of their textbooks.

While the focus on overview works is a more recent development, there is a longer tradition of detailed academic studies exploring individual early attempts to bring war criminals to justice. A fine example is James F. Willis's truly excellent exploration of the dynamics that drove the decision to make prosecuting war criminals a key feature of the peace negotiations after the First World War (*Prologue to Nuremberg: The Politics and Diplomacy of Punishing War Criminals of the First World War* (Westport: Greenwood, 1982)). Yet, the book was poorly reviewed or ignored when it was published because the topic was then unfashionable and considered largely irrelevant. The early trials in Turkey and Germany following the peace treaties are covered in an article by Alan Kramer ('The First Wave of International War Crimes Trials: Istanbul and Leipzig', *European Review* 14 (2006): 441–455) and a book by Gerd Hankel, which is unfortunately only available in German (*Die Leipziger Prozesse. Deutsche Kriegsverbrechen und ihre strafrechtliche Verfolgung nach dem Ersten Weltkrieg* (Hamburg: Hamburger Edition, 2003)). More recently, Kirsten Sellars has taken this period as the starting point for her investigation into the origins of the crime of aggression (*'Crimes against Peace' and International Law* (Cambridge: Cambridge University Press, 2013)). Marc Daniel Segesser provided a rare foray into the nineteenth century by tracking the debate among lawyers and politicians following the attempts by Gustave Moynier to establish an international legal forum for the prosecution of war crimes in response to the atrocities that marked the Franco-German War of 1870–1871 (*Recht statt Rache oder Rache durch Recht? Die Ahndung von Kriegsverbrechen in der internationalen wissenschaftlichen Debatte* (Paderborn: Schoeningh, 2010)).

The Nuremberg trials have received, by far, the largest share of scholarly attention, but earlier celebratory histories have now been replaced by more critical accounts such as Kevin Jon Heller's pioneering *The Nuremberg Military Tribunals and the Origins of International Criminal Law* (Oxford: Oxford University Press, 2011). His study was followed by works exploring the role of narratives in shaping the legacy of the trials (Alexa Stiller & Kim Christian Priemel, eds., *Reassessing the Nuremberg Military Tribunals: Transitional Justice, Trial Narratives, and Historiography* (New York: Berghahn, 2012)) or presenting the results of recent research for a wider audience (Andrew Williams, *A Passing Fury: Searching for Justice at the End of World War II* (London: Jonathan Cape, 2016)). In addition to offering a contemporary take on the fundamental question of whether the Nuremberg trials stand for vengeance or justice, the latter book offers a close look at the Belsen trial, the only one to directly examine individual crimes committed at Auschwitz.

The obvious next steps for the field are critical studies of the work of the tribunals of the 1990s—most prominently, the International Criminal Tribunals investigating the crimes that marked the wars in the former Yugoslavia or the Rwandan Genocide. Yet, as with the negotiations surrounding the Rome Statute and the early work of the ICC, we will have to wait until private and government papers documenting this key period become available.

Notes

1. Alexandra Kemmerer, "Histories of International Law," 6 (January 2015), available at http://www.ejiltalk.org/volkerrechtsgeschichten-histories-of-international-law/
2. See Alan Kramer, "The First Wave of International War Crimes Trials: Istanbul and Leipzig," *European Review* 14, no. 4 (October 2006): 441–455.
3. Georg Schwarzenberger, "A Forerunner of Nuremberg: The Breisach War Crime Trial of 1474," *Manchester Guardian*, 28 September 1946, 4.
4. Arthur Nussbaum, *A Concise History of the Law of Nations* (New York: The Macmillan Company, 1954), 320.
5. M. Cherif Bassiouni, "Perspectives on International Criminal Justice," *Virginia Journal of International Law* 50 (2010): 269, 298; idem, *International Criminal Law: Sources, Subjects and Contents* (Leiden: Martinus Nijhoff, 2008), 18; idem, ed., *Introduction to International Criminal Law* (Leiden: Martinus Nijhoff, 2012), 29, 416, 1048. See also William A. Schabas, *An Introduction to the International Criminal Court* (Cambridge: Cambridge University Press, 2011), 1; B. S. Brown, ed., *Research Handbook on International Criminal Law* (Cheltenham: Edward Elgar, 2011), 4.

6. Gregory S. Gordon, "The Trial of Peter Von Hagenbach: Reconciling History, Historiography, and International Criminal Law," in *The Hidden Histories of War Crimes Trials*, ed. Kevin Heller and Gerry Simpson (Oxford: Oxford University Press, 2013), 13. Note that Gordon upholds the trial's status as the first international war crime tribunal by describing the late Holy Roman Empire as 'an intergovernmental organisation with hundreds of independent member states.' (p. 42).
7. See for example Randall Lesaffer, "International Law and its History: The Story of an Unrequited Love," in *Time, History and International Law*, ed. Matthew Craven, Malgosia Fitzmaurice and Maria Vogiatzi (Leiden: Martinus Nijhoff, 2007), 27–41, 34–35.
8. Kevin Jon Heller, *The Nuremberg Military Tribunals and the Origins of International Criminal Law* (Oxford: Oxford University Press, 2011), 241. The judges in the *High Command* Trial felt more positive towards the precedent, but noted it was 'of academic interest only'—see United Nations War Crimes Commission, *Law Reports and Trials of War Criminals, Vol. XII, The German High Command Trial* (1949), 61.
9. The trial became a focal point of an ongoing dispute between North and South over the morality of the Civil War: James Madison Page, *The True Story of Andersonville Prison: A Defense of Major Henry Wirz* (1908) takes a very pro-Confederate line, with a pro-Union counterargument made in Norton Parker Chipman, *The Tragedy of Andersonville; Trial of Captain Henry Wirz, the Prison Keeper* (1911). For a modern account, see Marouf Hasian, *In the Name of Necessity: Military Tribunals and the Loss of American Civil Liberties* (Tuscaloosa: University of Alabama Press, 2012), chapter 5.
10. Guénaël Mettraux, "A Little-known Case from the American Civil War: The War Crimes Trial of Major General John H. Gee," *Journal of International Criminal Justice* 8, no. 4 (2010): 1059.
11. George A. Finch, "Superior Orders and War Crimes," *American Journal of International Law* 15, no. 3 (1921): 440, 444.
12. Daniel Marc Segesser, "'Unlawful Warfare is Uncivilised': The International Debate on the Punishment of War Crimes, 1872–1918," *European Review of History* 14, no. 2 (2007): 215; idem, *Recht statt Rache oder Rache durch Recht? Die Ahndung von Kriegsverbrechen in der internationalen wissenschaftlichen Debatte* (Paderborn: Ferdinand Schöningh, 2010).
13. The society published a string of pamphlets such as Alpheus Henry Snow, *The Development of the American Doctrine of Jurisdiction of Courts*

over States (1911), or George Wickersham, *The Supreme Court of the United States, a Prototype of a Court of Nations* (1913). See Paolo Amorosa, "James Brown Scott's International Adjudication between Tradition and Progress in the United States," *Journal of the History of International Law* 17, no. 1 (2015): 15.

14. Antony Anghie, *Imperialism, Sovereignty and the Making of International Law* (Cambridge: Cambridge University Press, 2007).
15. Bardo Fassbender and Anne Peters, "Towards A Global History of International Law," in *The Oxford Handbook of the History of International Law*, ed. Bardo Fassbender and Anne Peter (Oxford: Oxford University Press, 2012), 1–26.
16. David M. Crowe, *War Crimes, Genocide and Justice: A Global History* (New York: Palgrave Macmillan, 2014).
17. Gary Bass, *Stay the Hand of Vengeance: The Politics of War Crime Tribunals* (Princeton: Princeton University Press, 2002).
18. See Sönke Neitzel and Daniel Hohrath, eds., *Kriegsgreuel—Die Entgrenzung der Gewalt in kriegerischen Konflikten vom Mittelalter bis ins 20. Jahrhundert* (Paderborn: Ferdinand Schöningh, 2008).
19. See Jan Martin Lemnitzer, *Power, Law and the End of Privateering* (Basingstoke: Palgrave Macmillan, 2014).
20. Art. 24 and 25 of the Lieber code, printed in *The Laws of Armed Conflicts*, ed. Dietrich Schindler and Jiř Toman (Leiden: Martinus Nijhoff, 1988), 3–23.
21. John Fabian Witt, *Lincoln's Code: The Laws of War in American History* (New York: Free Press, 2012).
22. The Laws of War on Land, Manual published by the Institute of International Law, adopted by the Institute of International Law at Oxford, 9 September 1880, printed in *The Laws of Armed Conflicts*, 36–48. US historians tend to ascribe enormous importance to the influence of the Lieber code on the drafting of the Hague conventions, largely ignoring European legal developments between 1863 and 1899.
23. *Manchester Guardian*, 25 October 1904, 6. For a full account of the incident see Jan Martin Lemnitzer, "International Commissions of Inquiry and the North Sea Incident: A Model for a MH17 Tribunal?" *European Journal of International Law* 27, no. 4 (January 2017): 923–944.
24. Lansdowne to Hardinge, 27 October 1904, Parliamentary Papers, *Correspondence Relating to the North Sea Incident*, 1905 (Cd2350), Vol. CIII, 369, No. 17, 10.

25. *London Times*, 29 October 1904, 11–12.
26. *Manchester Guardian*, 28 October 1904, 7; *New York Times*, 28 October 1904, 8; *Economist*, 29 October 1904, 1727; *Economist*, 5 November 1904, 1766.
27. Lansdowne to Hardinge, 31 October 1904, Parliamentary Papers, *Correspondence relating to the North Sea incident*, 1905 (Cd2350), Vol. CIII, 369, No. 41, 25.
28. Lansdowne to Hardinge, 4 November 1904, ibid., No. 58, 35.
29. *London Times*, 27 February 1905, 3.
30. *Economist*, 4 March 1905, 342. *Chicago Tribune*, 26 February 1905, reprinted in *London Times*, 27 February 1905, 3.
31. Andre Mandelstam, "La commission internationale d'enquête sur l'incident de la Mer du Nord," *Revue Générale de Droit International Public* 12 (1905): 351, 414–415.
32. Amos S. Hershey, "Convention for the Peaceful Adjustment of International Differences," *American Journal of International Law* 2 (1908): 29, 36; Alexander Pearce Higgins, *The Hague Peace Conferences* (Cambridge: Cambridge University Press, 1909), 168–169.
33. Technically the non-ratification of the 1907 convention respecting the laws and customs of war on land (IV) by Serbia meant that it was not applicable because it was not in force for all belligerents of the conflict (see Art. 2 of the convention), but the very similar 1899 convention was undoubtedly in force for all participants of the conflict.
34. Nicoletta F. Gullace, "Sexual Violence and Family Honor: British Propaganda and International Law during the First World War," *American Historical Review* 102, no. 3 (1997): 714–747.
35. Hugh Bellot, "War Crimes: Their Prevention and Punishment," *Grotius Society, Problems of the War, Papers Read Before the Society in the Year 1916* 2 (1916): 31–55, 31.
36. House of Commons, 21 November 1917, Hansard, Vol. 99 Col. 1209–82, 1218.
37. Isabel Hull, *A Scrap of Paper: Making and Breaking International Law during the Great War* (Ithaca: Cornell University Press, 2014), 297, 298.
38. House of Lords, 5 May 1915, Hansard, Vol. 18 Col. 942–51, 946/7.
39. Ibid., 950.
40. House of Commons, 9 June 1915, Hansard, Vol. 72, Col. 267–8.
41. House of Commons, 16 July 1918, Hansard Vol. 108, Col. 897–8: 7 August 1918, Vol. 109, Col. 1351–2.

42. See for example House of Commons, 25 June 1840, Hansard Vol. 55 Col. 76–108, 94.
43. House of Commons, 31 March 1879, Hansard, Vol. 245, Col. 20–127, 32.
44. Ibid., 25 July 1882, Vol. 272, Col. 1691–1759, 1709.
45. Ibid., 23 October 1899, Hansard, Vol. 77, Col. 549–568, 558.
46. House of Lords, 14 March 1904, Hansard Vol. 131, Col. 919–948, 928.
47. House of Commons, 25 July 1912, Hansard, Vol. 41, Col. 1384–1501, 1469/70.
48. Ibid., 16 June 1910, Hansard, Vol. 17, Col. 1474–1526, 1485; 21 March 1912, Vol. 35, Col. 2077–201, 2131.
49. Printed in *Papers Relating to the foreign relations of the United States, 1915. Supplement, The World War*, 981.
50. House of Lords, 28 July 1915, Hansard, Vol. 19, Col. 774–778, 775.
51. Ibid, 778.
52. Art. 7, Rome Statute of the International Criminal Court, 17 July 1998, available at http://legal.un.org/icc/statute/romefra.htm
53. James F. Willis, *Prologue to Nuremberg: Politics and Diplomacy of Punishing War Criminals of the First World War* (Westport: Greenwood Press, 1982), chapter 4.
54. The first article seems to have been an editorial demanding to "Make German Guilt Personal," *New York Times*, 16 October 1918, 14. This was followed by a long article written by law professor Asa Bird Gardimer, *New York Times*, 8 December 1918, 45. See also the editorials of 15 December 1918, 25, and 21 January 1919, 6.
55. Art. 227 Versailles treaty.
56. Nigel J. Ashton and Duco Hellema, "Hanging the Kaiser: Anglo-Dutch Relations and the Fate of Wilhelm II, 1918–20," *Diplomacy & Statecraft* 11, no. 2 (2000): 53–78.
57. Gerd Hankel, *Die Leipziger Prozesse. Deutsche Kriegsverbrechen und ihre strafrechtliche Verfolgung nach dem Ersten Weltkrieg* (Hamburg: Hamburger Edition, 2003).
58. The general rules on a duty to assist the Allies in prosecuting war criminals were included in all of the treaties; see for example the Treaty of Neuilly with Bulgaria, Art. 118–20.
59. See Vahakn Dadrian and Taner Akçam, *Judgment at Istanbul: The Armenian Genocide Trials* (New York: Berghahn, 2011).
60. James L. Brierly, "Do We Need an International Criminal Court?" *British Yearbook of International Law* 8 (1927): 81–88, 87.

61. See Frederic Megret, "International Criminal Justice. A Critical Research Agenda," in *Critical Approaches to International Criminal Law: An Introduction*, ed. Christine E. J Schwöbel (London: Routledge, 2014), 17, 43.
62. Philip Currie to the Earl of Kimberley, 26 November 1894, *Parliamentary Papers, Correspondence relating to the Asiatic Provinces of Turkey, Part 1: Events at Sassoun, and Commission of Inquiry at Moush, 1905 (Cd7894)*, Vol. CIX. 239, No. 66, 41; Earl of Kimberley to P. Currie, 13 December 1894, ibid., No. 93,49.
63. Inclosure to P. Currie to Earl of Kimberley, 26 December 1894, ibid., No. 126, 62; P. Currie to Earl of Kimberley, 10 January 1895, No. 134, 68.
64. P. Currie to Earl of Kimberley, 26 January 1895, ibid., No. 144, 74; P. Currie to Earl of Kimberley, 28 January 1895, No. 146, 75.
65. P. Currie to Earl of Kimberley, 13 May 1895, ibid., No. 204, 111.
66. See annex to report of consular delegates on the Sasun commission of 20 July 1895, List of victims with table, page, ibid., 155–161.
67. See Larissa van den Herik and Catherine Harwood, "Sharing the Law: The Appeal of International Criminal Law for International Commissions of Inquiry," in *The Transformation of Human Rights Fact-Finding*, ed. Philip Alston and Sarah Knuckey (Oxford: Oxford University Press, 2016), 233, 249, for a discussion of this practice.
68. Annex to report of consular delegates on the Sasun commission of 20 July 1895, *Parliamentary Papers, Correspondence relating to the Asiatic Provinces of Turkey, Part 1: Events at Sassoun, and Commission of Inquiry at Moush, 1905 (Cd7894)*, Vol. CIX. 239, 166.
69. P. Currie to Earl of Kimberley, 21 May 1895, *Parliamentary Papers, Correspondence relating to the Asiatic Provinces of Turkey, Part 1: Events at Sassoun, and Commission of Inquiry at Moush, 1905 (Cd7894)*, Vol. CIX. 239, No. 209, 117; Kimberley to P. Currie, 3 June 1895, No. 221, 122; P. Currie to the Marquess of Salisbury, 27 July 1895, No. 245, 130; P. Currie to Salisbury, 23 August 1895, No. 254, 190.
70. See Davide Rodogno, *Against Massacre: Humanitarian Interventions in the Ottoman Empire 1815–1914* (Princeton: Princeton University Press, 2012), 194.
71. *New York Times*, 10 September 1895, 1.
72. "Report of a Visit to the Camps of Women and Children in the Cape and Orange River Colonies," June 1901.

73. Keith G. Robbins, "Lord Bryce and the First World War," *The Historical Journal* 10, no. 2 (1967): 255–278, 255.
74. Trevor Wilson, "Lord Bryce's Investigation into Alleged German Atrocities in Belgium, 1914–15," *Journal of Contemporary History* 14, no. 3 (1979): 378; *London Times*, 18 December 1914, 5.
75. Wilson, "Lord Bryce's Investigation", 373.
76. Ibid., 374, 380.
77. Ibid., 376–377.
78. Résumé of American press complied by Britain's propaganda headquarters Wellington House, 27 May 1915, cited in Wilson, ibid., 370; see also Michael L. Sanders, "Wellington House and British Propaganda During the First World War," *The Historical Journal* 18, no. 1 (1975): 119–146, 130.
79. James Bryce, *The Bryce Report on Alleged German Outrages* (12 May 1915).
80. See James Morgan Read, *Atrocity Propaganda, 1914–1919* (New Haven: Yale University Press, 1941); Arthur Ponsonby, *Falsehood in War-Time* (London: George Allen & Unwin, 1928); Harold Laswell, *Propaganda Technique in the World War* (London: K. Paul, Trench, Trubner & co., 1927); George G. Bruntz, *Allied Propaganda and the Collapse of the German Empire in 1918* (Stanford: Stanford University Press, 1938); George Sylvester Viereck, *Spreading Germs of Hate* (London: Duckworth, 1931); Michael F. Connors, *Dealing in Hate: The Development of Anti-German Propaganda* (London, n.d.); Clinton H. Grattan, *Why We Fought* (Indianapolis: Bobbs Merrill, 1928); Harry Elmer Barnes, In Quest of Truth and Justice (Chicago: National Historical Society, 1928); James Squires, *British Propaganda at Home and in the United States* (Cambridge: Harvard University Press, 1935); Horace C. Peterson, *Propaganda for War: The Campaign Against American Neutrality, 1914–1917* (Norman: University of Oklahoma Press, 1938).
81. Jeff Lipkes, *Rehearsals. The German Army in Belgium, August 1914* (Leuven: Leuven University Press, 2007); John Horne and Alan Kramer, *German Atrocities, 1914. A History of Denial* (New Haven: Yale University Press, 2001).
82. House of Lords, 6 October 1915, Hansard, Vol. 19, Col. 994–1004, 996.
83. Ibid., 996/7.

84. Michelle Tusan, "James Bryce's Blue Book as Evidence," *Journal of Levantine Studies* 5, no. 2 (2015): 35–50, 41.
85. Sanders, *Wellington House*, 144.
86. Miller, *History of the Blue Book*, 40.
87. Tusan, *Blue Book as Evidence*, 41.
88. Miller, *History of the Blue Book*, 40.
89. Memorandum of 26 September 1924, cited in Tusan, *Blue Book as Evidence*, 43.
90. Michelle Tusan, "'Crimes against Humanity': Human Rights, the British Empire and the Origins of the Response to the Armenian Genocide," *The American Historical Review* 119, no. 1 (2014): 47–77, 71.
91. Ibid., 69–73.
92. Tusan, *Blue Book as Evidence*, 35.
93. See in particular "Tall Armenian Tale," available at http://www.tallarmeniantale.com/atrocity-prop.htm; and http://armenians-1915.blogspot.com/2005/07/120-british-blue-book-james-bryce.html
94. See his article "The Bryce Report: British Propaganda and the Turks," available at http://www.ataa.org/reference/british_carthy.html
95. http://www.mfa.gov.tr/presentation-made-by-prof_-justin-mccarthy-_seminar-on-turkish-armenian-relations-organized-by-the-democratic-principles-association-15-march-2001-_istanbul_.en.mfa. The reprint he refers to is: Gomidas Institute/Ara Sarafian, The Treatment of Armenians in the Ottoman Empire, 1915–16: Documents Presented to Viscount Grey of Falloden by Viscount Bryce, Uncensored Edition (2000).
96. For the full text see http://www.mfa.gov.tr/presentation-by-prof_-justin-mccarthy-at-the-tgna-on-_the-reality-of-armenian-issue_-conference-on-march-24_-2005_.en.mfa
97. See http://www.gomidas.org/campaigns. See also Taner Akcam, "Anatomy of Genocide Denial: Academics, Politicians, and the "Re-Making" of History," available at http://www.chgs.umn.edu/histories/occasional/akcam_anatomy_of_denial.pdf
98. The council replaced the earlier Human Rights Commission, see the General Assembly resolution of 3 April 2006, A/RES/60/251.
99. The International Commission of Inquiry for the Democratic People's Republic of Korea, A/HRC/RES/S-22/13 (2013) and the Independent International Commission of Inquiry on the Syrian Arab Republic, A/HRC/RES/S-17/1 (2011) both had an explicit mandate to 'investigate crimes against humanity'.

100. Report of international commission of inquiry on Darfur, 25 January 2005, available at http://www.un.org/news/dh/sudan/com_inq_darfur.pdf
101. Second warrant of arrest issued by Pre-Trial chamber I, 12 July 2010, ICC-02/05–01/09, available at https://www.icc-cpi.int/iccdocs/doc/doc907140.pdf
102. Christian Delage, *Caught on Camera: Film in the Courtroom from the Nuremberg Trials to the Trials of the Khmer Rouge* (Philadelphia: University of Pennsylvania Press, 2014).

Jan Martin Lemnitzer is Assistant Professor at the Center for War Studies, University of Southern Denmark, and a research associate at the Changing Character of War Programme at Pembroke College, Oxford University. He completed his PhD thesis on the 1856 Declaration of Paris at the London School of Economics and won the British International History Group's award for the best thesis in 2010. It was published with Palgrave Macmillan under the title *Power, Law, and the End of Privateering*. He was a lecturer in modern history at Christ Church and Pembroke College, Oxford, and has published on the history of international law in *Diplomacy & Statecraft*, the *International History Review* and the *European Journal of International Law*.

6

History: War Crimes in the Past and Present—A Historian's Perspective

Peter Romijn

Historians and War Crimes: Introduction

In his history of the Peloponnesian Wars, the ancient Athenian historian Thucydides reported many acts of extreme violence committed against enemy soldiers and civilians, which today would, without any doubt, qualify as war crimes. His work, written between 430 and 400 BCE, contains appalling reports of the mass killing of prisoners of war, the extermination of citizens in enemy- or apostate-allied city-states, and the looting of their assets. These accounts from the earliest beginnings of recorded human history can appear to us as a grim prediction of terrible things to come. For Thucydides, who had seen military service himself, such cruelties were a fact of life and a part of the 'human condition'. Nevertheless, he points at immoral behaviour, particularly to cases in which promises of safe conduct were broken, envoys mistreated, or the gods insulted—in modern terms, the cases in which the (unwritten) rules of war were transgressed.[1]

P. Romijn (✉)
University of Amsterdam, Amsterdam, The Netherlands

J. Waterlow, J. Schuhmacher, *War Crimes Trials and Investigations*, St Antony's Series,
https://doi.org/10.1007/978-3-319-64072-3_6

Thucydides' narrative is a product of meticulous fact-finding and strictly analytical thinking. It is also a pioneering work in the search for explanations of human behaviour in war and provides a starting point for the psychology of mass violence and warfare.[2] This chapter discusses the contributions of present-day historians and their discipline to the study of both war crimes and the ways in which post-conflict societies have tried to cope and come to terms with a violent past. In our times, the historical profession is still committed to applying rigorous standards of fact-finding and analytical thinking about human behaviour in violent conflicts. The scope and societal impact of these contributions, however, are becoming much broader.

Present-day historians engage in scholarly debates within an interdisciplinary environment, but no less important are their roles as forensic experts and as opinion-makers in societies coping with the legacies of war crimes. This blending of functions is characteristic of the historical profession, in general, and for those historians working on the legacies of war crimes, in particular. Simultaneously, contemporary history as a discipline has become institutionalized as a way of clustering relevant and authoritative expertise on a problematic past. Working since 1985 in one of the leading European institutions dealing with the Second World War and other recent episodes of massive violence—the Amsterdam-based Netherlands Institute for War, Holocaust, and Genocide Studies (NIOD)—the author has become very familiar with the different roles of historians in this field.

For reasons that will be explained below, the Second World War and its legacies produced strong impulses for the study of atrocities in war and therefore will be the starting point for this chapter. I discuss the concept of war crimes within a broad temporal range and beyond its strictly legal connotations. In everyday language, the leadership of the Third Reich and leading collaborators in occupied countries have generally been branded 'war criminals', even though this does not hold in strictly legal terms. Formally, 'war crimes' concern violations of the laws and customs of war, as defined in international treaties since the late nineteenth century.[3] After the Second World War, the United Nations prosecuted these crimes by formulating and applying the statutes of the International Military Tribunals of Nuremburg and Tokyo. The categories of 'crimes against humanity' and 'crimes against peace' were formulated as parallel elements in the developing system of International Humanitarian Law. Grave offences, such as torture, deportation, and extermination, committed by a state against foreign nationals and even its own citizens were considered transgressions of international law, commonly denominated as 'war crimes'.

In the immediate aftermath of the Second World War, as legal scholar Ruti Teitel points out, the codification of such crimes against humanity by international tribunals actually remained limited to those related to war.[4] Thus, war crime trials in the strict sense became intertwined with the prosecution and punishment of what would soon be called genocide. As we know, the Holocaust was the implementation of a political agenda of ruthless leaders who deployed bureaucrats, police, and the military to plan and implement the extermination of Jews, Slavs, Sinti and Roma, and other 'racially undesirable' categories. As a logical consequence, the social perception of the war crimes of the Second World War and of the Holocaust became interconnected. The same occurred in historical research. International historiography has developed analytical tools for understanding and explaining mass atrocities committed in the context of war and violent conflict. Consequently, scholarly work on mass atrocities has for a long time been dominated by the horrific weight of the Holocaust. Recently, more integrated conceptions of organized mass violence have emerged, in which the Holocaust is seen as an extreme example.[5] The latter perspective has been challenged and contested,[6] but what matters here is that historians have come to analyse the Holocaust, genocide, and war crimes as closely connected subjects and by means of several overlapping approaches.

In this chapter I demonstrate how historians have worked in different capacities in dealing with war crimes—as scholars, forensic experts, and as contributors to historical dialogues in the public sphere. The chapter addresses the 'how' (by means of which methods, approaches, repertoires?) and the 'why' (which motivations, which social demands are the driving forces?). The Second World War and its aftermath are the point of departure, for the war unleashed an orgy of violence on the world at large. It deeply affected the lives and the thinking of those who experienced atrocities on a massive scale. It also provided strong impulses for a new international legal regime for dealing with those transgressions.

The specific case presented here is the Dutch one, which must, of course, be interpreted within its international context. This selection might at one level be attributed to my own Dutch background and experience as a researcher. At the same time, however, there are good intrinsic reasons for this choice. During the Second World War, the Dutch experienced a myriad of war crimes and crimes against humanity, both in Europe and in the Netherlands' Asian colonies. As a consequence, the collective memory of the war has been forged by these traumatic events. As history proceeded, during the extremely violent Indonesian War of Liberation (1945–1949), the Dutch both suffered and committed war crimes on a large scale. More recently, the Netherlands became entangled in the war leading to the dissolution of Yugoslavia—in particular in the gravest act of genocide in that war, the Bosnian–Serb massacre of the Bosnian Muslim population of the UN-proclaimed 'safe area' (Srebrenica 1995).

Thus, over the decades, the Dutch have had to struggle with assessing their own multiple roles—as victims, bystanders, and perpetrators in war crimes and crimes against humanity. A typical Dutch phenomenon was the very early institutionalization of contemporary history and its recognition as an instrument of working towards collective coping. Moreover, the Dutch ambition of providing an international infrastructure for administrating international justice—from the International Court of Justice to the Yugoslavia Tribunal and the International Criminal Court at The Hague—has progressively inspired thinking about conflict resolution and post-conflict settlements. The argument in this chapter is that historical knowledge and understanding are indispensable for successfully interpreting all these alarming phenomena—but precisely because war crimes are upsetting, historical narratives and insight alone cannot suffice to come to terms with the painful past.

The Historical Discipline: Background and Overview

Present-day historians have become entangled as much as Thucydides was with the efforts of their society to understand, prosecute, and punish war crimes. Their contributions to collective attempts to deal with these crimes and the aftermath were inspired by personal experiences, challenges to respond to societal needs, and the aspiration for innovation in the historical profession. According to Henry Rousso, the prominent French historian of the twentieth century, contemporary history as a discipline possesses a strong degree of sensitivity towards the traumatic events of our own time.[7] From his perspective, contemporary history is 'a dialogue between the living and the dead, like any history, but also a conversation between the living, the contemporaries' about how to interpret the present.[8] Indeed, the academic ideal of keeping a certain distance from the past has become ever more suspect in light of the traumas of the recent past that have continued to exert a painful influence over the present.

The first generation of Second World War historians often blended their personal experiences of violence, oppression, and persecution as witnesses and reporters with their professional role as producers of historical insight. Being historical subjects who study their own time and fate can be as inspiring as it is complicated. This became clear in the debates among German historians concerning the understanding of national socialist crimes. One example was the call by Martin Broszat, the director of the Munich Institute for Contemporary History, to study the Nazi regime like any other 'regular' topic in history in order to explain both the appeal and the character of the regime. Some considered this a very useful innovation in the historiography, but others branded it a project initiated by a 'fellow traveller' of the Hitler regime seeking exoneration through normalization.[9]

The historian's job has not remained limited to a search for understanding the causes of extreme violence, destruction, and mass killing. The next step is to address the persistent difficulties of societies in coming to terms with the traumatic events of the past. The expertise of historians has been sought during procedures for punishing perpetrators, compensating victims, and correcting administrative failures. Such input proved to be indispensable for collective efforts to deal with a troubled past. Thus, historians have felt challenged to accept roles outside their profession—be it as therapist or judge. This produced more public outreach than individual academic historians usually achieve when publishing for their peers. The Second World War was increasingly 'mediatized' from the 1960s onwards as professional historians used the rise of modern televised broadcasting to bring the experience, history, and memory of the war back into people's living rooms. A.J.P. Taylor (UK), Louis de Jong (the Netherlands), Maurice de Wilde (Belgium), Joachim Fest (West Germany), and Henry Michel (France)—to mention some of the pioneers—appeared as on-screen experts. They introduced documentary evidence, live witnesses, and film footage in support of powerful explanations of the shared past. Their common purpose was to present insights to the public at large, and thus these pioneering historians created public recognition for the academic specialism of contemporary history.

In essence, the political and moral dimensions of past experiences remain inseparable from the present in which the historians are at work. Regime change, political transition, and the application of justice are part of the legitimation and moral quality of the political regimes within their societies. The political significance of prosecuting and punishing the atrocities of predecessor regimes is to underline the idea that the old tyrants have been beaten and that the new rulers represent a clean slate. Nevertheless, while contemporary history writing is influenced by these present-day concerns, historians' work is often simultaneously oriented towards the future. New practices have emerged for coping with massive human rights violations after more recent regime changes in Latin America, South Africa, and East/Central Europe—like the establishment of truth commissions or lustration procedures.

This development has also extended the repertoire of the historical profession. Like many experts from other disciplines (e.g. international lawyers, psychologists, pastors, and political activists), historians have contributed ideas and reflections to what has become the field of 'Transitional Justice'. Whereas professional historians generally reject the popular notion that 'one can learn from the past' in order to avoid future evil, the promise of the new specialism seems to be that they can contribute to designing sets of 'best practices' for dealing with the traumatic aftermath of mass violence. Historian Annette Weinke argues that behind such optimism is a silent assumption of a clean slate after the collapse of a criminal regime.[10] This *Stunde Null* supposedly calls for the use of a toolkit that is future-oriented and aimed towards reconciliation and the reconstruction of nations; it, therefore, focuses on truth-telling, compensation and redress, and, in the end, forgiveness.

What distinguishes historians here is that they will search for context and continuities in order to explain which societal and political interests are having an impact on political transitions. Moreover, they are trained to evaluate trials and other procedures in terms of their significance over time. For instance, working for the prosecution in a war crimes tribunal prompts them to reflect on the problem of 'victor's justice', which is clearly related to providing legitimacy for the present and also for the future. Engaging in 'dialogues about the past' aims at the construction of bridges from the troubled past towards a future of greater justice and thus aspires to help societies come to terms with that past in an integrative manner. Creating shared narratives about past atrocities supposedly contributes to the integrative healing of a society consisting of victims as well as perpetrators.[11] Thus, historians are challenged by a persistent social demand to investigate the past, understand present concerns, *and* relate these to the future.

The continued search for historical knowledge and interpretation concerning war crimes and related mass violence events that challenge human understanding to the extreme has occupied historians both professionally and emotionally. Like Thucydides in his time, historians in the aftermath of the Second World War have felt the urge to report and explain the full extent of the agonies of their troubled times. Storytelling has always been a defining instrument in the historians' toolbox. Its strength is the power to capture audiences by offering seemingly immediate connections to those who lived in the past. Historiography (the practice of writing history) recaptures the experience of mass violence and proposes interpretations of why it happened. 'This is a history of political mass murder', historian Timothy Snyder announces in the introduction of *Bloodlands*—, his account of Nazi and Soviet mass-killing policies in Eastern Europe.[12] Presenting the bewildering facts is Snyder's first step towards grasping the historical significance of the mass killing of 14 million civilians, men, women, the elderly, and children.

Historical narratives such as Snyder's have a strong potential to make whole societies feel the need to engage in a process of coming to terms with the dark sides of their history. A potential drawback of historical storytelling—certainly not in Snyder's case—is the loss of analytical depth. Moreover, convincing narratives may become 'established' histories that discourage alternative points of view. At the same time, specialization and fragmentation have the potential to disconnect larger audiences from scholarly insight. In order to maintain its public impact, for example, historiography of the *Shoah* had been searching for the fundamental innovation of a 'grand narrative'. The controversies following Hannah Arendt's reporting of the Eichmann trial in Jerusalem would ultimately provide this, and the catchphrase about the 'banality of evil', although often misunderstood or misrepresented, still echoes into the present.[13]

As was the case in producing expertise on war crimes and atrocities, tribunals and trials for the criminal prosecution of such crimes played an important role in getting historiography started. Even before the Nuremburg International Military Tribunal began its deliberations, both victims and reporters published testimonies of the crimes in the mass media, as well as in brochures and books. These publications reflected an urge to know and to make known. Telling, showing (also in the form of images), and asking penetrating questions belonged to one and the same narrative. Historical fact-finding included the recovery, opening-up, and conservation of archival and other collections of documents and data. Such reporting produced the first narrative history of concentration camps and mass extermination. The post–Second World War trials of war crimes were primarily document-driven, and this is reflected in the historiography as well. Collections of relevant documents—like, for instance, the archives of Hitler's Foreign Ministry in the Berlin *Wilhelmstrasse*—were in need of immediate historical contextualization and interpretation after being taken and copied by the Allied occupiers. The early research has been dominated by the inductive analysis of empirical data. Historians delved into court files, official reports, and testimonies of victims, bystanders, and perpetrators, and discussed their findings in explanatory narratives.

In the late 1940s, an international community of historians developed an understanding that scholarship within the confines of national borders would be insufficient to understand a transnational crime like the Nazi atrocities.[14] The obvious interaction between scholarly impulses and social demand was demonstrated early on by Eugen Kogon's pathbreaking monograph *Der SS-Staat* ('The SS State'). The author, a former inmate of Buchenwald, had initially compiled his work to help the Allied liberators of Buchenwald understand the Nazi concentration camp system. Kogon later expanded his reports into a book and subsequently increased its scope. In the end, he saw his work not as a mere history of German concentration camps, nor as a compendium of atrocities, but 'primarily as a sociological study, in which the human, political, and moral implications are conceived as exemplary'.[15]

Immediately after the Second World War, across Europe, Jewish survivors of the Holocaust felt compelled to address the *Shoah*.[16] Dutch authors were among the forerunners in this area, and their work illuminates how strong a driving force personal experience of the devastating persecution was. Among the first monographs was *The War That Hitler Won*, published in 1947 by the German-Jewish journalist H. Wielek, who had lived in the Netherlands and who had been forced to go into hiding during the occupation.[17] The Dutch-Jewish lawyer Abel Herzberg published an early account of the persecution as a 'Chronicle' (1950). His argument was that the Holocaust was *Jewish* history, a part of a long-running experience of persecution, and that it was, therefore, not *Dutch* history. Under the German occupation, the Jews were on their own, he wrote, despite Dutch sympathy and efforts to help.[18] More than a decade later, the academic historian Jacob Presser was commissioned by the Dutch State Institute for War Documentation to write a monograph. He published his *Ondergang* ('The Destruction of Dutch Jewry') in 1965. The book offered an analytical interpretation of documents and testimonies, but as a matter of principle seen from the perspective of the victims.[19] Upon its appearance, the book sent a shockwave through Dutch society, due to its powerful narrative. Moreover, Presser addressed the question of complicity in the Dutch environment much more critically than Herzberg had done.

The motives, purposes, and constraints of historians working on genocide and mass atrocities are manifold—in particular when connected to personal experiences.[20] Herzberg had barely survived Bergen-Belsen, and Presser had been in hiding, while his wife was caught, deported, and killed. Herzberg was a leading Zionist, and from that point of view, he interpreted the role of the Dutch Jewish leadership in a largely positive sense. As a left-wing historian, Presser aspired to give a voice to the Jewish proletariat, the many underprivileged who had had to face persecution without protection. In 1965, Presser referred to Arendt's recent critical judgement of the Jewish Councils. He severely criticized the leadership of the Dutch Council for making themselves an instrument of diabolic German perpetrators, whereas Herzberg, as a lawyer, defended them in court against an indictment for collaboration.

In 1955, Louis de Jong, the managing director of the Dutch State Institute for War Documentation, was commissioned to write the history of the Netherlands during the Second World War. His idea was to write an integrative history of the Dutch, including the Jews, under occupation. His narrative described how society had been involved in the persecution—as villains, as heroes, as concerned or indifferent bystanders. De Jong chose to discuss the interactions between perpetrators and victims and the implications for society as a whole. In general, he was strongly inclined to judge individual and collective behaviour from a 'national' point of view—establishing who had contributed to the struggle for freedom and who had failed to do so. Only after finishing his multi-volume project, which was published between 1969 and 1981, did he confess that he had faced psychological constraints in discussing the fate of the Jewish community to which he himself belonged. De Jong had been in exile during the occupation but had had to cope with the violent death of his parents, siblings, and extended family. His first urge, he said, was to understand the Holocaust analytically and write about it. In the process, he discovered he could not do so without emotionally accounting for his responsibility to tell the story and to pass judgement.

The example of these authoritative Dutch authors points at the diversity of perspectives that historians could offer in pursuit of coming to terms with the worst crime ever to occur on Dutch territory. These historians helped make society at large ready to accept the facts and also consider them in terms of its own responsibility.[21] Their path-breaking narratives soon acquired an iconic status, even though they were very different in tone, scope, and interpretative framework. Nevertheless, both separately and taken together, they were seen to be above criticism and critical evaluation. This was the scene that up-and-coming academic historians faced at the time of the publication of Presser's account of the destruction of the Dutch Jewry. Whereas the mass media generally praised Presser for his emotional and evocative testimony of the experience of persecution, historian Ivo Schöffer raised eyebrows when he pointed to analytical weaknesses in Presser's striking narrative in a review, and his colleague Herman von der Dunk had his own critical review rejected by a leading historical journal 'for lack of respect' towards the book.[22] Nevertheless, within the historical profession, the urge to develop a fresh approach and greater conceptual clarity was growing. The fact that De Jong's series of monographs appeared on an annual basis from 1969 onwards provided an ever-stronger stimulus.

A historiographical landmark was the intervention of historian J.C.H. (Hans) Blom, at the time professor of Dutch history at the University of Amsterdam. From his point of view, the study of the history of the Second World War and the German occupation had been characterized for too long by an overdose of moralistic preoccupations. Blom was in no way a relativist, but he held that the time had come for conceptual and methodological innovation. His critique of De Jong, in particular, was an effort to modernize historiography by departing from moralistic reasoning in terms of searching for heroes and villains, of 'right and wrong'. He proposed international comparison and social science approaches. Such innovation, he argued, would liberate historical scholarship from being an instrument of memory politics. His first and enduring programmatic contribution was an article in which he tried to account for the disproportionally high number of Jews deported from the Netherlands, in comparison to Belgium and France.[23]

A new wave of historiography since the 1980s has provided more comprehensive interpretations of the legal hang-ups and political complications that surround the procedures for bringing war crimes and related atrocities to justice. Historical reconstruction restored crucial knowledge: how laws had been prepared for the punishment of war criminals and collaborators, how the jurisdiction had been organized, which procedures and norms had been applied, how punishment (and reintegration) had been implemented, who the perpetrators had been, how decisions about pardoning had been made, and how this had backfired on bilateral relations with the newly founded Federal Republic of Germany.[24] All such issues are defined by national laws and policies and at the same time became part of a developing transnational historiography.

Historians such as Donald Bloxham and Annette Weinke have argued that the prosecution of war criminals by the Nuremberg Tribunal has inspired the expanding specialization of *Tätergeschichte* ('Perpetrator Studies') and influenced the epistemology—Weinke mentions the search for Hitler's supposed command to exterminate all Jews in particular.[25] Meanwhile, the evaluation of trials, both national and international, has also produced a huge variety of histories of victimized communities, studies of concentration camps, and the ever-expanding subgenre of biographical studies. Internationalization was a distinctive feature of the search for more refined understanding. However, the ever-growing international community of scholarship also tended to develop into specialization of knowledge and fragmentation of insight. Thus, a danger came into existence of specialists knowing 'more and more about less',[26] while the general public is searching for trusted assumptions.

Consequently, in the Netherlands and elsewhere, the social demand for more integrative narratives continued to grow. Critical reflection was also stimulated by the 'linguistic turn' in historiography. The German historian Wulf Kansteiner argues that historiography, ever since the appearance of Hayden White's *Metahistory* (1973), cannot be discussed without systematically questioning the nature of the narratives and underlying methodologies. How do historians account for the choices they are making when organizing their narratives, applying instruments of style, and solving the complex relations between their research questions and selected sources, or between social and academic environments?[27] Since the 1990s, such issues have become apparent when new ways of accounting for the Holocaust were presented as integrated narratives. The Israeli-American historian Saul Friedländer's *Nazi-Germany and the Jews* (1998–2006) testifies to the successful innovation of the narrative style. Friedländer succeeds in bringing the fundamental uncertainty and disorientation of the victims to the centre of the narrative. By novel means of arranging time, place, and causality, the author centres his explanation in the suggestion that the victims found themselves encapsulated in a process that they could not understand and, therefore, could not develop counterstrategies to resist.[28]

Another contributor to conceptual innovation is the American historian Christopher Browning, who has integrated approaches from the social and behavioural sciences into the narrative of perpetrators in the Holocaust. In his path-breaking *Ordinary Men* (1992), he has reconfirmed the power of the genre.[29] Browning's history of the members of German Police Battalion 101 aimed to explain much about the whole framework of organized mass killings of Jews and Poles. He also made clear that it *had* been possible after all to withstand the *Notstandsbefehl* (superior orders under immediate threat of being shot). This turned the public perception in Germany and elsewhere upside-down. Likewise, in *Neighbours* (2001), the Polish-American historian Jan T. Gross confronted present-day Poland with a shocking narrative of guilt and responsibility with his powerful description of the July 1941 massacre of the Jewish population by villagers of Jedwabne.[30]

While 'Perpetrator Studies' originally occupied itself with the Third Reich,[31] such methods were expanded to other cases of war crimes, organized mass violence, and genocide.[32] German historian and social psychologist Harald Welzer has addressed the position of perpetrators in Vietnam, Rwanda, and the former Yugoslavia, pointing to the importance of shared standards of behaviour in connection with the situational context in which mass killing occurs.[33] In the Dutch case, the study of perpetrators has mainly focused on Dutch collaborators with the Nazi occupiers. One of the reasons is that this research trajectory has mainly been driven by documents and other sources created for the purpose of post-war trials. These trials, however, had a 'national interest' bias. For instance, the complicity of Dutch volunteers in the *Waffen-SS* mass killings in the East was hardly mentioned. These men were primarily considered and tried as traitors to the nation. Owing to the unfolding Cold War, legal exchanges between the East and the West were soon essentially non-existent. Consequently, early Dutch perpetrator studies primarily paid attention to atrocities in the context of combatting and suppressing Dutch resistance. These included psychological evaluations of the perpetrators in order to substantiate verdicts or decisions of clemency and reprieve.

Interdisciplinary Issues

In the immediate post-war period, reflection on the experience of the Second World War was a decisive impulse for establishing Contemporary History as a legitimate sub-discipline of historiography. Moreover, this new branch of historiography was institutionalized to serve the needs of society. Decades later, the field received fresh impulses from a new wave of museumization of the recent past. In 1993, the United States Holocaust Memorial Museum was opened in Washington DC, and an important research institute was attached to it. This was an influential example to be followed by many states that decided to commemorate and study the Holocaust and other historical cases of mass atrocities. The *Declaration of the Stockholm International Forum on the Holocaust* in 2000 confirmed the continuing commitment of governments to stimulate Holocaust education.

In the process, it has become obvious that professional historiography can only help to generate better understanding if it manages to enhance its analytical tools and, for that reason, is also prepared to engage with other disciplines.

As suggested above, connections to legal, political, social, cultural, and behavioural sciences are vital in the conduct of intensive debates on causality, responsibility, and impact. Moreover, the scholarly and socio-political function of research in this field is also influenced by the institutional environment. In several countries, including the Netherlands, specialized institutes were commissioned for the production of historical knowledge, including forensic evidence. These aspects prove to be largely interconnected, and, as a consequence, those working in the field continuously change their roles, shuttling between the activities of working in archives, writing monographs for academic audiences, testifying in court, participating in war pension boards, and presenting points of view in the mass media. Consequently, working in multi-disciplinary and multi-purpose units creates a permanent challenge to maintaining the standards of the historical profession.

The history of the *Institut d'Histoire du Temps Présent* in Paris leads back to a Committee for the History of the Occupation and Liberation of France, founded in 1944 under the auspices of General de Gaulle's provisional government. Likewise, two days after the Liberation in May 1945, the Dutch *Rijksinstituut voor Oorlogsdocumentatie* ('State Institute for War Documentation') was founded with the purpose of collecting archival and other collections to help post-war society, and posterity, to cope with and draw lessons from the experience of the Second World War. Other European institutions would share the purpose of working for the social interest, like the *Institut für Zeitgeschichte* in Munich, the Centre for Historical Research and Documentation on War and Society in Brussels, and the Institute of National Remembrance in Warsaw. In Israel, the *Yad Vashem* centre offered the example of a monument, a museum, and a research institute for the commemoration, exposition, and study of the *Shoah*.

In the work of the Amsterdam institute, the task of 'documentation' encompassed the whole range of collecting documents related to the Dutch in the Second World War, making these available for the public good, and bringing together a comprehensive body of sources for writing the history of occupation and repression.[34] There is a manifest, continuous, and very strong professional 'urge to know' within the different scholarly disciplines involved, as well as in the public sphere: journalists, politicians, administrators, or victimized communities. As a matter of fact, the public interest is a powerful motivation for historians and, at the same time, makes them subject to a very complicated set of responsibilities. Their professional engagement with the phenomenon of war crimes and their impact on contemporary society, as well as their legacies, may also lead to strong political, social, and moral pressures being exerted on their work.

From the beginning, the personal activism and professional ambitions of the staff of these institutions was crucial in supporting a politics of memory that political elites sought to establish in order to restore the political legitimacy and self-confidence of their resurgent nations. As the founding father of the Dutch institute, Louis de Jong formulated the purpose of his work—it was to teach the lessons of the experience of war and persecution and to create a stronger sense of national citizenship and democratic consciousness.[35] Although this concept came in many varieties, up to the present day it would represent the generic motivation for many initiatives in the multifaceted realm of memorialization of mass atrocities. Consequently, the purpose of such institutions, much like the research performed within them, produced a steady interaction between the political needs of the present and the urge to deal with the problematic past.

Historians were involved in these interactions in the immediate aftermath of the Second World War, within the framework of the international prosecution of war crimes and other cases of mass atrocities. From the beginning, historical expertise has been used to provide forensic evidence, not least by establishing the responsibility for atrocities and whether it lay with commanding officers or the personnel of political or state bodies. In this regard, the institutionalization of contemporary history proved to be an important asset for prosecutors and other instruments of justice. In the Dutch case, the War Documentation Institute brought together the relevant expertise—the staff was motivated to contribute to the prosecution and could be considered 'reliable' in both professional and political senses. Recent studies have demonstrated in detail how 'War Documentation' and Public Prosecutors interacted in the early post-war days.

The first step was collecting the archives of the occupation, both in the Netherlands and in occupied Germany. A Dutch mission explored the Allied collections of confiscated German archives in the Berlin Document Centre, and a liaison researcher was attached to the Nuremberg Tribunal.[36] This systematic acquisition of documents and copies of documents produced a significant addition to the institute's archival collection on the German occupation, for instance, concerning the involvement of the SS- and police apparatus in the regime of occupation. In the decades to come, these sources proved to be of much importance for historiography as well as for the legal prosecution of war crimes and Dutch collaboration.

Similar arrangements applied a decade later to the prosecution of Dutch and German perpetrators in West German courts. From the late 1950s onward, intensive cooperation between the War Documentation Institute and the (West) German authorities developed as the public prosecutor in Munich began procedures against so-called *Schreibtischtäter*, former German SS- and police officials, who had been responsible for organizing the persecution of Jews in the Netherlands. The example had been set by the Munich *Institut für Zeitgeschichte* within the framework of the Auschwitz trials in Frankfurt. In these reports, contemporary historians provided groundbreaking insight into the command structures of the Third Reich and the organization of its crimes against Jews, Soviet POWs, and other 'enemies of the Reich'.[37] What the Munich prosecutor in the Dutch case specifically needed to prove complicity in murder was evidence that the accused had known about the imminent fate of those who were to be deported. This is what the War Documentation Institute researchers focused upon, and they managed to dig up from the archives statements that the accused made during the war that helped to get them convicted.[38]

The Dutch experience of dealing with the legacy of war crimes includes several episodes in which the interaction between the media, the government, and the historical profession has generated heated debates and in-depth knowledge at the same time. Scholarship became linked with sentiments of public duty, moral outrage, and an 'urge to know'. A case that would bring war crimes back to the centre of political and scholarly interest was the trial of Pieter Menten, in the late 1970s. Menten was a Dutch millionaire art dealer who had gained a fortune through complicity with the SS-regime in occupied Poland. Over the case hung a cloud of sloppy prosecution and protection of the accused by prominent politicians.

In order to bring the case to an end, the government commissioned independent historians as experts to investigate. The researchers offered a contextual explanation, attributing the failure of justice to reasons connected with the political and legal confusion in post-war society. One of the underlying causes, they established, was a changing attitude in the late 1940s towards the legacy of war and occupation. According to them, 'the hangover of liberation' resulted from the fact that so many high hopes of creating a better and more 'pure' society had shattered against more urgent concerns. Continued economic austerity, the war in Indonesia, and the Cold War all caused popular frustration with the legacy of the war. The political purges and trials were also seen as unsatisfactory, and so people wanted to close the books and move on as quickly as possible.[39]

In the course of the 1960s, however, this state of mind had gradually reversed. The closing of the books had not resulted in collective satisfaction but in a sense of irreversible discontent. A new and critical generation started to ask penetrating questions about dealing with the past. They discovered imperfections in the purges and the trials, asked questions about the legitimacy of the procedures, and accused the post-war elites of opportunism and self-interest. This produced a re-evaluation of the trials based either upon the assumption of too much leniency (the 'spoiled purge') or excessive partiality ('victor's justice'). The Eichmann trial in Jerusalem and the Frankfurt Auschwitz trial were milestones in this process of rethinking the nature and meaning of the trials. In particular, the controversy following philosopher Hannah Arendt's report on the Eichmann trial pointed at the fact that historians were not alone in the practice of reflecting on the causes, impact, and legacies of war crimes.[40] Actually, they were not even in the forefront of the debates and were challenged by the political scientist Raoul Hilberg, who had analysed the German apparatus of persecution.[41] Nevertheless, the Eichmann controversy stimulated historians like Isaiah Trunk and Lucy S. Dawidowicz as well as sociologist Helen Fein in their pioneering research on Jewish victimization and its social, political, and administrative contexts.[42]

Besides providing expertise for the pre-trial stages, historians have been involved in war crime trials as expert witnesses. Such a role is more public, and may simultaneously tickle professional pride as well as create feelings of unease. A well-known controversy between French historians—among them Marc Olivier Baruch and Henry Rousso—on whether to participate as expert witnesses in the 1997 trial of Maurice Papon is informative in this regard. The importance of providing factual expertise and historical context was countered by the argument that knowledge about the past should be and remain clearly distinguished from knowledge about legal norms.[43] As a consequence, when invited or challenged to present historical expertise, historians are required by their professional standards to account for the epistemological and didactic limits of their knowledge—in particular the question of which facts can be established and which lessons can be drawn from historical research.

This is often not a very satisfactory public role to play. Judges, prosecutors, and barristers may shrug their shoulders impatiently ('just tell us what you know and what we can learn'), use parts of the testimony selectively for their own purposes, or completely ignore it. Being an expert witness as a historian involves soul-searching about maintaining professional standards, negotiating the modalities and limitations of the assignment with those who require the expertise, and finally considering which message gets through to the general public. Even as they aspire to contribute to solving vexing problems in court cases, contemporary historians are trained to keep their distance from thinking in terms of 'learning from the past' and from the political contamination of their work. Nevertheless, the tension between active participation of historians in war crimes and related trials, on one hand, and staying aloof for the sake of 'purity' has not been solved. Individual researchers have to weigh the pros and cons of participating in trials, considering that their expertise may be used to create usable narratives and interpretations or even to distort facts.

A third way of deploying forensic expertise is the provision of evidence that may lead to material compensation for victims of war and persecution. But these contributions are also not value-free or of a technical nature only. Formally, these are not judicial procedures, but under certain conditions, the application of these administrative procedures may have the same impact as criminal law.[44] The motivating questions in this area were not limited to finding evidence that a particular person had been victimized in a specific atrocity. Another consideration proved to be just as important—the question of 'national dignity', or whether the applicant had behaved like a true patriot. Such overlapping functions were bound to generate criticism about the relevant judgements. In a steady interplay between the justice system and the executive, the War Documentation Institute in Amsterdam built up an increasing degree of public authority over all matters concerning the Second World War and its legacy. At the same time, some senior staff here assumed the responsibility to judge their fellow citizens in terms of patriotism and civic virtues as displayed during the war. They felt competent to distinguish between 'right' and 'wrong', between 'good' and 'bad', and in their various assignments they did not hesitate to do so.[45] Seen from this perspective, their work was an extension of the politics of memory engaged by the post-war elites.

Overarching Theme: Coming to Terms with the Past

Contributing forensic expertise to trials, tribunals, and procedures of redress belongs to the politics of transition that are part of regime change. To punish the crimes of predecessor regimes underlines the fact that new rulers are in power and that these rulers are intent on making a new start. Related to the politics of transition, but not identical, is the politics of memory as a means to define the interpretation to the troubled past.[46] War Documentation Institute in Amsterdam and all related institutes have contributed to the resurrection of their post–Second World War nation-states, which urgently needed to give some sense to national experiences of oppression, defeat, and victory. 'Lessons learned' and the restoration of national pride were two sides of the same coin. Historians have simultaneously been challenged to develop counternarratives and to be confrontational about the 'difficult' aspects of the past. Thus, within the framework of present-day coping with historical evil and injustice, historians are called upon to inform debates about the Atlantic slave trade and slavery itself, the violation of aboriginal rights, or destruction of indigenous peoples, and of genocides as a component of contemporary repression and warfare.[47]

These repertoires also pertain when providing redress by means of remembering, restoring legal rights, and providing compensation for damages. In Germany, historical expertise was sought to inform decisions to compensate forced labourers in Hitler's war economy. Historians were asked to investigate the contaminated past of specific institutions and companies such as the foreign ministry, universities, and Volkswagen. In the Netherlands and elsewhere, historical expertise was sought in rendering justice concerning looted financial assets, art, real estate, and Jewish property in particular. Closely connected to such historical fact-finding was in-depth reflection on the way in which societies had dealt with victimized categories of citizens. Thus, historians made vital contributions to the establishment of truth, recognizing victimhood, and negotiating reconciliation. Here was an analogue with the globally admired work of the truth and reconciliation commissions of Latin America and South Africa.

In line with the same high-minded purposes, the Dutch government in the 1990s commissioned the former War Documentation Institute, presently the NIOD Institute for War, Holocaust, and Genocide Studies, to study several cases of 'unfinished business' from the Second World War. One project addressed the Dutch, European, and Eurasian communities in the former Dutch East Indies (presently Indonesia) that had been victimized under the Japanese occupation (1942–1945) and in the subsequent Indonesian War of Independence (1945–1949). These post-colonial communities felt themselves to be 'second class victims' and claimed recognition, compensation, and war pension benefits on an equal basis to other victimized and traumatized Dutch citizens. The second project concerned the 'cold-shoulder' attitude of post-war Dutch society towards several categories of war victims, including Jews returning from the concentration camps, forced labourers returning from their workplaces in Germany, and returnees from the colonies. Many of these returnees encountered insensitive neighbours and fellow-citizens and, above all, an impassive state bureaucracy unable or unwilling to tackle practical problems and share their psychological burden. These disheartening experiences had become part of the collective memory of the post-war period.

These historical research projects proved to be inspiring challenges for the institutions and scholars involved. They dove into the archives, conducted many interviews, and organized inspiring workshops. In terms of knowledge-gathering, they made huge progress and gained much insight. At the same time, scholarly output did not change many minds. Communities connected by a sense of victimhood did not readily shed their identities, even if they were able to relate better to the causes of their victimhood. Obviously, the politics of group identity clashed with historicization. As one of the protagonists expressed, 'what use is the truth if it hurts us?'[48] These cases illuminate the general phenomenon that historical scholarship cannot promote coping with the problematic past in a mechanical way. In open societies, the political agendas of rulers and specific interest groups may seek support in historical scholarship, but neither the outcome nor the reception should be pre-mediated. In fact, the published studies met with firm scholarly appreciation but a significant lack of public reflection.

Case Study: 'Our Boys' as War Criminals?

In the public debate, war crimes have the persistent potential to provoke strong feelings. This is particularly the case when one's own side is involved, and the attribution of individual guilt and collective responsibility may be a highly emotional affair.[49] This is illuminated by the alarmed reception to the photographic exhibition of the Wehrmacht's war crimes committed during the Second World War on the Eastern Front.[50] The exhibition produced arresting images of the crimes and of regular German soldiers as perpetrators. Criticism by some historians of the use of sources transformed into a passionate national debate on the criminal character of the German 'war of ideology' on the Eastern Front. Similar issues emerged in the long-running Dutch debates on war crimes committed by Dutch soldiers in the Indonesian War of Independence.

In 1969, a Dutch veteran caused national outrage by openly confessing on TV that he had participated in war crimes in Indonesia. His position that such crimes had been an endemic element of the war angered veterans as well as the mainstream mass media, which defended 'our boys' against the accusations.[51] The outrage was followed by a preliminary government report that did not deny that transgressions had occurred.[52] The report stated, however, that these crimes had occurred 'infrequently'. Moreover, the report used the official euphemism for war crimes—'excessive violence'. Subsequently, several individual cases were studied, among them the mass executions in southern Sulawesi in early 1947.[53] Two sociologists, also veterans of the war, wrote an in-depth study of the origins of the Dutch war crimes. They abstracted from specific places, persons, and time markers, and therefore, it remained impossible to get the stories confirmed or to find perpetrators.[54] Subsequently, historical interest in decolonization tended to shift in the direction of discussing the Dutch political decision-making process in the struggle with the Indonesians—in other words, away from issues of violence to the question of who had failed to bring the war to a desired end.

In 1981, however, the public debate made a turnaround as the 'national historian' of the Second World War, Louis de Jong, addressed the war of decolonization in Indonesia. His work on the German occupation had brought him widespread respect and public admiration, in which he had discussed crimes of war committed by German SS-, police, and military units and their Dutch collaborators. A particularly notorious case was the destruction of the small town of Putten. On 1 October 1944, German troops, by way of reprisal for a resistance attack, burned down the town's houses, shot inhabitants, and deported the male population to German concentration camps, where a large number of them perished. Like Oradour-sur-Glane and Lidice, Putten became a *lieu de memoire* ('site of memory') in the history of Nazi cruelty during the Second World War.[55] Now, arriving at the final volume of his series, De Jong proceeded to address massive atrocities committed during the Indonesian War of Independence. However, when he described how Dutch soldiers executed prisoners of war and burned down villages as the Germans had done in Putten, he was met with a public outcry.

As a draft of his manuscript was leaked to the press, war veterans and their supporters argued that it was completely inappropriate to refer to these incidents as 'crimes of war'. They maintained it had not been a formal war in the first place, as the Dutch troops had been deployed in order to restore internal peace and stability in the colony. De Jong's critics admitted that atrocities had occurred, but not on a structural basis. They held that the force of circumstances and, in particular, the guerrilla tactics of the enemy were the reasons for 'excessive violence' on the Dutch side. Clearly, the veterans and those speaking on their behalf felt scandalized by the fact that the 'national historian' had put them in a position they detested. They put so much pressure on De Jong that he felt he had to abandon the concept of war crimes in his draft manuscript. He adopted the terminology of his critics and changed the accusatory 'war crimes' to the euphemistic 'excessive violence'.[56]

Looking back, historian Stef Scagliola argues that for decades, Dutch historians have not paid enough attention to this issue—'Clio slept'.[57] Only since the turn of the century has research into Dutch war crimes in Indonesia been taken up once again. It may also be that historical research is primarily source-driven, and that historians, therefore, only feel ready to meet the social demand if new sources become available. Anyway, this new wave of interest occurred against a changing background of legal steps taken by the surviving relatives of Indonesian victims aspiring to gain compensation from the Dutch government, and of debates about the need for the Dutch government to formally apologize. New revelations in the press about serious atrocities committed by their own troops made clear to the public that the colonial war had not just been a 'policing' operation to secure peace and order for the benefit of the subjects.

Historians have begun to fill in the gaps by exploring open sources, testimonies of veterans, and recently declassified archives. At the same time, the subject could be linked to similar cases of violence in other wars of decolonization, such as those in Indo-China, Algeria, or Kenya. In 2012, several Dutch research institutes, among them the NIOD, proposed a project to investigate the violence of the colonial war. The government was reluctant to provide funding lest it endanger relations with Indonesia or disturb the veterans. As research was taken up with the available means, the government's decision remained pending for four more years, before being granted only in late 2016. All in all, the debate has finally opened up, almost seven decades after the events in question. The stories of victims and veterans alike are told and heard, uneasy matters are addressed, and using the term 'war crimes' no longer immediately enrages the participants. Surviving veterans who meanwhile have reached the age of 90 or more, or their families, even send in testimonies, diaries, letters, and pictures to the press and to the research institutes.

The newly studied sources reveal clearly that war crimes were committed by both sides in the Dutch–Indonesian war and have been an intrinsic part of that asymmetric conflict. They took the character of reprisals (e.g. burning down villages considered to be on the side of the enemy), counter-insurgency (extra-legal executions of suspect people), shootings of POWs, and the torture and killing of enemy combatants for the sake of extorting tactical information. Aside from fact-finding, there is a need to understand how both sides were brutalized by the struggle.[58] It has become clear that soldiers were permanently challenged to transgress the norms of regular warfare, as comrades-in-arms were brutally mutilated and killed, enemy snipers in the jungle eroded their nerves, and dangerous patrols across vast areas became routine. At the same time, such situational explanations served the goal of self-justification. They were publicly used as an antidote for critical voices and as a means for rhetorically turning perpetrators into victims.

Research questions now include more detailed study of the nature and the extent of the war crimes, of the circumstances that produced or encouraged transgressions, and in the legal, military, administrative, and political reasons and mechanisms behind decisions for (not) prosecuting war crimes committed within their own ranks. Finally, fundamental considerations of whether this was a 'just war' should be taken into account. Wars of decolonization were driven by deeply rooted value orientations, both within the independence movements and in the colonial states as well. These values include thinking in terms of racial superiority and believing in the righteous and beneficial impact of colonial rule. From this point of view, independence fighters were branded 'extremists' and criminals. Analysing such discourses of justifications for the war is, therefore, an indispensable element of the historiography of war crimes.

In the post–Cold War world, redress for historical injustices has become a moral norm and a political practice.[59] A noticeable case related to the Dutch–Indonesian war is a procedure started by activists and human rights lawyers. They are suing the Dutch state on behalf of the widows of the Rawagedeh massacre of 1947, in which almost 400 men were killed. International law, in conjunction with Dutch civil law, is now at the forefront of an effort to provide redress to the victims. Whereas it is too late to punish individual perpetrators, there is still an opportunity to address collective responsibility. The Dutch government has long hesitated to formally express regret. Finally, in 2005, the minister of foreign affairs, Ben Bot, apologized to his Indonesian counterpart for the fact that, during the war of decolonization, the Netherlands had been 'on the wrong side of history'.[60] This obviously well-intentioned explanation still implied that the Dutch could not have done differently, owing to the force of circumstances—a form of reasoning that should not appeal to historians. Subsequently, in 2013, the Dutch ambassador to Indonesia has apologized for the atrocities committed by Dutch troops. According to historian Paul Bijl, this step marks 'a move towards a more critical attitude in the Netherlands to its past human rights record'.[61]

Concluding Remarks

In 1989, after heated debates, the last two Germans serving life sentences for war crimes were released from their Dutch prison. The controversies about the question of whether or not they should be released kept the memory of executions, reprisal killings, and deportations alive. The continued punishment of these men gave evil a face and kept it locked in prison. Initially, thinking about war crimes was tied to war crimes committed by enemies only. However, the Dutch had to come to terms with their own responsibility as well. Historians have engaged in providing a deeper understanding of the nature of war crimes and the circumstances in which they occurred. They have addressed the position of victims and perpetrators, the social environment and political context, as well as the long-lasting legacies. The experience of the Second World War was a starting point for both coping and analysing. Following the Dutch case, we have seen how forensic expertise and narrative historiography first developed and became intertwined against a background of institutionalization.

This point of departure has, in the Netherlands and elsewhere, defined much of the historiography of war crimes. For many years, debates on 'other war crimes', like those committed by the Dutch troops in Indonesia, remained dominated by the Second World War paradigm. 'Our boys are no SS-men' was the aggressive defence of Dutch soldiers accused of atrocities. Even in the aftermath of the Srebrenica massacre of 1995, the Second World War discourse returned as a metaphor. As Dutch UN peacekeepers were criticized for failing to protect the Bosnian Muslim population of the 'safe area', it was observed that 'the nation of Anne Frank failed once again to protect people like her'.[62]

What have historians to offer in taking up Thucydides' legacy? Narrative history is important as it directly connects in-depth research on human exploits to the public sphere. Meticulous reconstruction of historical processes informs debates on prosecution and prevention of war crimes while weighing the importance of socio-economic, political, and cultural contexts, as well as interpreting actions, constraints, and motives. Moreover, historians can challenge presentist and teleological outlooks, and, at the same time, have an open eye for the role of the individual within a collective. Furthermore, they are able to make connections to concerns and approaches in other disciplines, like, for instance, legal studies. For example, their interdisciplinary contribution to this field is restoring knowledge about how in the past legal systems, procedures, and cultures (including normativity) were constructed and operated. This is extremely important for a deeper understanding of the legal frameworks, the norms applied, and the verdicts of trials and tribunals dealing with war crimes.

Historians have contributed in many different ways to reflections on the causes, the nature, and the impact of war crimes. Their pioneering epic narratives produced in the first decades after the Second World War were read as eye-openers because they helped to relive the history. Present-day historical research is no longer a one-direction, top-down movement from the expert to an audience hungry for insight, between a 'national teacher' and a 'national classroom'. And neither are historians on their own: they are part of a multi-disciplinary effort for interpretation, which includes legal scholars and professionals, social and political scientists, and scholars working in cultural and media studies. Very recently, new sub-disciplines and cross-disciplines have emerged within the ambit of historiography. Heritage studies address the need for the conservation of material evidence (as in the Cambodian 'killing fields'), court and tribunal records (like those of the Nuremberg, Tokyo, and other international tribunals, but also of national justice procedures), and oral testimonies (like the collections of the *Gacaca* 'community justice' procedures in Rwanda).

The rapidly expanding digital availability of enormous amounts of these trial records challenges us to develop new methods of mass data-mining and analysis. Thus, historiography has been diversified by means of interdisciplinary research—internationalized along with all forms of scholarship and democratized as a result of much more involvement, presently by means of increased access to open sources and data collections—even though the latter factor also leaves much to be desired. In any case, the capacity of historians to provide research strategies and interpretations will remain indispensable for collective understanding of war crimes as one of the worst manifestations of the human character.

Bibliographical Essay

The body of scholarly literature on societies dealing with the impact and legacies of war and mass violence is as diverse and extensive as the phenomena themselves. In their efforts to conceptualize the many-faceted socio-political aspects of war crimes and related matters, historians are borrowing from other disciplines, in particular from the legal, social, and political sciences. The following notes cannot pretend to be more than a set of informed suggestions on the part of the present author, and make no claim to cover or represent the field as a whole.

War, War Crimes, and Mass Violence

Many monographs offer a broad scope of insight into the history of war and warfare; a very useful first introduction can be found in an edited volume that will help interested readers to find further avenues of reading: Charles Townsend (ed.), *The Oxford History of Modern War* (Oxford: Oxford University Press, 1997; 2005). A comprehensive exploration of sociological concepts concerning 'war, violence and the social' is Sinisa Malesevic's *The Sociology of War and Violence* (Cambridge: Cambridge University Press, 2010). In a formal, legal sense, crimes of war are one element of a broad repertoire of organized mass violence and murder against large groups of people, including both soldiers and civilians. A path-breaking contribution to historical understanding of the whole spectrum of atrocities of the recent past is Christian Gerlach's *Extremely Violent Societies: Mass Violence in the Twentieth Century World* (Cambridge: Cambridge University Press, 2010).

The history of the Holocaust is discussed broadly by historians and social scientists. One of the defining studies is Christopher R. Browning and Jürgen Matthäus' *The Origins of the Final Solution: the Evolution of Nazi Jewish Policy 1939–1942* (Jerusalem and Lincoln, Nebraska: Yad Vashem and University of Nebraska Press, 2004). A historiographical standard is the two-volume monograph: Saul Friedländer, *Nazi Germany and the Jews* (New York: HarperCollins, 1997 and 2007). An all-encompassing effort to edit the most important sources of the Nazi-persecution and extermination of the Jews all over occupied Europe is a series planned to encompass 16 Volumes, edited by Susanne Heim, Ulrich Herbert, Michael Hollmann, Hans-Dieter Kreikamp, Horst Möller, Gertrud Pickhan, Dieter Pohl, and Andreas Wirsching: *Die Verfolgung und Ermordung der Europäischen Juden durch das nationalsozialistische Deutschland 1933–1945* (Munich: Oldenbourg Verlag, 2008–). Meanwhile, the historiography of genocide has followed the establishment of the new international regime of criminal law during the second part of the twentieth century. An excellent survey of many different cases and dimensions is edited by a prominent scholar in the field: Dan Stone (ed.), *The Historiography of Genocide* (Basingstoke and New York: Palgrave Macmillan, 2008).

Legal Responses, Trials, and Tribunals

The origins of international law intended to regulate the conduct of war and the punishment of transgressions belong to the nineteenth century and were codified in international treaties, like the Hague Convention of 1907, the successive Geneva Conventions, and the Rome Statute founding the International Criminal Court (1998). A broad overview is Alexander Zahar and Göran Sluiter's *International Criminal Law: A Critical Introduction* (Oxford: Oxford University Press, 2008). The development of international law concerning the protection of individuals against organized state- and state-related violence is Ruti Teitel's *Humanity's Law* (Oxford: Oxford University Press, 2011). In the aftermath of the Second World War, the International Military Tribunals of Nuremberg and Tokyo have had a profound influence on the conceptualization of war crimes and genocide. An evaluation, with particular emphasis on historiographical questions, is Kim C. Priemel and Alexa Stiller's (eds.) *Reassessing the Nuremberg Military Tribunals: Transitional Justice, Trial Narratives, and Historiography* (New York & Oxford, 2012). The more general idea of transitional justice includes a variety of practices and repertoires for dealing with disruptive mass violence which lie both within and outside the legal sphere. An authoritative survey is Jon Elster's *Closing the Books: Transitional Justice in Historical Perspective* (Cambridge: Cambridge University Press, 2004). The political trials conducted in different European states, including the Netherlands, aimed at dealing with the legacies of National Socialist and fascist rule is the subject of Istvan Deak, Jan T. Gross, and Tony Judt (eds.), *The Politics of Retribution in Europe: World War II and its Aftermath* (Princeton: Princeton University Press, 2000).

War Crimes on Trial: History and Memory

As legacies of disruptive mass violence, retributive justice and the politics of memory are separate and at the same time closely connected issues. The different repertoires for dealing with historical injustice are the subject of Elazar Barkan, *The Guilt of Nations: Restitution and Negotiating Historical Injustices* (New York & London: W.W. Norton and Company, 2000), and Manfred Berg and Bernd Schaefer (eds.), *Historical Justice in International Perspective: How Societies Are Trying to Right the Wrongs of the Past* (Cambridge: Cambridge University Press, 2009). Donald Bloxham's *Genocide on Trial: War Crimes Trials and the Formation of Holocaust History and Memory* (Oxford: Oxford University Press, 2001) discusses the role and importance of international criminal law for shaping the memory of the Holocaust. Richard A. Wilson, *Writing History in International Criminal Trials* (Cambridge: Cambridge University Press, 2011), discusses the connections between historical expertise and criminal legal procedures in international courts and tribunals.

A broad overview of the politics of memory in post-1945 Europe can be found in Richard Ned Lebow, Wulf Kansteiner, and Claudio Fugu (eds.), *The Politics of Memory in Post-war Europe* (Durham & London: Duke University Press, 2006). A collection of national cases (including the Dutch one) is Nico Wouters' (ed.), *Transitional Justice and Memory in Europe (1945–2013)* (Cambridge, Antwerp, and Portland: Intersentia, 2014). The historiography of the Holocaust in the Netherlands is discussed in Conny M. Kristel, 'Survivors as Historians: Abel Herzberg, Jacques Presser and Loe de Jong on the Nazi Persecution of the Jews in the Netherlands', in David Bankier & Dan Michman (eds.), *Holocaust Historiography in Context: Emergence, Challenges, Polemics, and Achievements* (New York & Jerusalem: Berghahn Books & Yad Vashem, 2008), pp. 207–224.

Notes

1. Thucydides, *The History of the Peloponnesian War*, for instance: Book 1, Kylon (126–127); Book 2, the Thebeans and Plataeans (5–6), Cleon/Mytiline.
2. Michael Grant, *The Ancient Historians* (London: Weidenfeld & Nicholson, 1970), 95–97. On violent regime change in Athens at the time: John Elster, *Closing the Books. Transitional Justice in Historical Perspective* (Cambridge: Cambridge University Press, 2004), 7–16.
3. The Statute of the International Criminal Court defines war crimes as, inter alia, 'serious violations of the laws and customs applicable in international armed conflict' and 'serious violations of the laws and customs applicable in an armed conflict not of an international character'—ICC Statute, Article 8 (Vol. II, Ch. 44, § 3). For more on the complex evolution of the terminology and legal status of 'war crimes' and 'crimes against humanity', see Jan Martin Lemnitzer's chapter in the present volume.
4. Ruti G. Teitel, *Transitional Justice* (New York/Oxford: Oxford University Press, 2000), 60–61.
5. Christian Gerlach, *Extremely Violent Societies. Mass Violence in the Twentieth-Century World* (Cambridge: Cambridge University Press, 2010); idem, *The Extermination of the European Jews* (Cambridge: Cambridge University Press, 2016); Donald Bloxham, *The Final Solution. A Genocide* (Oxford: Oxford University Press, 2009); Jacques Semelin, *Purify and Destroy. The Political Uses of Massacre and Genocide* (London: Hurst & co., 2007).
6. Yehuda Bauer, *Rethinking the Holocaust* (New Haven: Yale University Press, 2001), chapter 3.
7. Henry Rousso, "Therapeut und Richter. Was ist Zeitgeschichte in Frankreich zu Beginn des 21. Jahrhunderts?" in *Was heißt und zu welchem Ende studiert man Geschichte des 20. Jahrhunderts?*, ed. Norbert Frei (Göttingen: Wallstein Verlag, 2007), 53.
8. Henry Rousso, *La hantisse du passé. Entretien avec Philippe Petit* (Paris: les Editions Textuel, 1998), 63.
9. Norbert Frei, "Nach Broszat," in *Martin Broszat, der "Staat Hitlers" und die Historisierung des Nationalsozialismus*, ed. Norbert Frei (Weimar: Wallstein, 2007), 7–16.
10. Annette Weinke, *Gewalt, Geschichte, Gerechtigkeit. Transnationale Debatten über deutsche Staatsverbrechen im 20. Jahrhundert* (Göttingen: Wallstein Verlag, 2016), 258–260.

11. Elazar Barkan, *The Guilt of Nations. Restitution and Negotiating Historical Injustices* (New York/London: W.W. Norton & Co., 2000).
12. Timothy Snyder, *Bloodlands. Europe between Hitler and Stalin* (London: The Bodley Head, 2010), x.
13. Hanna Arendt, *Eichmann in Jerusalem. A Report on the Banality of Evil* (New York: Viking Press, 1963) as an author, and as the protagonist in Margarethe von Trotta's feature film *Hannah Arendt* (2014).
14. A leading figure being the Polish-Jewish historian Philip Freedman (1901–1960) according to: Conny M. Kristel, *Geschiedschrijving als opdracht. Abel Herzberg, Jaques Presser en Loe de Jong over de Jodenvervolging* (Amsterdam: Meulenhoff, 1998), 12–14.
15. Eugen Kogon, *Der SS-Staat. Das System der deutschen Konzentrationslager* (Munich: Wilhelm Heyne Verlag, 1991–1923. Auflage), 11.
16. Conny M. Kristel, *Geschiedschrijving als opdracht*, 12–21.
17. H. Wielek (pseudonym of W. Kweksilber), *De oorlog die Hitler won* (Amsterdam, 1947).
18. Abel Herzberg, *Kroniek der Jodenvervolging 1940–1945* (Amsterdam: E. Querido, 1950 (1985—5th revised Ed.)), 19.
19. Jacques Presser, *Ondergang. De vervolging en verdelging van het Nederlandse Jodendom 1940–1945* (Den Haag: Staatsuitgeverij, 1965); English translation: *Ashes in the Wind* (London: Souvenir Press, 1968) and *The Destruction of the Dutch Jews* (New York: Dutton, 1969).
20. Kristel, *Geschiedschrijving als opdracht*, 292–305.
21. Louis de Jong, *Het Koninkrijk der Nederlanden in de Tweede Wereldoorlog* (14 Volumes—Den Haag and Amsterdam: Staatsuitgeverij/Martinus Nijhoff/SDU, 1969 (Vol I)—1991 (Vol. 14).
22. Kristel, *Geschiedschrijving als opdracht*, 246–248.
23. Johan C.H. Blom, "The Persecution of the Jews in the Netherlands: A Comparative Western European Perspective," *European History Quarterly* 19, no. 3 (July 1989): 333–351. Blom inspired a number of historical studies in this specific field, culminating as an all-encompassing comparison in: Pim Griffioen and Ron Zeller, *Jodenvervolging in Nederland, Frankrijk en België, 1940–1945* (Amsterdam: Boom, 2011).
24. August David. Belinfante, *In plaats van bijltjesdag. De geschiedenis van de bijzondere rechtspleging na de Tweede Wereldoorlog* (Assen: Van Gorcum, 1978); Christiaan F. Rüter, *Enkele aspecten van oorlogsmisdaden en misdaden tegen de menselijkheid* (Amsterdam: Associated Publishers, 1973); Peter Romijn, *Snel, Streng en rechtvaardig. Politiek beleid inzake de bestraffing en reclassering van 'foute' Nederlanders* (Houten: Unieboek, 1989).

25. Donald Bloxham, *Genocide on Trial. War Crimes Trials and the Formation of Holocaust History and Memory* (Oxford: Oxford University Press, 2001), 200–208.
26. David Bathrick, Brad Prager and Michael D. Richardson, eds., *Visualizing the Holocaust: Documents, Aesthetics, Memory* (Woodbridge: Camden House, 2008).
27. Wulf Kansteiner, "Gefühlte Wahrheit and ästetischer Relativismus. Über die Annäherung von Holocaust-Geschichtsschreibung und Geschichsttheorie," in *Den Holocaust Erzählen. Historiographie zwischen wissenschaftlicher Empirie und narrativer Kreativität*, ed. Norbert Frei and Wulf Kansteiner (Göttingen: Wallstein, 2013), 13
28. Ibid., 28–29.
29. Christopher R. Browning, *Ordinary Men. Reserve Police Battalion 101 and the Final Solution in Poland* (New York: HarperCollins, 1992).
30. Jan T. Gross, *Neighbors. The Destruction of the Jewish Community in Jedwabne, Poland* (Princeton: Princeton university Press, 2001).
31. As represented in Klaus-Michael Mallmann and Gerhard Paul, eds., *Karrieren der Gewalt. Nationalsozialistische Täterbiographien* (Darmstadt: Wissenschaftliche Buchgesellschaft, 2004).
32. A. Dirk Moses and Bart Luttikhuis, eds., *Colonial Counterinsurgency and Mass Violence. The Dutch Empire in Indonesia* (Abingdon/New York: Routledge, 2014).
33. Harald Welzer, *Täter. Wie aus ganz normalen Menschen Massenmörder werden* (Frankfurt: Fischer, 2005).
34. As regulated in a *Royal Decree concerning the Rijksinstituut voor Oorlogsdocumentatie* (1981) and in the transfer of the NIOD to the Royal Academy of Arts and Sciences in 1999.
35. Boudewijn Smits, *Loe de Jong 1914–2005: Historicus met een missie* (Amsterdam: Boom, 2014).
36. Annemieke van Bockxmeer, *De oorlog verzameld. Het ontstaan van de collectie van het Rijksinstituut voor Oorlogsdocumentatie* (Amsterdam: De Bezige Bij, 2014), 162–170.
37. Christian Ritz, *Schreibtischtäter vor Gericht. Das Verfahren vor dem Münchener Landgericht wegen der Deportation der niederländischen Juden (1959–1967)* (Paderborn: Ferdinand Schöning, 2012), 178–180.
38. Ibid., 149, 170–177.
39. *De affaire-Menten 1945–1976* (Den Haag: Staatsuitgeverij, s.a., 1979).
40. Hannah Arendt, *Eichmann in Jerusalem: A Report on the Banality of Evil* (New York: Viking Press, 1963).

41. Raoul Hilberg, *The Destruction of the European Jews* (New York, 1961; revised version: Holmes & Meier, 1985).
42. Isaiah Trunk, *Judenrat. The Jewish Councils in Eastern Europe Under Nazi Occupation* (New York: Macmillan, 1972); Lucy S. Dawidowicz, *The War against the Jews 1933–1945* (London: Penguin, 1975, 2nd Ed. 1987); Helen Fein, *Accounting for Genocide: National Responses and Jewish Victimization during the Holocaust* (Chicago/London: Chicago University Press, 1979).
43. Henry Russo, *La hantisse du passé* (Paris: le Seuil, 1998), 85–138.
44. Teitel, *Transitional Justice*, 149–189.
45. Elly Touwen, *Op zoek naar grenzen. Toepassing en uitvoering van de wetten voor oorlogsslachtoffers* (Amsterdam: Boom, 2010).
46. Konrad H. Jarausch and Thomas Lindenberger, *Conflicted Memories. Europeanizing Contemporary Histories* (New York/Oxford: Berghahn, 2007); Norbert Frei, ed., *Transnationale Vergangenheitspolitik. Der Umgang mit deutschen Kriegsverbrechern in Europa nach dem zweiten Weltkrieg* (Göttingen: Wallstein, 2006).
47. Berber Bevernage, *History, Memory, and State-Sponsored Violence. Time and Justice* (New York: Routledge, 2012), 1–16.
48. Johan C.H. Blom, "Wat hebben wij aan de waarheid als die ons hindert?: verificatie in de wetsuitvoering," *Cogiscope: Tijdschrift over de gevolgen van oorlog en geweld* 2, no. 2 (2006): 14–23.
49. Peter Romijn, *Der lange Krieg der Niederlande. Besatzung, Gewalt und Neuorientierung in den vierziger jahren* (Göttingen: Wallstein Verlag, 2017).
50. The exhibition "Verbrechen der Wehrmacht. Dimensionen des Vernichtungskrieges 1941–1944" of the Hamburg *Institut für Sozialforschung*, shown 1995–1999; in a revised form, 2001–2004.
51. Stef I. Scagliola, "'Clio's 'unfinished business': Coming to Terms with Dutch war Crimes in Indonesia's War of Independence," in *Colonial Counterinsurgency and Mass Violence. The Dutch Empire in Indonesia*, ed. A. Dirk Moses and Bart Luttikhuis (London: Routledge, 2014), 240–260.
52. *De excessennota* (with an introduction by Jan Bank—Den Haag: SDU, 1985).
53. Willem IJzereef, *De Zuid-Celebes affaire. Kapitein Westerling en de standrechtelijke executies* (Dieren: de Bataafse Leeuw, 1984).
54. Jacques A.A. van Doorn and Wim J. Hendrix, *Ontsporing van geweld: over het Nederlands-Indische/Indonesisch conflict* (Rotterdam, 1970).

55. De Jong, *Het Koninkrijk, Vol. 10b 'Het laatste jaar'* (Den Haag, 1981), 50–67.
56. Ibid. and *Vol. 12—Epiloog* (Den Haag, 1988), 1011–1061 and Annex 2.
57. Hans Blom, see footnote 48.
58. Rémi Limpach, "Business as Usual: Dutch Mass Violence in the Indonesian War of Independence 1945–49," and Peter Romijn, "Learning on 'the job': Dutch War Volunteers Entering the Indonesian War of Independence 1945–1946," both in *Colonial Counterinsurgency and Mass Violence. The Dutch Empire in Indonesia*, ed. A. Dirk Moses and Bart Luttikhuis (London: Routledge, 2014), 64–90 and 91–110.
59. Elazar Barkan, *The Guilt of Nations. Restitution and Negotiating Historical Injustices* (New York/London: W.W. Norton and Co., 2000), Preface, xi.
60. *De Volkskrant*, August 16, 2005; "De verkeerde kant van de geschiedenis".
61. Paul Bijl, "Colonial memory and forgetting in the Netherlands and Indonesia," in *Colonial Counterinsurgency and Mass Violence. The Dutch Empire in Indonesia*, ed. A. Dirk Moses and Bart Luttikhuis (London: Routledge, 2014), 301.
62. Christ Klep, "A Tale of Two Commissions. Dutch Parliamentary Inquiries During the Srebrenica Aftermath," in *Investigating Srebrenica: Institutions, Responsibilities, Facts*, ed. Isabella Delpla (Oxford/New York: Berghahn, 2012), 68.

Peter Romijn is Head of Research at the NIOD Institute for War, Holocaust, and Genocide Studies (The Netherlands) and Professor of twentieth-century history at the University of Amsterdam. His research interests are the history of politics and administration in times of war and crises, including regime change and political purges, during the Second World War and Decolonization.

7

Violence Studies: Social Theoretical Considerations Towards Understanding of War Crimes

Christian Gudehus

From War Crimes to Social Theory

Fundamentally, war crimes are actions or clusters of action that are labelled as such on the basis of a juridical and moral evaluation.[1] Beyond these very specific evaluations, which are not always unambiguous, they are actions or, more precisely, acts of a violent nature. It is these acts, and the approaches used to analyse them, that are subject of this chapter. Key social scientific and social psychological concepts are introduced and considered as to how far they bear the potential to contribute to our understanding of war crimes. There are two points to keep in mind. Firstly, only the smaller part of these approaches deals with war crimes or even with violence. Rather, they are theories dealing with actions in a more general manner. Secondly, the body of theories outlined here is

For the translation from German I am grateful to Jessica Holste (J.H.).

C. Gudehus (✉)
Institute for International Law of Peace and Armed Conflict, Ruhr-Universität Bochum, Bochum, Germany

J. Waterlow, J. Schuhmacher, *War Crimes Trials and Investigations*, St Antony's Series,
https://doi.org/10.1007/978-3-319-64072-3_7

complex and rooted in enduring scholarly debates, so they are introduced only selectively with reference to some specific authors. However, their application is repeatedly outlined and, towards the end of the chapter, exemplified by two case studies. Crucially, these theories are used by scholars and practitioners who investigate war crimes from various disciplinary backgrounds, yet they frequently do so without a deep understanding of the nature and limitations of these frameworks.

The concepts originate from various disciplines and focus on different aspects of human action. Therefore, this chapter addresses several epistemologies, methodologies, and practices. These are employed to examine the subject of violence/war crimes and thus may be integrated into one strand of the diversified field of violence studies. Similar to memory or gender studies, violence studies is not an academic discipline in the traditional sense of the word, but a field to which the researchers of many disciplines contribute. This research becomes interdisciplinary whenever approaches, explanatory models, methods, and so on, of different disciplines are used systematically and integrative—that is, in a truly concerted rather than in a merely complementary manner—to explain violence. Attempts by one discipline to draw on another are common—for example, when historiographical or sociological research draws on social-psychological classics.[2] They are employed to help interpret violent actions that other disciplines struggle to explain. Frequently, concepts such as conformity, obedience, or peer pressure are used in particular research projects to explain the individual motivation of actions. Nonetheless, in such cases, the approach may in principle still be confined to a particular discipline. As an alternative to this confinement or segregation, I would like to adopt an approach that focuses on individual action and its conditions. This approach is necessarily interdisciplinary as it incorporates different levels of human sociality and explains them. To put it more precisely, these are social and cognitive frames that open up and limit courses of action, social interpersonal relationships of actors, situational factors, and, eventually, individual features. Since the larger part of the elements relevant for such an approach belongs to social theory, this—as a field, not a discipline per se—should be discussed first.

Social Theory: Action and Social Change

The German sociologists Hans Joas and Wolfgang Knöbl sum up the core questions of social theory as follows: 'We believe that the theoretical development of the social sciences can be understood as revolving around three very specific questions. These are "What is action?"; "What is social order?"; and "What determines social change?" All theorists—and this applies to both the *classical* authors of sociological theory as well as *modern* social theorists—have taken up these three questions. We should add that these are of course always closely linked: the *actions* of human beings are never entirely random. *Social orders* always develop, and these are subject to historical *change*.'[3] Accordingly, the subjects of social theory are, firstly, the permanent stabilization and simultaneous change of social constellations. Secondly, it explores the role of individual actions as part of these dynamics. It is immediately apparent that the objects of investigation—society, action, sociality, and so on—are not even considered independently of temporal change for heuristic reasons, but that instead their fundamental principles are transition, change, and the processual and dynamic forces.

In many respects, wars are places of massive societal—that is, social and therewith also psychological—change. (1) Their aim—not necessarily also their cause—is usually either violently to bring about or to avoid a particular state of social relations.[4] For if an agreement existed between the actors—if only as regards the modes of a violence-free arrangement of relations—a war would not be necessary. Even wars initiated for domestic political reasons aim at a change of relations with the opponent (or opponents). (2) Wars change societies and the individuals constituting them. This change does not exclusively entail apparently negative consequences like death, physical mutilation, or a number of psychological damages that have corresponding effects on social relationships. War requires the readiness and ability to resort to violence. People must learn to use violence competently.[5] This is an ability of a physical, cognitive, emotional, and also social nature that is largely dysfunctional and thus undesirable beyond war or other defined spaces and contexts of violence (e.g. sports, slaughterhouses, torture, execution). Accordingly, what is required is the creation of the competence to be violent and its simultaneous containment. It is precisely in this space that the object of scrutiny—war crimes—is situated: they are deeds of violence that are (at least temporarily) undesired in specific instances in the context of, in principle, not only desired but also required violence. The failure to exert violence is as much subject to sanction as is wrongly executed violence. Violence can be deemed wrong due to the timing of its execution, its intensity, as well as the choice of its target. Accordingly, actions of this type are neither prohibited nor allowed in principle, and, hence, their legitimacy and often their legality depend on context. However, contexts frequently consist of a complex network of social norms, situational requirements, codified rules, social relationships, and a panoply of various frameworks. They are, accordingly, everything but unambiguous and require interpretation. To reconstruct and understand this interpretative activity requires tools that do not merely facilitate the differentiation between wrong and right but that investigate the formation of actions in specific contexts. Furthermore, any such research has to focus on the question of how far individual actions contribute to the formation of contexts. Action and context are one.

All theories of human action have to analyse the relationship between the individual who, being a single person, seems to be empirically graspable, and the social and physical world surrounding them. This question interests historians as much as jurists, sociologists, brain researchers, socio-biologists, or philosophers. A look at the theoretical and empirical approaches of social scientific and psychological research shows that these relationships are predominantly explained by recourse to three levels of approach: These are the person, the situation, and the frame. Only the latter will be addressed in the context of this publication.[6]

Frame

Unfortunately, *frame* is a term used as much in everyday life as it is a defined concept in academic discussions. This highlights a difficulty: Few neutral terms exist in this field. Either we find that even such a seemingly unequivocal word as ‘action’ is closely connected to specific theoretical positions, or the metaphorical character of many terms blurs their meaning. In the context of this chapter, 'frame' is used as a general term for the idea that modes of perception and interpretation—and, thereby, one's options to act—are not necessarily created on an individual basis. Rather, individuals are situated in a network of customs, habits, rules, patterns of action, things conceivable, etc., in which they each develop their specific ways to act.

At first it might be confusing that in addition to this general usage of the frame metaphor, another specific one exists. The choice of term is particularly inspired by the thought of the sociologist Erving Goffman, who defines it as follows: Each framework 'allows its user to locate, perceive, identify, and label a seemingly infinite number of concrete occurrences defined in its terms. He is likely to be unaware of such organized features as the framework has and unable to describe the framework with any completeness if asked, yet these handicaps are no bar to his easily and fully applying it.'[7] In this way, frames are points of reference for every perception, interpretation, and action. They contain notions as to 'how the world functions' and 'what people are like' as well as 'what to do and what not.' In fact, such notions are a type of knowledge that in some cases is explicable and hence available, whereas in others it is implicit and hence not available to acting individuals. This frame knowledge—that is, the competence to refer to frames, to understand them, to act in them and to know 'what, one manages or does not manage to do, talk and arrange when, where with whom'[8]—fulfils a series of psychological functions: "It is a means of orientation and provides 'unproblematic, common and supposedly warranted *background convictions*'; it provides 'ontological safety'; and it is the basis of the fear-absorbing processing of irritations that are translated back into known and accustomed patterns."[9]

Mentality

Another concept commonly employed in everyday speech is that of mentality. It is used to ascribe a typical mode of behaviour to groups that is conditioned by the way they feel, think, or view the world. No matter how superficial or often simply wrong such ascriptions may be in individual cases, they are nonetheless at their core useful in two ways. First, collectively shared modes of how situations are perceived and interpreted actually exist. They are the result of experiences likewise shared by the collective (hence, they are experienced by all or most individuals belonging to the collective and have subsequently been sedimented). Second, mentality as an aid to interpretation ('they have such and such a mentality') is itself proof for the usefulness of ready-made modes of perception in everyday life, since these help to categorize and comprehend (certainly at times wrongly) events with little effort and thus pave the way for being able to act. As the term implies, it refers to mental, intellectual—in this case cognitive—processes. When the term mentality is used in the academic context of the science of history, many definitions circle around this comprehension. They refer to dispositions, unconscious assumptions, structurings that precede action.[10]

Research on mentality focuses on the reconstruction of the modes of perception and interpretation of historical actors. In this way, a methodical circle is established: Mentality prefabricates options or potentialities to act, yet it is difficult to empirically prove this influence. In order to research and prove them, an analysis of collective action is required. Its recognizable patterns and common features shed light on the mentality that, in this conception, precedes action.[11] However, the usage of the term varies. Gerhard Schreiber, who investigated German war crimes that took place in Italy during the Second World War, understands mentality to be a consequence—and, as such, a cluster—of a whole array of factors: 'Explanations for this killing legitimated by the government [...]—motivations determined by the situation notwithstanding—result, as mentioned above, from factors related to military considerations, power politics, occupational politics, ethnic considerations and race ideology that in total—especially when dealing with the resistance—lowered the inhibition threshold to destroy Italian life in a direct or indirect fashion, i.e. that brought into existence a mentality facilitating the ordering, execution or tolerance of murder on Italian soil.'[12] Schreiber understands mentality as a constellation of social, political, and cultural characteristics that suggests certain options to act. Felix Römer, an expert in military history, refers to mentality exclusively in the plural. In the final analysis, though, he also draws up a cluster of factors that he considers responsible for the propensity to violence, including the committing of crimes. These comprise nationalism, racism, camaraderie, and militarism as much as a soldierly ethos that demands toughness, the dedication to act, and a strong sense of obligation.[13] All in all, mentality might be described as a socially generated psychological space of action.

Figuration

Figuration, a concept developed by the sociologist Norbert Elias on the basis of historical but also qualitative empirical research, espouses the notion that relations of people, groups (of various sizes), or institutions towards each other influence the individuals' repertoires of action.[14] Accordingly, humans are involved in social networks. Amongst other influences, their actions result from their relations as members of social groups of different types towards each other. With reference to Elias, Michaela Christ illustrated how the figurations of actors in a Ukrainian town continuously changed with the approach of the German troops; the siege of the town; the German occupation; the successive realization of German racist politics; the ghettoization of the Jews; their murder; and, eventually, the conquest of the town by Soviet troops. As a consequence of these changes, the actors' perceptions of the situations shifted and therewith the perceived—and hence also the considered—options to act.[15] An illustrative example is the time between the withdrawal of the Red Army from Berdichev and the Wehrmacht's occupation. It created a vacuum of power that was used by the town's citizens to raid the homes and businesses of those refugees—often Jews who, aware of their imperilment, had fled from the Soviets. Consequently, according to Christ, the power relations between Jews and non-Jews changed in favour of the latter. While the Jews were witnessing the distinct instability and fragility of their position, the others saw a potentially expanding range of possibilities to become rich at the Jews' expense and without punishment. Yet figurations define the individuals' modes of thinking and acting on a much more fundamental level. Consider, for instance, when Elias discusses the French court of the eighteenth century and, in this context, describes how norms are not merely rules obeyed or ignored but are an integral part of historical figurations 'whose commands individuals can escape only if they renounce contact with their social circle and membership of their social group. These norms cannot be explained by a secret buried in the breasts of large numbers of individual people; they are explainable only in the context of the specific figuration formed by these individuals and the specific interdependences binding them together.'[16] Similarly, he describes prejudice as 'a normal aspect of the social beliefs of an established group in defense of its status and power against what is felt as an attack of outsiders against them.'[17] It is in exactly such constellations that a relational concept of freedom and determination surfaces. Elias thinks 'of "the freedom" of each individual as part of a chain of interdependences linking people to one another and limiting individual possibilities of decision and action.'[18] Accordingly, every kind of framework bears the potential to free and to limit at the same time. It is liberating to live in social constellations that provide relatively stable orientations for the execution of small elements of action (e.g. greetings) as well as complete life designs. However, these very same things may be perceived as restrictive, if not oppressive, depending especially upon the respective positions of individuals in a given social network. This is aggravated by social sanctions placed on dissidents that guarantee the relative stability of such formations. Those who do not adhere to shared interpretations must thus be ready to pay the price in the corresponding social and psychological currency—the loss of recognition. In peaceful, pluralistic, affluent societies that also are not subject to rigid social controls, deviance is easy. This is even more so the case since there is always the chance of social change that might bring about the general recognition of one's own interpretation. This is undoubtedly different in situations such as war where belonging and solidarity, expressed as value, emotion, or action (for instance, in the form of customs), are of central importance to any social organization—and probably also to physical survival.

Social Norms

The aforementioned shared interpretations, their relevance for perceived or real options to act, and the role of social sanctions already represent central elements of a theory of social norms. What is now of interest are the explanations as to how such norms develop, how they are related to individual actions, how they, on the one hand, are stabilized and what, on the other, causes their modification or even their removal. The German sociologist Heinrich Popitz explicitly freed himself from the constraints of sociological traditions, and his work is therefore easily accessible to the layman. Popitz defines norms as those expected forms of regular behaviour whose absence or violation causes social sanctions.[19] The repertoire of sanctions ranges from disapproval over repressions, discrimination to punishment.

However, in complex societies, the extension of norms, if not their violation, occurs on a regular basis. Individuals violate others' expectations for various reasons. They might do so intentionally (I violate a norm knowingly and deliberately), the violation might be a side effect (the violation of the norm was not the goal of my action), or completely unintended (I simply acted). It might be the consequence of creative processes (this could be done differently) or simply of laziness and a lack of interest. People know of a norm when they expect sanctions in the case of its violation or when they react to other people's violations with sanctions. In a simple case, a violation of a norm is followed by a negative reaction. As a consequence, the norm is kept intact and the social order in question is stabilized. Accordingly, not only the degree to which a norm is followed indicates its validity, but also the readiness to protect it. This is precisely the key to processes of change. Norms fade—lose their influence on actions—when their violation is sanctioned only hesitatingly or, eventually, not at all. Correspondingly, the expectation to be sanctioned is lowered and thus the authority of the norm fades. The fact that individuals in many cases do not know whether other members of a community obey norms also contributes to the stability of norms.[20] There are many reasons for the absence of sanctions. One is that the absence of disapproval of violations entails considerably fewer sanctions, as does the violation of the norm itself. At the outset, however, it is, according to Popitz, of secondary importance whether people violate norms or else do not sanction a violation because they are lazy, disinterested, or do it intentionally. It is much more important that all of this takes place in the form of *actions*. Norms are produced by actions; they are stabilized by them, questioned, violated, and so on. It is in this sense, incidentally, that non-acting does not exist. Not to sanction the violation of a norm might lead to the violation continuing. Accordingly, the focus is not on values that inform actions, but on social relations within which norms that inform actions are performatively negotiated.[21] Consequently, norms cannot be empirically recorded when people state which norms are valid in their opinion, but only when actual actions are observed.

With the aid of examples, Popitz illustrates how far actions can fundamentally change power relations and social orders. He presents the example of a ship on which only a limited number of deck chairs is available but whose distribution is, at first, unproblematic.[22] They are used as they are required, and since the ways and times to use them differ, a casual arrangement develops. However, when new people arrive on board and others leave the ship, a minority—the new arrivals—changes this practice. These people reserve the unused deck chairs for each other. This action already establishes a norm: It results in a mutual confirmation of claims. What is done is right because others do it too, and it is done for one another. There are multiple consequences. First, two groups are created—the privileged and the excluded. While the action of the first group generates an organizational structure, this is missing in the second group that should organize itself, seek confrontation, and that, eventually, should defend its newly proclaimed right. Even if the confrontation resulted in victory, completely new social orders and social norms would have been established in action, that is, performatively. This example is another case in point, illustrating just how little effect specific intentions regarding a set of actions may have on actual consequences. The starting point was nothing but the wish to have a deck chair available at all times, a lack of trust in the old order, or simply a lack of knowledge concerning the hitherto prevailing practice.

Theories of Action

Frames, figurations, and mentality conceptualize the social conditions of individual actions. On the one hand, they all claim that options to act, even their mere perception, are considerably influenced by these *sedimented experiences*.[23] Yet, at the same time, all of these concepts emphasize that individuals are not determined by but rather continuously position and reposition themselves in relation to their environment. In this context, frames may be as much consolidated as they might be varied or even extensively modified. The same holds true for social norms that are an essential element of such sedimented experiences themselves. This positioning and repositioning is the core of what might be understood as action. Theories of action are interested in exactly this process. In fact, a whole array of social scientific theories of action exist whose representatives at times attack each other and who, more importantly, emphasize the—from their point of view—fundamental and often allegedly insurmountable differences in their respective theories. This is, at least to some degree, certainly due to the prestige-generating relevance of theory construction, which is especially typical for sociology. If one, metaphorically speaking, takes a step back, though, and looks at the fundamental assumptions from a distance, convergences come into view.

In research on the psychology of action, *acting*, *doing*, and *behaviour* (in German, *Handeln*, *Tun*, and *Verhalten*) are differentiated. *Acting* refers exclusively to those actions that are the result of processes of reflection, hence they are profoundly intentional. In contrast, *behaviour* rather indicates actions carried out as a reflex, involuntarily. *Doing* is a category for cases that will not fit within the other two concepts, hence it at least seems to be a somewhat hapless category, where an action might be planned, but the motives causing the action are hidden to the actor.[24] Whether or not one accepts this differentiation, it already contains essential elements of the theorization of human acting. First, we are once more confronted with the problem of labelling, because all three terms are used almost synonymously in everyday speech and because an umbrella term does not exist, which is itself quite revealing. As a temporary aid, the term *performance* (in German, *agieren*) could be used. More important are the previously mentioned, essential criteria of differentiation—*rationality* and *availability*. *Rationality* indicates to what degree actions can be the result of considerations and, thereby, of plans. *Availability* refers to what individuals know or can know about their motives to act but also about the conditions of their actions—thus it alludes to *frames*. There is hardly a theory of action belonging to the social or cognitive sciences conceivable that would not discuss these points. The principle opposing or complementing a profound rationality is, however, not so much irrationality or ignorance, but rather something that is already implied in the approaches outlined above. The function of frames to serve as an aid to orientation does not, after all, imply that they have to be considered in much detail before an action is carried out. In fact, the relation between individual action and sedimented experience—be it *figuration* or *habitus*,[25] to mention another prominent concept of the social sciences that is used in violence studies[26]—manifests itself in a set of so-called scripts, routines, or automatisms of a considerably varying stability and range. The terms vary depending on the theoretical provenance. They illustrate that performance does not imply a constant, complete recreation, but rather a more or less varying repetition of tested modes of perception, comprehension, and action. Or, as Hartmut Esser, a sociologist supporting a rational choice approach, formulates it, 'Frames and scripts are mental *models* of typical situations and sequences of action, which are stored in the memory, tied to specific contents, focused on certain aspects, and simplifying "reality" drastically.'[27]

Theories of action are concerned with the evidently central difference between automatism and deliberation. Even what seem to be fundamentally different approaches converge on the view that there exist automatized, routinized modes that are barely or even not at all subject to deliberation, carried out in order to assess situations and to appropriate them or to develop an action (according to a social theory perspective),[28] or to choose one (according to the rational choice approach).[29] In contrast, there are those who consider a high level of conscious, reflexive, and, in the empathetic sense of the word, thoughtful confrontation with the situation of action a necessity in order to do justice to the variously combined exigencies in each situation.

Hartmut Esser has worked out the points of agreement between the rational choice theories and the social theory of Alfred Schütz. In this context, both approaches are most interested in the common differentiations of routinized, habituation-based modes, on the one hand, and, on the other, those that are preceded by a deliberate 'choosing between projects of action like an accountant.'[30] Clemens Kroneberg, Esser's student, undertakes a comparable differentiation and distinguishes a *reflexive-calculative* mode of processing of information in the framework of action processes from an *automatic-spontaneous* one.[31] Comparable insights can also be found in the writings of another sociologist, Hans Joas, albeit formulated quite differently: 'Given that the fundamental forms of our capacity for action lie in the intentional movement of our body in connection with locomotion, object-manipulation and communication, our world is initially structured according to these dimensions. We divide the world into categories such as accessible and inaccessible, familiar and unfamiliar, controllable and uncontrollable, responsive and unresponsive. If these action-related expectations inherent in our perception of the world are not met, we do indeed dissociate ourselves from a part of the world which now surprisingly transpires to be inaccessible and unfamiliar, uncontrollable or unresponsive, and accord it the status of an external object.'[32] 'This means,' Joas argues, 'that even acts of the utmost creativity assume the pre-existence of a bedrock of underlying routine actions and external conditions which are simply taken as given.'[33] The sociologist Anselm Strauss also complies with this differentiation when he argues that, at the bottom line, no action exists that is not in one way or another based on routines: 'Routine aspects are encapsulated even in an act carried out for the first time, in the form of bodily skills such as walking, culturally devised gestures, listening and speaking. Stretching the term *routine*, perhaps, one could claim that perception and memory, which are thoroughly social in character and which enter into and make possible most if not all nonreflexive action, have been routinized through repeated experiences with the world.'[34] Again, the differences between the various approaches should by no means be negated, yet the convergence between different modes of decision making is striking and ultimately articulates the relation between reflexive and automatized elements in any theory of action.

At the very least, these considerations imply that the relation between the reflexive and the routinized is not exclusively an opposition. The determination of the actual relation ultimately depends on the individual cases under scrutiny. And it is precisely at this point a difference between theories that claim general validity—as they explain action on a fundamental level—and the empathetic reconstruction of actual war crimes can be discerned. The theories aim to sensitize, and they indicate possibilities as to how actions might be understood. They cannot be transferred readily. It is a common mistake to assume that all actors are equally conditioned or even determined by frameworks and routines. However, theoretical as well as empirical research should, firstly, delineate spaces for creativity, and it should, secondly, not ignore individual differences.

Adjustment, Appropriation, and Creativity

People learn societies—that is, how to orient themselves in social and physical environments—in manifold and complex ways. One decisive dynamic for many of these processes comprises *adjustment* and *appropriation*. Everyone must continuously relate to the social and physical world surrounding her/him (the quality of the latter naturally is also the result of social processes that may be analysed). For the most part, this ultimately happens in a process combining adjustment and appropriation.[35] *Adjustment* means—I orient my performance towards the expectations I assume others have.[36] It is immediately obvious that this interpretive process requires a minimum of analytical skills and, indeed, of creativity. The more ambiguous these expectations in the shape of social norms or role requirements are,[37] the more room is left for creativity. From an analytical vantage point, *appropriation* is, strictly speaking, the following step. The foreign is internalized. I do not only adjust, but I habitualize what is new to me. It becomes (for me and for others) something taken for granted. Accordingly, adjustment and appropriation are two closely related aspects of the same thing. Both require interpretation and creativity. The result of such processes, however, can only to a certain degree be predicted because these appropriations are, in the terms of the narrative of *Alltagsgeschichte* (the history of everyday life), *idiosyncratic* (*eigensinnig*). Its most prominent representative, Alf Lüdtke, accordingly declares the reconstruction of forms and practices of appropriation to be the essence of the historical research following this school of thought.[38]

This also stimulates the research on (war) crimes. The historian Elissa Mailänder has, for instance, described the process of adjustment and appropriation undergone by female guards in the German concentration camps very vividly.[39] The often quite young women presumably take up their posts without a clear idea of the modes of behaviour that will be expected of them. Accordingly, at the outset, many are surprised, in some cases even shocked, when, for the first time, they are confronted with the violence their colleagues use against the prisoners.[40] At first, they do not behave according to the social norms of the camp that do not correspond to those outside and therefore act 'wrongly.' For instance, some newcomers initially greet prisoners who tried to make space for them. Within a short time—some days or weeks—though, a change also of the *habitus* becomes perceptible for the prisoners. The guards grow into their uniforms and their boots—they change their gait, their look, their facial expression, and the corresponding behaviour.[41] 'Idiosyncratic' also implies that bureaucratic and juridical norms are deliberately shunned. Mailänder shows exactly these idiosyncrasies when some of the guards disobey orders in various contexts, who complain and refuse, who occasionally even argue vehemently with their male colleagues or superiors.[42] All these observations indicate a space in which performance is by no means determined, but may be appropriated. Incidentally, there were a number of women who quit their work in the camps quite quickly for reasons that cannot now be determined. In these cases, the process of adjustment and appropriation was interrupted.

Interruptions like these, as well as the aforementioned processes, indicate individual differences and spaces of creativity. The latter may be due to a number of factors and take on various forms. The most common form of creativity (1) is the continuous navigation within requirements and routines. It is the daily adjustment in largely established social contexts accomplished by everybody. Furthermore, (2) creativity is necessary when there is no prefabricated script or routine, or otherwise when there are competing scripts and routines available to solve a problem. This applies especially in contexts of a violent nature, such as wars and war crimes. Far more rarely, (3) creativity occurs as innovation, that is, as a variation or further development of a rule, a technique, a process, and so forth, that exceeds the mere continuation or differentiation of what is accustomed. The first two variants of creativity occur within systems of rules that are handed down from one generation to the next, whereas the third may gradually exceed these. Another ideal-typical mode is (4) the intentional questioning of valid processes and the development of new points of view and questions. *New* is always a relational concept. The types of creativity vary by degrees. In the social world, nothing is ever exactly the same. Similarly, innovations are based on preconditions because they depend on techniques, technologies, modes of thinking, social orders, and the like. Consequently, from the vantage point of action theory, custom (or routine) and creativity are not opposites.[43]

Practices

As was shown in the introduction to Heinrich Popitz's approach, social norms and power relations are not only conditions but are in fact the consequences of individual action. Popitz thus anticipated a development that in the social sciences is called the *performative turn*.[44] This development, also discussed under the umbrella term of praxeology, signifies a shift of attention in the research on human interaction. The relevance of ideas for the accomplishment of human actions is put into proportion by a focus on actions as processes of interpretation of appropriation that eventually constitute reality. These tendencies are already implied by many of the theories outlined so far. The theory of practice goes one step further.

The different forms of sedimented experience—among others, mentality, figuration, habitus, but also some action-theoretical concepts—are available to individuals in different ways. They may to some degree become subject to reflection. At the same time, individuals differ in their ability to do this. However, this cognitive penetration of the social environment and its conditions that motivates and frames one's own performance is but one possible technique of interpretation. Another such mode of referring to the external world is of a distinctly different nature and points to the core of how human action is understood. What this means can be illustrated with the corresponding considerations of creativity: 'In the presented action model we ground creativity *in* action. Therewith, we do not search for the variable, indeterminate quality of social practices in anteceding tendencies or abilities of subjects, but in the sequence of practices themselves: in their success or failure, in their continuous new launches and the modifications of the already existent. Not the actor, but the practices with their sequences of, and problems with, action are the starting point of analysis.'[45]

Practice theory even goes one step further and turns its focus away from the acting subject and towards practices. Andreas Reckwitz, a renowned representative of this approach, defines practices as follows: 'A practice is thus a routinized way in which bodies are moved, objects are handled, subjects are treated, things are described and the world is understood.'[46] With reference to the acting subjects, he points out: 'It invites us to regard agents as carriers of routinized, oversubjective complexes of bodily movements, of forms of interpreting, knowing how and wanting and of the usage of things.'[47] Once more, the objects of investigation are not even specific actions anymore, but, for instance, beating or torture understood as already acquired knowledge 'out there'[48] that only needs to be individually appropriated, as Theodore Schatzki, another leading representative of this theory, has put it. In this interpretation, these practices are available as a type of non-cognitive knowledge and may be 'understood as know-how-dependent routines of behaviour linked up by a practical type of "comprehension". Knowledge of them is, on the one hand, "incorporated" in the bodies of the acting subjects and, on the other, regularly takes on the form of routinized relationships between subjects and the material artefacts "used" by them.'[49] At this point, two aspects must be emphasized. First, the relevance attributed to artefacts. They belong to a physical world that is not merely used and manipulated, but that may itself have an action-guiding, if not action-forcing, character. If we consider war machinery and weapons as such artefacts, this immediately makes sense. Second, routines are also a part of practice theory. In no way are they described as immutable. 'What is much more important for what eventually becomes routine, however, is the "process of working through" (in German, *Abarbeitung*) of practical problems and specific situations in which resistance is experienced, new things are learned, applied and linked up with other elements of practical knowledge.'[50] Not only their individual appropriation but also the complexity of social and object relations necessitate variation.[51] What is more, 'Apart from the fact that the mere "application" of a practice might put to the test the practical abilities of the actor because it is conditioned by context and time, it is primarily the structural feature of a subject to be a heterogeneous cluster of knowledge (in German, *Wissensbündel*) that constitutes an element of unpredictability.'[52] In other words, individuals are exposed to so many different requirements and possibilities to cope with these that it is absolutely necessary for them to be idiosyncratic or innovative. Whether practice theory really presents a new paradigm or whether it is rather a new emphasis within already-existing elements of theories is a question that continues to be discussed.[53] For the purpose of understanding war crimes, it provides further arguments in favour of the notion that *doing*, its formation, its routine-like aspects, and its creative components, should be the focus of analysis.

The historian Sven Reichardt, undoubtedly one of the pioneers of using praxeology in studying history, develops an epistemology that comprises all elements mentioned: 'The connection between bodily routines of behaviour, collective patterns and subjective attributions of meaning of historical actors as well as the historical anchoring of their identities and symbols become the central subjects of analysis and theory formation.'[54] Yet, Reichhardt does not only theorize, he also applies. In his historical analyses of German and Italian fascist combat leagues, he tests the usefulness of praxeological theory. And indeed, it is the action—the shared, often violent acting—that becomes the specific feature of these groups. 'Not the ideology or a coherent, political programme made fascism an independent and clearly distinguishable phenomenon, but the combination of the forms of its political practice with the political attitudes.'[55] Violence—and this is the reason why this is a relevant example for the research on war crimes—in this context is not merely understood to be a consequence of ideology or pressure, to be a side effect, or even only an element of community formation. It is simultaneously its engine and the adhesive gluing everything together. The physicality of violence is evident. Its execution becomes routine, a normal element of this sociality. 'It was violence itself that created communality.'[56] A similar line of argumentation is applied to the National Socialist 'people's community' that was effectively far more than an ideological concept and again was created performatively, also and especially by violent acts of varying intensity.[57]

The approaches outlined here help to explain human action in general. It is important to bear in mind that they allow a grasp of the topic, offer a frame of interpretation, pursue and enable a specific form of understanding. But they do not generate hard facts, they do not prove, but imply, argue, and make plausible. This vagueness diminishes their appeal for some researchers who are looking for reliable, provable if-X-then-Y relations.[58] Yet, because they can appear to deliver just these, some classic social psychological experiments are frequently referred to whenever explanations are sought for the participation of people in extremely widespread violence. They are cited to illustrate factors such as autonomy, conformity, obedience, or peer pressure that themselves are intended to bridge gaps in explanatory models. However, if they are to be applied legitimately, some potential problems must be kept in mind. Thus, some specific features of the generation of social scientific insights must be accounted for since they are not readily compatible with other approaches of social science, not to mention the arts. Therefore, similar to primary sources, they must be critically scrutinized in order to find out what they actually claim or prove and what lies beyond their reach. Furthermore, their methods and results are subject to interpretation and hence may be understood and employed in differing ways. Accordingly, it might prove useful to undertake an exemplary, critical investigation of the potential of such a study to explore this point further.

Experimental Social Psychology: Concerning a Regularly Used Classic

Experimental social psychology sheds light on the average behaviour of individuals in settings that are (allegedly) reduced in their complexity. This reduction is intended to control all factors—called variables—that are relevant to behaviour. As such, the aim is to create a social situation in which conditions may be entirely controlled, if possible. It is assumed that the frequency or intensity of each investigated aspect of behaviour can be traced back to few, often even just one variable. Is this really possible?

One of the most prominent social psychological experiments is a good example of the many pitfalls that threaten these approaches as well as their transfer to other contexts. The Milgram experiment has not only very frequently been referred to in order to explain violent action,[59] it is still the subject of academic discussion[60] and has, over the decades, been used in schooling, as well as being the subject of a number of films and other artistic projects.[61] The title of the most important publication on the study, 'Obedience to Authority,'[62] immediately demonstrates the issue. The experimental assembly is well known, as is the result of one key variant: A majority of test subjects punishes the mistakes other people make when solving tasks with eventually very large and probably dangerous electric shocks.[63] They do this, according to the usual explanation, because they follow the examiner's orders or leave the responsibility for possible consequences up to him.[64] It is interesting to consider a number of further observations that are made in the 18 variants of the experiment, for example: (1) The more the examiner distances himself from the situation (e.g. by instructing the test person over the phone) or the more his position is doubted (a second scientist disagrees), the more people interrupt the experiment. (2) The closer the task-solving individual is to the test subject, the more people interrupt the experiment. (3) Especially in the filmed version, we witness people bringing the test to an end without any visible signs of stress, yet the majority sooner or later hesitate or try to begin a discussion with the attending scientist. There are, of course, further aspects to consider, yet already the discussion of these three examples indicates an abundance of additional possible interpretations besides obedience.

The test subjects are in an either-or-situation unusual for everyday life. They have a social obligation towards the test or the examiner. They, at first, do what was agreed upon or, more precisely, what they think is expected of them. The equipment, notably the sequence of switches to be flipped, might imply another logic of continued doing. This doing is highly repetitive, so that routine might quickly set in. The valid script is that agreements must be followed. To sum up: One does what the overall situational constellation suggests.[65] Considered from this vantage point, obedience is not the right concept. An intersubjective agreement exists stating that the examiner informs the test subject what to do. As the examiner is the one who is not new to the situation, it can be assumed that he knows what has to be done. Moral considerations—what is good, what is bad—only come into play as regards the observance of social conventions since what the test subject primarily does is to be in a social situation and to act in it. The flipping of the switch, however, is a kind of secondary action. The irritation occurs when the student to be punished expresses that he will not comply with the agreed rules. This directly contradicts the already established routines. Accordingly, often quite a number of disapprovals are necessary before the test subjects react visibly or audibly. They get caught in a dilemma. The compliance with the social agreement is revoked by one side, yet the other side insists on its validity. What gives the reactions of many participants such a smack of scandal is that the injury of another person is considered taboo and that this injury becomes central to the situation. Correspondingly, it seems inhuman not to interrupt the injury. Yet there is no previously determined option to deal with the situation. An interruption was not discussed and thus is unprovided for. Despite this, many, probably even most, participants would like to stop the injury, but not necessarily the experiment. However, they cannot even negotiate this. Neither the examiner, who constantly repeats prefabricated sentences,[66] nor the problem-solving individual, who eventually completely refuses to answer, allows the test subject to negotiate agreed-upon options to act.[67]

This distinguishes the situation from most constellations in everyday life—there is no way out that does not require the defiance of a social norm or the lack of compliance with a social obligation. At least, that is what it looks like. In this context, the filmed documentation of the experiment visibly illustrates another feature of human performance. A test subject clearly expresses their intention, verbally and physically, to interrupt, yet is repeatedly asked to continue. Eventually, the subject finishes the experiment. In the following debriefing, the man answers the question posed by Milgram himself, 'Why didn't you stop anyway?' 'I wa—I did stop, but he kept going, keep going.' 'But why didn't you just disregard what he said?' 'He says it['s] got to go on, the experiment.'[68] It becomes apparent that the individually recognizable options to act vary within seemingly stable situations. Hence the man does not fail to interrupt because he is a bad person or enjoys violence. He simply does not recognize the possibility to do this. If the Milgram experiment really addresses the issue of obedience, then it does this in a very specific sense: Obedience here is a social agreement, a social norm (sanctions are expected), and indeed also a routine. It becomes effective when an individual, for whatever reason, has difficulties in obeying the agreement, to execute the routine. Only when disobedience becomes an issue does it make sense to speak of obedience. Prior to this, what is done is simply what has been agreed upon.

Obedience—in the context of wars, the following of orders—is itself an agreement.[69] The experiment hence yields insights into a very specific constellation: How do people behave in a situation of contradictory action orientation? The answer is: The majority at first tries to negotiate (obviously without success). When this has failed, the participants follow what they consider the more dominant action orientation. However, this is not apparent and cannot be calculated reliably by either the actor or the observer. In this reduced situation, the action orientation is formed in the interplay of space, routines, elements of communication, and—this is where we leave the field of experimental social psychology—of psychological traits and experiences that people have acquired prior to the situation. The latter concerns the individual and their way of navigating in the world. While this may vary depending on the situation, it is, for instance, likely that someone who has developed a strategy of avoiding unpleasant situations will fall back on it under the given circumstances. In contrast, someone else might tend to endure unpleasant moments. All these are speculations that we shall now abandon. It should now be clear how the interpretation of a seemingly unequivocal experiment might well deviate from explanations that have been communicated hundreds of times. Accordingly, the re-reading of the Milgram experiment is a first application of some of the hitherto discussed approaches.[70]

Applications and Clarifications

It transpires that, from a methodological point of view, the focus on actions and/or practices derived from social theoretical considerations at first entails the task of describing their specific features. *Who does what in which way?* is, therefore, the first question. It is followed by an interpretation drawing on a matrix of analytical considerations that offers possible explanations, but does not impose them on the situation. Elements of analysis are the identification of routines or scripts, reconstructions of figuration or habitus, the detection of dynamic forces, the tracing of processes. Although this approach starts with the reconstruction of situations, this does not mean that frames exceeding them are not relevant.[71] Allen Kramer has analysed a case of German atrocities in Belgium during the First World War with similar means.[72] Close to a Belgian town, German soldiers were constructing a pontoon bridge across a river. The town had previously been searched and civilians taken hostage—which provides the context in which the people involved would perform next.

They were afraid of (civil) snipers (*Heckenschützen*) who allegedly illegally killed German soldiers in a way that the latter perceived as sly or unfair. Kramer attributes this myth of the *franc-tireurs*, to events that had occurred 40 years earlier when such actions really were performed by the French: 'German histories of the war 1870–1, historical novels, magazine articles, and military education manuals all helped to ensure there was a predisposition to expect *franc-tireurs* in 1914.'[73] The officers were ordered to react strongly to civilian resistance. Diverse narratives[74] concerning such attacks that were (wrongly) considered illegal circulated. As a matter of fact, German soldiers were indeed fired upon. Although in this situation it was obvious for at least some Germans that the aggression originated from regular troops, the frame of interpretation, the fear, the orders (in German, *Befehlslage*), the fact that hostages had been taken, and so forth, created a fatal dynamic that would conclude with the shooting of more than 70 people—among them toddlers, children, women, and men. Kramer rightly emphasizes that a dynamic cannot take the part of a subject. It is people who act. They do this rooted-in experiences that are sedimented to various degrees and that do not only create their modes of perception but also their sensibility.[75] They fall back on practices in which sequences such as the taking of hostages or mass shootings are already prefigured. The dynamic element certainly does not imply inevitability. On the contrary, what happens cannot be determined until it takes place. The muttered opinion of a German soldier that civilians definitely could not have fired the shots might have been ignored or recorded. This is open to debate. Again, it is apparent that—notwithstanding frames, social obligations, routines, and so forth—options to act are not determined. This is all the more so because frames, social obligations, routines, and so forth simultaneously allow for different actions. For this reason, for example, some people helped Jews to evade National Socialist persecution.[76]

Once more, the approaches introduced here can help to explain and understand events that the experts in question call war crimes. They are by no means the only promising approaches and, more importantly, are not exclusive. Research modes as different as individual psychology or statistics likewise contribute to the investigation of these and other phenomena. However, in this chapter, the primary focus was on action and its formation. This systematic linkage of existing concepts with empirical evidence is clearly one direction the study of large-scale violence takes.[77] It should be clear by this point that in order to make full use of theories that explain individual and collective action, one must engage with their epistemologies and develop an understanding of their reach and limits. Just to use whichever parts of a theoretical concept (or parts of different concepts) that help to bridge a particular explanatory gap is the equivalent of cherry-picking facts to support one's preferred interpretation. The equivalent of cherry-picking when it comes to facts that support a theory is to just use the part of a theoretical concept (or parts of different concepts) that helps to bridge a certain explanatory gap.[78] Therefore, this chapter does not suggest we mix all approaches at will, but rather has presented some alternative ways to conceptualize war crimes.

Bibliographical Essay In my chapter, I have presented social theoretical consideration that may be of use to understand violence, in general, and war crimes, in particular. This bibliographical essay will refer to some of the literature that was already mentioned. It will further introduce works from a range of disciplines not discussed in this book that deal with collective violence. Doing so I hope to give scholars from other fields and disciplines the possibility to get a glimpse of what else is out there.

Social Theory The lectures of Hans Joas and Wolfgang Knöbl are an excellent introduction to social theory. Addressing students, these texts are easily understandable for scholars from other fields. The chapters discuss concepts that deal with action, social order, and social change (*Social Theory. Twenty Introductory Lectures*, New York: Cambridge University Press, 2009). Seminal reading for an understanding of social figurations and their shaping impact on individual action is Norbert Elias and John L. Scotson, *The Established and the Outsiders* (revised edition, Dublin: University College Dublin Press, 2008 [1965]). Heinrich Popitz explains the genesis, stabilization, and change of social norms in a very comprehensive manner. His considerations are extremely helpful for understanding the dynamics that may lead to criminal violence (Heinrich Popitz, *Phenomena of Power*, trans. Gianfranco Poggi, ed. Andreas Göttlich and Jochen Dreher, New York: Columbia University Press, 2017).

In recent years, scholars have used social theoretical concepts in order to explain violence. Jutta Bakonyi and Berit Blieseman de Guevara edited a volume that discusses half a dozen cases within such a theoretical framework (*A Micro-Sociology of Violence. Deciphering Patterns and Dynamics of Collective Violence*, London and New York: Routledge, 2012). Daniel Bultmann explicitly focuses on habitus-types, examining how commanders get their soldiers to follow them in the context of civil war in Cambodia (*Inside Cambodian Insurgency. A Sociological Perspective on Civil Wars and Conflict*, London and New York: Routledge, 2016). A good and brief introduction to practice theory is Andreas Reckwitz, 'Toward a Theory of Social Practices. A Development in Culturalist Theorizing,' *European Journal of Social Theory* 5/2 (2002). Sven Reichardt is one of the few scholars who has applied such concepts with a focus on how violence performatively creates community: 'Violence and Community: A Micro-Study on Nazi Storm Troopers,' *Central European History* 46 (2013).

Sociology The last 20 years have seen a considerable evolution in the sociology of violence. More and more, the concrete action, the violence carried out by individuals, has become the centre of interest. Explanatory models, therefore, derive from the observations instead of using theories to explain violent behaviour. Randall Collins, for example, discusses the dynamics of violence in such cases as lynching, war atrocities, and crowd violence (*Violence. A Micro-Sociological Theory*, Princeton and Oxford: Princeton University Press, 2008).

Psychology Psychological approaches discuss mainly motivations and, therefore, factors that either increase or decrease the probability that a specific action will be carried out. The discipline further studies aggression, and not violence. Social psychology focuses more on social aspects that moderate action as, for example, conformity, group pressure, and so on. Barbara Krahé provides a very matter-of-fact overview: *The Social Psychology of Aggression*, Hove and Philadelphia: Psychology Press, 2013). However, many of the models presented in this and similar publications are of a rather mechanical nature and only partially explain the complexity of social situations leading to collective violence. Alvarez and Bachman have written another introduction to the study of violence that refers to knowledge from a range of disciplines, including social theoretical thought: *Violence. The Enduring Problem* (Los Angeles: Sage, 2014). James Waller studies the factors and motivations that made individuals take part in mass violence, specifically genocides: *Becoming Evil. How Ordinary People Commit Genocide and Mass Killing* (Oxford and New York: Oxford University Press, 2007).

Notes

1. For a comprehensive history of the legal aspects, see David M. Crowe, *War Crimes, Genocide, and Justice. A Global History* (New York: Palgrave Macmillan, 2014).
2. To name but three examples in three languages and three disciplines stretching over a quarter of a century: Christopher Browning, *Ordinary Men. Reserve Police Battalion 101 and the Final Solution in Poland* (New York: Harper Collins, 1992); Gerhard Kümmel and Paul Klein, "Gewalt im Militär," in *Internationales Handbuch der Gewaltforschung*, ed. Wilhelm Heitmeyer and John Hagan (Wiesbaden: Westdeutscher Verlag, 2001), 214–234; Xavier Crettiez, *Les formes de la violence* (Paris: Éditions La Découverte, 2008).
3. Hans Joas and Wolfgang Knöbl, *Social Theory. Twenty Introductory Lectures* (New York: Cambridge University Press, 2009), 18.
4. A detailed account of "Cultural Preconditions of War" provided from a psychological perspective may be found in Ervin Staub, *The Roots of Evil. The Origins of Genocide and other Group Violence* (Cambridge: Cambridge University Press, 1989), 250–260.

5. Randall Collins, *Violence. A Micro-Sociological Theory* (Princeton: Princeton University Press, 2008).
6. A focus on situational action can be found in Per-Olof Wikström and Kyle H. Treiber, "Violence as Situational Action," *International Journal for Conflict and Violence* 3, no. 1 (2009): 75–96.
7. Erving Goffman, *Frame Analysis. An Essay on the Organization of Experience* (New York: Harper Colophon Books, 1974), 21.
8. Hans-Georg Soeffner, *Auslegung des Alltags—Der Alltag der Auslegung* (Frankfurt: Suhrkamp, 1989), 143 (Translation J.H.).
9. Herbert Willems, *Rahmen und Habitus. Zum theoretischen und methodischen Ansatz Erving Goffmans: Vergleiche, Anschlüsse und Anwendungen* (Frankfurt: Suhrkamp, 1997), 51 (Translation J.H.).
10. Peter Burke, "Stärken und Schwächen der Mentalitätsgeschichte," in *Mentalitäten-Geschichte: Zur historischen Rekonstruktion geistiger Prozesse*, ed. Ulrich Raulff (Berlin: Wagenbach, 1989), 127–145; Ingrid Gilcher-Holtey, "Plädoyer für eine dynamische Mentalitätsgeschichte," *Geschichte und Gesellschaft* 24 (1998): 476–497.
11. Volker Sellin, "Mentalität und Mentalitätsgeschichte," *Historische Zeitschrift* 241 (1985): 555–598.
12. Gerhard Schreiber, *Deutsche Kriegsverbrechen in Italien: Täter-Opfer-Strafverfolgung* (Munich: C. H. Beck, 1996), 38 (Translation J.H.).
13. Felix Römer, *Kameraden. Die Wehrmacht von innen* (Munich: Piper, 2012), 470.
14. Norbert Elias, *Die höfische Gesellschaft* (Frankfurt: Suhrkamp, 1997[1969]); Norbert Elias and John L. Scotson, *Etablierte und Außenseiter* (Frankfurt: Suhrkamp, 2002 [1965]); Norbert Elias, *What Is Sociology?* (New York: Columbia University Press, 1978 [German ed. 1970]).
15. Michaela Christ, *Die Dynamik des Tötens. Die Ermordung der Juden von Berditschew* (Frankfurt: S.Fischer, 2011).
16. Norbert Elias, *The Court Society*, rev. ed. trans. Edmund Jephcott (Dublin: University College Dublin Press, 2006[1969]), 73.
17. Norbert Elias and John L. Scotson, *The Established and the Outsiders*, rev. ed. (Dublin: University College Dublin Press, 2008[1965]), 185.
18. Roger Chartier, "Social Figuration and Habitus," in *Cultural History: Between Practices and Representations*, ed. Roger Chartier (Cambridge: Polity Press, 1988), 71–94, 78.
19. Also for the following: Heinrich Popitz, *Soziale Normen* (Frankfurt: Suhrkamp, 2006), 69–75.

20. Andreas Diekmann, Wojtek Przepiorka and Heike Rauhut, "Die Präventivwirkung von Nichtwissen im Experiment," *Zeitschrift für Soziologie* 40, no. 1 (2011): 74–84.
21. About norm transformation in the context of genocidal violence, see Paul Morrow, who, however, does not discuss the crucial role actions play in such processes: "The Thesis of Norm Transformation in the Theory of Mass Atrocity," *Genocide Studies and Prevention* 9, no. 1 (2015).
22. Also for the following: Heinrich Popitz, *Phänomene der Macht* (Tübingen: J. C. B. Mohr, 1992), 185–200. [Heinrich Popitz, *Phenomena of Power*, trans. Gianfranco Poggi, ed. Andreas Göttlich and Jochen Dreher (New York: Columbia University Press, 2017.]
23. A more elaborate account of sedimented experiences can be found in Christian Gudehus, "On the Significance of the Past for Present and Future Action," in *Theorizing Social Memories: Concepts and Contexts*, ed. Gerd Sebald and Jan Wagle (London & New York: Routledge, 2016).
24. Hans-Jürgen Kaiser and Hans Werbik, *Handlungspsychologie* (Göttingen: Vandenhoeck & Ruprecht, 2012), 41–42; more detailed is Jürgen Straub and Doris Weidemann, *Handelnde Subjekte. "Subjektive Theorien" als Gegenstand der verstehend-erklärenden Psychologie* (Gießen: Psychosozial, 2015), 29–37.
25. Pierre Bourdieu, *Outline of a Theory of Practice* (Cambridge: Cambridge University Press, 1972).
26. As a central concept, for instance, in Jutta Bakonyi and Berit Bliesemann de Guevara, eds., *A Micro-Sociology of Violence. Deciphering Patterns and Dynamics of Collective Violence* (London: Routledge, 2012). Greta Uehling, "Genocide's Aftermath: Neostalinism in Contemporary Crimea," *Genocide Studies and Prevention* 9, no. 1 (2015).
27. Hartmut Esser, *Soziologie. Spezielle Grundlagen*, Band 6: Sinn und Kultur (Frankfurt/New York: Campus, 2001), 262.
28. Hans Joas, *The Creativity of Action* (Chicago: University of Chicago Press, 1996).
29. Clemens Kroneberg, *Die Erklärung sozialen Handelns. Grundlagen und Anwendung einer integrativen Theorie* (Wiesbaden: VS Verlag, 2011), 17.
30. Hartmut Esser, "The Rationality of Everyday Behavior: A Rational Choice Reconstruction of the Theory of Action by Alfred Schütz," *Rationality and Society* 5, no. 7 (1993): 17.
31. Clemens Kroneberg, *Die Erklärung sozialen Handelns. Grundlagen und Anwendung einer integrativen Theorie* (Wiesbaden: VS Verlag, 2011), 145.

32. Hans Joas, *The Creativity of Action* (Chicago: University of Chicago Press, 1996), 158–159.
33. Ibid., 197.
34. Anselm Strauss, *Continual Permutations of Action* (New York: Aldine de Gruyter, 1993), 193.
35. Drawing on a different vocabulary, this process is discussed in various classical social theories. For instance, proponents of a reading from the vantage point of the sociology of knowledge are Peter L. Berger and Thomas Luckmann, *The Social Construction of Reality. A Treatise in the Sociology of Knowledge* (New York: First Anchor Books, 1967 [first edition Doubleday: New York 1966]), 129–173.
36. This aspect is, for instance, discussed by Newman in the context of a social psychological approach towards genocide: Leonard S. Newman, "What is a 'Social Psychological' Account of Perpetrator Behavior? The Person Versus the Situation in Goldhagen's *Hitler's Willing Executioners*," in *Understanding Genocide. The Social Psychology of the Holocaust*, ed. Leonard S. Newman and Ralph Erber (Oxford: Oxford University Press, 2002), 61.
37. Also in this case, a reading of Popitz is recommended: Heinrich Popitz, *Soziale Normen* (Frankfurt: Suhrkamp, 2006), 117–157.
38. Alf Lüdtke, "Alltagsgeschichte: Aneignung und Akteure. Oder—es hat noch kaum begonnen!," *werkstattgeschichte* 17 (1997) 87.
39. Elissa Mailänder-Koslov, *Gewalt im Dienstalltag. Die SS- Aufseherinnen des Konzentrations- und Vernichtungslagers Majdanek 1942–1944* (Hamburg: Hamburger Edition, 2009).
40. Alexander Hinton observes similar dynamics with some of the individuals working at the Tuol Sleng prison and torture facilities: "Some Tuol Sleng cadres seem to have had an initial reluctance to brutalize prisoners." Alexander Laban Hinton, *Why Did They Kill? Cambodia in the Shadow of Genocide* (Berkeley: University of California Press, 2005), 237.
41. A classic theorization of such processes may be found in Erving Goffman, *Asylums. Essays on the Social Situation of Mental Patients and Other Inmates* (Garden City: Anchor Books, 1961).
42. Elissa Mailänder-Koslov, *Gewalt im Dienstalltag. Die SS- Aufseherinnen des Konzentrations- und Vernichtungslagers Majdanek 1942–1944* (Hamburg: Hamburger Edition, 2009), 279ff.
43. Hilmar Schäfer, "Kreativität und Gewohnheit. Ein Vergleich zwischen Praxistheorie und Pragmatismus," in *Kreativität und Improvisation. Soziologische Positionen*, ed. Udo Göttlich Kurt Ronald Springer (Wiesbaden: VS, 2012), 17–43.

44. Doris Bachmann-Medick, *Cultural Turns. Neuorientierungen in den Kulturwissenschaften* (Reinbek bei Hamburg: Rowohlt, 2006), 104–143
45. Karl H. Hörning, "Soziale Praxis zwischen Beharrung und Neuschöpfung. Ein Erkenntnis- und Theorieproblem," in *Doing Culture—Neue Positionen zum Verhältnis von Kultur und sozialer Praxis*, ed. Karl H. Hörning and Julia Reuter (Bielefeld: Transcript, 2004), 19–39 (Translation J.H.).
46. Andreas Reckwitz, "Toward a Theory of Social Practices. A Development in Culturalist Theorizing," *European Journal of Social Theory* 5, no. 2 (2002): 250.
47. Ibid., 259.
48. Theodore Schatzki, *Social Practices—A Wittgensteinian Approach to Human Activity and the Social* (Cambridge: Cambridge University Press, 1996), 106.
49. Andreas Reckwitz, "Grundelemente einer Theorie sozialer Praktiken: Eine sozialtheoretische Perspektive," *Zeitschrift für Soziologie* 32, no. 4 (2003): 289 (Translation J.H.).
50. Melanie Jaeger-Erben, *Zwischen Routine, Reflektion und Transformation—die Veränderung von alltäglichem Konsum durch Lebensereignisse und die Rolle von Nachhaltigkeit* (Ph.D thesis: TU Berlin, 2010), 260 (http://opus4.kobv.de/opus4-tuberlin/frontdoor/index/index/docId/2661) (Translation J.H.).
51. Andreas Reckwitz, "Grundelemente einer Theorie sozialer Praktiken: Eine sozialtheoretische Perspektive," *Zeitschrift für Soziologie* 32, no. 4 (2003): 294–295.
52. Ibid., 296 (Translation J.H.).
53. Criticism comes, for instance, from Ingo Schulz-Schaeffer, "Praxis, handlungstheoretisch betrachtet," *Zeitschrift für Soziologie* 39 (2010), 319–336; Gregor Bongaerts, "Soziale Praxis und Verhalten—Überlegungen zum Practice Turn," *Social Theory. Zeitschrift für Soziologie* 36 (2007): 246–260.
54. Sven Reichardt, "Praxeologische Geschichtswissenschaft. Eine Diskussionsanregung," *Sozial Geschichte* 22 (2007): 3, 44 (Translation J.H.).
55. Sven Reichardt, *Faschistische Kampfbünde. Gewalt und Gemeinschaft im italienischen Squadrismus und in der deutschen SA* (Köln/Weimar/Wien: Böhlau, 2002), 717 (Translation J.H.).
56. Sven Reichardt, "Praxeologie und Faschismus. Gewalt und Gemeinschaft als Elemente eines praxeologischen Faschismusbegriffs," in *Doing*

Culture—Neue Positionen zum Verhältnis von Kultur und sozialer Praxis, ed. Karl H. Hörning and Julia Reuter (Bielefeld: Transcript, 2004), 141 (Translation J.H.).
57. Michael Wildt, *Volksgemeinschaft als Selbstermächtigung. Gewalt gegen Juden in der deutschen Provinz 1919 bis 1939* (Hamburg: Hamburger Edition, 2007); Frank Bajohr and Michael Wildt, eds., *Volksgemeinschaft. Neue Forschungen zur Gesellschaft des Nationalsozialismus* (Frankfurt: S.Fischer, 2009); Michael Wildt, "Picturing Exclusion: Race, Honor, and Anti-Semitic Violence in Nazi Germany before the Second World War," in *Violence and Visibility in Modern History*, ed. Jürgen Martschukat and Silvan Niedermeier (New York: Palgrave Macmillan, 2013), 137–155.
58. In this context, Alvarez and Bachman are a positive example. In their textbook, they draw on social theoretical concepts as well as on some classical experiments and contextualize both. Alex Alvarez and Ronet Bachman, *Violence. The Enduring Problem* (Los Angeles: Sage, 2014).
59. As Newman states correctly, apart from Milgram's work, the research of Solomon Asch and David Zimbardo is also regularly referred to in order to prove—often in a determining manner—the relevance of situational factors for allegedly immoral actions. Leonard S. Newman, "Beyond Situationalism. The Social Psychology of Genocide and Mass Killing," in *NS-Täter aus interdisziplinärer Perspektive*, ed. Helgard Kramer (Munich: Verlag Martin Meidenbauer, 2006), 107–119.
60. A noteworthy actualization in the context of a programme broadcast on French television is a filmed experiment that, among other aspects, investigates which power media formats develop: Dominique Oberlé, Jean-Léon Beauvois and Didier Courbet, "Une transposition du paradigme d'obéissance de Milgram à la télévision: enjeux, résultats et perspectives," *Connexions* 95, no. 1 (2011): 71–88 (http://archivesic.ccsd.cnrs.fr/sic_00720889/document).
61. In a TV broadcast, the magician/mentalist Derren Brown draws on the experiment to influence people in such a way that they commit a robbery.
62. Stanley Milgram, *Obedience to Authority. An Experimental View* (New York: Harper & Row, 1974). The film produced at the time (1962) that shows parts of the test series bears the plain title "Obedience" (University Park, PA: Penn State Audio Visual Services, 1965).
63. Baumeister justly states that the test subjects are not requested to behave aggressively, but solely to help someone to learn. Roy F. Baumeister, *Evil. Inside Human Violence and Cruelty* (New York: Henry Holt and Company, 2001), 256.

64. In an almost hagiographic manner, Blass traces the influence of this interpretation, which he confirms: Thomas Blass, "Perpetrator Behavior as Destructive Obedience. An Evaluation of Stanley Milgram's Perspective, the Most Influential Social-Psychological Approach to the Holocaust," in *Understanding Genocide. The Social Psychology of the Holocaust*, ed. Leonard S. Newman and Ralph Erber (Oxford: Oxford University Press, 2002), 91–108.
65. These points—the repetitive character and social obligations—were already mentioned by Milgram himself: Stanley Milgram, *Obedience to Authority. An Experimental View* (London: Pinter & Martin, 2013 [first published by Harper & Row: New York 1974]), 151–153.
66. The philosopher Hans Bernhard Schmid extensively discusses this communicative confusion. According to him, the test subjects misinterpret the almost automated answers of the examiner triggered by their questions as a meaningful dialogue. Hans Bernhard Schmid, *Moralische Integrität. Kritik eines Konstrukts* (Frankfurt: Suhrkamp, 2011), 269–270.
67. The psychologist Ernst Boesch is one of the first academics to have presented their own interpretations of the experiment. For example, he argues that the discussion between the teacher-participant and the 'Scientist' is a strategy to deal with this conflict. By arguing, the participants may have the experience that they are at least doing something. That does not solve the conflict between following the protocol and not wanting to hurt a person, but may make it more bearable. Ernst E. Boesch, *Psychopathologie des Alltags. Zur Ökopsychologie des Handelns und seiner Störungen* (Bern/Stuttgart/Wien: Verlag Hans Huber, 1976), 273.
68. My transcription. The sequence is at minute 36.
69. Interestingly enough, this point was already addressed in the 1970s. Mantell and Panzarella carried out a variation of the experiment in Germany. They argued that 'Commands were effective to the degree that they were supported by the subject's voluntary commitment to a subordinate role which he perceived as justified and safeguarded by the competence and the experience of the experimenter.' David Mark Mantell and Robert Panzarella, "Obedience and Responsibility," *British Journal Clinical Psychology* 15 (1976): 244.
70. This approach is in contrast to those that dismiss the experiment as too narrowly focused on 'situationist obedience,' whereas I argue that this applies rather to many of its interpretations. George R. Mastroianni, "Obedience in Perspective: Psychology and the Holocaust," *Theory & Psychology* 25, no. 5 (2015): 657–669.

71. Elaborated in Christian Gudehus, "Rahmungen individuellen Handelns. Ein Analysemodell," in *"Der Führer war wieder viel zu human, viel zu gefühlvoll". Der Zweite Weltkrieg aus Sicht deutscher und italienischer Soldaten*, ed. Harald Welzer, Sönke Neitzel and Christian Gudehus (Frankfurt: S.Fischer, 2011), 26–54.
72. Allen Kramer, "The War of Atrocities. Murderous Scares and Extreme Combat," in *No Man's Land of Violence. Extreme Wars in the 20th Century*, ed. Alf Lüdtke and Bernd Weisbrod (Göttingen: Wallstein, 2006), 11–33.
73. Ibid., 20.
74. For information on the part that rumours play in processes of violence, see Tim Buchen, *Antisemitismus in Galizien. Agitation, Gewalt und Politik gegen Juden in der Habsburgermonarchie um 1900* (Berlin: Metropol, 2012), 167–215.
75. In his study of the actions of German troops of the most diverse backgrounds in France, Peter Lieb explored in much more detail the specific war experiences and focused on factors that described contexts of action. These deliver convincing indicators of how, under certain conditions, war crimes occur. He lists ideological indoctrination, experience (e.g. which forms of violence have been experienced and practised in the past), social dynamics within the units as well as situational constellations (e.g. time pressure—it may be that the prisoners restrict the mobility of the group and thus endanger it). Peter Lieb, *Konventioneller Krieg oder NS-Weltanschauungskrieg? Kriegführung und Partisanenbekämpfung in Frankreich 1943/44* (Munich: Oldenbourg, 2007).
76. On *helping* as action, see Christian Gudehus, "Helping the Persecuted. Heuristics and Perspectives (Exemplified by the Holocaust)," in *Online Encyclopedia of Mass Violence*, published on 7 March 2016, www.sciencespo.fr/mass-violence-war-massacre-resistance/en/document/helping-persecuted-heuristics-and-perspectives-exemplified-holocaust
77. A current example is Daniel Bultmann, *Inside Cambodian Insurgency. A Sociological Perspective on Civil Wars and Conflict* (London: Routledge, 2016).
78. Steven Pinker has been criticized for such cherry-picking when referring to anthropological and archaeological findings: Brian R. Ferguson, "Pinker's List. Exaggerating Prehistoric War Mortality," in *War, Peace, and Human Nature. The Convergence of Evolutionary and Cultural Views*, ed. Douglas P. Fry (Oxford: Oxford University Press, 2013).

Christian Gudehus holds a PhD in social science and works at the Institute for International Law of Peace and Armed Conflict at Ruhr-Universität Bochum. His teaching and research focus on violence as well as on individual and collective forms of memory. He has taught and undertaken research in several institutions in Argentina, Austria, France, Germany, and Israel. From 2014 onwards, he is Editor-in-Chief of the journal *Genocide Studies and Prevention*.

8

International Relations: Between Theory and Practice, the National and International

Yuna Han

Background and Overview

International Relations (IR) as a field of social science[1] has historically been primarily concerned with the study of states, their respective foreign policy decisions, patterns of interactions emerging from the structure and nature of the international domain of politics, and the organization of world politics.[2] In this context, the interest in war crimes trials from the perspective of IR is chiefly centred on the establishment and development of international criminal law (ICL) and international criminal tribunals by states, beginning with the establishment of the International Military Tribunals (IMTs) of Nuremberg and Tokyo[3] following the end of World War II (WWII). While there is an undoubtedly temporal dimension to the discipline's understanding of the establishment of the IMTs as a noteworthy juncture, given the fact that the political experience of the two World Wars provided

Y. Han (✉)
London School of Economics and Political Science, London, United Kingdom

J. Waterlow, J. Schuhmacher, *War Crimes Trials and Investigations*, St Antony's Series,
https://doi.org/10.1007/978-3-319-64072-3_8

the real-world impetus for the modern study of IR, the establishment of international criminal tribunals in the twentieth century signal a much more fundamental development of international politics, challenging the classical theoretical approaches of IR. Theoretically, as noted, IR as a discipline had assumed that the 'state' was the primary agent of political behaviour in the international sphere since the Peace of Westphalia in the seventeenth century.[4] Sovereign states in this 'Westphalian' international system were understood to have clearly demarcated internal and external dimensions, where internally the state had a unified, indivisible, comprehensive, and direct authority over its territory and peoples, and externally was independent from and impermeable to foreign authorities.[5] While it is questionable as to whether this idealized notion of a Westphalian sovereign state ever existed in reality, it is certain that since the seventeenth century, sovereign states have increasingly become a significant player in the international realm of politics, particularly with respect to the development of international law. International law was almost exclusively understood as a set of institutional structures and normative principles that were created by states to protect and realize the external dimensions of sovereignty.

The establishment of the IMTs was part of a rapid and radical development within international law that substantially departed from this traditional understanding of international politics and law. First, the establishment of international courts with criminal jurisdiction represented a significant challenge to the traditional notions of sovereign authority and international law. By allowing the direct prosecution of individuals under international law by international judicial bodies, the development of international criminal justice raises the question of why states would relinquish their internal authority over their own citizens. Second, the introduction of the individual as a legal personality under international law produces an additional challenge to the analytical framework of IR, while presenting a potentially new mode of international politics in practice. This aspect of the IMTs provides theoretical justification for the tribunals' status as a critical juncture in international politics within the discipline of IR.

Explaining the Establishment of International Criminal Justice

The study of international criminal justice in general has therefore focused on explaining why and how states establish and initiate international criminal justice processes despite the significant challenge international criminal justice poses to the exercise of sovereign authority (or the 'high sovereignty cost'). Existing literature can be categorized into three types of explanatory theories: first, theories of international norm dissemination; second, theories of power relations and coercion; and third, theories of rational choice.

Social-Norms-Based Explanations

Perhaps the most prominent strand of theoretical explanations in the field of international criminal justice relies on the international dissemination of particular 'norms,' or the 'collective expectations about proper behaviour for a given identity.'[6] Sikkink's influential account of the 'justice cascade,' for example, posits that the spread of the norm of individual criminal accountability—or a societal belief that individuals should face criminal trial for their responsibility regarding mass atrocities, including war crimes, crimes against humanity, and genocide—as well as the concurrent decline of the norm of sovereign immunity—or the international societal belief that state officials were immune from prosecution for domestic policies—explains the increasing willingness of states to initiate criminal trials or establish international criminal tribunals over time.[7] In other words, due to the 'active domestic entrepreneurship' of advocates regarding the initial emergence of the idea that such violations needed to be criminally prosecuted, and 'transnational emulation and transnational norm entrepreneurship,' states have come to see criminal prosecution of individuals for mass atrocities as something that 'ought' to be done.[8] The norm of individual criminal accountability, however, as presented in Sikkink's argument, does not specify the institutional form in which the norm is enacted, resulting in an incomplete explanation as to why and when states would choose the institutional forum that would incur the highest 'sovereignty cost,' such as foreign or international tribunals.[9]

Furthermore, history and experience has demonstrated that both the dissemination and power of the norm of individual criminal responsibility are modulated by more 'secular' political concerns. For example, based on the history of the WWII IMTs and ad hoc tribunals, commentators such as Bass and Rudolph have argued that international criminal tribunals are a negotiated result of domestic preferences based on liberal norms and the self-interest of powerful, mostly Western states.[10] On the one hand, the expansion of liberal norms of rule-of-law and human rights protection is argued to be the driving force behind the international legal regime governing mass atrocities, such a genocide and crimes against humanity.[11] Because states are assumed to prefer their respective domestic values and processes to be played out in the international context, liberal states are argued to inherently prefer legal procedures over illiberal measures of accountability, such as show trials or executions.[12]

On the other hand, the assumed liberal preference for international criminal justice is seen to be confined within the boundaries of self-interest. For Bass, this means that liberal states will only propose war crimes trials when their domestic public is the most outraged and therefore more willing to subsume the cost of establishing such tribunals.[13] For Neier, war crimes tribunals were established precisely because they were the cheapest way of responding to public moral outrage.[14] Rudolph goes a step further to suggest that normative preference will not trump economic and strategic concerns, and thus liberal states will selectively initiate legalist responses to mass violence only in situations of less strategic importance.[15] Furthermore, Bosco has illustrated how, in the more recent history of the establishment and development of the International Criminal Court (ICC), powerful states that ostensibly accept the idea of international criminal justice use explicit and implicit measures to control the operations of the court to suit their immediate interests.[16] Kaufman, in his recent study regarding America's policy on transitional justice—defined to include war crimes trials—has systematized this interaction between normative commitments and political interests as a theory of 'prudentialism,' or the dynamic interaction between 'beliefs, politics, and pragmatics.'[17]

What underlies the social-norms-based explanations is the fact that the development of international war crimes trials represents a fundamental shift in international politics, not only by introducing new actions states can take following wars or other forms of mass violence, but also by enforcing new ideas of acceptable and unacceptable political behaviour.

Power-Based Explanations

A second strand of literature relies on the asymmetrical dissemination of power within the international system to explain why and when states decide to prosecute individuals for state crimes. Analysis of specific international criminal tribunals often highlight the role of explicit coercion by relatively more powerful international actors, such as donor nations or international organizations, on weaker 'host' states in which the atrocities in question had taken place. In other words, an imbalance of power forces weaker states to subsume the sovereignty cost of international criminal justice. The establishment of the IMTs, for example, was no doubt made possible by the unambiguous victory of the Allied Forces. Perhaps for this reason, the earlier generation of norms-driven theories have suggested that the driving force behind international criminal justice will be powerful Western liberal states, who would be relatively more willing to prosecute foreign nationals while reluctant to subject its own citizens to the same standards.[18]

Indeed, international pressure, especially from powerful Western states, has played a significant role in the expansion of the international criminal justice system and in inducing cooperation from less-powerful states. For example, states within the EU have made cooperation with the International Criminal Tribunal for the former Yugoslavia (ICTY) in particular a condition of economic aid and eventual membership into the EU for the former Yugoslavian states, in order to induce their active cooperation with war crimes trials.[19] Furthermore, international pressure can come directly from international criminal tribunals. For instance, some commentators have argued that the decision of the ICC Office of the Prosecutor to investigate the conflict in the Democratic Republic of Congo (DRC) played a pivotal role in pushing the DRC government to voluntarily surrender jurisdiction to the ICC.[20]

A second strand in the power-based literature focuses on more complex forms of structural or discursive power relations within the international system. This type of theory places emphasis on the intangible power of liberal norms themselves—such as the norm of rule-of-law and individual criminal responsibility—in the international sphere. It acknowledges that while specific liberal norms do play a significant role in a state's decision to prosecute individuals for mass atrocities, such norms are not disseminated and socialized in a power vacuum. In other words, liberal norms of rule-of-law and human rights are picked up by states not only through the conscious persuasive action of international criminal justice advocates, as in the case of social-norms-based theories discussed in the section above, but because they are compelled to do so precisely because such norms are backed by powerful—often Western—states.[21] Moghalu, for example, has argued that the idea of criminalization of war crimes in the Western liberal tradition is a 'hegemonic' norm, suggesting that not only do Northern states use international criminal justice to maintain and construct hegemony, but the emergence of the idea that individuals should be held criminally accountable in and of itself is a manifestation of Northern power.[22]

Rationalist Explanations

Finally, a third strand of literature conceptualizes the decision to establish or initiate international war crimes trials as resulting from a form of cooperation problem with between states, or between states and non-state actors.[23] In this view, states would voluntarily establish international criminal tribunals and initiate trials despite a high sovereignty cost due to the collective benefit an international criminal trial could bring. Abbott and Mayerfield, for example, argued that international criminal tribunals are established as a solution to a particular cooperation between states.[24] In a decentralized international criminal justice system, individual states will have less incentive to unilaterally bring perpetrators to justice, even if they respectively believe individuals should be held criminally accountable for mass crimes.[25] An international criminal tribunal, therefore, will centralize prosecution and therefore facilitate cooperation between states. This argument is problematic, as Fehl has pointed out, in that it presupposes a near-universal normative consensus regarding individual criminal accountability for mass atrocities without accounting for the continued controversy precipitated by various mechanisms of international criminal justice.[26]

Simmons and Danner's study on the ratification of the Rome Statute for the ICC, on the other hand, suggests that international criminal justice institutions serve as a self-binding mechanism of the government vis-à-vis domestic actors, including potential rebel groups or opposition.[27] Using the framework of credible commitment theory, Simmons and Danner argue that ratification of the Rome Statute raises the expected *ex post* costs of reneging—in other words, committing unlimited violence against opponents in the case of internal conflicts—by governments, as the ICC theoretically provides for punishment of government agents as well,[28] thereby sending a strong signal to non-state actors the government is acting in good faith.

What the previous strand of Rationalist studies has in common is the basic assumption that actors will utilize international war crimes trials to achieve goals broadly consistent with the perceived goals of international criminal justice—such as the prosecution of war criminals and establishment of peace. It is, however, also possible to conceive of international war crimes trials as a strategic tool of political actors for instrumental means unrelated to the perceived goals of international criminal justice. For example, Hillebrecht and Straus argue, in their study of state cooperation with the ICC, that states may cooperate with international criminal trials to remove or delegitimize potential domestic rivals to power, or to gain reputational gains by overtly cooperating with international institutions.[29] In a similar vein, I have argued that international criminal justice can be evoked as a strategic tool to increase state power by de-politicizing internal rivals, such as rebel groups, and asserting autonomy in international institutions, such as international criminal tribunals.[30]

Explaining the Effects of Individualization

The effects of the individualization of responsibility for mass atrocities under ICL remain relatively less studied than the dense theorizations regarding the establishment of international criminal justice processes as noted above. The insertion of the individual as a direct international legal personality—as a direct subject under international law without the mediation of domestic law—is a radical departure from the conventional norms of modern international law and politics not only because of its challenge to the traditional, absolutist notion of sovereign authority, but also because it suggests an advent of a new form of international politics in which the individual is directly implicated. IR as a discipline has largely operated under the analytical assumption that the international system is inhabited by collective political entities, such as states, non-state actors, and international organizations. While certain theoretical paradigms allowed for individual agency to be analysed, such as norms-based arguments advanced by Sikkink, individuals as political actors were frequently relegated sphere of domestic politics alone.

The introduction of the individual as a direct legal subject under international law in the context of international criminal justice possesses another dimension. The fact that *individuals* are being criminally prosecuted for crimes that inherently have a widespread or systematic nature suggests the de-collectivization, or individualization, of social and moral guilt that is associated with mass atrocities. This, in turn, presents the possibility that certain individuals will be prosecuted as a symbolic gesture to address the collective responsibility of a political group, system, or the state itself, strongly suggesting that inherent in the individualization of criminal responsibility under ICL is an opportunity for politicization.

This possibility of politicization seemed to have been a conscious concern for actual political actors during the Rome Conference. There was a widespread consensus amongst the delegates that the abuse of ICL by individuals should be prevented, leading to the decision to limit the states' ability to trigger jurisdiction of the ICC to broadly defined 'situations' rather than individuals.[31] The fear of political abuse also seemed to have been the reason why, aside from the notable exception of the Mexican delegation's proposal, no serious consideration had been given to the possibility of private prosecutions or a complaint system for individuals.[32] Legal research has considered this possibility of positive politicization, arguing that international criminal trials can provide a society with an opportunity to engage in a symbolic purging of the past, allowing it to successfully implement political transition.[33]

The possibilities for politicization of international criminal trials have been examined in the context of domestic politics. Ainley, for example, has suggested that individualization of responsibility under ICL has the effect of securing the state's 'monopoly over legitimate violence' while punishing individuals, most likely non-state actors, for specific transgressions.[34] Subotic demonstrated empirically how this plays out in the context of transitional politics following the Yugoslav Wars in the 1990s. Serbia, according to Subotic, seemed fully aware of the political effect of international criminal justice when transferring suspects indicted by the ICTY for war crimes, as those individuals were hailed as heroes who were being sacrificed in return for international aid and recognition for the country.[35] Analyses of Ugandan domestic politics surrounding its self-referral to the ICC regarding the Lord's Resistance Army (LRA) conflict also consider the possibility that Ugandan political leaders were using the international criminal justice process to eliminate internal opponents, and secure their dominance over the state security forces,[36] as we shall explore in more detail below. I have argued that the general effect of such domestic politics of individualization is the entrenchment of state power in moments of acute sovereignty crisis—triggered by either internal situations such as civil conflicts or by external interventions.[37]

Nonetheless, direct theorization regarding the political effect of the introduction of individuals as direct international legal subjects as well as the individualization of criminal responsibility under ICL in the context of IR remains thin. Does the advent of international criminal justice increase the importance of non-state and even non-collective actors, such as individual perpetrators, within the international political system? And, if so, how permanent and significant is this change? Does the politics of individualization domestically determine the state's behaviour internationally? Such questions require further systematic inquiry.

However, related studies within IR do provide insight and tools for further research. Literature on international human rights, for example, has already highlighted the ways in which international legal instruments also '*alter* politics, especially in fluid domestic settings,'[38] by empowering individuals and thereby creating domestic constituencies that drive change on the domestic political level.[39] Furthermore, previous studies on the linkages between domestic and international politics have shown how international developments create diverse responses and interest groups within the domestic political arena, and shape the state's international behaviour.[40] Given that the introduction of the individual as a direct legal subject under ICL disaggregates the assumption of the state as a unitary actor in practice, and would feasibly elicit diverse reactions and interests amongst different domestic actors, this approach can provide the necessary tools to understand the full scope of the effects of pursuing individual criminal responsibility for mass violence, including the conduct of war.

Interdisciplinary Issues

IR can be argued to be inherently interdisciplinary, which as it was defined more by the specific subject matter of global politics—specifically, politics without central authority—rather than by common theoretical or methodological approaches.[41] Regardless, three specific areas within the study of international criminal justice that would benefit from further interdisciplinarity can be identified.

Specifying the Subject

First, as noted above, within IR and Political Science, war crimes trials are considered almost exclusively in conjunction to other forms of mass atrocities, such as genocide and crimes against humanity, as part of ICL. While this perhaps adequately reflects political practice and the operations of more contemporaneous international tribunals, the lack of specificity in terms of the analytical framework can result in an incomplete understanding regarding the institutional and political development within international criminal justice. For example, a holistic consideration of atrocity crimes cannot adequately reflect the fact that each core crime under ICL possesses a different historical origin, level of international support from states, legal foundations, and legal developments. Consequently, a more detailed and nuanced framework of analysis could be a welcome benefit of engagements with legal and historical research.

Understanding Individualization

Second, we would gain a more sophisticated analysis of the political effects of individualization of criminal responsibility from a deeper understanding of the nature of collective violence. Micro-level comparative politics, such as the work of Straus,[42] has already tested theories of mass mobilization for violence in a political framework with respect to genocides. But there are still gaps within the discipline regarding the nature of collective mobilization regarding other forms of violence. For example, can the micro-politics of mobilization for genocide shed light on why people join other forms of mass violence, such as internal conflicts, rebel movements, or terrorist organizations? Or do different forms and aims of violence require different types of mobilization strategies? If so, how do such differences impact the organizational structure of the group? What is the role of political leadership in mass atrocities? Such questions, many of which are considered by Christian Gudehus in this volume, can provide greater insight into the status of individual autonomy and agency within a wider system of violence. This understanding, in turn, will inform the study of the political effects of individualizing responsibility for mass atrocities, both in terms of its impact on domestic politics during political transitions as well as international behaviour of states.[43]

Understanding Punishment and Stigma

Finally, a better understanding of the nature of punishment and stigma would greatly broaden the scope of possible analysis with respect to IR and international criminal justice. Questions regarding the effects of international criminal justice are intricately tied up with the notion of specific punishment that international criminal tribunals entail. The prevailing assumption, especially in legal literature and activist discourse, is that punishment rendered by an international criminal justice tribunal would mirror the normative structure and effect of a domestic criminal tribunal—in other words, the convicted would be considered to have engaged in behaviour that deviates from 'normal' social behaviour and is therefore subject to legitimate sanction by the state. This normative legitimacy of criminal punishment is, however, based on the acceptance of the state as the central authority in society, as well as a complex web of social practices that bind its members together. This raises the question of whether the 'domestic analogy' applies to international criminal justice at all.[44] Does the mere fact that a state has participated in the establishment of the ICC, for example, provide the necessary justification for the Court to legitimately sanction individuals? Is active transnational and domestic civil society participation necessary to create the required support and acceptance of the authority of a given international criminal tribunal? How effectively can a state manipulate the legitimacy of punishment by international criminal tribunals, and does it have the capacity to influence the degree of stigma surrounding punishment? Recent developments, such as the case of the ICC indictment of the Kenyan president Uhuru Kenyatta—who was elected as president despite the ICC indictment[45]—increases the pertinence of such questions, and calls for a sustained analysis drawing from a variety of fields, such as social psychology, legal theory, and history.

Overarching Themes and Issues

One of the overarching issues discussed during the first workshop that preceded this volume pertained to the historical origins of the practice of international war crimes trials. On the one hand, the Western origins of the first modern international war crimes tribunals, namely the WWII IMTs, suggest that the exercise of international criminal justice since then is a legal transplantation, or perhaps what we might call the importation of Western practices to non-Western settings. This aspect of the development of international criminal justice calls into question the efficacy and impact of transplanting largely foreign legal practices—*can* legal practices be transplanted? What becomes 'lost in translation'?

Considering Neo-imperialism

On a perhaps a more pernicious level, the Western origins of early international criminal justice practice suggest the possibility that the criminal prosecution of individuals for mass atrocities is an exercise in power relations between powerful, liberal Western states and non-Western states. Indeed, the majority of international criminal justice initiatives have been concerned with non-Western states of the 'Global South,' or states understood to inhabit a weaker position in the international system of states. Furthermore, most of these tribunals, both in terms of fully international tribunals and 'hybrid' tribunals,[46] have received strong support from Western, or 'Northern,' states. This view is reflected in both direct and indirect ways in the power-based explanations of why and when international criminal justice processes are initiated, as discussed above. Some commentators assert that the power asymmetry influencing the practice of international criminal justice is tantamount to a project of neo-imperialism,[47] meaning discourse and mechanisms through which indirect imperial conquest is manifested and legitimated.[48]

Uncovering Weak State Agency

The argument of neo-imperialism and power relations, however, advances a far too simplistic criticism regarding the development of international criminal justice. Previous research within IR and Political Science, as noted in the previous sections, has considered the effects of power imbalances on the practice of international criminal justice, specifically with regard to the decision to establish or initiate international criminal justice processes. Such power-based theories, however, exhibit two critical flaws.

Accounting for Absent Coercers

First, such arguments are overly deterministic as they claim that in every expression of agency by a Southern state to initiate international criminal trials, a more powerful state is exerting pressure behind the scenes.

However, this fails to account for the variance in the degree and type of pressure exerted by more powerful states in each case. Furthermore, an explanatory theory that focuses on the role of the more powerful state cannot account for the diversity of normative preferences amongst powerful states. Especially with the rise of China, and its increasing ambitions abroad, it is difficult to maintain the assumption that powerful states share a normative preference for judicial processes as accountability measures for mass atrocities.

Exposing Subversive Agency

Second, they generate overly deterministic accounts based on a minimalist understanding of agency and passivity. The focus on the discursive dominance and interest of the more powerful 'Northern' states in effect negates the possibility of less-powerful Southern states having agency, states which are oftentimes the subject and site of international criminal justice processes. Empirically, however, a significant number of international criminal justice cases have been initiated at the explicit request of the 'host' state, or the state from which the perpetrators and violence originated. A simplistic understanding of power relations within international criminal justice, therefore, would relegate the explicit initiatives of the weaker 'host' states to be superficial performances. While it is important to acknowledge the extent and effect of external influences—after all, the reality of the hierarchical power structure of the international system means that one would be hard pressed to find an explanation of external behaviour of the Global South that totally excludes external influence—it seems equally pertinent to contextualize this alleged 'passivity.'[49]

Indeed, literature from the tradition of African and Third World Comparative Politics have argued that weaker political actors, even under the condition of explicit colonialism, have exhibited a long practice of exercising agency through strategies of perversion, circumvention, and subversion, suggesting that the condition of weakness does not negate the possibility of purposeful strategic action.[50]

Case Study: Politics of International Criminal Justice in Uganda

The case of Uganda's self-referral to the ICC (the voluntary surrender of jurisdiction to the ICC by a member state) will serve as an empirical example to demonstrate how the specific issues of interdisciplinarity raised in this chapter—namely the clarification of the subject matter, the effects of individualization of responsibility for mass violence, and the effects of punishment and stigma for international crimes—can enhance our understanding of the politics of international criminal justice. Furthermore, as a case of a relatively weaker state actor proactively engaging with the ICC, the Ugandan example helps us understand how existing power dynamics interact with, and are altered by, the very system and nature of international criminal justice.

Background

On 16 December 2003, President Yoweri Museveni voluntarily referred the situation concerning the LRA to the Prosecutor of the ICC.[51] By this action, Uganda became the first state party to vest the ICC with jurisdiction over its territory.[52]

The decision by the Ugandan government to self-refer to the ICC seems counterintuitive at first sight—particularly from the perspective of traditional Westphalian sovereignty, which had dominated IR theory as noted in the introduction of this chapter. Why would the state give up its ability to prosecute its own citizens, particularly in the context of an internal conflict? In other words, why would it subsume the 'sovereignty cost' of international criminal justice? One hypothesis would be to consider whether the Uganda self-referral was a result of external pressure from more powerful actors. This assumption would require a power-based explanation that takes on the concerns of power asymmetry, as discussed in the previous sections. Indeed, Uganda's decision to self-refer to the ICC did not happen in the absence of international interest in pursuing international criminal justice in the context of the

LRA conflict. The idea to open an ICC case for the LRA conflict initially originated from international actors. Already in 1998, as the Rome Conference for the establishment for the ICC was under way, the UNICEF staff in New York had suggested that the Court should consider the LRA and Joseph Kony, the rebel group's leader, as its first investigation target.[53] Once the ICC became operational in 2002, the first Prosecutor, Luis Moreno Ocampo, lobbied the Ugandan government to consider referring the case to the ICC.[54]

However, Uganda's self-referral demonstrates a more complex relationship between power and the pursuit of international criminal justice. Many commentators have argued that Uganda and its Museveni adeptly instrumentalized the ICC for political gains, such as diverting international attention away from the humanitarian crisis of the Internally Displaced Persons (IDP) camps in Northern Uganda, or creating a pretext for military incursions into neighbouring countries.[55] For example, Branch asserts that Uganda stood to gain 'very secular benefits from the ICC intervention,' particularly with regard to the economic and political gains that came with a prolonged conflict, such as increased legitimacy for oppressive domestic political practices and justification for a bloated military budget.[56] Nouwen and Werner also argued that the self-referral was part of the a 'military strategy and international reputation campaign' that was aimed at intimidating the LRA and gain international legitimacy—or at least encourage tactful inattention—for the increasingly brutal tactics used by the government on its political opposition.[57] Furthermore, commentators such as Allen and Vlassenroot have suggested that the ICC referral has served as a convenient distraction from the increasing domestic and international criticism regarding the brutality of the Ugandan armed forces, known as the Ugandan People's Defence Force (UPDF).[58]

The question thus arises: how was it possible for the ICC to be instrumentalized, and to what end? I will argue in the following section that the self-referral demonstrated that the individualization and criminalization of responsibility for mass violence has the effect of de-politicizing the context of the violence, as well as shifting the blame of a more complex conflict dynamic to a recognizable individual. This cumulative political effect of international criminal justice, in the context of Uganda, allowed the government to regain flexibility in pursuing strategies that increased its relative power and autonomy vis-à-vis domestic actors, such as civil society members and political opposition, and international actors, such as donor nations and international organizations. This instrumental use of the ICC was, in turn, made possible by the ICC's reliance on state cooperation for its day-to-day operations, including the court's ability to carry out investigations, access evidence, and apprehend suspects.

Politics of ICC Referral

The Ugandan government, which at the time was a one-party state dominated by the National Resistance Movement (NRM), was facing three forms of pressure regarding the LRA conflict, from both its external and internal constituents—namely from the international community, the domestic public, and domestic military elites. These pressures put greater demands and scrutiny on the practices of the NRM government, limiting the range of actions it could take to secure its own survival and authority, particularly in the context of continued internal conflict with the LRA.

International Pressure

First, the international community was increasingly becoming aware and concerned with the humanitarian crisis in Northern Uganda, signalling the possibility that external pressures on the Ugandan government may increase. Just a month before the referral, the UN Under-Secretary for Humanitarian Affairs, Jan Egeland, declared the LRA conflict to be the 'most forgotten and neglected crisis in the world'[59] during his visit to the IDP camps in the conflict area. Most significantly, Egeland's report emphasized the UPDF's inability—or unwillingness—to provide adequate protection for the IDPs, thereby suggesting the complicity of the government in aggravating civilian suffering in Northern Uganda. This critique stood in stark contrast with the previous international discourse on the conflict, which had primarily focused on atrocities committed by the LRA, such as practices of child abduction and forced conscription.[60]

This shift in the international discourse was particularly relevant given the increasing scrutiny on the NRM government's overall human rights track record. Throughout the 1990s, Uganda was hailed as a leading success story of post-conflict development, and Museveni himself was hailed as one of the 'new breed' of African leaders that were thought to be effectively combining economic and political liberalization.[61] This international support was critical for the NRM government in gaining access to economic assistance and political support. However, beginning in the late 1990s, donor countries and international organizations had become increasingly concerned with the growing authoritarian tendencies of President Museveni,[62] as well as the protracted internal conflict with the LRA.[63]

Domestic Pressure: War-Weary Public

Simultaneously, the domestic public was increasingly supporting the political opposition in protest of, amongst other grievances, the protracted conflict against the LRA. This was particularly true in the districts hardest hit by the LRA conflict, which overwhelmingly supported the political opposition in both the 1996 Presidential elections and the 2001 general elections.[64]

From the perspective of the domestic public, particularly those who were living in the conflict area, the NRM government and the UPDF were just as complicit as the LRA in causing civilian suffering during the conflict. The government's military strategy during the 1990s of creating 'protected villages,' which amounted to forcibly creating IDP camps, further aggravated the situation.[65] The camps lacked in basic supplies for survival, and residents became easy targets for the LRA. Those who left the camps, however, could be targeted by the military as potential LRA supporters. Furthermore, the UPDF was often seen to be ineffective or unwilling to protect the civilians in IDP camps. Many IDP camp residents reported that the UPDF frequently was late or absent during the most violent LRA attacks on the camps.[66] This led to the widespread suspicion that the NRM government had 'deliberately isolated' and aggravated the conflict, in order to continue reaping monetary profits from corrupt military practices,[67] as well as justifying the oppression of political opposition as LRA sympathizers.[68] Such mistrust and dissatisfaction was aggravated by Museveni's dismissal of various efforts by the Northern communities themselves to reach a peaceful, negotiated resolution with the LRA.[69]

Domestic Pressure: Elite Preference for War

The LRA conflict was thus becoming an increasingly unpopular endeavour for the NRM government, with regard to both its international and domestic audience. The unpopularity of the war led to a few concessions on the part of President Museveni, who acquiesced to a number of conciliatory measures designed to facilitate a negotiated end to the conflict. The Amnesty Act passed in 2000 was one such example, which provided amnesties to returning LRA combatants.[70]

However, at the same time, the NRM government faced sustained political and economic motivations to continue engaging with the LRA in military combat. The LRA conflict, as noted above, was useful for the government in order to justify increasingly oppressive political practices. For instance, politicians, or even private citizens, were often labelled 'Konyists' when they voiced criticism about the government.[71] Journalists that were critical of the NRM and Museveni were frequently accused of having links to the LRA and prosecuted for their alleged 'terrorist' activities,[72] and prominent political opponents to Museveni were accused of colluding with the LRA.[73] Furthermore, the continued military campaigns against the LRA provided a myriad of opportunities for profiteering and corruption amongst the NRM elite, as well as the rank-and-file military officers. The local population in conflict areas has long reported how military officers used the conflict as land grabbing or cattle rustling opportunities,[74] and high-profile corruption scandals in the late 1990s—implicating even the president's half-brother—revealed how commanders were padding military payrolls with dead or missing soldiers and pocketing the extra pay.[75]

The military elites within the NRM government further intensified the incentive to continue the war for the government, particularly president Museveni, by using the conflict as a means to criticize the political leadership of Museveni and the NRM political elites. For example, General Tinyefuza—a prominent member of the military since the NRM's days as an armed rebel group—claimed that, based on his personal experience in directing dearly military campaigns against the LRA, the president and current government needlessly prolonged the conflict by employing fruitless strategies.[76] As a former armed rebel group that came into power by effectively capturing the capital, the military leaders have long sustained a privileged position within the NRM government,[77] and their critique of the president carried particular weight. Against this backdrop, it is not surprising that the intensity of the military offensive grew greater with the rise of critiques from the armed forces. For example, during the 2001 Iron Fist I campaign, the Museveni personally directed some of the offensives and made frequent public appearances in military fatigues, creating a public perception of a hands-on, high-stakes military operation.[78]

The ICC Referral: Shifting the Narrative

The ICC referral in this context allowed the Ugandan government to retain flexibility in its strategies without having to immediately respond to one source of pressure over another, and therefore optimize its chance of re-establishing authority, both at home and abroad. In particular, the ICC, unlike peace negotiations and the full implementation of the Amnesty Act, provided an opportunity for the NRM government to continue military action if necessary. The involvement of the ICC provided additional justification for military action as a campaign to enforce international law,[79] rather than as an internal security issue. This function of the ICC as a normative buttress for further military action was apparent in the evidence provided by the Ugandan government to prove the LRA conflict situation's admissibility under the Rome Statute's principle of complementarity. The government argued that its inability to physically apprehend the suspects proved that it was 'unable' to prosecute the alleged perpetrators, and therefore satisfied the criteria of complementarity. Legally, this was a controversial argument, as there is a near-universal consensus since the Rome Conference that the ICC should only have jurisdiction when national *trial* procedures are not 'available or may be ineffective.'[80] By formulating the plea for judicial intervention on the grounds that they have not yet captured Joseph Kony and other LRA commanders, the Ugandan government effectively strengthened the case for the continued military pursuit after the LRA rebels.

Furthermore, by initiating an international criminal justice process, the ICC referral was able to shift discourse surrounding the conflict on to specific individuals who were deemed responsible for the suffering of the IDPs and other victims—most notably, LRA leader Joseph Kony—and depict the conflict dynamics in terms of criminality and moral aberration. This, in turn, influenced the ideological and discursive underpinnings of the conflict itself, shifting the focus away from the ineptitude and transgressions of the Ugandan government, transforming the LRA into a criminal group (rather than a rebel group challenging the government), the northern Ugandan population into passive victims (rather than aggrieved citizens with agency), and the government as an enforcer of justice (rather than a complicit actor).[81]

These effects of the ICC referral bring us back to the questions regarding the effects of individualization raised in the previous sections of this chapter. The effects of individualization of responsibility for mass violence in the case of the LRA conflict seem to confirm, for example, Ainley's argument presented earlier that individualization can serve to further legitimize the state's exercise of violence—in this case, as a means of conducting military operations to capture Joseph Kony, a wanted international criminal. This, as I have suggested, seem to have had the cumulative effect of strengthening the state's position, vis-à-vis internal and external critiques. But the effects of individualization of responsibility in Uganda also raise further questions that can benefit from greater interdisciplinary insight into the nature of individualization. For example, whether the structure of the armed group, in which there was a recognizable and self-identified leader, and the nature of the conflict dynamic, in which the public was largely marginalized as passive victims, matter in how individualization impacted the narrative? Would the effect look different in a mass violence situation in which the leadership of the violent party is fractured or diffused, or if potential perpetrators received widespread support from the public? Such possible variances in the effects of individualization can be better explored with a fuller understanding of individual agency and collective violence.

Enabling Instrumentalization: Necessity of State Cooperation

This refocusing of the conflict narrative was only possible because the ICC limited its investigative and prosecutorial focus to the LRA, leaving out the UPDF and other state actors. Technically, a government cannot surrender its jurisdiction for the prosecution of a single conflict party or individual. Rather, a government can only refer a conflict or violent *situation*, after which the ICC OTP has the responsibility to consider all conflict parties as potential prosecutorial targets. However, in this particular case, there is significant evidence that suggests that the Ugandan government exerted both implicit and explicit pressure on the newly formed ICC to limit is ambit to the LRA. Schiff, for example, argued that Museveni steered the OTP away from investigating the UPDF from the beginning.[82] According to Branch, the Ugandan government also repeatedly threatened to 'withdraw' its referral to the ICC, indicating that it would cease to cooperate with the court if it decided to also investigate military or government actors.[83] In fact, the government was so confident that the OTP would not investigate their own troops, which government and military officials publically stated that the UPDF was not guilty of any crimes, and would not be prosecuted by the ICC.[84]

The Ugandan government was able to pressure the ICC in this way because of the basic fact that the ICC is heavily reliant on the referring government for access to critical information and evidence to build its case.[85] In fact, I have argued that the structures of international criminal justice, in which international courts directly prosecute domestic crimes, inherently create 'structural power' for the state, or leverage stemming from the necessity of state cooperation for prosecution that can be used by the state to instrumentalize international criminal justice.[86] In the case of Uganda, this theoretical leverage of a government over the ICC proceedings was amplified by the fact that it was the first poster-case for the nascent institution, and therefore garnered widespread international goodwill. Indeed, despite widespread knowledge of the problematic behaviour of the UPDF, the ICC 'cleared' the UPDF of any wrongdoing in the early stages of its investigations.[87]

This ability of a state to instrumentalize international criminal justice, as shown in the case of Uganda, brings us back to one of the questions raised in the overarching themes introduced in this volume—how do power asymmetries manifest themselves in international criminal justice? While our workshops focused on potential impact of the broader asymmetries of power that results from historical developments in international politics generally, the case of Uganda highlights how power dynamics manifest in more multidirectional and complex ways. In fact, in the case of Uganda, not only did power politics influence the decision to prosecute individuals for mass atrocities, but also the process of international criminal justice itself became the source of power for the NRM government. By harnessing the normative discourse underpinning the ICC, the Ugandan government was able to negotiate an enlarged space for strategic action vis-à-vis international actors as well as domestic constituents.

Instrumentalizing International Criminal Justice: An Evaluation

Was Uganda successful in instrumentalizing international criminal justice for its own strategic political aims? On the one hand, the ICC referral did have an impact in redirecting the international narrative regarding the conflict. This led to concrete benefits in terms of military strategy, as the involvement of the ICC garnered valuable cooperation from neighbouring Sudan. With Sudan's willing cooperation, the UPDF was able to conduct far-reaching military operations into Sudanese soil in pursuit of the LRA.[88] On the other hand, the domestic public considered the ICC to be conducting a biased investigation that did not reflect their collective experience of the LRA conflict, omitting the egregious negligence and alleged violations committed by the Ugandan army. Additionally, many prominent members of civil society believed that the ICC investigation was actually hindering the process of peace, providing adverse incentives for both the leadership of the LRA and the rank-and-file combatants.[89]

The mixed result of the Uganda case brings us back to the question of stigma and punishment. How does stigma operate in relation to international criminal justice? Uganda's experience highlights how stigma emanating from becoming the target of ICC investigation can have different relevance in domestic and international levels of politics. While the specific case of Uganda suggests that this variance is related to the institutional legitimacy of the ICC itself, as well as the Ugandan government, further determinants may be identified through a better understanding of how stigma created through international prosecutions operates in both international and domestic settings.

Conclusion

This chapter has given a brief overview of IR and the study of war crimes trials, particularly in the form of international criminal justice. It was by no means an exhaustive list of IR 'approaches' to the study of international criminal justice. In fact, delineating a uniquely IR approach may well be a quixotic task, given the inherently interdisciplinary and vast nature of IR as an academic field. The chapter, instead, provided a broad overview of some of the key literature on two specific areas of international criminal justice that is of interest to IR—namely the establishment/initiation of international criminal tribunals/trials, and the political effects of individualization. The main theoretical tension that underlies the various theories and studies introduced in this chapter is the clash between the traditional image of international politics as a domain of states and the introduction of new actors and mechanisms of interactions—a development that is not unique to, but is particularly emphasized by, the nature of international criminal justice. The case study of Uganda helps to demonstrate the benefit of posing the question by highlighting this tension between the powers of the state and the introduction of the individual as an international legal entity. It uncovered some of the unintended or indirect consequences of international criminal justice, such as the expanded ability to conduct war or deflect criticisms regarding the state, and emphasized areas in which politics alone could not provide adequate theoretical foundations to understand the effects. In sum, the conceptualization of international criminal justice as antithetical to the traditional IR image of the state clarifies the question: what is at stake in international criminal justice?

Bibliographical Essay The field of international criminal justice is an increasingly popular area of study in both IR and comparative politics. Early literature focused on the establishment of international criminal tribunals, such as the post-WWII IMTs of Nuremberg and Tokyo or the ad hoc tribunals of former Yugoslavia (ICTY) and Rwanda (ICTR). The most prominent example of such early literature would be Gary Jonathan Bass, *Stay the Hand of Vengeance: The Politics of War Crimes Tribunals* (Princeton: Princeton University Press, 2000). Bass provides a comparative study of war crimes trials, including the pre-WWII efforts such as the Napoleonic trials, the trials at Leipzig after World War I, and the trials at Constantinople after the massacre of Armenians, as well as the establishment of the WWII tribunals and the ICTR. While Bass concedes that the establishment of war crimes tribunals have often been a result of power politics and national self-interest, he argues that the motivation for trials also stems from legal principles drawn from liberal domestic political and universal notions of rights, or 'legalism.'

Benjamin Schiff, *Building the International Criminal Court* (New York: Cambridge University Press, 2008) is a comprehensive and interdisciplinary account of the politics behind the establishment of the ICC, and serves as a good starting point for research on the court. More recently, David Bosco, *Rough Justice: The International Criminal Court in a World of Power Politics* (New York: Oxford University Press, 2014) traced the geopolitical and domestic developments that led to the establishment of the ICC in an impressively researched monograph. Bosco's main focus is the relationship between the ICC and major powers. How do we understand the variance in relationships between the ICC and major powers, such as the US, both across time and amongst countries? Bosco argues that this relationship is defined by a 'mutual accommodation' of sorts, in which major powers accommodated the existence of this potentially threatening court in the practice of international politics, while the court exercised self-restraint in its practice to gain support of even the most sceptical major powers. The main contribution of this volume is that not only does Bosco's framework of analysis conceptualize the possible strategies of major powers, but also considers the strategies of the ICC formulated in response, resulting in a more comprehensive and dynamic account of the politics of the ICC.

Perhaps one of the most influential accounts published in the recent years is Kathryn Sikkink, *The Justice Cascade: How Human Rights Prosecutions are Changing World Politics* (New York: W.W. Norton & Co., 2011). Sikkink's publication has spawned a veritable cottage industry—both attempting to further substantiate or develop her claims, or to refute it. Sikkink develops the concept of a 'justice cascade,' defined as the 'interrelated, dramatic new trend in world politics toward holding individual state officials, including heads of state, accountable for human rights violations.' While not exclusively concerned with war crimes trials, the justice cascade empirically includes international war crimes trials as well. Sikkink's principal argument is that the emergence and subsequent diffusion of the justice cascade is the result of the influence of the new human rights norm of individual criminal prosecution. This norm in turn is argued to be developed and disseminated by the strategic, purposeful, and agentic actions of individuals—such as human rights activists, scholars, and practitioners—referred to as 'norm entrepreneurs.' Albeit empirically limited to the ICC, Beth A. Simmons and Allison Danner provide an alternative account as to why states establish international criminal tribunals and agree to join such institutions in 'Credible Commitments and the International Criminal Court,' *International Organization* 64 (Spring, 2010). Simmons and Danner argue that some governments sign up to the ICC as a mechanism of committing to deescalating the level of violence. This leads to the counterintuitive phenomenon of countries which are most likely to be subject to an ICC prosecution, such as countries that are experiencing civil war, will be more likely to join the court.

Although it was not dealt with directly in the chapter, whether international criminal justice can deter violence is another critical topic area in IR. In this field, Hyeran Jo and Beth A. Simmons, 'Can the International Criminal Court Deter Atrocity?,' *International Organization* 70, no. 3 (July 2016) has generated significant discussion. The article considers the potential deterrent effect of the ICC on both state and non-state actors, and finds that there is a conditional effect of the ICC on governments and rebel groups, if they are seeking legitimacy.

Notes

1. This chapter adopts a broad definition of IR as the social-scientific study of international politics. It differentiates the modern study of international politics from the more classical study of politics, such as that of Thucydides. The question of whether IR is a separate discipline or a sub-discipline under Political Science has been a matter of continuous contention within the discipline itself. This debate is partially rooted in the different historical developments across different countries as well as institutions (although this has been largely limited to the West). For example, IR was institutionalized as a separate discipline in the United Kingdom after World War I, while in the United States, Germany, and France, it was considered as a sub-discipline of Political Science. For further discussion regarding the disciplinary boundary of IR and its intellectual history, see: Brian C. Schmidt, "On the History and Historiography of International Relations," in *Handbook of International Relations*, ed. Walter Carlsnaes, Thomas Risse, and Beth A. Simmons (London: Sage, 2002), 189–206; Ole Waever, "Still a Discipline after All These Debates?," in *International Relations Theories: Discipline and Diversity*, ed. Tim Dunne, Milja Kurki, and Steve Smith, 4th ed. (Oxford: Oxford University Press, 2016), 300–332.
2. Michael Barnett and Kathryn Sikkink, "From International Relations to Global Society," in *Oxford Handbook on International Relations*, ed. Chris Reus-Smit and Duncan Snidal (Oxford: Oxford University Press, 2008), 63.
3. Officially known as the International Military Tribunal of the Far East (IMTFE)
4. David A. Lake, "The State and International Relations," in *The Oxford Handbook of International Relations*, ed. Chris Reus-Smit and Duncan Snidal (Oxford: Oxford University Press, 2008), 41–61.
5. Jean L. Cohen, *Globalization and Sovereignty: Rethinking Legality, Legitimacy, and Constitutionalism* (Cambridge: Cambridge University Press, 2012), 26–27.
6. Ronald L. Jepperson, Alexander Wendt and Peter J. Katzenstein, "Norms, Identity and Culture in International Security," in *The Culture of National Security: Norms, Identity in World Politics*, ed. Peter J. Katzenstein (New York: Columbia University Press, 1996), 54.
7. Kathryn Sikkink, *The Justice Cascade: How Human Rights Prosecutions Are Changing World Politics* (New York: W.W. Norton & Co., 2011).

8. Ibid., 246.
9. Ibid., 248.
10. Gary J. Bass, *Stay the Hand of Vengeance: The Politics of War Crimes Tribunals* (Princeton: Princeton University Press, 2000); Christopher Rudolph, "Constructing an Atrocities Regime: The Politics of War Crimes Tribunals," *International Organization* 55, no. 3 (2001): 655–691.
11. Rudolph refers to this as the 'atrocities regime'; this would generally include international criminal law, international humanitarian law, and specific aspects of international human rights law focused on bodily harm.
12. Bass, *Stay the Hand of Vengeance*, 20–23, 28–36. Keck and Sikkink, in a study of transnational advocacy for human rights, reached a similar conclusion that in general, states with liberal, law-based traditions have difficulties resisting normative arguments for legalist accountability measures. Margaret E. Keck and Kathryn Sikkink, *Activists Beyond Borders: Advocacy Networks in International Politics.* (Ithaca: Cornell University Press, 1998), 117–119, 207–209.
13. Bass, *Stay the Hand*, 8.
14. Aryeh Neier, *War Crimes: Brutality, Genocide, Terror, and the Struggle for Justice* (New York: Times Books, 1998), 129. See also: Caroline Fehl, "Explaining the International Criminal Court: A 'Practice Test' for Rationalist and Constructivist Approaches," *European Journal of International Relations* 10, no. 3 (2004): 373; Eric Neumayer, "A New Moral Hazard? Military Intervention, Peacekeeping and Ratification of the International Criminal Court," *Journal of Peace Research* 46, no. 5 (2009): 659–670.
15. Rudolph, "Constructing an Atrocities Regime," 683.
16. David Bosco, *Rough Justice: The International Criminal Court in a World of Power Politics* (Oxford: Oxford University Press, 2014).
17. Zachary D. Kaufman, *United States Law and Policy on Transitional Justice: Principles, Politics, and Pragmatics* (Oxford: University of Oxford Press, 2016), 5–6; 42–64.
18. See above section.
19. Victor Peskin and Mieczysław P. Boduszyński. "Balancing International Justice in the Balkans: Surrogate Enforcers, Uncertain Transitions and the Road to Europe," *International Journal of Transitional Justice* 5, no. 1 (2011): 53–54.

20. Benjamin N. Schiff, *Building the International Criminal Court* (Cambridge: Cambridge University Press, 2008), 213. See also: Jacqueline Gies and Alex Mundt, *When to Indict: International Criminal Indictments, Peace Processes, and Humanitarian Action* (Groningen: Brookings-Bern Project on International Development, 2009).
21. Stern argued that, in the context of establishing *opinion juris*, involves two different kinds of rationale, depending on the individual state's 'position of power within the international order.' While more powerful states are likely to feel freely bound to international law, other weaker states will 'feel bound because they cannot not want to be, because the rule is imposed upon them.' Brigitte Stern, "Custom at the Heart of International Law," trans. Michael Byer and Anne Denise, *Duke Journal of Comparative and International Law* 11, no. 1 (2001): 108. See also: Michael Beyers, "International Law," in *The Oxford Handbook of International Relations*, ed. Chris Reus-Smit and Duncan Snidal (Oxford: Oxford University Press, 2008), 624; Martti Koskenniemi, *The Politics of International Law* (Oxford and Portland: Hart Publishing, 2011), 222.
22. Kingsley Chiedu Moghalu, *Global Justice: The Politics of War Crimes Trials* (Westport: Greenwood Publishing Group, 2006), 13. On the argument that human rights norms in general is an example of a pervasive Western 'world-culture,' see also: Martha W. Finnemore, "Norms, Culture, and World Politics: Insights from Sociology's Institutionalism," *International Organization* 50, no. 2 (1996): 325–347; Thomas Risse and Kathryn Sikkink, "The Socialization of International Human Rights Norms into Domestic Practices: Introduction," in *The Power of Human Rights: International Norms and Domestic Change*, ed. Thomas Risse, Stephen C. Rapp, and Kathryn Sikkink (Cambridge: Cambridge University Press, 1999), 1–38.
23. Rationalism on the broadest level is a methodological approach that explains 'both individual and collective (social) outcomes in terms of *individual goal-seeking under constraints*.' This broad notion of Rationalism provides the baseline methodological foundation for multiple IR theories, including neo-liberalism/neo-liberal institutionalism (theory of state cooperation and international institutions) and neo/structural-realism (structural theory of state behaviour under the condition of anarchy) Duncan Snidal, "Rational Choice and International Relations," in *Handbook of International Relations*, ed. Walter Carlsnaes, Thomas Risse, and Beth A. Simmons (London: Sage, 2002), 87–88.

24. Kenneth W. Abbott, "International Relations Theory, International Law, and the Regime Governing Atrocities in Internal Conflicts," *The American Journal of International Law* 93, no. 2 (1999): 361–379; Jamie Mayerfield, "Who Shall be Judge?: The United States, the International Criminal Court, and the Global Enforcement of Human Rights," *Human Rights Quarterly* 25, no. 1 (2003): 93–129.
25. Abbott, "International Relations Theory," 374–375.
26. Fehl, "Explaining the International Criminal Court: A 'Practice Test' for Rationalist and Constructivist Approaches," 369–370.
27. Beth A. Simmons and Allison Danner, "Credible Commitments and the International Criminal Court," *International Organization* 64, no. 2 (2010): 225–256.
28. Ibid., 234.
29. Courtney Hillebrecht and Scott Straus, "Who Pursues the Perpetrators? State Cooperation with the ICC," *Human Rights Quarterly* 39, no. 1 (2017): 162–188.
30. Yuna Han, "International Criminal Justice and the Global South: Extraversion and State Agency," (DPhil diss., University of Oxford, 2016); "International Criminal Justice as Political Strategy: Asymmetry of Opportunity?" in *Human Rights and Justice: Implementing and Accessing Justice*, ed. Kurt Mills and Melissa Labonte (London: Routledge, Forthcoming).
31. *United Nations Diplomatic Conference of Plenipotentiaries on the Establishment of an International Criminal Court*, vol. II (New York: United Nations, 2002), 196 (para. 34). For statements by individual states, see or example: Ibid., 65 (para. 21; Norway), 185 (para. 68; Norway), 187(para. 11; Spain), 195 (para.2 1; USA).
32. *United Nations Diplomatic Conference of Plenipotentiaries on the Establishment of an International Criminal Court*, 191 (para. 63).
33. Gerry Simpson, *Law, War and Crime: War Crimes Trials and the Reinvention of International Law* (Cambridge: Polity Press, 2007), 13.
34. Kirsten Ainley, "Responsibility for Atrocity: Individual Criminal Agency and the International Criminal Court," in *Evil, Law and the State. Perspectives on State Power and Violence*, ed. John T. Perry (Amsterdam and New York: Rodopi, 2006), 4.
35. Jelena Subotić, "The Paradox of International Justice Compliance," *The International Journal of Transitional Justice* 3, no. 3 (2009): 370–371.
36. For example: Adam Branch, "Uganda's Civil War and the Politics of ICC Intervention," *Ethics and International Affairs* 21 no. 2 (2007): 179–198.

37. Han, *International Criminal Justice and the Global South: Extraversion and State Agency*; idem, "International Criminal Justice as Political Strategy: Asymmetry of Opportunity?".
38. Beth A. Simmons, *Mobilizing for Human Rights: International Law in Domestic Politics* (Cambridge, UK: Cambridge University Press, 2009), 12. Emphasis original.
39. Ibid.
40. Andrew Moravcsik, "Taking Preferences Seriously: A Liberal Theory of International Politics," *International Organization* 51, no. 4 (1997): 513–553.
41. Ibid.; Robert D. Putnam, "Diplomacy and Domestic Politics: The Logic of Two-Level Games," *International Organization* 42, no. 03 (1988): 427–460; James D. Fearon, "Domestic Politics, Foreign Policy, and Theories of International Relations," *Annual Review of Political Science* 1, no. 1 (1998): 289–313.
42. Schmidt, "On the History and Historiography of International Relations," 6.
43. The criminological implications of mass atrocities and individual responsibility have been considered from the perspective of international law. See: Mark Drumbl, *Atrocity, Punishment and International Law* (Cambridge: Cambridge University Press, 2007).
44. Scott Straus, *The Order of Genocide: Race, Power, and War in Rwanda* (Ithaca and London: Cornell University Press, 2006).
45. Summary of the relationship between the ICC and Kenya can be found here: http://www.iccnow.org/?mod=kenya
46. A 'hybrid' tribunal refers to a court where both the institutional apparatus and applicable law combine international and domestic aspects. International judges and prosecutors work alongside domestic counterparts; domestic law and international law is applied. See: Laura A. Dickinson, "The Promise of Hybrid Courts," *The American Journal of International Law* 97, no. 2 (2003): 295; Sarah Nouwen, "'Hybrid Courts': The Hybrid Category of a New Type of International Crimes Courts," *Utrecht Law Review* 2, no. 2 (2006): 190–214; Suzanne Katzenstein, "Hybrid Tribunals: Searching for Justice in East Timor," *Harvard Human Rights Journal* 16 (2003): 245–278. Also referred to as 'internationalized' tribunals.
47. Michael Hardt and Antonio Negri, *Empire* (Cambridge: Harvard University Press, 2001); Jedediah Purdy et al., eds., "The Revival of Empire," Special Section, *Ethics and International Relations* 17 no. 2

(2003): 34–88; Nico Krisch, "International Law in Times of Hegemony: Unequal Power and the Shaping of the International Legal Order," *European Journal of International Law* 16, no. 3 (2005): 369–408.

48. Michael Ignatieff, "The American Empire. The Burden," *New York Times Magazine* (2003); Robert Hunter Wade, "The Invisible Hand of the American Empire," *Ethics & International Affairs* 17, no. 2 (2003): 77–88. For a summary of the neo-imperial argument see: Jean L. Cohen, "Whose Sovereignty? Empire versus International Law," *Ethics & International Affairs* 18, no. 3 (2004): 2.
49. See, for example: Stephanie Neuman, "International Relations Theory and the Third World: An Oxymoron?," in *International Relations Theory in the Third World*, ed. Stephanie Neuman (New York: St Martin's Press, 1998); Carlos Escudé, "An Introduction to Peripheral Realism and Its Implications for the Interstate System: Argentina and the Condor II Missile Project," in *International Relations Theory in the Third World*, ed. Stephanie Neuman. On hierarchy in international relations in general see: David A. Lake, *Hierarchy in International Relations* (Ithaca: Cornell University Press, 2009); Ian Clark, *The Hierarchy of States: Reform and Resistance in the International Order* (Cambridge: Cambridge University Press, 1998); Edward Keene, *Beyond the Anarchical Society: Grotius, Colonialism and Order in World Politics* (Cambridge: Cambridge University Press, 2002).
50. Christopher S. Clapham, *Third World Politics: An Introduction* (Madison: University of Wisconsin Press, 1985), 3–5; idem, *Africa and the International System: The Politics of State Survival* (Cambridge: Cambridge University Press, 1996), 4–7; Jean-François Bayart and Stephen Ellis, "Africa in the World: A History of Extraversion," *African affairs* 99, no. 395 (2000): 218–219; Jean-Pascal Daloz and Patrick Chabal, *Africa Works: Disorder as Political Instrument* (Oxford: James Curry, 1999), xix–xx.
51. President of Uganda Refers Situation Concerning the Lord's Resistance Army (LRA) to the ICC *International Criminal Court* (January 29, 2004): http://www.icc-cpi.int/en_menus/icc/press%20and%20media/press%20releases/2004/Pages/president%20of%20uganda%20refers%20situation%20concerning%20the%20lord_s%20resistance%20army%20_lra_%20to%20the%20icc.aspx
52. Payam Akhavan, "The Lord's Resistance Army Case: Uganda's Submission of the First State Referral to the International Criminal Court," *The American Journal of International Law* 99, no. 2 (2005): 403.

53. Tim Allen, *Trial Justice: The International Criminal Court and the Lord's Resistance Army* (London and New York: Zed Books, 2006), 83.
54. Phil Clark, "Law Politics and Pragmatisim: The ICC and Case Selection in the Democratic Republic of Congo and Uganda," in *Courting Conflict? Justice, Peace and the ICC in Africa*, ed. Nicholas Waddel and Phil Clark (London: Royal African Society, 2008), 43
55. Schiff, *Building the International Criminal Court*, 199
56. Adam Branch, "Uganda's Civil War and the Politics of ICC Intervention," *Ethics & International Affairs* 21, no. 2 (2007): 179, 183.
57. Sarah M. H. Nouwen and Wouter G. Werner, "Doing Justice to the Political: The International Criminal Court in Uganda and Sudan," *The European Journal of International Law* 21, no. 4 (2010): 949.
58. Tim Allen and Koen Vlassenroot, "Introduction," in *The Lord's Resistance Army: Myth and Reality*, ed. Tim Allen and Koen Vlassenroot (London: Zed Books, 2010), 16.
59. "Kony War a Forgotten Crisis," *The Monitor*, 11 November 2003.
60. Human Rights Watch, "Uganda in the Drc: Fueling Political and Ethnic Strife," (New York: Human Rights Watch, 2001).
61. J. Oloka-Onyango, "New-Breed' Leadership, Conflict, and Reconstruction in the Great Lakes Region in Africa: A Sociopolitical Biography of Uganda's Yoweri Kaguta Museveni," *Africa Today* 50, no. 3 (2004): 2.
62. Sabiti Makara, Lise Rakner and Lars Svåsand, "Turnaround: The National Resistance Movement and the Re-introduction of a Multiparty System in Uganda," *CMI Working Paper* (2007), 5.
63. Allen, *Trial Justice*, 73.
64. Joshua B. Rubongoya, *Regime Hegemony in Museveni's Uganda: Pax Musevenica.* (Basingstoke: Palgrave Macmillan, 2007), 84.
65. Sverker Finnstrom, *Living with Bad Surrounding: War and Existential Uncertainty in Acholiland, Northern Uganda* (Uppsala: Uppsala Studies in Cultural Anthropology, 2003), 133.
66. Aili Mari Tripp, *Museveni's Uganda: Paradoxes of Power in a Hybrid Regime* (Boulder: Lynne Rienner Publishers, 2010), 161.
67. Refugee Law Project, "Behind the Violence," 23–24.
68. Adam Branch, *Displacing Human Rights: War and Intervention in Northern Uganda* (Oxford: Oxford University Press, 2011), 92.
69. Tripp, *Museveni's Uganda*: 166.
70. Allen, *Trial Justice*, 74.
71. Joshua B. Rubongoya, *Regime Hegemony in Museveni's Uganda: Pax Musevenica* (Basingstoke: Palgrave Macmillan, 2007), 84.

72. For example, a number of journalists were prosecuted because their phone numbers were allegedly found on the body of a dead LRA commander. *Northern Uganda: Understanding and Solving the Conflict* (Brussels: International Crisis Group, 2004).
73. Charles Etukuri and Emmy Allio, "Besigye Denies Lra," *New Vision*, 7 July 2007
74. Frank van Acker, "Uganda and the Lord's Resistance Army: The New Order No One Ordered," *African Affairs* 103, no. 412 (2004): 353–354.
75. An internal audit by the UPDF in 1997 estimated that there were about 10,000 non-existent soldiers on the payroll, known as 'ghost soldiers.' Ibid., 354
76. Tripp, *Museveni's Uganda*, 65.
77. Tripp, *Museveni's Uganda*, 24; Carbone, *No Party Democracy?*, 41.
78. Allen, *Trial Justice*, 52.
79. Branch, "Uganda's Civil War,' 184.
80. John T. Holmes, "Principle of Complementarity," in *The Making of the Rome Statute: Issues, Negotiations, Results*, ed. Roy S. Lee (Cambridge: Kluwer Law International, 1999), 47.
81. Branch, "Uganda's Civil War," 190.
82. Schiff, *Building the International Criminal Court*, 199.
83. Branch, *Displacing Human Rights*, 187.
84. Ibid.
85. Immi Tallgren, "The Sense and Sensibility of International Criminal Law," *European Journal of International Law* 13, no. 3 (2002): 561–595; Bosco, *Rough Justice*.
86. Han, "International Criminal Justice as Political Strategy: Asymmetry of Opportunity?".
87. Clark, "Law, Politics and Pragmatism," 42–43.
88. Allen, *Trial Justice*, 91.
89. Allen, *Trial Justice*, 84–85; Branch, "Uganda's Civil War," 184–185.

Yuna Han is a Research Associate at the European University Institute. Her research focuses on the intersection of international law and politics, specifically regarding international criminal justice and human rights prosecutions in weaker states within the international system. She is interested in understanding what impact the individual criminal responsibility for mass atrocities has on the international system, particularly with regard to state authority. She received her DPhil (PhD) in International Relations from the University of Oxford. She also holds a bachelor's degree in Government from Harvard University and an MPhil in Politics from the University of Cambridge.

9

Responsibility to Protect: Justice and Responsibility—Related but Not Synonymous

Alex J. Bellamy

It is sometimes said that the Responsibility to Protect (R2P) and international criminal justice are like cousins.[1] They are closely related but should never marry. This chapter seeks to explain why. It offers a perspective on international criminal justice from the vantage point of an advocate and academic working on the prevention of atrocity crimes and protection of populations from them through the implementation of R2P. I will argue that R2P and international criminal justice for atrocity crimes are complementary projects that are, on the whole, mutually supportive.[2] But they are not, however, synonymous and should not be treated as such. Nor should one be instrumentalized to serve the purposes of the other. There are two main reasons for this view. First, each has its own individual mandates and strengths. Each contributes most to the overall goal of greater human protection when allowed to pursue their own agendas unfettered by the requirements of the other. Establishing a global culture of legal accountability for atrocity crimes

---

A.J. Bellamy (✉)
School of Political Science and International Studies, The University of Queensland, Brisbane, QLD, Australia

J. Waterlow, J. Schuhmacher, *War Crimes Trials and Investigations*, St Antony's Series,
https://doi.org/10.1007/978-3-319-64072-3_9

would undoubtedly contribute to the goals of R2P. Likewise, progress on the prevention of atrocity crimes—promised by R2P—would undoubtedly help the International Criminal Court (ICC) and similar institutions achieve their goals of ensuring legal accountability for atrocity crimes and ending impunity. Making international criminal justice the handmaiden of R2P, though, risks making it selective and political without necessarily adding to the prevention of imminent atrocities.[3] Second, there are situations in which the demands of immediate protection and the prevention of imminent crimes (R2P) may require actions that undermine principles of legal accountability. For example, negotiators may have to cut deals with the perpetrators of atrocity crimes, peacekeepers may be dependent on cooperation with groups that have perpetrated atrocity crimes and may have to make conscious decisions not to apprehend alleged perpetrators of atrocity crimes for fear of disturbing the peace. What is more, as the political fortunes of R2P and international criminal justice ebb and flow, so does their utility to one another. In its early years, R2P was widely seen as a politically toxic concept because of its alleged association with Western interventionism not always motivated by humanitarian concern, a concept best avoided by others operating in the human protection space. However, since 2011, the concept has been normalized in the work of the United Nations (UN) Security Council to the point where it is now an established norm.[4] At the same time, the ICC has become more controversial. Where ICC advocates may have once been reluctant to utilize R2P for fear of undermining global consensus, in more recent times R2P advocates have looked to distance themselves from the ICC.[5] In both 2014 and 2015, for example, governments and R2P advocates were prepared to drop controversial references supportive of the ICC from draft Security Council resolutions that included references to R2P.[6]

With these points in mind, the chapter examines the pursuit of criminal justice for atrocity crimes from the perspective of R2P with the aim of understanding the complex relationship between them.[7] It does so in four parts. The first provides a general background to the emergence of R2P as an international norm. The second section examines the commonalities and differences between R2P and international criminal justice. The third section considers how these played out in relation to two significant cases: Kenya and Libya. The final, concluding, section examines the evolution of this relationship into the future. Overall, the chapter argues that although R2P and international criminal justice are generally related, the nature of that relationship differs from case to case. As Kurt Mills perceptively observed, they may be used separately or together, sequentially or simultaneously, and may be mutually supportive or mutually undermining depending on the context.[8]

Responsibility to Protect: Background and Overview

Stemming from the horrors of Srebrenica, a UN 'safe area' from which over 7000 men and boys were taken and slaughtered by Bosnian Serb forces in 1995, and Rwanda, which, a year earlier, had experienced full blown genocide, R2P is a disarmingly simple idea. It holds that sovereign states have a responsibility to protect their own populations from four crimes that indisputably 'shock the conscience of humankind': genocide, war crimes, ethnic cleansing and crimes against humanity.[9] It requires that the international community assist individual states to fulfil their responsibility, because some states lack the physical capacity and resources of legitimacy needed to protect their populations from these crimes. Finally, R2P says that when states 'manifestly fail' to protect their populations from these four crimes, whether through lack of capacity or will or as a result of deliberate intent, the international community should respond in a 'timely and decisive' fashion with diplomatic, humanitarian and other peaceful means and, failing that, with all the tools that are available to the UN Security Council. This can include the use of military force, which is sometimes a tragic necessity. R2P calls specifically for the prevention of the four crimes and—significantly—their incitement.

These are the three pillars of the Responsibility to Protect: (1) the primary responsibility of the state to protect its own population from genocide, war crimes, ethnic cleansing and crimes against humanity; (2) the international community's duty to assist; (3) the international responsibility to take timely and decisive action to protect populations from these crimes when the state fails to do so. The principle is a simple one; it is the politics that surround it and the challenge of realizing its ambition in practice that is so difficult.[10]

The phrase 'responsibility to protect'—R2P—was first coined in 2001 by the inelegantly titled 'International Commission on Intervention and State Sovereignty' (ICISS), a group of retired politicians, diplomats and humanitarians chaired by former Australian Foreign Minister Gareth Evans and the highly respected former Algerian diplomat Mohammed Sahnoun. The Commission was tasked by the Canadian government with the job of reconciling the tensions between state sovereignty and humanitarian necessity made abundantly obvious by NATO's 1999 intervention in Kosovo. Specifically, the Canadian government asked the Commission to find a way of avoiding repetitions of, on the one hand, cases like the 1994 Rwandan genocide, where the world stood aside and did nothing as 800,000 people were butchered in just 100 days and, on the other hand, cases like Kosovo where a group of states took it upon themselves to use force to protect people without a mandate from the UN Security Council.[11]

The Commission's answer came in the form of R2P—a call for a shift away from sterile debates about the prerogatives of interveners and inalienable rights of sovereigns towards a focus on protection for vulnerable populations and the responsibilities of individual governments and the international community as a whole.[12] The Commission argued that there was a duty to prevent as well as respond to these crimes and maintained that armed intervention should be reserved for the most severe cases and guided by a set of prudential criteria drawn from the Christian Just War tradition. This would ensure that force would only be used for the right reasons and only when likely to do more good than harm. R2P, Thakur explains, was 'the ICISS answer to reconciling the neuralgic rejection of humanitarian intervention by the global South with the determination by the North to end atrocities'.[13]

The journey of translating R2P from idea to political principle and diplomatic practice began with former UN Secretary-General, Kofi Annan. Annan welcomed the advent of R2P, describing it in his memoir as 'a brilliant innovation'.[14] He judged that by reframing debates about how the world should respond to mass atrocities and focusing on the responsibilities of sovereignty, R2P held the promise of reconciling two fundamental principles of the UN Charter that had all too often worked to opposite ends: state sovereignty and the protection of fundamental human rights.[15]

The opportunity to elevate R2P from intellectual curiosity to international diplomacy came in 2004. With the UN besieged by a neo-conservative administration in the US, hamstrung by a membership deeply divided by the US-led invasion of Iraq, and engulfed in the oil-for-food scandal, Annan decided to promote debate about broad-sweeping UN reforms. In preparation for what became known as the 'World Summit', Annan commissioned a High-Level Panel to review options for reforming the UN. The Panel called for the adoption of R2P as a guiding principle.[16] When Kofi Annan included the Panel's recommendations on R2P in his own blueprint for UN reform, a report entitled *In Larger Freedom*, the idea was placed squarely on the international agenda.[17]

In September 2005, more than 150 Heads of State and Government—the largest ever gathering at this level—arrived in New York to conclude negotiations on a blueprint for UN reform. In paragraphs 138 and 139 of the World Summit's Outcome Document, subsequently adopted as a General Assembly resolution, the UN's Member States committed themselves to R2P and its three 'pillars'. This commitment was subsequently reaffirmed by the Security Council in Resolution 1674 (2006), Resolution 1894 (2009), Resolution 2171 (2014) and Resolution 2220 (2015)—amongst others. In 2009, the General Assembly passed a unanimous resolution in which it pledged to continue its consideration of the implementation of R2P. Since then, the Secretary-General has issued a report on R2P each year and the General Assembly has debated it in an informal and interactive dialogue.

Since then, R2P has also become part of the diplomatic language used, albeit unevenly and with patchy results, to prevent and respond to atrocity crimes. The practical use of R2P got off to a slow and discouraging start. In the almost five years between Security Council Resolution 1674 (2006) and Resolution 1970 on Libya (2009), the Council referred to the concept only once (though it did refer to R2P prior to Resolution 1674, in Resolution 1653 (2006) on the Great Lakes Region of Africa). This came in a highly contentious preambular paragraph in Resolution 1706 (2006) on the situation in Darfur, where Sudanese government forces and their notorious allies the 'Janjaweed' militia had let rip a reign of terror resulting in the death of some 200,000 people and forced displacement of over two million more. Several Council members were cautious about the inclusion of R2P in the resolution (China abstained) and about the diplomatic pressure that was brought to bear to secure it. The diplomatic victory over the passage of Resolution 1706 was pyrrhic.[18]

With the UN and its Member States so hesitant to implement their 2005 commitment to R2P, few—if any—anticipated the role that the principle would play in the dramatic events of 2011. In February 2011, the 'Arab Spring' reached Libya. Protests there quickly turned into a major uprising that threatened to topple the dictator Muammar Gaddafi, who had ruled with an iron fist for over forty years. Gaddafi's forces responded to the challenge with typical brutality and the Libyan leader issued chilling threats of retribution reminiscent of the terms used to incite the Rwandan genocide nearly twenty years earlier. The following month, in March 2011, the Security Council responded to the unfolding crisis by throwing almost its entire portfolio of preventive measures at the situation in Libya in Resolution 1970. When the Gaddafi regime failed to comply with the Council's demands and looked likely to topple the rebel stronghold of Benghazi and commit a massacre there, the Council took the unprecedented step of authorizing the use of force against a state to protect civilians from imminent danger, enforce a no-fly zone, and enforce an arms embargo (Resolution 1973). NATO and its allies hastily arranged a coalition of the willing which prevented the fall of Benghazi and the widely anticipated massacre there. The conflict dragged on into a stalemate but eventually the regime collapsed and Gaddafi himself was killed, provoking a new storm of controversy.

A few days after the adoption of its landmark resolution on Libya, the Security Council unanimously adopted Resolution 1975 on Côte d'Ivoire. Having lost an election, the country's now-former president, Laurent Gbagbo, refused to stand down. Following the advice of international election monitors, the Council declared Alassane Ouattarra to be the country's President and authorized the use of force to protect the civilian population. UN forces already stationed in Côte d'Ivoire as part of the United Nations Operation deployed to oversee an end to the country's civil war and transition to a new, democratic, government acted alongside French forces to stop the escalating violence, remove Gbagbo and allow the elected president to take his place at the head of the new government.

The Council's responses to the crises in Libya and Cote d'Ivoire demonstrated a newly found determination to act on the responsibility to protect populations from atrocity crimes, including through the use of force when necessary. But the responses proved highly controversial. Critics complained that NATO and the UN had overstepped their mandates by contributing to regime change, that they had used disproportionate force which increased civilian casualties and that they had ignored or outright rejected opportunities for further political dialogue. Russia in particular argued that the Libyan experience coloured its thinking on the subsequent crisis in Syria, pushing it to resist Western pressure on the al-Assad regime on the grounds that it might open the door to forced regime change.[19]

Although the Council has indeed been deadlocked on Syria and has failed to respond adequately to a crisis which has resulted in the deaths of more than 200,000 people and forced in excess of four million people from their homes, controversies about the implementation of protection mandates in Libya and Côte d'Ivoire did not inhibit the constructive use of R2P in other contexts. Resolution 1996, adopted in July 2011, established a UN peace operation for South Sudan and called upon the international community to provide assistance to help the new government there to fulfil its responsibility to protect. Resolution 2014, adopted in October 2011, reminded the government of Yemen of its primary responsibility to protect its population. In its September 2011 Presidential Statement on preventive diplomacy, the Council again recalled its commitment to R2P. More recently, Resolution 2085 (2012) on Mali authorized an international mission to assist the government there in fulfilling its responsibility to protect, among other things, Resolution 2117 (2013) on small arms and light weapons recognized their capacity to result in the commission of R2P crimes, and Resolution 2121 (2013) on the Central African Republic underscored the government's responsibility to protect its own population.

Thus, in a remarkably short space of time R2P has been transformed from a concept proposed by an international commission into an international norm endorsed by the world's governments and usefully employed in more than a dozen situations. It is a principle that increasingly frames how the world thinks about the prevention of genocide and mass atrocities and responses to them. Translating that principle into consistent practice has proven more difficult, however, and the practical record is mixed. That is primarily because R2P does not exist in a social vacuum but instead interacts with other norms and interests and is subject to political contestation. For example, even if actors agree on the substance of R2P as a principle, they may still disagree radically on the best way of achieving its ambitions or on whether doing so is more, or less, important than achieving other goals, such as stability and order. Justin Morris coined the apt phrase 'dual responsibility' to point to the fact that the world's great powers have not just a responsibility to protect but also a responsibility to maintain international peace and security, and there are times in which the two imperatives might not correspond.[20] Moreover, we tend to greatly exaggerate the international community's capacity to influence domestic politics through means short of comprehensive interventions, which are themselves costly and risky undertakings.[21]

The Intersection of R2P and International Criminal Justice: Disciplinary Issues

Many advocates and scholars on both sides of the disciplinary divide between R2P and international criminal justice regard the ICC and other criminal tribunals as 'tools' for implementing R2P. The ICISS report described the ICC as one potential 'tool' for the prevention of atrocities and claimed that the Court's Rome Statute was one of the 'sources' of the R2P.[22] In his 2009 report, the UN Secretary-General noted that:

> By seeking to end impunity, the International Criminal Court and the United Nations-assisted tribunals have added an essential tool for implementing the responsibility to protect, one that is already reinforcing efforts at dissuasion and deterrence.[23]

Contarino and Negron-Gonzales agree, seeing the ICC as 'a powerful tool for the enforcement of the R2P norm'; Weiss and Serrano situate the ICC in the UN Security Council's 'toolbox' for implementing R2P; and Wallace sees the Court playing a powerful role in R2P's 'operationalization'.[24] But it is not only R2P scholars and advocates that have viewed the principle's relationship with the ICC in largely instrumental terms. Even the ICC's Chief Prosecutor, Fatou Bensouda, has commented that the Court is a 'critical tool' for implementing R2P.[25] Her predecessor, Moreno-Ocampo, suggested an alternative—but no less instrumental—view of the relationship, proposing that the ICC 'could add legitimacy to the Security Council's decision to apply the Responsibility to Protect concept'.[26]

It is certainly true that R2P and international criminal justice can be mutually supportive. Each state's primary responsibility to protect entails a duty to investigate and prosecute alleged atrocities, reinforcing the international criminal justice principle of complementarity. The ICC's Chief Prosecutor Luis Moreno Ocampo made the point emphatically when he observed that:

> the scheme envisioned by the Responsibility to Protect where each individual State has the primary responsibility to protect its populations from genocide, war crimes, ethnic cleansing and crimes against humanity, including the prevention of such crimes, and the idea that the international community will only step in when a State is failing to do [it] is very much the scheme retained in Rome for the International Criminal Court, the same concept, including the gravity threshold retained for the Responsibility to Protect is also close to our own legal standards under the Rome Statute.[27]

Likewise, the second pillar of R2P (relating to international assistance) entails responsibilities to provide practical assistance to the ICC and other criminal tribunals and to promote capacity building to augment each state's capacity to prosecute its own perpetrators of mass atrocities.[28]

The two projects also share much in common. They share a similar background and normative intent, both stemming from the failures to protect people from atrocity crimes in Rwanda, Bosnia, and elsewhere in the 1990s and a commitment to improving human protection. They share a grounding in state sovereignty and an interest in promoting responsible sovereignty.[29] They both espouse a 'humanity-based defence of international authority' and are underpinned by the principle of complementarity. Above all, however, R2P and international criminal justice share a mutual concern with the prevention and punishment of international *crimes*. Thus, the UN adopted the phrase 'atrocity crimes' to explain R2P's scope and coverage and the Special Advisor to the UN Secretary-General, Jennifer Welsh, articulated a 'crimes-prevention' approach to implementing R2P, drawing from the field of criminology.[30]

But despite the ubiquity of the claim, a marriage of this sort carries dangers for international criminal justice and R2P which could inhibit the capacity of both to deliver on their core mandate. That is because whilst they share these similarities, R2P and international criminal justice are also different in important respects.[31] Unless international society reaches a utopian condition in which all states become responsible sovereigns that protect populations from atrocities and accept the universal jurisdiction of the ICC, these differences will mean that it will not always be the case that what is required practically to achieve the goal of one (e.g. the protection of a particular population) will necessarily help the cause of the other (e.g. the prosecution of a particular perpetrator). Potential contradictions arise in practice, and how they play out in individual cases will need to be carefully managed to ensure that the pursuit of one objective (be it R2P or criminal accountability) does not fundamentally undermine the pursuit of the other.

There are at least four key differences that warrant further discussion. First, although the overall vision of R2P and international criminal justice is arguably the same (a world without mass atrocities), their specific *purposes* are different. R2P focuses on the prevention of atrocity crimes and their incitement and on the protection of vulnerable populations. The ICC, on the other hand, was established to prosecute the perpetrators of those crimes.[32] Thus, whilst—in theory at least—R2P is forward looking and proactive, international criminal justice is by necessity backwards looking and reactive. Criminal justice is concerned with principles of accountability and judicial independence, which are at most only secondary considerations for R2P.[33] Proponents of international criminal justice complain that the appropriation of crimes language by non-judicial bodies, such as human rights monitoring missions or UN officials, has led to the uneven application of criminal law standards and raised questions about due process (in relation to the naming of individual suspects) and investigative methodologies (i.e. witness protection).[34]

Viewed another way, we might say that R2P intends to marshal direct action to prevent atrocity crimes and protect vulnerable populations, whereas the ICC's contribution is largely indirect. Thus, R2P requires that when a state manifestly fails to protect its own population from atrocity crimes, the international community should adopt measures through the UN Security Council and relevant regional organizations. In this context, states should cooperate to provide physical protection to vulnerable populations (in the form of peacekeepers, civilian monitors, humanitarian aid) whilst seeking to both coerce the actual or would-be perpetrators into changing their course of action (through diplomacy and moral suasion, sanctions and embargoes, military measures) and diminish their capacity to commit atrocities (through arms and other embargoes, etc.). International criminal justice has a much less direct effect. Proponents argue that a permanent standing court such as the ICC can deter future would-be perpetrators by reducing impunity, but the initial evidence suggests that any preventive effect is indirect and applicable only under certain conditions.[35] There is now evidence that the Court's investigations can have a strong deterrent effect on governments and non-state armed groups that seek international legitimacy, but its wider effects remain unclear.[36] Nonetheless, this can only ever be an indirect and long-term cumulative effect, not the sort of direct and immediate influence required by R2P. But in a sense, the whole debate over whether international criminal justice prevents atrocities misses the point, namely that its purpose is the pursuit of *justice*, not the prevention of crimes or protection of populations from them.

Second, R2P and international criminal justice have different normative and institutional characteristics. Whereas R2P is a *political* commitment to implement existing legal obligations that states have under International Humanitarian Law (IHL) through existing international institutions, the ICC is a novel and permanent legal institution designed to prosecute and punish grave violations of IHL.[37] The latter is based on the solid foundations of international treaty law, whereas R2P's normative status is more intangible and—hence—indeterminate. Whatever its long-term merits or problems, R2P's indeterminacy makes the norm more flexible than hard-law institutions such as the ICC and thus more readily tailored to individual situations. R2P draws upon a variety of political concepts (e.g. 'sovereignty as responsibility' and the 'international duty of care'[38]) and legal foundations and is wedded only to the rules and institutional settings established by the UN Charter, which are themselves adaptable in the face of changing global conditions. The flexibility that derives from norm ambiguity can help build consensus amongst states with different perspectives (by allowing multiple interpretations of the norm), protect the norm from damage resulting from its application in especially controversial or difficult cases, and can facilitate incremental reform aimed at securing greater compliance.[39] As a result, for example, controversy over the implementation of R2P in relation to Libya did not inhibit the norm's use by the Security Council in subsequent crises in South Sudan, Mali, Central African Republic, Somalia, Yemen, and even Syria.[40]

Beyond this, the ICC is, in principle, hostile to the international use of force, preferring peaceful judicial processes. Amendments to the Rome Statute (Article 121.5) could extend the Court's jurisdiction to the crime of aggression. By mid-2016, 28 states had ratified or acceded to the amendment, with 30 needed to bring the amendment into force. Should the new clause come into force, the ICC might even act to deter states from using armed intervention to save populations from atrocity crimes, including genocide.[41] Whilst exhibiting a strong preference for prevention and peaceful responses to atrocity crimes, R2P acknowledges that the use of force may sometimes be necessary as a last resort—though by insisting that this be authorized collectively by the UN Security Council, such intervention would not fall foul of the ICC's definition of aggression.

Third, R2P and the international criminal tribunals have different 'jurisdictions'. As a political commitment, made by all UN member states, R2P 'applies' everywhere, and all the time. As the UN Secretary-General has pointed out, there is never a situation in which states *do not* have a responsibility to protect or in which the international community does not have a responsibility to take action in response to atrocity crimes.[42] For R2P, the appropriate question is not one of *whether there is* responsibility for protection, but how that responsibility is best *exercised.* By contrast, whereas the ICC's legal and institutional character is a source of strength, they also serve to limit the Court's jurisdiction. Only alleged crimes committed within the territory of state parties or referred to the Court by the UN Security Council fall within its jurisdiction, limiting the scope of its coverage. Not surprisingly, in practice almost all atrocity crimes since 2005 have been committed in countries that are not state parties to the Rome Statute. In order words, in most cases where R2P is put to work, the ICC has no automatic jurisdiction. As such, given that decision-making in the Security Council about whether or not to refer a situation to the Court is always highly political, the Court's involvement in situations of ongoing atrocity crimes almost always adds political complications in practice.

Fourth, R2P and international criminal justice have a different *focus*: R2P is unashamedly victim oriented. As Ramesh Thakur explains, the whole purpose of R2P is to take the side of the victim; to ensure that the state or international community stands between perpetrators of atrocity crimes and their victims, ultimately by whatever means necessary, including the full range of coercive and enforcement powers at the disposal of the UN Security Council.[43] By contrast, international criminal justice is perpetrator centred.

At is most fundamental, the difference between R2P and the ICC is that one is *political* and the other *legal*, yet in practice sometimes the legal is put into the service of the political and vice-versa. This raises a number of obvious problems and objections. For example, diplomats and peacekeepers working under a mandate to protect populations from atrocity crimes sometimes require a degree of flexibility that the law cannot provide. In 2006, for example, the UN dispatched its chief humanitarian, Jan Egeland, to Uganda to negotiate a peace agreement with the notorious Lord's Resistance Army (LRA). The LRA and its leadership was, at the time, under indictment by the Prosecutor of the ICC after a self-referral from Uganda. It is possible that it was the ICC investigation that triggered the LRA's interest in negotiations but that notwithstanding, Egeland was convinced that the group was seriously interested in peace overtures. However, the LRA insisted that the indictment against its leader be lifted as part of any agreement. This is where the clash between the political and the legal became obvious, since Egeland had no authority to even request such an arrangement and once that became clear to the LRA, the negotiations collapsed.[44] From an entirely pragmatic R2P perspective, it might be argued that the inflexibility of the ICC cost an opportunity to negotiate an end to atrocities by the LRA. From the legal perspective, however, any such compromise would have fundamentally damaged the Court's independence and its battle against impunity.

This is where we come to one of the principal critiques of R2P itself, which is that being a norm constituted by international society it is unable to marshal the fundamental political reforms needed to end mass atrocities. Critics such as Heather Roff maintain that R2P is flawed precisely because it does not impose legally binding demands on states. It is easy, the critics contend, for states to commit to a nebulous international responsibility to protect since—unlike international jurisprudence—the norm places no specific demands on any particular actor.[45] Nor are its nebulous demands legal in character, limiting the extent to which they can generate state compliance. As such, some international lawyers have tended to dismiss R2P as mere political rhetoric incapable of shifting state behaviour.[46]

This line of critique raises fundamental questions about the drivers of change in world politics and the relationship between laws and norms in state compliance. Advocates of R2P have tended to embrace the concept's political foundations and embeddedness within the existing order, albeit whilst recognizing the constraints that this imposes. Part of this is to do with political pragmatism and the urgency of responding to the problem of mass atrocities. If what is required is a legally binding set of duties to save strangers from atrocities, then we need a fundamentally different type of international society—one comprised of Kantian republics prepared to put the common good ahead of their own self-interests. States that are deeply cautious about a flexible political commitment such as R2P are hardly likely to commit themselves to binding international legislation. If possible at all, therefore, this more thoroughgoing reform is a long-term political project which leaves us with the question of what to do in the here and now.

R2P is still in its formative stages, as both a practice and field of study. There is a clear policy imperative for the careful tailoring of different measures to address the problem of preventing and responding to atrocity crimes in different contexts, yet we do not yet have a sufficient evidentiary base on which to draw conclusions about the types of actions most likely to support protection. This is abundantly clear, for example, in the relationship between R2P and the ICC. We have a range of case studies and anecdotes but as yet only limited systematic understanding of the relationship between prevention, protection, and prosecution. What is required is a more finely grained and interdisciplinary approach to understanding particular cases in greater depth and a more systematic approach to comparative analysis and the generation of generalizable insights about practice. Perhaps inevitably for a field so young, the study of R2P and atrocity crimes has thus far focused almost exclusively on the normative and practical value of the norm itself. What the field needs is a turn to the more careful and sober study of specific practices and cases, drawing upon a range of disciplines, so that we may get a clearer sense of causal chains. The following section sketches out what this might look like in relation to two critical cases, those of Kenya and Libya.

Case Studies in Perspective: Kenya and Libya

The best way to get a clear understanding of the relationship between protection and prosecution—the R2P and the ICC—is by examining their interaction in practice. This section considers two key cases—Kenya and Libya. I focus on these cases because the R2P and ICC were simultaneously employed in both. In doing so, the section amplifies the point that whilst the overall goals of R2P and the ICC may be similar, their operational practices are distinct and not always mutually reinforcing.

The international community's response to the ethnic violence that erupted in the aftermath of the disputed 30 December 2007 elections in Kenya is widely trumpeted as one of the best examples of R2P in practice.[47] That it occurred in a country that was also a state party to the Rome Statute meant that R2P and the ICC could be employed together without the involvement of the UN Security Council. Whilst up to 1500 people were killed and 300,000 displaced, a coordinated diplomatic effort by a troika of eminent persons mandated by the African Union (AU), spearheaded by Kofi Annan and supported by the UN Secretary-General, persuaded the country's president, Mwai Kibaki, and main opponent, Raila Odinga, to conclude a power-sharing agreement and rein in the violent mobs. This prevented what many feared could have been the beginning of a much worse campaign of mass atrocities. Reflecting on his successful diplomatic mission, Annan later observed that he:

> Saw the crisis in the R2P prism with a Kenyan government unable to contain the situation or protect its people. I knew that if the international community did not intervene, things would go hopelessly wrong. The problem is when we say 'intervention', people think military, when in fact that's a last resort. Kenya is a successful example of R2P at work.[48]

UN Secretary-General Ban Ki-moon was also quick to characterize the situation as relevant to R2P and to remind Kenya's leaders of their responsibilities.[49] The Secretary-General's Special Adviser for the Prevention of Genocide, Francis Deng, called upon Kenya's leadership to exercise their responsibility to protect, reminding them that if they failed to do so they would be held to account by the international community.[50] Several other senior UN officials also weighed in: Under-Secretary-General for Political Affairs, Lynn Pascoe, expressed concern about ethnic violence and the High Commissioner for Human Rights, Louise Arbour, demanded that there must be no impunity for those responsible. Significantly, these efforts were given strong diplomatic support by the UN Security Council, which issued a Presidential Statement reminding the leaders of their 'responsibility to engage fully in finding a sustainable political solution and taking action to immediately end violence'.[51]

It is widely acknowledged that this concerted diplomatic effort prompted the two leaders to agree to share power and rein in their militia, saving Kenya from civil war. The UN Secretary-General's first Special Advisor on R2P, Edward Luck, told reporters that: 'So the only time the UN has actually applied this [the R2P], was in the case of Kenya, early in 2008 after the disputed elections. When there's seven or eight hundred people … killed, it was not clear there was full-scale ethnic cleansing, but it could well become that or even something greater, and the UN decided to apply R2P criteria and to really make it the focus of the efforts there'.[52] But whilst those involved contend that Kenya provides an illustration of what R2P could deliver in terms of preventive action, others argue that R2P itself played a marginal role.[53] Another note of caution was sounded by AU Commissioner Jean Ping, who questioned whether it was appropriate to apply R2P in this case, suggesting that it raised serious questions as to the threshold of violence that constituted an R2P situation. Ping worried about potential selectivity when the response to Kenya was compared to the much weaker response in Somalia.[54]

In its response to post-election violence in Kenya, the international community tried to weave R2P together with international criminal justice. At the outset, Annan observed that 'we cannot accept that this sort of incident takes place every five years or so and no one is held to account ... or we will be back here again after three or four years'.[55] The agreement Annan negotiated contained a commitment to establish a Commission of Inquiry into the post-election violence. Kenyan Judge Philip Waki led the Commission and recommended the establishment of a special tribunal to prosecute those accused of committing serious violations of IHL. Kibaki and Odinga supported the proposal, but it was opposed by the National Assembly. Waki then gave a sealed list of people who should be indicted to Annan with instructions that he should pass this on to the ICC should a national tribunal not be established. In the end, the Waki commission delivered the names and case files directly to the ICC, which issued an ultimatum to the government of Kenya that if it did not establish a local tribunal, the papers would be transferred to the ICC prosecutor.

The government chose not to establish a national tribunal and so the matter was referred to the prosecutor's office. Investigations were opened and charges laid against six defendants, including prominent politicians Uhuru Kenyatta and William Reto. Backed by the AU, Kenya responded by demanding a cessation to the investigation and threatening to withdraw from the Court. In 2013, Kenyatta was elected President of Kenya—his popularity boosted by the ICC's indictment and the charge that the court was victimizing Kenya.[56] In 2014, supporters of the two most high-profile indictees, Uhuru Kenyatta (now Kenya's president) and William

Ruto, began a relentless campaign against the Court, insisting that the institution had become a tool of neo-imperialism—a curious argument given the fact that a majority of African cases before the ICC have resulted from self-referrals. In October 2014, the AU agreed that all heads of state—including those of states, like Kenya, that are signatories to the Rome Statute—should be immune from prosecution by the Court.[57] In the face of this political storm and unable to secure the evidence it needed, in late 2014, the ICC dropped charges it had laid against the principal defendant, Uhuru Kenyatta.

Yet despite the clear sense that R2P and the ICC would be mutually reinforcing in this case, their application was incoherent and mutually undermining. Serena Sharma concluded that 'measures designed to protect the population in Kenya appear to have undermined the efforts to prosecute perpetrators'.[58] The longer-term implications remain unclear. On the one hand, determined action at the annual Assembly of State Parties by friends of the ICC has ensured that there has been no en masse African departure from the Court. On the other hand, the AU has established a commission to investigate the whole issue of transitional justice, which is reportedly leaning firmly towards a focus on reconciliation rather than criminal accountability for atrocity crimes.[59]

Turning to Libya, in early 2011, the Arab Spring developed into a violent uprising against the Gaddafi regime. The rebel Interim National Transitional Council (NTC) enjoyed rapid successes in mid-February, declaring that its forces had taken control of most of the major cities. However, in late February and early March, Gaddafi's forces tipped the balance back in their favour and by mid-March were threatening to crush the rebellion's eastern epicentre in Benghazi. Senior UN officials warned of the imminent threat of mass atrocities and framed their responses in R2P terms. On 22 February, the UN's High Commissioner for Human Rights, Navi Pillay, emphasized the need to protect civilians and called on the authorities to stop using violence against demonstrators, which 'may amount to crimes against humanity'. On the same day, the Special Advisers to the UN Secretary-General on genocide prevention and R2P stated that the Libyan regime's behaviour could amount to crimes against humanity and that it must exercise its responsibility to protect. The following day the UN Secretary-General framed the ensuing debate as one about the prevention of mass atrocities and protection of vulnerable populations.

On 26 February, the Security Council voted unanimously to pass Resolution 1970. Among other things, this condemned 'the widespread and systematic attacks' against civilians, which it suspected 'may amount to crimes against humanity'. Acting under Chapter VII of the UN Charter, the Council demanded an immediate end to the violence; urged Gaddafi's government to ensure safe passage for humanitarian and medical supplies; established an arms embargo on the country; imposed indefinite travel bans on 16 individuals of the Libyan regime; froze indefinitely the assets of six members of the ruling regime; established a sanctions committee to monitor the implementation of these measures; and called upon Member States to make available humanitarian and related assistance for Libya. Significantly, for our purposes, it also referred the situation in Libya since 15 February to the Prosecutor of the ICC.[60] However, as Jennifer Welsh points out, the combination of judicial measures with targeted sanctions designed to coerce the Libyan government created strategic ambiguity on the Council's part in that it was unclear whether it wanted to deal with the regime's leaders or prosecute them.[61]

As in the Kenyan case, the AU took a more ambiguous stance on the questions of protection and prosecution. Its Peace and Security Council defined the situation in Libya 'a serious threat to peace and security in that country and in the region as a whole', and 'the indiscriminate use of force and lethal weapons ... and the transformation of pacific demonstrations into an armed rebellion'.[62] It went on to emphasize its 'strong commitment to the respect of the unity and territorial integrity of Libya, as well as its rejection of any foreign military intervention, whatever its form'.[63]

On the diplomatic front, Gaddafi's regime rejected the demands set out in Security Council Resolution 1970 and refused to permit humanitarian aid convoys into besieged towns such as Misrata and Ajdabiya. The UN Secretary-General personally contacted the Libyan leader and in a 40-minute conversation tried—and failed—to persuade Gaddafi to comply with the Council's demands. Thus, while the search for a diplomatic solution through the UN Special Envoy and the AU High-Level

Committee enjoyed widespread support, many governments, commentators and UN officials alike were coming to the view that diplomacy alone would not prevent a massacre should Benghazi fall.

It was in this context that Security Council members debated whether to authorize the use of force to establish a no-fly zone and protect civilians.[64] One of the central arguments made in the Council, and outside, was that the situation in Libya was both an ongoing threat to international peace and security and a humanitarian crisis which was likely to get significantly worse without urgent and decisive action. Gaddafi's description of the protesters as 'cockroaches', his promise to 'cleanse Libya house by house', and his threat to attack Benghazi and show its residents 'no mercy', provided clear evidence of the regime's intent to commit mass atrocities.

The vote on 17 March saw resolution 1973 pass with ten votes in favour (Bosnia and Herzegovina, Colombia, France, Gabon, Lebanon, Portugal, Nigeria, South Africa, the United Kingdom, and the United States), zero votes against, and five abstentions (Brazil, China, Germany, India, and Russia). The resolution reiterated the Council's concern that crimes against humanity may have been committed, deplored the ongoing humanitarian crisis, and took note of the criticisms of Gaddafi's regime made by a variety of international organizations, particularly the League of Arab States (Arab League, LAS). Acting under Chapter VII of the UN Charter, it demanded, among other things, an immediate ceasefire and intensified efforts to find a political solution to the crisis. It also authorized the use of 'all necessary means' (i.e. the use of force) to protect civilians and enforce the arms embargo imposed by Resolution 1970.

Resolution 1973 was a landmark moment in the Council's history, though differences of interpretation and recriminations over its implementation came to the fore almost immediately. NATO-led operations prevented the fall of the rebel stronghold of Benghazi and a widely anticipated massacre and after a period in which the frontline moved backwards and forward with alarming rapidity, the conflict settled into a period of stalemate. During this period, NATO and its allies continued to use force against Libyan targets, including command and control facilities. On 19 August, forces loyal to the rebel NTC stormed Tripoli and the city was taken in the space of a week. Fighting continued around government strongholds until October, when the town of Sirte fell to rebel forces and Gaddafi himself was captured and executed.

As in the Kenyan case, it was after the main hostilities were over that the ICC came into play, with the arrest of two senior regime figures, Abdullah al-Senussi and Saif al-Islam Gaddafi. As Mark Kersten shows, the new Libyan government and the ICC prosecutor disagreed about the best way of prosecuting these cases. Keen to establish its sovereignty, the new government in Tripoli called for the pair to the prosecuted in the national courts. Doubting that they could get a fair trial, the ICC prosecutor's office argued that they should be transferred to The Hague for prosecution.[65] Though the dispute was finally resolved in favour of the Libyan government, the affair 'may hamper the objectives and interests of both the ICC and Libyans'.[66]

Overarching Themes and Issues: Learning from the Practice

From the preceding case studies, a number of critical points about the relationship between R2P and international criminal justice emerge into focus. The first, and arguably most important, is that the assumption that R2P and international criminal justice will positively reinforce one another in the face of atrocity crimes does not always hold. In neither case is it clear, for example, that international criminal justice—or the prospect of it—played any direct role in preventing atrocity crimes or protecting vulnerable populations. Certainly, the work of the Waki Commission in Kenya—which increased the transparency of atrocity crimes and raised the prospect of legal accountability—helped put downwards pressure on the likelihood of post-election violence in 2013, but it is not at all clear that accountability concerns influenced negotiations positively in 2008. In Libya, where timelines were even shorter, the ICC referral contained in Resolution 1970 had little, if any, positive effect on the ground. At the time that the UN Security Council met to consider Resolution 1973, there was no confidence at all inside the Council that the threat of criminal accountability would be sufficient to prevent a massacre in Benghazi should it fall. Simply put, despite all the talk of international criminal justice being a useful 'tool' with which to achieve R2P's goals, there is little evidence to suggest that—absent other protective measures or certain enabling conditions—it is an especially useful tool. More broadly, to the extent that R2P has been associated with efforts succeeded in limiting atrocity crimes, as in Kenya, Cote d'Ivoire, Mali, Libya, and the Central African Republic, international criminal justice has played a relatively modest role.

Part of the problem is that politics and criminal law deal in different ontologies.[67] The assumptions that underpin the criminal law approach to atrocities often do not hold in settings where atrocities are committed. Criminal law deals in terms of perpetrators, victims and witnesses (actual or expert). It is concerned with crimes committed *by* perpetrators *against* victims. Not only are these categories fixed, they are consequential in law. The practical reality, however, is that these are not fixed categories. Victims in one context may become perpetrators in other, and vice versa. It is quite common for atrocity crimes to be committed as revenge for past crimes. Using fixed categories can limit diplomatic room for manoeuvre and reduce the scope for creative international responses aimed at preventing or terminating atrocities.

Another key ontological assumption in criminal justice relates to the fact of law itself. In domestic settings, not only is law said to reflect community expectations and standards, it is embedded within and constitutive of the community itself. Violations of the law are therefore violations of common community standards. That assumption does not necessarily hold for IHL, especially on territories where weak states exerted limited authority for protracted periods. In those spaces, standards of international law may be alien and not at all consistent with community expectations. Thus, it is not uncommon to find social settings where vengeance killing is *expected* and legal principles such as civilian immunity are not well embedded. Still more extreme are cases where states legislate to support mass killing (e.g. Nazi Germany, the Stalinist Soviet Union, Khmer Rouge Cambodia) and are not parties to conventions prohibiting it. In these situations, individual perpetrators may violate prevailing interpretations of their own domestic law by *refusing* to commit atrocities.

A second problem is the misappropriation of international criminal justice for political purposes. There is a risk that by aligning criminal justice with political agendas—and by using justice as a 'tool' to achieve other social goods—relevant institutions become political rather than judicial actors, weakening their long-term legitimacy and viability.[68] In the Kenyan case, for example, the issue of referral to the ICC became a political football used first to coerce the Kenyan authorities, including its national parliament, into a particular course of action (establishing a special tribunal), and then to influence the course of a national election.[69] In the Libyan case, the court took only a few days to decide that it would launch an investigation, a decision that some believe was intended to further de-legitimize the Gaddafi regime and support the UN Security Council's strategy.[70] In turn, this raised concerns about the *procedures* used to determine which situations should be referred to the Court and which should not and a mounting sense that the Council found it easier to refer African cases than it did to refer other, non-African, situations (e.g. Syria, Yemen, Palestinian Territories).[71] Once the regime was overthrown, the Court rapidly changed course and permitted the new Libyan authorities to lead the investigations and prosecutions.[72] Although they might deliver short-term gains in terms of assisting humanitarian diplomacy, such machinations only damage the Court's long-term reputation as a dispenser of impartial justice. As Stahn points out:

> [It] is risky to rely on calculated political effects to motivate prosecutorial choices. Placing human security concerns at the centre of justice-related decision-making processes is likely to result in disappointment and failure. It might ultimately lead to a mission creep of international criminal justice. Viewing international criminal justice as a project to build responsible sovereignty is overambitious.[73]

Particularly significant are charges that the Court has been politicized (and is therefore biased), aired most vocally by the AU in its decision to defy the Court by granting immunity to Heads of State but also evident in academic commentary.[74] Of course, because it lacks universal jurisdiction but can have matters referred to it by the UN Security Council, the Court was, by design, always partly political. Some argue that it is this power of the UN Security Council to refer matters to the Court that is the source of its political difficulties.[75] Others point to longstanding—but as yet unfounded—fears that the language of criminality ('atrocity crimes' and their perpetrators) could be used as a quasi-judicial justification for armed intervention.[76] Yet, in reality, the most controversial cases in this regard—that of Kenya, and Uganda's inability to recall proceedings against the LRA—both stemmed from self-referrals arising out of accession to the Rome Statute, and not referrals from the UN Security Council.

Furthermore, it would be naïve to believe that the establishment of international criminal justice mechanisms above the sovereign state, designed, in part, to hold sovereigns to account, could be somehow apolitical and avoid controversy. From this perspective, it is hardly surprising that heads of government should object vociferously to moves to hold them, individually, accountable for their role in the commission of grave violations of IHL. Irrespective of R2P, the very notion that sovereigns should be individually accountable in this way is among the most radical propositions advanced since the Treaty of Westphalia declared the *Rex* to be master of his/her own territory.[77] My point here is not to suggest that politicization is not a complicating factor, but that the project of international criminal justice is itself a radical political departure from past practice. It does not need R2P to make it politicized or controversial, it achieves that all by itself.

On the upside, fears that the Court might shift protection responsibilities away from the UN Security Council have proven unfounded.[78] At the time of writing, the Council had confronted more than a dozen crises through the lens of R2P, and not once had it opted to refer a matter to the ICC as a substitute. In Libya and elsewhere, the Council has used R2P and the ICC in tandem. Where they are not used together, R2P is more commonly used than the ICC. Roach argues that the politicization problem may be addressed by the Court shedding its allegiance to being apolitical and by, instead, embracing its political character. That would allow the court to focus on achieving outcomes based on mutual accommodation, increasing its flexibility and potentially preventing the types of dispute seen over Kenya and Libya.[79] But that is not a solution likely to find much support among jurists.

Conclusion

In this chapter, I have suggested that although R2P and international criminal justice are related, they are not synonymous and ought to pursue their objectives independently of one another. They are cousins that ought not marry. In doing so, I identified a number of specific challenges that have arisen through the interplay of R2P and international criminal justice. How might these issues be addressed in the future? Two specific proposals are that proponents of R2P should reassess their use of 'crimes' language, perhaps focusing instead on specific practices or indicators of atrocities and cordoning off the use of criminological terms and concepts for judicial bodies. This would help clarify the distinctions between the criminal-legal and the political ways of approaching the problem of mass atrocities and inhibit creep. A second suggestion is that R2P and international criminal justice should focus on 'positive complementarity'—that is, supporting national capacity building and reform.[80] This, of course, is the essence of R2P's second pillar, which is focused on helping and encouraging states to fulfil their responsibility to protect. Saxon argues that it will be a key function of the ICC too: 'Over the long term, the ICC's strongest tool for the prevention of crime may be its ability to convince states to reform their own judicial institutions so that these bodies have the capacity to protect fundamental human rights'.[81]

Looking more broadly, it is important to set aside all thought of marriage (and divorce) and recognize that R2P and international criminal justice are cousins. As such, they ought to be permitted to pursue their own separate paths towards their common goal of universal, responsible and accountable sovereignty. This means that each element ought to be supported and developed in its own right and that each should be pursued vigorously without much regard for how it might impact, in the short term, on the other. In simple terms, that means that the ICC Prosecutor should vigorously pursue all lines of investigation falling within the Court's jurisdiction, irrespective of what diplomatic fallout this might have for those more focused on R2P. The Court will only achieve its goals of justice and deterrence if it becomes an established part of international life, across generations. Just as national courts can be awkward, disruptive and controversial for government agendas, so too must international courts. A Court charged with holding heads of government to account for atrocity crimes *ought to be* controversial, contested and difficult. If it is not, then it is probably not doing its job. At the same time, R2P should be advanced as a policy agenda and political mobilizer without concern for how it might enable or assist international criminal justice. References to the ICC should not be added to general resolutions supporting R2P unless there is sufficient consensus and clear benefit. The same applies to country-specific resolutions. Situations should be referred by the Security Council to the ICC only where there are apparent advantages. What is more, timely and decisive responses to atrocity crimes should never be delayed by the need to win consensus on an ICC referral. It is important to acknowledge that the Rome Statute includes potentially awkward elements with respect to the UN Security Council. Each needs to be supported and developed in its own right, independently of the other.

Finally, however, more attention needs to be paid to the political and historical context. The whole endeavour of ridding the world of atrocity crimes needs to be imbued with a sense of modesty and a clear understanding of the limits of what can be achieved through international initiatives such as R2P and the ICC. We need to first recognize that there are important limits to what norms and laws can do in world politics. In an anarchic international system, laws and norms cannot by themselves *compel* people or states to take particular actions or physically *prevent* them from doing so. Instead, they influence behaviour indirectly by shaping governments' own judgements about appropriate and inappropriate behaviour and influencing the way in which other governments will respond to that behaviour. Behaviour compliant with shared norms is likely to be welcomed and praised; non-compliance is likely to be met with criticism, punishment and social exclusion.[82] But what counts as a breach of a norm, and the consequences that flow from that, are not decided objectively or in mechanistic fashion. Instead, judgements are contingent on their context and are highly political—usually influenced by situations themselves.[83] In international society laws and norms influence behaviour indirectly through social pressures that promote compliance and threats of punishment and exclusion. They do not determine or compel behaviour and therefore cannot guarantee particular outcomes.

Even when the normative and political context allow for it, the effective protection of populations from atrocity crimes confronts significant practical challenges. Even if there were abundant enthusiasm, consensus, and resources available for protection and atrocities prevention, it would likely still prove impossible to prevent every atrocity and protect every individual—absent some fundamental reforms to the human condition. There are significant limits to what outsiders can do to prevent atrocity crimes. Many internal conflicts are not readily susceptible to outside mediation, whether (as in the case of Rwanda or Iraq (Islamic State)) because one or more of the parties have embarked implacably on a course of action leading to atrocities or (as in the case of Syria and South Sudan) because a situation is so complex and fraught with danger as to defy easy resolution.[84] Although concerted international action can sometimes protect populations or prevent mass atrocities (e.g. as in Cote d'Ivoire, Kenya, Libya), the primary determinants of violence or peace typically rest within the country itself and the disposition of its leaders.[85]

This problem is compounded by the fact that R2P and international criminal justice tend to be reserved for use in the most difficult cases.[86] Situations usually reach the UN Security Council and ICC only when others have tried, and failed, to resolve them. In such circumstances, a modest success rate might partly reflect the sheer difficulty of the cases presented.

It is also important to recognize that R2P and international criminal justice are political all the way down. Their practice is both enabled and constrained by politics and can generate acute controversies and disputes by, for instance, requiring that some states be identified as being at risk of atrocities and some state leaders culpable in their commission. Often, even long-term preventive and capacity building measures entail a significant degree of intrusion into the domestic affairs of states, which is not likely to be always welcome.[87] In this context, it is important to recognize that 'in the nation-state era there will be limits to both the practicality and the wisdom of formally breaching the proper boundaries of sovereignty.'[88] Typically, states jealously guard their sovereign prerogatives and are sensitive about perceived incursions on their rights or criticisms of their conduct or domestic conditions. As such, they rarely invite assistance or look kindly upon external efforts to prevent atrocities within their jurisdiction. It is false to assume that preventive or judicial action will always be less contentious than intervention.[89] For that reason, engagement with politics and history will be an ongoing feature of both the study and practice of R2P and international criminal justice.

Bibliographical Essay From relatively modest beginnings, since 2011 the academic literature on the Responsibility to Protect has developed and grown significantly. Initially, literature focused on the emergence of R2P itself and the politics surrounding it, but as the focus has turned to the practice of atrocity prevention and response, interest in the relationship between R2P and international criminal justice has grown, resulting in a number of standalone monographs focused exclusively on this issue. Among the first two books to appear on R2P were Gareth Evans, *The Responsibility to Protect: Ending Mass Atrocity Crimes Once and for All* (Washington, DC: The Brookings Institution, 2008) and Alex J. Bellamy, *The Responsibility to Protect: The Global Effort to End Mass Atrocities* (Oxford: Polity, 2009). These books cover similar ground but bring different perspectives. Evans was arguably the principal norm entrepreneur for R2P and his account offers a powerful defence of the principle's rationale and place in world politics, as well as providing an insightful explanation of how atrocities may be ended and the dilemmas this politics provokes. My account provides a more detailed examination of the emergence of R2P, charting preceding ideas such as 'sovereignty as responsibility', assessing the work and findings of the ICISS and describing the diplomacy behind the 2005 World Summit agreement on R2P. Both of these works make passing reference to the ICC and issues of international criminal justice, but neither includes a sustained analysis of this relationship.

As interest in R2P grew—alongside the emerging practice—the academic literature on the subject burgeoned. The best way of getting a sense of the sheer weight and diversity of the literature on R2P is through Alex J. Bellamy and Tim Dunne, eds., *The Oxford Handbook on the Responsibility to Protect* (Oxford: Oxford University Press, 2016). Intended as a 'one-stop-shop' for analysis of R2P, its origins, development, and practice as well as its intersection with other fields—including international criminal justice—the Oxford Handbook comprises more than fifty chapters by scholars drawn from every continent. Of particular interest for readers of this chapter will be contributions on the relationship between R2P and international criminal justice, as well as chapters on the relationship between human rights and R2P, gender and atrocity prevention, and the evolution of key international institutions. Published shortly before the Handbook were two other major edited collections that significantly advanced our understanding of the preventive dimensions of R2P. These were Sheri P. Rosenberg, Tibi Galis, and Alex Zucker, eds., *Reconstructing Atrocity Prevention* (Cambridge: Cambridge University Press, 2016) and Serena K. Sharma and Jennifer M. Welsh, eds., *The Responsibility to Prevent: Overcoming the Challenges to Atrocity Prevention* (Oxford: Oxford University Press, 2015). Collections of the highest quality, not only do these volumes contain chapters specifically focused on the relationship between R2P and international criminal justice—including one by former Special Adviser to the UN Secretary-General, Jennifer Welsh—they also situate international criminal justice within the broader effort to prevent atrocity crimes. Thus, Dan Saxon's contribution to *The Responsibility to Prevent* highlights some of the ways, outside prosecutions, in which the ICC contributes towards atrocity prevention.

Finally, we come to a selection of books that are specifically focused on the core relationship examined in this chapter, or at least variations thereof. Mark Drumbl's, *Atrocity, Punishment and International Law* (Cambridge: Cambridge University Press, 2007) provides a detailed examination of the question of how those responsible for atrocity crimes should be punished. Putting forth a somewhat controversial answer, Drumbl argues that international prosecutions rarely achieve their stated goals and that a more flexible, bottom-up approach to the punishment of perpetrators that takes account of social needs and local traditions may be necessary. Turning specifically to the role of the ICC in situations where R2P might be invoked is Mark Kersten, *Justice in Conflict: The Effects of the International Criminal Court's Interventions on Ending War and Building Peace* (Oxford: Oxford University Press, 2016). This is a powerful and compelling book that demonstrates the need to push beyond simple binaries and acknowledge that the ICC's engagement in on-going situations is likely to be complex and the outcomes varied, depending on the political situation and the vagaries of each context. Likewise, Kurt

Mills, *International Responses to Mass Atrocities in Africa: Responsibility to Protect, Prosecute and Palliate* (Philadelphia: University of Pennsylvania Press, 2015) shows that the interaction of R2P and the ICC can produce a range of different outcomes. Indeed, Mills goes further and points to the different qualities and types of interaction as well, giving us fresh depth in understanding this relationship. Finally Serena K. Sharma's, *The Responsibility to Protect and the International Criminal Court: The Case of Kenya* (London: Routledge, 2016) provides the definitive account of the ICC's engagement with the Kenyan case—often taken to be R2P's greatest success.

Notes

1. By international criminal justice I am specifically referring to the various courts and special tribunals established to prosecute individuals for grave violations of International Humanitarian Law.
2. It is most common to see the two as complementary projects. See Fatou Bensouda, speech at conference on 'R2P: the next decade', 18 January 2012, available at http://www.fora.tv/2012/01/18/R2P_in_2022, and Michael Contarino, Melinda Negron-Gonzales and Kevin T. Mason, "The ICC and Consolidation of the R2P as an International Norm," *Global Responsibility to Protect* 4, no. 3 (2012): 275–308. By 'atrocity crimes', I mean the four crimes associated with R2P: genocide, war crimes, ethnic cleansing and crimes against humanity.
3. Points made by Anthony Dworkin, "International Justice and the Prevention of Atrocity," European Council on Foreign Relations, October 2014, 34, available at http://www.ecfr.eu/page/-/ECFR115_International_Justice_Report.pdf
4. For a full defence of this view see Alex J. Bellamy, "The Responsibility to Protect Turns Ten," *Ethics and International Affairs* 29, no. 2 (2015): 161–185.
5. In this sense, whilst both R2P and the ICC have faced crises, it is not necessarily clear that they confront the *same* crisis or are in crisis for the same reasons. See Kirsten Ainley, "The Responsibility to Protect and the International Criminal Court: Counteracting the Crisis," *International Affairs* 91, no. 1 (2015): 37–54.

6. Based on the author's own observations of the drafting and negotiating process. It is somewhat ironic, therefore, that calls for the divorcing of R2P and the ICC are almost always couched in terms of the need to protect the latter from the political controversies surrounding the former. See, for example, David Chandler, "Born Posthumously: Re-Thinking the Shared Characteristics of the ICC and R2P," *Finnish Yearbook of International Law* 21 (2010): 1–9.
7. In suggesting that the relationship is complex, the nature of which changes from case to case, I am following Mark Kersten, *Justice in Conflict: The Effects of the International Criminal Court's Interventions on Ending War and Building Peace* (Oxford: Oxford University Press, 2016).
8. Kurt Mills, *International Responses to Mass Atrocities in Africa: Responsibility to Protect, Prosecute and Palliate* (Philadelphia: University of Pennsylvania Press, 2015).
9. This phrase borrowed from Michael Walzer, *Just and Unjust Wars: A Moral Argument with Historical Illustrations* (New York: Basic Books, 1977).
10. First set out in *Implementing the Responsibility to Protect: Report of the Secretary-General*, A/63/677, 12 January 2009.
11. For accounts of the rise of R2P see Alex J. Bellamy, *The Responsibility to Protect: The Global Effort to End Mass Atrocities* (Oxford: Polity, 2009) and Gareth Evans, *The Responsibility to Protect: Ending Mass Atrocity Crimes Once and for All* (Washington, DC: The Brookings Institution, 2008).
12. International Commission on Intervention and State Sovereignty, *The Responsibility to Protect* (Ottawa: IDRC, 2001).
13. Ramesh Thakur, "Review Article: The Responsibility to Protect at 15," *International Affairs* 92, no. 2 (2016): 417.
14. Kofi Annan, *Interventions: A Life in War and Peace* (New York: Allen Lane, 2012), 118.
15. Annan, *Interventions*, 118.
16. High Level Panel on Threats, Challenges and Change, *A More Secure World: Our Shared Responsibility*, A/59/565, December 2004, 65–66. For an account of the Panel's work see David Hannay, *New World Disorder: The UN after the Cold War—An Insider's View* (London: I. B. Tauris, 2008).
17. *In Larger Freedom: Towards Development, Security and Human Rights for all. Report of the Secretary-General*. A/59/2005. Add.3, 26 May 2005.

18. Colum Lynch, "The Ten Worst UN Security Council Resolutions Ever," *Foreign Policy*, accessed 21 March 2010. http://turtlebay.foreignpolicy.com/posts/2010/05/21/the_10_worst_un_security_council_resolutions_ever
19. Derek Averre and Lance Davies, "Russia, Humanitarian Intervention and the Responsibility to Protect: The Case of Syria," *International Affairs* 91, no. 2 (2015): 813–834.
20. Justin Morris, "The Responsibility to Protect and the Great Powers: The Tensions of Dual Responsibility," *Global Responsibility to Protect* 7, no. 3–4 (2015): 401–424.
21. See, for example, Scott Straus, *Making and Unmaking Nations: War, Leadership and Genocide in Modern Africa* (Ithaca: Cornell University Press, 2015), 326.
22. ICISS, *Responsibility to Protect*, paras. 3.30 and 6.17, respectively.
23. Ban, *Implementing*, para. 18.
24. Respectively, Michael Contarino and Melinda Negron-Gonzales, "The International Criminal Court," in *An Institutional Approach to the Responsibility to Protect*, ed. Gentian Zyberi (Cambridge: Cambridge University Press, 2013), 411; and Don Wallace, "The International Criminal Court," in *International Organizations and the Implementation of the Responsibility to Protect: The Humanitarian Crisis in Syria*, ed. Daniel Silander and Don Wallace (London: Routledge, 2015).
25. Cited in Serena Sharma, *The Responsibility to Protect and the International Criminal Court: The Case of Kenya* (London: Routledge, 2016).
26. Luis Moreno-Ocampo, "The Responsibility to Protect: Engaging America," 17 November 2006, accessed 13 May 2016. http://www.r2pcoalition.org/content/view/61/86
27. Luis Moreno Ocampo, Keynote Address, Chicago, 17 November 2006, Chicago, accessed 14 May 2016. http://www.r2pcoalition.org/content/view/61/86/
28. *Implementing the Responsibility to Protect. Report of the Secretary-General*, 2009, para. 44.
29. Or 'good sovereignty' as Megret puts it. See Frederic Megret, "ICC, R2P, and the International Community's Evolving Interventionist Toolkit," *Finnish Yearbook of International Law* 21 (2010): 21–51.
30. See Serena K. Sharma, Ruben Reike and Jennifer M. Welsh, "Conceptualizing the Responsibility to Prevent," in *The Responsibility to Prevent: Overcoming the Challenges to Atrocity Prevention*, ed. Serena K. Sharma and Jennifer M. Welsh (Oxford: Oxford University Press,

2015); and Jennifer M. Welsh, "The 'Narrow but Deep' Approach to Implementing the Responsibility to Protect: Reassessing the Focus on International Crimes," in *Reconstructing Atrocity Prevention*, ed. Sheri P. Rosenberg, Tibi Galis and Alex Zucker (Cambridge: Cambridge University Press, 2016), 81–94. Also Ruben Reike, "The 'Responsibility to Prevent': An International Crimes Approach to the Prevention of Mass Atrocities," *Ethics and International Affairs*, 28, no. 4 (2014): 451–476.

31. Carsten Stahn, "Marital Stress or Grounds for Divorce? Rethinking the Relationship between R2P and International Criminal Justice," *Criminal Law Forum* 26, no. 1 (2015): 13–50.
32. Kurt Mills, "R2P: Protecting, Prosecuting or Palliating in Mass Atrocity Situations," *Journal of Human Rights* 12 (2013): 333.
33. Stahn, "Marital Stress," 16.
34. Stahn, "Marital Stress," 32.
35. Such as strong domestic institutions. See Dan Saxon, "The International Criminal Court and the Prevention of Atrocities," in *The Responsibility to Prevent: Overcoming the Challenges of Atrocity Prevention*, ed. Serena K. Sharma and Jennifer M. Welsh (Oxford: Oxford University Press, 2015), 157. Also, Kurt Mills, "R2P and the ICC: At Odds or in Sync?" *Criminal Law Forum* 26 (2015): 77. Payan Akhavan, "Can International Criminal Justice Prevent Future Atrocities?" *Leiden Journal of International Law* 95 (2001); and Leslie Vinjamuri, "Deterrence, Democracy, and the Pursuit of International Justice," *Ethics & International Affairs* 24, no. 2 (2010): 191.
36. Hyeran Jo and Beth Simmons, "Can the International Criminal Court Deter Atrocity?" unpublished paper, 18 December 2014, Social Science Research Network.
37. According to Dieter Fleck, R2P challenges states to meet their existing legal obligations. See Dieter Fleck, "The Law Applicable to Peace Operations," in *The Oxford Handbook of International Law in Armed Conflict*, ed. Andrew Clapham and Paola Gaeta (Oxford: Oxford University Press, 2014), 216. On the importance of these key differences see Jason Ralph, "The International Criminal Court," in *The Oxford Handbook on the Responsibility to Protect*, ed. Alex J. Bellamy and Tim Dunne (Oxford: Oxford University Press, 2016).
38. On which, see Louise Arbour, "The Responsibility to Protect as a Duty of Care in International Law and Practice," *Review of International Studies* 34 (2008): 445–458.

39. Wes W. Widmaier and Luke Glanville, "The Benefits of Norm Ambiguity: Constructing the Responsibility to Protect Across Rwanda, Iraq and Libya," *Contemporary Politics* 21, no. 4 (2015): 367–383.
40. Alex J. Bellamy, "From Tripoli to Damascus: Lesson Learning and the Implementation of the Responsibility to Protect," *International Politics* 51, no. 1 (2014): 23–44.
41. On which, see Larry May, *Aggression and Crimes against Peace* (Cambridge: Cambridge University Press, 2008); and C. McDougall, *The Crime of Aggression under the Rome Statute of the International Criminal Court* (Cambridge: Cambridge University Press, 2013).
42. *Responsibility to Protect: Timely and Decisive Response. Report of the Secretary-General.* A/66/874-S/2012/578, 25 July 2012, para. 13.
43. 'R2P…addresses the issue from the perspective of the victims'. Ramesh Thakur, "Review Article: The Responsibility to Protect at 15," *International Affairs* 92, no. 2 (2016): 418.
44. See Jan Egeland, *A Billion Lives: An Eyewitness Report from the Frontlines of Humanity* (New York: Simon and Schuster, 2010).
45. Heather Roff, *Global Justice, Kant, and the Responsibility to Protect: A Provisional Duty* (London: Routledge, 2014).
46. Carsten Stahn, "Responsibility to Protect: Political Rhetoric or Emerging Legal Norm?" *American Journal of International Law* 101, no. 1 (2007): 99–120.
47. E.g. Evans, *Responsibility to Protect*, 106; Desmond Tutu, "Taking the Responsibility to Protect," *New York Times*, 9 November 2008; Donald Steinberg, "Responsibility to Protect: Coming of Age?" *Global Responsibility to Protect* 1, no. 4 (2009): 432–441. For the most comprehensive account to date see Elizabeth Lindenmayer and Josie Lianna Kaye, "A Choice for Peace? The Story of Forty-One Days of Mediation in Kenya," International Peace Institute, August 2009.
48. Cited in Roger Cohen, "How Kofi Annan Rescued Kenya," *New York Review of Books* 55, no. 13 (14 August 2008).
49. Statement attributable to the Spokesperson for the Secretary-General on the situation in Kenya, New York, 2 January 2008.
50. Ban Ki-moon, Address to the Summit of the African Union, Addis Ababa, 31 January 2008. See International Crisis Group, "Kenya in Crisis," *Africa Report*, no. 137, 21 February 2008. Public Radio International, "The Responsibility to Protect," 7 March 2009.
51. S/PRST/2008/4, 6 February 2008

52. International Crisis Group, "Kenya in Crisis," *Africa Report*, no. 137, 21 February 2008. Public Radio International, "The Responsibility to Protect," 7 March 2009.
53. These views are expressed in Sean Harder, "How they Stopped the Killing," The Stanley Foundation, June 2009.
54. Keynote Address by Jean Ping, Chairperson of the AU Commission, at the Roundtable High-Level Meeting of Experts on "The Responsibility to Protect in Africa," Addis Ababa, 23 October 2008.
55. Cited in Sharma, *R2P and the ICC*, xx.
56. On the role played by the Court, see Gabrielle Lynch and Misa Zgonec-Rozej, "The ICC Intervention in Kenya," Chatham House, February 2013.
57. Michela Wrong, "Has Kenya Destroyed the ICC?" *Foreign Policy*, 15 July 2014. It is important here to distinguish the AU's move to limit the jurisdiction of the court over state-parties to the Rome Stature from those states, such as the US, China, Russia and India, that have limited the court's jurisdiction by simply refusing to accede to the Rome Statute.
58. Sharma, *R2P and the ICC*, xx
59. Wrong, "Has Kenya Killed the ICC?".
60. On 3 March, the ICC Prosecutor, Luis Moreno-Ocampo, said his office was investigating crimes against humanity that may have been committed by Gaddafi's regime. This was the first time the Security Council had referred to both the ICC and R2P in a single substantive resolution. See Carsten Stahn, "Libya, the International Criminal Court and Complementarity: A Test for Shared Responsibility," *Journal of International Criminal Justice* 10, no. 2 (2012): 325–349.
61. Welsh, "Narrow But Deep Approach," 91.
62. This was in line with the AU's general commitment to condemn all efforts to engage in 'unconstitutional forms of government' on the continent.
63. AU document PSC/PR/COMM.2(CCLXV), 10 March 2011.
64. See S/PV.6498, 17 March 2011.
65. Mark Kersten, "Justice after the War: The International Criminal Court and post-Gaddafi Libya," in *Transitional Justice and the Arab Spring*, ed. Kirsten J. Fisher and Robert Stewart (London: Routledge, 2014), 188.
66. Ibid., 188.
67. Some of these are set out by Mark Drumbl, *Atrocity, Punishment and International Law* (Cambridge: Cambridge University Press, 2007).

68. Stahn, "Marital Stress," 33.
69. See Sabine Hohn, "New Start or False Start? The ICC and Electoral Violence in Kenya," *Development and Change* 45 (2014): 565–588.
70. There is no direct evidence of this, it must be acknowledged. See Carsten Stahn, "Libya, the ICC and Complementarity: A Test for 'Shared Responsibility'," *Journal of International Criminal Justice* 10, no. 2 (2010): 325–351.
71. Jason Ralph and Adrian Gallagher, "Legitimacy Faultlines in International Society: The Responsibility to Protect and Prosecute after Libya," *Review of International Studies* 41, no. 3 (2015): 553–573.
72. Stahn, "Libya, the ICC and Complementarity".
73. Stahn, "Marital Strain," 40.
74. For example, Mahmood Mamdani, "Responsibility to Protect or Right to Punish?" *Journal of Intervention and Statebuilding* 4, no. 1 (2010): 53–67.
75. Louise Arbour, "The Relationship Between the ICC and the UN Security Council," *Global Governance* 20, no. 2 (2014): 195–201; and Andrea Birdsall, "The Responsibility to Prosecute and the ICC: A Problematic Relationship?" *Criminal Law Forum* 26, no. 1 (2015): 51–72.
76. E.g. Anne Orford, *Reading Humanitarian Intervention* (Cambridge: Cambridge University Press, 2003).
77. David Luban, "After the Honeymoon: Reflections on the Current State of International Criminal Justice," *Journal of International Criminal Justice* 11, no. 3 (2013): 505–515.
78. Benjamin Schiff, "The ICC's Potential for Doing Bad When Pursuing Good," *Ethics and International Affairs* 26, no. 1 (2012): 73–81.
79. Steven C. Roach, "How Political is the ICC? Pressing Challenges and the Need for Diplomatic Efficacy," *Global Governance* 19, no. 4 (2013): 507–523.
80. Ainley, "Responsibility to Protect".
81. Saxon, "International Criminal Court," 158.
82. Thomas Franck, *The Power of Legitimacy Among Nations* (New York: Oxford University Press, 1990), 52.
83. Alex J. Bellamy, *Massacres and Morality: Mass Killing in an Age of Civilian Immunity* (Oxford: Oxford University Press, 2012).
84. Edward C. Luck, *The UN Security Council: Practice and Promise* (London: Routledge, 2006).

85. Scott Straus, *The Order of Genocide: Race, Power and War in Rwanda* (Ithaca: Cornell University Press, 2008); and Stephen McLoughlin and Deborah Mayersen, "Reconsidering Root Causes: A New Framework for the Structural Prevention of Genocide and Mass Atrocities," in *Genocide, Risk and Resilience: An Interdisciplinary Approach*, ed. Bert Ingelaere, Stephan Parmentier, Jacques Haers and Barbara Segaert (Basingstoke: Palgrave, 2013), 49–67.
86. For instance, see Michael Gilligan and Stephen John Stedman, "Where Do Peacekeepers Go?" *International Studies Review* 5, no. 4 (2003): 37–54; and Kyle Beardsley and Holger Schmidt, "Following the Flag or Following the Charter? Examining the Determinants of UN Involvement in International Crises, 1945–2002," *International Studies Quarterly* 56, no. 1 (2012): 33–49. Using different datasets, both papers find that scale and potential for escalation are key determinants of whether the UN Security Council will engage on an issue.
87. The central argument advanced by Ruben Reike, "The Responsibility to Prevent: An International Crimes Approach to the Prevention of Mass Atrocities," *Ethics & International Affairs* 28, no. 4 (2014): 451–476.
88. Edward C. Luck, "Sovereignty, Choice and the Responsibility to Protect," *Global Responsibility to Protect* 1, no. 1 (2009): 20–21.
89. Reike, "Responsibility to Prevent".

Alex J. Bellamy is Professor of Peace and Conflict Studies and Director of the Asia Pacific Centre for the Responsibility to Protect at The University of Queensland, Australia. He is also Senior Adviser at the International Peace Institute, New York, and Fellow of the Academy of Social Sciences in Australia.

10

Moral Philosophy: The Ethics of War—Before, During and After

Brian Orend

Background and Overview

On the one hand, 'the ethics of war and peace' is as old as the hills, and spread across every major cultural and religious tradition (Aboriginal, Buddhist, Christian/Western, Hindu/Indian, Islamic, Oriental, etc.). To that extent, one might say that moral philosophy—that is, speculative theory focussed on practical issues of what makes human conduct right or wrong—does indeed have a long and deep history of reflection on wartime justice: amongst the oldest of any of the disciplines on display in this book.[1] On the other hand, when it comes to the more specific issue of war crimes *trials*, philosophy has not, historically, been particularly innovative or influential (not at least until very recently). In fact, it's fair to say that moral philosophy has been a very late-comer to this particular party, and thus has been outperformed by the lawyers, politicians, social activists, practical moral reformers, and institution-builders, and even by senior commanding officers in various militaries.[2]

B. Orend (✉)
University of Waterloo, Waterloo, ON, Canada

J. Waterlow, J. Schuhmacher, *War Crimes Trials and Investigations*, St Antony's Series,
https://doi.org/10.1007/978-3-319-64072-3_10

Indeed, with the notable exception of the Dutch thinker Hugo Grotius (1583–1645), not one major, truly card-carrying philosopher proposed or discussed war crimes trials with any real sophistication *until after* such trials were first held in Nuremberg and Tokyo (1945–1946) after the Second World War. (And even Grotius was as much a lawyer as he was a philosopher. His great work in this field (from 1625) was, after all, entitled *The Law of War and Peace* [my emphasis], and he is not today taught in any philosophy classes, rather, only in international law courses.)[3] Even a legendary philosopher like the German Enlightenment thinker Immanuel Kant (1724–1804), commonly considered one of the greatest and most important moral philosophers, and who wrote directly about war and peace (e.g., 'On Perpetual Peace' from 1795), and who advocated such prescient institutional innovations as a cosmopolitan federation, nowhere mentioned anything like criminal trials in the aftermath of war.[4]

And so, contrary to its preferred self-image as a conceptual innovator—proposing ideas often decades, or even centuries, ahead of their time—when it comes to war crimes trials we find this curious yet true phenomenon of philosophy playing catch-up, and being utterly derivative, to other disciplines. Perhaps the first focussed, systemic, and original reflections directly on actual war crimes trials by a card-carrying political philosopher were those in Hannah Arendt's 1963 book, *Eichmann in Jerusalem: A Report on The Banality of Evil*.[5] But, since then, there has been a true effervescence of ethical reflections on wartime justice, and war crimes trials, spurred by such actual, controversial wars as Vietnam and Iraq, as well as by such masterworks as Michael Walzer's 1977 classic, *Just and Unjust Wars*.[6] Indeed, today we might even say there's an embarrassment of riches which philosophy offers in this regard, to the point where it's actually becoming more of a task keeping up with all the new proposals for both conceptual and institutional reform.

Our task in this chapter is to explore and explain this evolution, as well as to consider and describe in detail the actual content of what moral philosophy has had to offer the subject of war crimes trials, alongside considering how philosophy's contributions rate against, and interact with, those of such other disciplines as are on offer here in this volume.

Interdisciplinary Issues

Having caught up—eventually—to the 'war crimes trials game,' today moral philosophy does now draw upon, and interacts strongly with, a number of other disciplines. Perhaps the two most resonant ones are history and the law (particularly international law). History is so important because it's really from there that philosophy draws what case study evidence it can. Obviously, philosophers do not perform on-site forensic investigations of war crime scenes, nor do they conduct detailed interviews with victims of mass atrocity. Because the concern is more sweeping and theoretical, and there has—until very recently—been a reluctance on the part of philosophers to make bold proclamations here, for instance in regard to future institutional reform and/or sharp judgements about guilt, *philosophers have tended to stick rather conservatively to past cases, as described and vetted by historians, when it comes to adducing evidence about just or unjust conduct in wartime.* On the one hand, this has led to a robust engagement with empirical, worldly evidence which other parts of philosophy, such as metaphysics, clearly lack. On the other, the moral philosophers wouldn't be taken seriously unless they had some such reference anyway—plus, it importantly means that they are beholden, in a significant way, to how historians have sorted and sifted through the evidence, and offered interpretations of it, for the judgements at which they themselves arrive. This is perhaps not questioned enough by the philosophers writing in this discipline, and good questions can always be raised to them about their sources, and about where, and why exactly, they make the factual claims about historical events which they do. They have not had the same kind of explicit training in that regard as the historians.[7]

Since applied moral philosophers are often in the business of trying to consider (or even construct) proposed rules of human conduct, it makes sense that any of them looking into war, and war crimes, would draw upon the law and its rules for guidance. And, luckily—until very recently—the law in question has been more of the nature of general principles of international law (aspirational, sweeping, easily readable to the non-lawyer) as opposed to detailed and rigorous case law, for instance involving complex crimes either of a violent or fraudulent nature (which non-lawyers can struggle with). Thus, there has been both a comfort level, and quite a similarity of both scope and content, between international law and applied moral philosophy that practitioners of the latter often make heavy use of, and refer to—sometimes even as a sensible initial point of departure—the rules of international law. Now, it goes deeper than that, of course: as the so-called laws of armed conflict (LOAC, such as The Hague and Geneva Conventions) have grown, historically, in many ways out of the ethics of war and peace (in particular, one branch of it known as 'just war theory,' about which more below). Thus, the similarity is not mere happenstance, and is quite natural and to be welcomed, as both draw on each other and help further development, with international lawyers and moral philosophers often appearing together at various conferences where issues of wartime justice are discussed and debated; they read each other's work, and test out ideas for reform against each other's principles, and so on.[8]

There are also clear and robust connections to the Responsibility to Protect (R2P) doctrine, as well as to Transitional Justice. To get a better sense of why, we need to define quickly what just war theory is, and appreciate how it's the most comprehensive and developed (though certainly not the only) perspective on the ethics of war and peace. The core proposition of just war theory is that *it is sometimes morally permissible to go to war* (e.g., to resist, punish, and repeal a prior act of violent aggression). This sets just war theory apart from both realism (which denies that morality and warfare have anything to do with each other) and pacifism (which denies that it can ever be morally permissible to go to war). We will explore realism and pacifism further below. To flesh out the notion that war-fighting can be morally justified in certain circumstances, just war theory goes on to specify (as it must) what those circumstances and conditions might be. Since there are three phases to any given armed conflict—beginning, middle, and end—just war theory has, over the centuries, crafted three sets of rules to guide belligerents and define such circumstances. These are known by the Latin terms *jus ad bellum* (the justice of beginning a war, or starting to fight); *jus in bello* (the justice of proper conduct in the midst of battle); and, more recently, *jus post bellum* (justice in the aftermath of war, during the transition time from fighting back to peace).[9] Obviously, this last subject of *jus post bellum* has much in common with the concerns of Transitional Justice.[10] And there's much in common between the R2P doctrine and *jus ad bellum*, as of course R2P, amongst other things, concerns itself with the justification of, and/or the authorization to, resort to armed force so as to stop and/or prevent a mass atrocity crime (MAC) such as genocide. Indeed, R2P defines and defends one so-called just cause for going to war, namely, armed humanitarian intervention on behalf of vulnerable victims of MACs, who need armed protection, either from the depredations of their own state government, or else from those of some other enemy group whilst their own state government is either incapable, or unwilling, to protect them.[11]

One final, perhaps unexpected, interdisciplinary connection has grown in recent years—and is of manifest concern to the subject of war crimes trials. This has to do with the explosion of interest in, and official education and training regarding, the ethics of war and peace by various military academies around the world. Many have credited this clear movement to senior US military officers—in the army, navy, and air force—starting in the late 1970s and especially through the 1980s and beyond. Why then? Informally, the understanding is that many of these officers, who were themselves young soldiers during the Vietnam War in the late 1960s and early 1970s, had many critical questions and lingering doubts and disappointments about that war, both in terms of its political cause (*jus ad bellum*) as well as with how it was fought (*jus in bello*). Stung by those experiences, when such officers reached positions of authority themselves, they swore that the next generation of soldiers would have different and better training, and were able to mandate such ethical education. The result has been an explosion of interest in just war theory (and the LOAC) by real-world militaries around the world, and explicit instruction in such, and invitations to debate around such. This is to say that just war theorists and other moral philosophers are also interacting not merely with historians, lawyers, other theorists and ethicists: they are interacting increasingly with soldiers and officers who have vital on-the-ground experience. The benefits go both ways: the soldiers and officers come to deeper understandings of the professional ethics of what they do, alongside larger questions about the justice of warfare in general; and the ethicists come to a much greater factual awareness of what battle is like, how soldiers actually get trained, the sorts of weaponry and information/intelligence involved, and the kinds of ultra-pressured circumstances in which soldiers are placed and yet are still expected to make upstanding decisions.[12] I've been privileged enough to be invited to such sessions, and am told that this is quite unlike the experiences within this volume's other academic disciplines. Perhaps it's because moral philosophy is an express invitation to debate and consider issues of right conduct, unlike (say) with the law, where such may be simply proscribed and thus not as subject to debate, and unlike in military strategy, where debate about what to do is there, but is conceived purely in pragmatic and not ethical terms. In my experience, soldiers very much want to do the right thing, or at the very least wish to avoid committing war crimes, and so they are increasing, with enthusiasm, their exposure to theories about such things. Indeed, one might say that a major overall objective of this fruitful interdisciplinary dialogue would be for everyone to come to a much better understanding of *what truly counts as a war crime* deserving of trial and punishment.

Overarching Themes and Debates

There are important philosophical debates *between* just war theory and its main rivals, realism and pacifism, on the one hand, and—on the other—debates *within* the just war tradition itself, both in general and with specific application to war crimes trials. Let's consider the first, starting with the rival theories.

Realism

Realism is most influential amongst political scientists, as well as scholars and practitioners of International Relations. While realism is a complex and often sophisticated doctrine, its core propositions express a strong suspicion about applying moral concepts, like justice, to the conduct of international affairs. Realists believe that moral concepts should be employed neither as descriptions of, nor as prescriptions for, state behaviour on the international plane. Realists emphasize power and security issues, the need for a state to maximize its expected self-interest and, above all, their view of the international arena as a kind of anarchy, in which the will to power enjoys primacy.[13]

Referring specifically to war, realists believe that it is an inevitable part of an anarchical world system; that it ought to be resorted to only if it makes sense in terms of national self-interest; and that, once war has begun, a state ought to do whatever it can to win. In other words, 'all's fair in love and war.' During the grim circumstances of war, 'anything goes.' So if adhering to the rules of just war theory, or the LOAC, hinders a state during wartime, it should disregard them and stick steadfastly to its fundamental interests in power, security, and economic growth. Prominent classical realists include Thucydides, Machiavelli, and Thomas Hobbes. Modern realists include Hans Morgenthau, George Kennan, Reinhold Niebuhr, and Henry Kissinger, as well as so-called neo-realists, such as Kenneth Waltz.[14]

Thus characterized, *most realists would view war crimes trials as thinly disguised nonsense.* If 'anything goes' in wartime, after all, it's neither fair nor sensical to judge anyone for their conduct after a war is over. All too often, war crimes trials will thus be mere 'show-trials,' or the winners of the war asymmetrically imposing such on the losers, in a superb marketing show—nothing more—of double-standards and hypocrisy, a way to try to cement in everyone's mind that the winner not merely won, but was justified in winning.

The essence of the just war reply to this attitude is that realism, apart from the cynicism of its general outlook, is moreover a recipe for escalation in warfare. Belligerents aren't likely merely to 'sit there and take it,' as the opponent does whatever it best sees fit. They are most likely to retaliate in kind, or even disproportionately, which would then invite the other side to do likewise. Thus, even if one only cares about the concrete consequences of action, and not moral principles in the abstract, one can nevertheless see how having such rules and principles—and holding people accountable to them after war—is meant to a play a vital role ensuring that warfare not degenerate into an exercise in mutual ruin.[15]

Pacifism

Different pacifists define pacifism differently, and offer various kinds of justification for their beliefs. But what unites all forms of pacifism—the basic proposition, or lowest common denominator—is opposition to warfare. The logical core of pacifism, as Jenny Teichman says, is 'anti-war-ism.'[16] No matter what kind of pacifist you are, you believe that *war is always wrong*; there is always some better approach to the problem than warfare. So, unlike realists, pacifists believe that it *is* possible and meaningful to apply moral judgement to international affairs. In this, they agree with just war theorists. But they disagree with just war theorists regarding the application of moral judgement to warfare. Just war theorists say war is *sometimes* morally permissible, whereas pacifists say war is *never* morally permissible. Quite literally and straightforwardly, a pacifist rejects war in favour of peace. It is not violence in all its forms which the most challenging kind of pacifist objects to; rather, it is the specific *kind and degree of violence that war involves* to which the pacifist objects. A pacifist objects to killing (not just violence) in general and, in particular, objects to the mass killing, for political reasons, which is part and parcel of the wartime experience. So, a pacifist rejects war, believing that there are no moral grounds which can justify resorting to war. War, for the pacifist, is always wrong.[17]

Having come to a working definition of pacifism as anti-war-ism, we can now consider some of the reasons offered in its favour. Many such reasons have been offered but not all of them are appropriate to our concern. For example, many pacifists are so for religious reasons. This chapter will stick to secular justifications for pacifism, which try to appeal to *any* rational person *regardless* of religious affiliation. The most relevant and potent pro-pacifist arguments here include the following: (1) a more *teleological* form of pacifism (or TP), which asserts that war and killing are at odds with human excellence and flourishing; (2) a more *consequentialist* form of pacifism (or CP), which maintains that the benefits accruing from war can never outweigh the costs of fighting it; and (3) a more *deontological* form of pacifism (or DP), which contends that the very activity of war is intrinsically unjust, since it violates foremost duties of morality and justice, such as either: not killing other human beings; or, more narrowly, not killing *innocent* people (as every war generates so-called collateral civilian casualties). Most common and compelling amongst contemporary secular pacifists, such as Robert Holmes and Richard Norman, is a mixed doctrine which combines, in some way, all three.[18]

Pacifists would therefore actually have a complicated view of war crimes trials. On the one hand, a pacifist would say that *all* activity carried out in advance of *any* war aim constitutes the height of injustice, and so *of course* should face trial and punishment afterwards. In principle, that counts as a ringing endorsement and, if anything, the pacifist would say that there's not been nearly enough war crimes trials; and they would note with some sympathy realist claims how, certainly from a historical perspective, the whole practice of war crimes trials has been rife with double-standards, cherry-picking only certain kinds of defendant (notably, low-level soldiers and officers, as opposed to political leaders) and hypocritical asymmetry. At the same time, however, pacifists may well question whether war crimes trials actually make sense: the preferred viewpoint for them, of course, is not to engage in war in the first place, as opposed to running a series of trials at war's end. As stated, for a pacifist, any war action is going to count as a crime, and so they would say that *the practice mistakenly puts the emphasis completely on the wrong end of the war*, so to speak: war crimes trials are there, at war's end, to punish a few people who have (apparently) done 'appalling wrong' in what is otherwise a completely appalling endeavour. *The emphasis, instead, should be on preventing the whole endeavour to begin with*, for example, through systematic non-violent resistance to aggression.[19] A pacifist may well, therefore, refuse to endorse war crimes trials at all, on the grounds that such trials are logically predicated on the notion that, in wartime, there's a meaningful distinction between good or at least excusable behaviour (which *shouldn't* be put on trial) and that there's bad and unacceptable behaviour (which *should*). But since the pacifist thinks that *it's all bad behaviour in wartime*, there really isn't the logical or ethical grounds for making that sort of good/bad distinction: *that's more a just war theory perspective*, and thus not something a pacifist is about to support or go along with. It's *either* war crimes trials for everyone and everything, *or else* it's putting all that kind of effort into the much more important prior issue of preventing armed conflict in the first place.

The core of the just war response to pacifism is essentially to accuse it of excess optimism regarding the efficacy of the proffered 'alternative' of non-violent resistance, especially against particularly brutal aggressors like the Nazis. Walzer, for example, says that pacifism is either: 'essentially untried' historically (as non-violent protests, he opines, have only 'worked' against democratic governments responsive to moral idealism); or, worse, amounts to 'a disguised form of surrender' to aggression.[20] Thus, to suggest that we should give up on having war crimes trials to invest everything 'up front' in preventative nonviolent resistance is not something we should expect to have a high probability of success. And thus we are left with trials at war's end, and the just war theorist simply disagrees with the sweeping pacifist claim that every action within warfare constitutes a crime. A defensive war action, for example, carried out carefully with limited violence against legitimate military targets, is morally not on the same level of judgement as, say, an intentional attack on civilians by a first-striking aggressor.

As a result, we see that the only major tradition of thought on the ethics of war and peace which clearly supports war crimes trials—and which must—is just war theory (and the LOAC which have developed out of it). Let's now programmatically develop just war theory, to get a fuller sense of this claim, alongside a bolder picture of what actually counts as a war crime under its purview. (Indeed, it's fair to say that, *historically, these two things have really been the main contribution of moral philosophy, and just war theory, to the notion of war crimes trials*: (1) just the raw *support* for there being such things; and then (2) coming to a wider and deeper *definition* as to what should count as a war crime.)

Just War Theory

Jus ad bellum

The rules of *jus ad bellum* are addressed, first and foremost, to heads of state. Since political leaders are the ones who inaugurate wars, setting their armed forces in motion, they are to be held accountable to *jus ad bellum* principles. If they fail in that responsibility, then they commit war crimes. In the language of the Nuremberg prosecutors, aggressive leaders who launch unjust wars commit 'crimes against peace.'[21] What constitutes a just or unjust resort to armed force is disclosed to us by the rules of *jus ad bellum*. Just war theory contends that, for any resort to war to be justified, a political community, or state, must fulfil each and every one of the following six requirements:

1. *Just Cause*. This is clearly the most important rule; it sets the tone for everything which follows. A state may launch a war only for the right reason. The just causes most frequently mentioned include: self-defence from external attack; the defence of others from such; the protection of innocents from brutal, aggressive regimes; and punishment for a grievous wrongdoing which remains uncorrected.[22] Spanish theologian Francisco de Vitoria (1492–1546) suggested that all the just causes be subsumed under the one category of 'a wrong received.' Walzer, and most modern just war theorists, speak of the one just cause for resorting to war being the resistance of aggression. Aggression is the use of armed force in violation of someone else's basic rights.[23]

   The basic rights of two kinds of entity are involved here: those of states; and those of their individual citizens. International law affirms that states have many rights, notably those to political sovereignty (i.e., self-governance) and territorial integrity (i.e., to a secure space for both living and self-governance). The LOAC thus affirm that aggression involves the use of armed forces—armies, navies, air forces, marines, missiles—in violation of these rights. Classic cases would be Nazi Germany into Poland in 1939, and Iraq into Kuwait in 1990, wherein the Aggressor used its armed forces to invade the territory of the Victim, overthrow its government and establish a new regime in its place. Crucially, the commission of aggression causes the aggressor to forfeit its own state rights, thereby permitting violent resistance. *An aggressor has no right not to be warred against in defence*; indeed, it has the duty to stop its rights-violating aggression.[24]
2. *Right Intention*. A state must intend to fight the war only for the sake of its just cause. Having the right reason for launching a war is not enough: the actual motivation behind the resort to war must also be

morally appropriate. Ulterior motives, such as a power or land grab, or irrational motives, such as revenge or ethnic hatred, are ruled out. The only right intention allowed is to see the just cause for resorting to war secured and consolidated. If another intention crowds in, moral corruption sets in. International law does not include this rule, probably because of the evidentiary difficulties involved in determining a state's intent.[25]

3. *Proper Authority and Public Declaration.* A state may go to war only if the decision has been made by the appropriate authorities, according to the proper process, and made public, notably to its own citizens and to the enemy state(s). The 'appropriate authority' is usually specified in that country's constitution: in democracies, it is usually the legislature whereas in non-democracies it is usually the executive head-of-state.[26]
4. *Last Resort.* A state may resort to war only if it has exhausted all plausible, peaceful alternatives to resolving the conflict in question, in particular diplomatic negotiation. One wants to make sure something as momentous and serious as war is declared only when it seems the last practical and reasonable shot at effectively resisting aggression.[27]
5. *Probability of Success.* A state may not resort to war if it can foresee that doing so will have no measurable impact on the situation. The aim here is to block mass violence which is going to be futile. International law does not include this requirement, as it is seen as biased against small, weaker states.[28]
6. *Proportionality.* A state must, prior to getting involved in warfare, weigh the *universal* goods expected to result from it, such as securing the just cause, against the *universal* evils expected to result, notably casualties. Only if the benefits are proportional to, or 'worth,' the costs may the war action proceed. (The universal must be stressed since, often in war, states only tally *their own* expected benefits and costs, radically discounting those accruing to the enemy and to any innocent third parties.) Since war is so bloody and costly, it may be asked (e.g., by the pacifist): what can be so bad as to have war seem like a 'proportionate solution' to the problem? The answer is precisely violent aggression, and the need to defend people from it.[29]

Jus in bello

Jus in bello, we've seen, refers to justice in war, to right conduct in the midst of battle. Responsibility for state adherence to *jus in bello* norms falls primarily on the shoulders of those military commanders, officers, and soldiers who formulate and execute the war policy of a particular state. They are to be held responsible for any breach of the principles which follow below. Such accountability may involve being put on trial for war crimes, whether by one's own national military justice system or perhaps by the International Criminal Court (ICC) (created by the 1998 Treaty of Rome).[30]

There are several general principles of *jus in bello*. They have been codified into hundreds of specific rules within such LOAC as The Hague (1899–1907) and Geneva (1946–1949) Conventions:[31]

1. *Obey All International Laws on Weapons Prohibition.* Chemical and biological weapons, in particular, are forbidden by many treaties.[32]
2. *Discrimination and Non-Combatant Immunity.* Soldiers are only entitled to use their (non-prohibited) weapons to target those who are, in Walzer's words, 'engaged in harm.' Thus, when they take aim, soldiers must discriminate between the civilian population, which is morally immune from direct and intentional attack, and those legitimate military, political, and industrial targets involved in rights-violating harm. While some *collateral* civilian casualties are excusable,[33] it is wrong to take deliberate aim at civilian targets. An example would be saturation bombing of residential areas. (It is worth noting that almost all wars since 1900 have featured larger civilian, than military, casualties. Perhaps this is one reason why this rule is the most frequently and stridently codified rule in all the laws of armed conflict, as international law seeks to protect unarmed civilians as best it can.)[34]
3. *Benevolent Quarantine for Prisoners of War (POWs).* If enemy soldiers surrender and become captives, they cease being lethal threats to basic rights. They are no longer 'engaged in harm.' Thus it is wrong to target them with death, starvation, rape, torture, medical experimentation, and so on. They are to be provided, as The Geneva Conventions spell

out, with benevolent—not malevolent—quarantine away from battle zones and until the war ends, when they should be exchanged for one's own POWs.[35]

4. *Proportionality*. Soldiers may only use force proportional to the end they seek. They must restrain their force to that amount appropriate to achieving their aim or target. Weapons of mass destruction, for example, are usually seen as being out of proportion to legitimate military ends.[36]
5. *No Means Mala in Se*. Soldiers may not use weapons or methods which are 'evil in themselves.' These include: mass rape campaigns; genocide or ethnic cleansing; using poison or treachery (like disguising soldiers to look like the Red Cross); forcing captured soldiers to fight against their own side; making use of child soldiers; and using weapons whose effects cannot be controlled, like biological agents.[37]
6. *No Reprisals*. A reprisal is when country A violates *jus in bello* in war with country B. Country B then retaliates with its own violation of *jus in bello*, seeking to chasten A into obeying the rules. There are strong moral and evidentiary reasons to believe that reprisals don't work, and they instead serve to escalate death and make the destruction of war increasingly indiscriminate. Reprisals are prohibited, and the claim made that 'winning well is the best revenge.'[38]

As stated, violation of any *jus in bello* principle is thought to constitute a war crime, with perhaps the clearest instances being either the use of a weapon which is outlawed, and/or taking deliberate aim at civilians, notably engaging in civilian massacre (such as the 1968 My Lai massacre during the Vietnam War (more below) or the Serb shelling of Sarajevo during the latter stages of the Bosnian civil war, 1992–1995).[39]

Jus post bellum

Unlike the prior two phases of war, there's next-to-no legal regulation of the aftermath of armed conflict (presumably as winners of wars don't want restrictions on their conduct, postwar). This is regrettable, for reasons I've explained elsewhere.[40] Yet, historically we can discern not only two major contrasting policies of postwar justice—namely, retribution and rehabilitation—but also an overlapping consensus between them, wherein war crimes trials may be located and supported. Let's quickly list the elements of these three theories of postwar justice, so we can move efficiently to a deeper consideration of war crimes trials in the next section.

We can refer to the overlapping consensus between the two robust theories of postwar justice as the one 'thin' theory amidst the two 'thick' ones. And we can characterize its core principles briefly as follows:

1. *Overlapping Consensus: The Thin Theory of Postwar Justice*

- *GOAL*: vindicating the rights whose violation triggered the war, forcing the defeated Aggressor[41] to accept a proportionate policy on surrender which includes:
  - Public Terms of Settlement (as no part of any peace treaty ought to be kept secret from the people it affects);
  - Mutual Exchange of Prisoners-of-War (POWs);
  - Aggressor to Apologize (for the act of aggression which began the war);
  - Aggressor to Give Up any Unjust Gains won during the war;
  - Aggressor to (at least partially) Demilitarize; and
  - War Crimes Trials (Jus ad Bellum trials for Aggressor; Jus in Bello trials for all sides)[42]

More on war crimes trials below. For now, we need to complete the two 'thick' theories of postwar justice. Both include the 'thin' elements listed above, which is important in connection with war crimes trials. Unlike, say, with some of the Transitional Justice literature (or even the realist literature), no one in the just war, or international law traditions wonders or worries about whether having such trials might de-stabilize the broader postwar settlement/situation and thus not 'be worth it.' Such completely forward-looking calculations fall on deaf ears when it comes to just war theory and international law, which insist we not forget completely about what happened in the past. The latter traditions are firmly committed to the notion of war crimes trials as a non-negotiable matter of justice. As Walzer says: 'There can be no justice in war if there are not, ultimately, responsible men and women.'[43]

2. *Thick Theory #1: RETRIBUTION*

- *GOAL*: to make the defeated Aggressor *worse-off* than prior to the war (as backward-looking punishment).
- *MEANS*: all of the thin theory above, plus:
  - Compensation Payments from Aggressor to Victim, and possibly to the International Community more broadly;
  - Sanctions put on Aggressor, to hamper its future economic growth; and
  - No aid or assistance with postwar reconstruction. Such is left up to the locals, with no forcible regime change imposed on Aggressor.

Classic examples of the retributive theory of postwar justice in action would be both the 1919 Treaty of Versailles, ending the First World War (1914–1918); and the terms of settlement ending the first Iraq War, better known as The Persian Gulf War, in 1991.[44]

3. *Thick Theory #2: REHABILITATION*

- *GOAL*: to make the defeated Aggressor *better-off* than prior to the war (as forward-looking reconstruction).
- *MEANS*: all of the thin theory above, plus:
  - No Compensation Payments
  - No Sanctions
  - Aid and Assistance with postwar reconstruction, including possible Forcible Regime Change imposed on defeated Aggressor.

The highest-profile real-world cases of the rehabilitative model of postwar justice would be those of (West) Germany and Japan, from 1945 to 1955 following the end of the Second World War. Plus, elements of attempted rehabilitation were clearly tried following the overthrow of the regimes in Afghanistan (in early 2002) and Iraq (in mid-2003), but to much more unclear of an overall outcome than the shining successes of Germany and Japan in the 1950s.[45]

Now, it's fascinating to consider the pros and cons of each of these models of postwar justice alongside such historical cases. I have done so elsewhere,[46] but they are not really to the point here. What *is* on point is the notion that *both thick theories support the holdings of war crimes trials in the aftermath of war*. As our case study, let's consider how just war theory views and defends such trials against their critics.

Case Study: War Crimes Trials Through the Lens of Just War Theory

The normative need for such trials, from a just war perspective, follows from Walzer's maxim above that: 'There can be no justice in war if there are not, ultimately, responsible men and women.'[47] Individuals who play a prominent role during wartime must be held accountable for their actions and what they bring about. There are, we've seen, two broad categories of war crimes: those which violate *jus ad bellum* and those which violate *jus in bello*. (We should note that, once norms of *jus post bellum* become more settled and endorsed, that their violation would also need to count as a war crime of some kind.)

Jus ad bellum war crimes have to do with 'planning, preparing, initiating, and waging' aggressive war, as we have defined it above. Responsibility for the commission of any such crime falls on the shoulders of the political leader(s) of the aggressor regime. Such crimes, in the language of the Nuremberg prosecutors, are 'crimes against peace.'[48]

Nuremberg

The Nuremberg trials, of course, refer to the very first set of modern war crimes trials, held right after the Second World War in the German city of that name. (There were Japanese war crimes trials too, in Tokyo, as noted.) In Nuremberg, much of what was left of the Nazi hierarchy was put on trial, whether for 'a crime against peace' (i.e., starting an aggressive war) or else for bad conduct during the war.[49]

While some complained that the Nuremberg trials were 'victor's justice'—and, certainly, the Allies did not put any of their own people on trial for such controversial actions as the bombings of Dresden or Hiroshima/Nagasaki—*it's hard to agree that that's all they were.* The process, after all, was rigorous, open, and fair. All those charged had lawyers, could cross-examine witnesses and experts, and present their own evidence. The trials operated on rules known to all. Consider also the raw numbers: 22 Nazi elites were tried over the course of a year, 3 were found innocent, 19 guilty. Of the guilty, 11 were sentenced to death and 8 to prison sentences of varying lengths. This conviction rate, of just over 86%, is actually in line with the average rate of conviction for non-war-crimes in most developed societies.[50] (If that seems high, consider: (1) that prosecutors often drop charges against those they feel they can't convict; and (2) there are many social and psychological factors—apart from the case's evidence—which incline judges and juries to convict, such as desires to re-establish order and to offer the victim some solace.) Combine this percentage at Nuremberg with the variety of outcomes in sentencing there, and it looks like you have a fairly well-developed, reasonable judicial process looking at the evidence in each individual's case—as opposed to one which sweepingly condemns and convicts them all because they happened to be on the losing side.[51] Plus, the first international war crimes trials had to happen *sometime.* The notion that the Nuremberg trials operated on principles just then being invented is silly: there had been talk since the 1800s of having postwar criminal tribunals, and the codes of proper military conduct, such as The Hague Conventions (1899–1907)—to say nothing of basic moral decency—were known to all who were charged. Whenever there is a new institution or innovation, there is bound to be controversy, especially when something like war is involved. It wasn't perfect, but the Nuremberg trial process was decent and defensible. Decent, because it followed standard due process regulations. (Ironic and notable, indeed, that these Nazis, when in power, denounced the rule of law and due process—and yet benefited from them during these trials.) And defensible, because the Nazis were culpable for horrendous crimes, and at the time *the only people capable of running a trial for them were the winners of the war.* It was a bold institutional move, for proper moral motives, which has resonated down to today.[52]

Contemporary Tribunals

Resonated how, exactly? In a threefold sense. First, the Nuremberg trials directly inspired some future war crimes trials. After the brutal Bosnian civil war of 1992–1995, and the genocidal Rwandan massacres of 1994, the international community decided to convene war crimes, and crimes against humanity, proceedings. The one regarding Bosnia is actually still ongoing, and takes place at The Hague in the Netherlands, long a place associated with international diplomacy and institutions. The other, regarding Rwanda, is situated in neighbouring Tanzania and is likewise still ongoing. Both tribunals unfortunately confront huge backlogs in trials and workloads. These ad hoc—or 'one-time'—criminal procedures feature the same commitment to rigorous due process as Nuremberg did. (This is one, partial reason for the backlog.) They have also, unlike Nuremberg, tried some of the biggest fish: the ex-prime minister of Rwanda; and the ex-president of Serbia/Yugoslavia, both seen as heavily complicit in the respective conflicts. The results: ex-Serb president, Slobodan Milosevic, died (of natural causes) during his trial before sentencing could be determined; but Jean Kambanda, ex-prime minister of Rwanda, plead guilty to genocide charges, and is now serving a life term in prison.[53]

Partly to overcome the limitations of ad hoc trials and to institute something more lasting, there arose in the late 1990s a movement to create a *permanent* International Criminal Court (or ICC). In 1998, the Treaty of Rome was signed, paving the way for the ICC to be formed, also at The Hague. Since it will be permanent, and fully international, the ICC repels accusations regarding 'revenge motives' and 'victor's justice.' Its permanence and global resources should also allow it to become a more experienced and efficient court process than, say, either the Bosnian or Rwandan efforts, which continue to be starved of resources. Although Americans continue to object to the ICC—fearing that it could be 'politically hijacked' to feature 'show trials' of US servicemen—the ICC has gone ahead anyway, and there are principled reasons to support the court:[54]

- First, there's *the deterrence benefit*. If all war crimes, in all wars, are prosecuted and punished by an impartial world court, then it stands to reason that future, would-be war criminals might well be deterred from committing their ghastly actions if they know that they will, themselves, pay a personal price for their crimes.
- Second, there's *the war termination benefit*. Having a permanent and non-partisan world court can assist nations in wrapping up their armed conflicts, punishing acts which need punishment in an impartial manner which applies to all of them equally.
- Third, there's what we might call *the world system benefit*. The global community has already witnessed the huge benefits of having an international system based on rules of law which are reasonable, impartial, and applicable to all. The trade sector is perhaps the clearest and most recent example of this. The construction of a permanent world criminal court helps complete the international landscape, thereby adding to the existence of a global system which can run smoothly on a consistent and comprehensive set of shared values, notably human rights. History shows that specialist agencies of the United Nations (UN)—that is, those manned by trained professionals and focussing on a specific task—enjoy a much higher success rate than the generalist and politicized agencies, such as the General Assembly and Security Council.[55]
- Finally, there's *the commitment benefit*. The construction of a permanent war crimes court allows the world community to better keep its commitments to the core values of peace, security, and human rights. A world court enhances peace by punishing deeds which, if left unpunished, could sow the seeds of future wars. This augments global security more broadly. Finally, the existence of a world court

for war crimes, and crimes against humanity, marks another much needed advance in the compelling cause of human rights protection around the world.[56]

The third effect of Nuremberg—apart from the recent ad hoc trials and the ICC—concerns the much more active willingness of national armed forces, at least in developed nations, to investigate and prosecute members *of their own services* for alleged war crimes. The activity here is real and quite remarkable. Consider the American military prosecuting and punishing those of its own soldiers who engaged in the infamous My Lai Massacre during the Vietnam War. Frustrated by civilian support for, and hiding of, Viet Cong soldiers, one American unit—under Lt. William Calley—morally snapped and deliberately massacred the inhabitants of the village of My Lai. More recently, the Canadian Armed Forces prosecuted and punished some members of its Airborne Unit which served in the 1993 intervention in Somalia. Thuggish members of that Unit caught a Somali civilian stealing from their supplies and beat him to death. Then there's the US reservists facing charges in the 2004 Abu-Ghraib prisoner abuse scandal in Iraq. Convictions came down in Spring 2005. The list here can go on and on: the developed world's armed services drill their soldiers in the rules of engagement, and the ethics of war and peace (as mentioned above), and they quite vigilantly oversee them. In some engagements, I've actually heard servicemen say—only half-jokingly—that they are more afraid of their own service's military *lawyers* than they are of enemy *soldiers*. (It should be noted, for those still anxious about the ICC, that it's empowered to act *only* when a given national armed service fails to act on and investigate an alleged war crime. It does *not* replace or supercede the national military justice systems. Still, as many of us know, the United States has nevertheless been reluctant since 1998 to give the ICC the resources it needs, resulting in very large backlogs there, too, perhaps even to the point of: (1) running afoul of the famous legal maxim that 'justice delayed means justice denied'; and (2) seriously dampening enthusiasm and momentum on behalf of consistent and successful war crimes prosecution. These facts, from a just war perspective, are quite regrettable.)[57]

One Last Challenge: 'Western-ism'?

How does moral philosophy, and just war theory, handle the notion that many of the above norms and values appear 'uniquely Western,' and thus either may not 'apply' to other ethical traditions or else are objectionable purely on that basis? It's fair to that say that just war theory isn't impressed by such a challenge. First, as to outright scepticism about these values, recall the section above on realism, and see there the just war response to it. Second, moral philosophy in general tends to reject relativism, including cultural relativism, when it comes to moral and political issues, as: (1) relativism is a dead-end to rational debate (as it then becomes a mere matter of taste and preference); and (2) relativism winds up in practice being a surrender either to power and/or to traditionally existing practice. Relativism, at the least, is a complacent perspective at odds with reformist improvements, as by definition there are no firm standards against which to judge practices and values, and thereby motivate change. And, at the worst, relativism can serve as a bad-faith cloak, and pretence at 'justification,' for those who don't want to be held accountable for their beliefs and actions.[58]

As for the above values being uniquely Western, and thus objectionable, the following replies occur. First, one must of course be sensitive and respectful of the history of controversial interaction between Western and non-Western cultures. Second, even if just war values were somehow uniquely Western, *it's hard to see what that proves in the end*. While it *does* seem true that many of the original just war theorists—Aristotle, Cicero, Augustine—were Western thinkers, it is (as philosophers would say) 'a genetic fallacy' to object to ideas simply on the basis of where they came from. Now, this isn't, at all, to imply that just war theory is perfect: merely that a critical evaluation of it should focus on its principles and their consequences, as opposed to the cultural- and political geography of where it 'came from.' Wisdom, arguably, consists (at least in part) in being open to the idea that good ideas can come from anywhere. And the ideas behind just war theory revolve around limiting and restraining the use of killing force, and it seems hard to believe that such objectives only have relevance to Westerners.[59] Finally, even if just war theory *started out* as Western we must note how *it has since spread world-wide*, both in terms of theory (see, e.g., such recent books as *Chinese Just War Ethics*)[60] as well as through the LOAC. It's not just Western countries which have freely passed, and ratified, the various treaties and conventions which together comprise the LOAC: almost every country in the world has, for example, ratified The Hague and Geneva Conventions. This is to say that nations from every cultural grouping in the world have at least offered official, formal endorsement of these general sorts of values, including principles behind the wrongness of certain actions in wartime, and the need for accountability to follow in their wake.[61]

Conclusion

Moral philosophy, and the ethics of war and peace more narrowly, support war crimes trials in the aftermath of war. This, alongside fleshing out fuller definitions of what count as war crimes (i.e., violations of any of the principles of *jus- ad bellum, in bello*, and *post bellum*) count as the main historical contribution of the discipline to the subject. Realism and pacifism either do not support war crimes trials, or do so only in an indirect sense, whereas the support of just war theory and international law are full-throated, logically mandated, and enthusiastic.

We've seen that, historically and curiously, moral philosophy has not been on the cutting edge of the subject of war crimes, and has been heavily reliant on, and intertwined with, such other disciplines as history and international law (and, more recently, such niche disciplines as Transitional Justice and R2P. However, having caught up to the real world, moral philosophy now finds itself in the slightly awkward position of providing support for, and looking to advance the cause of, war crimes trials, in a time—post-Afghanistan and Iraq—where American war fatigue, and broader scepticism about supra-national and global institutions, has put substantial obstacles and inefficiencies in front of the progression of war crimes prosecution. In other words, having finally made it to 'the party,' moral philosophy finds that everything's not as it should be and, in particular, that many of the key 'movers-and-shakers' are no longer there, deflating the atmosphere quite substantially. It's like we're at something of a crossroads, where either this leads to mere sadness and lament, or else to frustration and thus focussed motivation to move forward with new ideas and new proposals for improving things. Will philosophy again leave the task to others, or rather join with its allies to be in the lead?

I suppose that the history, as sketched above, does not leave one very confident in this regard, unless we suppose that philosophy has learned from its mistakes. Just war theory, furthermore, tends actually to thrive during periods of adversity—where bad wars spur new reflections—and, more broadly, it's clear that, with strong recent trends *against* international institutions and *in favour* of assertive new nationalisms, the adversity is real and substantial. So there may be—and, I think, should be—a renewed and spirited case to be made in favour of the sense and justice of putting on trial those accused of some of the very worst things human beings can do.

Bibliographical Essay It's hard to beat Machiavelli's *The Prince*, or Hobbes' *Leviathan*, as classic expressions of realism, as well as for showing how a hard-nosed policy of moral scepticism, combined with ruthless tending to the interests of the self/nation, can nevertheless lead to general norms and a viable framework for international order and security (importantly assuming that the various actors are rational and forward-looking, which states usually are—but don't always have to be—and there are, of course, non-state actors, such as radical terrorist organizations, who may not fall under that description at all). The combination of rationality, moral scepticism, and selfishness can produce relatively stable rules for action, including for wartime conduct, as are articulated, for instance, in George Kennan's sophisticated classic, *Realities of American Foreign Policy* (Princeton: Princeton University Press, 1954). An often over-looked, but philosophically excellent, account of this rational choice approach would be G. Malvrodes, "Conventions and The Laws of War", *Philosophy and Public Affairs* (1975), 117–131.

The two best secular works of pacifism in recent decades are, in my view: Robert Holmes, *On War and Morality* (Princeton: Princeton University Press, 1989); and Richard Norman, *Ethics, Killing and War* (Cambridge: Cambridge University Press, 1995). They patiently—and with utter lack of any strident, judgemental ideology—make systematic arguments as to how any policy other than pacifism, in connection with armed conflict, is morally indefensible. They are impressive efforts. But, as noted in the essay, since their focus is all on preventing the outbreak of armed conflict in the first place, they don't directly wrestle with the issues involved in war crimes trials, because of course for them either: it is all unjust activity in war; or else all the attention and effort need to go into preventing the start of war, as opposed to wrapping wars up, with trials and so forth. Still, perhaps they have a point regarding where our finite time and resources ought mainly to be focussed, and especially so when we consider all the formidable problems with constructing well-run war crimes trials, which this volume has analysed.

The modern classic expression of just war theory remains Michael Walzer's *Just and Unjust Wars* (New York: Basic Books, 1977, but with four editions since, with new introductions for each). Not only is it the authoritative explanation and defence of just war theory, it is chock-a-block full of excellent historical examples, and sets a standard for enjoyable reading which almost no one in the field has ever rivalled. Moreover, it deals with war crimes trials in a very substantial way—as indeed Walzer says that it is the holding of those responsible, postwar, via fair trial, which is absolutely key to upholding norms of morality and justice in connection with armed conflict. He considers both Nuremberg and Tokyo in detail, as well as the various military justice trials of US servicemen like William Calley in connection with Vietnam. (Indeed, the whole sub-plot of Walzer's book is that Vietnam represents unjust, whereas the Second World War represents just, wars.) My own *The Morality of War* (Peterborough: Broadview, 2nd edition, 2013), is indebted to Walzer, and is a continuation and updating of his general approach to these issues, and is certainly likewise committed to the justice of holding trials in the aftermath of war. It also develops a different understanding of Walzer's so-called (and controversial) supreme emergency exemption, according to which the ordinary rules and laws of war may be over-ridden under very exceptional circumstances. By contrast, I argue that such situations constitute moral tragedies which may perhaps be excused but never justified, and they imply robust duties of international intervention: for example, of the sort articulated by the R2P movement.

Recently, there has arisen a robust and sophisticated so-called revisionist understanding of just war theory, which departs from the more standard expression of the doctrine as found in Walzer and Orend above. In particular, the revisionist account concerns itself with linkages between the start of war (*jus ad bellum*), and conduct during war (*jus in bello*), with the result that there is a defence of holding many more people accountable via war crimes trials than is perhaps usual. Historically, it was said that only political and military leaders should be held accountable for *jus ad bellum* violations, whereas ordinary officers and soldiers should be held accountable for *jus in bello* violations. The revisionists argue that also holding soldiers accountable for *ad bellum* violations may have the happy effect of dampening down the outbreak of aggressive war, and that when political leaders get involved in planning actual attacks, then they should stand in judgement for *in bello* violations, too. There are philosophically superb works in this revisionist tradition, such as: David Rodin and Henry Shue, *Just and Unjust Warriors* (Oxford: Oxford University Press, 2010); Rodin's *War and Self-Defence* (Oxford: Oxford University Press, 2005); Jeff McMahan, *Killing in War* (Oxford: Oxford University Press, 2011); Seth Lazar, *Sparing Civilians* (Oxford: Oxford University Press, 2015); and Cecile Fabre's two studies: *Cosmopolitan War* (Oxford: Oxford University Press, 2014); and *Cosmopolitan Peace* (Oxford: Oxford University Press, 2016).

On the ethics of war and peace generally, plus many more sources, consider the two free online entries on 'War' at the *Stanford Encyclopedia of Philosophy* (https://plato.stanford.edu/): the older one by myself; the newer one by Lazar.

Notes

1. Brian Orend, *The Morality of War*, 2nd ed. (Peterborough: Broadview, 2013), 9–33. In general, the works of James Turner Johnson and John Kelsay are excellent for cross-cultural histories in this regard.
2. Charles A. Smith, *The Rise and Fall of War Crimes Trials* (Cambridge: Cambridge University Press, 2012).
3. Hugo Grotius, *The Law of War and Peace*, trans. L.R. Loomis (Roslyn: WJ Black Inc., 1949).

4. Immanuel Kant, *On Perpetual Peace*, ed. B. Orend, trans. by I. Johnston (Peterborough: Broadview, 2015).
5. Hannah Arendt, *Eichmann in Jerusalem: A Report on The Banality of Evil* (New York: Penguin Classics, 2006).
6. Michael Walzer, *Just and Unjust Wars* (New York: Basic Books, 1977), with four further editions since.
7. Mark Day, *The Philosophy of History* (London: Bloomsbury Academic, 2008).
8. Alexander Gillespie, *History of The Laws of War*, 3rd ed. (New York: Hart, 2011); Stephen C. Neff, *War and The Law of Nations* (Cambridge: Cambridge University Press, 2008); Gary D. Solis, *The Law of Armed Conflict* (Cambridge: Cambridge University Press, 2010).
9. Orend, *Morality, passim*; Walzer, *Wars, passim*.
10. Ruti Teitel, *Transitional Justice* (Oxford: Oxford University Press, 2002).
11. The International Commission on Intervention and State Sovereignty, *Report: The Responsibility to Protect* (Ottawa: International Development Research Centre, 2001); Alex Bellamy, *Responsibility to Protect* (London: Polity, 2009).
12. Martin Cook, *Issues in Military Ethics* (Albany: SUNY Press, 2013); G. Lucas, *Military Ethics: What Everyone Needs to Know* (Oxford: Oxford University Press, 2016).
13. Jeff McMahan, "Realism, Morality and War," in *The Ethics of War and Peace: Religious and Secular Perspectives*, ed. Terry Nardin (Princeton: Princeton University Press, 1996), 78–92. David R. Mapel, "Realism and the Ethics of War and Peace," in *The Ethics of War and Peace: Religious and Secular Perspectives*, ed. Terry Nardin (Princeton: Princeton University Press, 1996), 180–200. Steven Forde, "Classical Realism," in *Traditions in International Ethics*, ed. Terry Nardin and David R. Mapel (Cambridge: Cambridge University Press, 1992), 62–84. Jack Donnelly, "Twentieth Century Realism," in *Traditions in International Ethics*, ed. Terry Nardin and David R. Mapel (Cambridge: Cambridge University Press, 1992), 85–111.
14. Henry Morgenthau, *Politics Among Nations*, 5th ed. (New York: Knopf, 1973); George F. Kennan, *Realities of American Foreign Policy* (Princeton: Princeton University Press, 1954); Reinhold Niebuhr, *Christianity and Power Politics* (New York: Charles Scribner's Sons, 1940); Hedley Bull, *The Anarchical Society: A Study of Order in World Politics* (New York: Columbia University Press, 1977); Kenneth Waltz, *Man, The State and*

War (Princeton: Princeton University Press, 1978); Henry Kissinger, *Diplomacy* (New York: Harper Collins, 1995).
15. Orend, *Morality*, 251–273.
16. Jenny Teichman, *Pacifism and the Just War* (Oxford: Basil Blackwell, 1986), 3.
17. Jan Narveson, "Pacifism: A Philosophical Analysis," in *Morality and War*, ed. Richard A Wasserstrom (Belmont: Wadsworth, 1970), 63–77.
18. Robert L. Holmes, *On War and Morality* (Princeton: Princeton University Press, 1989); Richard Norman, *Ethics, Killing and War* (Cambridge: Cambridge University Press, 1995).
19. Robert L. Holmes and Barry S. Gan, eds. *Nonviolence in Theory and Practice*, 2nd. ed. (Long Grove: Waveland, 2005).
20. Walzer, *Wars*, 329–336; Orend, *Morality*, 273–297.
21. Joseph E. Persico, *Nuremberg: Infamy on Trial* (New York: Penguin, 1995); Michael R. Marrus, *The Nuremberg War Crimes Trials 1945–6* (New York: St. Martin's Press, 1997).
22. It should be noted, as a difficult debate amongst just war theorists, regarding the divide between so-called defensive wars against prior aggression (such 'classic cases' as WWII) and, shall we say, non-defensive wars against aggression which is feared yet not realized (such 'non-classic' armed conflicts like the invasion of Iraq in 2003).
23. Orend, *Morality*, 33–70.
24. Orend, *Morality*, 33–48; Walzer, *Wars, Passim*; Adam Roberts and Richard Guelff, eds., *Documents on The Laws of War*, 3rd ed. (Oxford: Oxford University Press, 2000).
25. Orend, *Morality*, 48–52.
26. Ibid., 52–59.
27. Ibid., 59–61.
28. Ibid., 61.
29. Ibid., 62–63.
30. Ibid., 111–152.
31. W. Michael Reisman and Chris T. Antoniou, eds., *The Laws of War* (New York: Vintage, 1994).
32. William H. Boothby, *Weapons and The Laws of Armed Conflict* (Oxford: Oxford University Press, 2009).
33. Provided such satisfy the controversial Doctrine of Double Effect. See Orend, *Morality*, 121–125. Paul A. Woodward, ed., *The Doctrine of Double Effect* (Notre Dame: University of Notre Dame Press, 2001).

34. Walzer, *Wars*, 126–140; Orend, Morality, 112–125.
35. Erik Saar, *Inside the Wire* (New York: Penguin, 2005); Michael Ratner and Ellen Ray, *Guantanamo: What The World Should Know* (New York: Chelsea Green, 2004); Derek Jinks, *The Rules of War* (Oxford: Oxford University Press, 2013).
36. Orend, *Morality*, 125–127.
37. Ibid., 125–130.
38. Ibid., 130–133.
39. Seymour Hersh, *My Lai 4* (New York: Doubleday, 1970); David Rieff, *Slaughterhouse: Bosnia and The Failure of The West* (New York: Simon and Schuster, 1995).
40. Orend, *Morality*, 185–215; Brian Orend, "Justice after War," *Ethics and International Affairs* 16, no. 2 (2002): 43–57; Brian. Orend, *War and International Justice: A Kantian Perspective* (Waterloo: Wilfrid Laurier University Press, 2000).
41. Note that such an assumption is part of what makes this a theory of postwar *justice*. This isn't to deny there aren't real-world cases where the Aggressor might win, or there might not be a clear cut 'winner' at all: merely to note that in either such case—but emphatically the first—this will *not* be an instance where justice is served at the end of the war. For more on starting assumptions behind postwar justice, see: Orend, *Morality*, 187–190.
42. For more detail on each of these principles, and some relevant facts and cases, and the complexities of such, see: Orend, *Morality*, 185–201.
43. Walzer, *Wars*, 288.
44. Orend, *Morality*, 185–214; Manfred F. Boemke, ed., *The Treaty of Versailles* (Cambridge: Cambridge University Press, 1998); Margaret Macmillan, *Paris 1919* (New York: Macmillan, 2003); James Turner Johnson and George Weigel, eds., *Just War and Gulf War* (Washington, DC: University Press of America, 1991); and Alan Geyer and Barbara G. Green, eds., *Lines in the Sand: Justice and the Gulf War* (Louisville: John Knox, 1992).
45. Orend, *Morality*, 215–250; Howard B. Schonberger, *Aftermath of War: Americans and The Remaking of Japan* (Ohio: Kent State University Press, 1989); Eugene Davidson, *The Death and Life of Germany: An Account of the American Occupation* (St. Louis: University of Missouri Press, 1999); US Government, *Afghanistan Reconstruction* (Washington, DC: Bibliogov, 2011); US Special Inspector General, *Hard Lessons: The Iraq*

Reconstruction Experience (Washington, DC: US Independent Agencies and Commissions, 2009).
46. Orend, *Morality*, 215–250.
47. Walzer, *Wars*, 288.
48. Ibid., 292–301.
49. Walzer, *Wars*, 319–322; Reisman and Antoniou, *The Laws of War*, 337–350; Yuku Tanaka, *Hidden Horrors: Japanese War Crimes in World War II* (Boulder: Westview Press, 1997); Timothy P. Maga, *Judgment at Tokyo: The Japanese War Crimes Trial* (Lexington: University of Kentucky Press, 2001).
50. Reisman and Antoniou, *The Laws of War*, 332–333.
51. Admittedly, however, there was a 100% conviction rate in the Tokyo trials, which rightly raises eyebrows. See Maya, *Judgment, passim.*
52. Walzer, *Wars*, 292–296; Reisman and Antoniou. *The Laws of Wars*, 318–337; Persico, *Infamy, passim;* Marrus, *Nuremberg, passim.*
53. Victor Peskin, *International Justice in Rwanda and The Balkans* (Cambridge: Cambridge University Press, 2008); Richard H. Steinberg, *Assessing the Legacy of the ICTY* (London: Brill Academic, 2011); Gerald Gahima, *Transitional Justice in Rwanda* (London: Routledge, 2012).
54. William Schabas, *The International Criminal Court* (Oxford: Oxford University Press, 2010).
55. Brian Orend, *Introduction to International Studies* (Oxford: Oxford University Press, 2012), chapter 5, "International Law and Organization."
56. Brian Orend, *Human Rights: Concept and Context* (Peterborough: Broadview, 2002).
57. Smith, *Rise and Fall*, passim; Walzer, *Wars*, 309–316; Reisman and Antoniou, *The Laws of War*, 357–370; Peter A. French and Jane Sternett, eds., *Individual and Collective Responsibility: The Massacre at My Lai* (Cambridge: Harvard University Press, 1972); Seymour Hersh, *Chain of Command: The Road from 9/11 to Abu Ghraib* (New York: Harper Collins, 2004).
58. Michael Krausz, ed., *Relativism: Interpretation and Confrontation* (Notre Dame, IN: University of Notre Dame Press, 1989).
59. Morris R. Cohen and Ernest Nagel, *Logic and Scientific Method* (New York: Simons, 1934). See Orend, *Human Rights*, 155–190, for an extended discussion of the related accusation that human rights values are 'Western' and thus purportedly objectionable on that basis.
60. Ping-Cheung Lo and Sumner B. Twiss, *Chinese Just War Ethics* (London: Routledge, 2015).
61. Reisman and Antoniou, eds., *The Laws of War*, 18–23.

Brian Orend is Professor of Philosophy at the University of Waterloo in Canada. His core fields of research include: human rights, international relations, and the ethics of war and peace. He is perhaps best known for his work on postwar justice, and the book *The Morality of War* (Broadview, 2nd ed., 2013). Recent publications include being the editor of a new edition of Kant's *Perpetual Peace* (Broadview, 2015). Forthcoming books include: the updated second edition to his *Introduction to International Studies* (OUP, 2018); an edited anthology on *War Ethics* (Broadview, 2018); plus a monograph, *War and Political Theory* (Polity, 2018).

Erratum to: War Crimes Trials and Investigations

Jonathan Waterlow and Jacques Schuhmacher

J. Waterlow, J. Schuhmacher, *War Crimes Trials and Investigations*, St Antony's Series https://doi.org/10.1007/978-3-319-64072-3

The original version of the book contained an error that has been corrected.
The cross references to the book chapter numbers were incorrect.
They have been corrected.

The updated original online version for this book can be found https://doi.org/10.1007/978-3-319-64072-3

J. Waterlow, J. Schuhmacher, *War Crimes Trials and Investigations*, St Antony's Series, https://doi.org/10.1007/978-3-319-64072-3_11

Index[1]

[1] Note: Page number followed by 'n' denotes note.

J. Waterlow, J. Schuhmacher, *War Crimes Trials and Investigations*, St Antony's Series,
https://doi.org/10.1007/978-3-319-64072-3

FSC
www.fsc.org
MIX
Papier | Fördert
gute Waldnutzung
FSC® C083411

Kolibri 360 GmbH
Ferdinand-Jühlke-Straße 7
99095 Erfurt, Deutschland
produktsicherheit@kolibri360.de